Sociology

A Modular Approach

Alison Bowes, Denis Gleeson & Pauline Smith

GENERAL EDITOR
Denis Gleeson

Oxford University Press

Oxford University Press,
Walton Street, Oxford OX2 6DP

Oxford New York Toronto
Delhi Bombay Calcutta Madras Karachi
Petaling Jaya Singapore Hong Kong Tokyo
Nairobi Dar es Salaam Cape Town
Melbourne Auckland

and associated companies in
Berlin Ibadan

Oxford is a trade mark of Oxford University Press

ISBN 019 913331 X

Typeset by Tradepools Ltd., Frome, Somerset
Printed in Great Britain by
Butler & Tanner Ltd, Frome and London

Author's note

Sociology: A Modular Approach owes much to the inspiration and example of teachers, lecturers, pupils and students in local 'Potteries' schools and colleges in and around Stoke-on-Trent. A debt of gratitude is also owed to past and present students of the University of Keele, Department of Education, whose ideas have contributed to the book in many different ways. We also thank Rob Scriven and Lucy Hooper, of Oxford University Press, for their guidance and encouragement, and Gladys Pye, for her invaluable secretarial expertise.

Preface

This book is specifically designed to meet the needs and requirements of students on GCSE or introductory sociology courses. It is intended to have wide appeal to a broad cross-section of students of different ages and ability in school and further education. Each module contains exciting stimulus material including photographs, cartoons, diagrams and lively ideas for student coursework, research and assessment. In addition, *Sociology: A Modular Approach* integrates various key themes into the main body of the text, including Race, Gender and Health, as well as incorporating research and comparative perspectives throughout. Essentially, the book is activity based and student centred, inviting interaction, participation and active involvement at every step.

While *Sociology: A Modular Approach* comprehensively deals with sociological concepts and criteria expected at this level, it does so in a variety of new and challenging ways. First, it introduces practical ideas for student coursework alongside more detailed suggestions regarding research methods, project ideas, tasks, questions and assignments. Secondly, it integrates student research and assessment as a continuous rather than as a separate feature of sociological understanding. Finally, instead of working through the book in a conventional 'linear' fashion, *Sociology: A Modular Approach* is organised on a free-standing modular basis. Following initial guidance and advice in the opening module, students may choose the starting point and pattern by which they will plan their studies. Further suggestions for this planning are also provided throughout the text by comprehensive cross-referencing between the various modules and the units which comprise them.

In addition to the flexibility and freedom which this approach allows in developing self-supporting study skills, it also encourages students to make the links between different topics in sociology, such as race and stratification, population and urbanisation, gender and education, development and health. In so doing, the modular approach is designed to meet the requirements of students undertaking additional or related GCSE, professional, pre-vocational or open learning courses (including Industrial Studies; Business Education; Integrated Humanities; Social Science; Social Policy and Health Studies) where a significant sociological input is required. *Sociology: A Modular Approach* also covers the knowledge and understanding required for Levels 1–3 in the Health and Social Care NVQ.

The National Curriculum requires coverage of cross-curricular themes, dimensions and skills. *Sociology: A Modular Approach* provides this particularly in the areas of citizenship and personal and social skills, whilst emphasising the active development of student study skills.

Denis Gleeson
General Editor

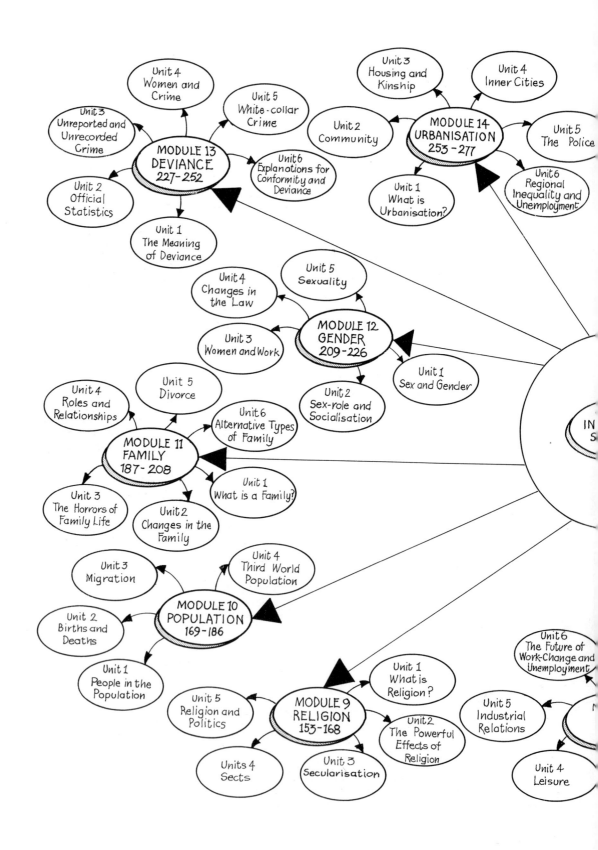

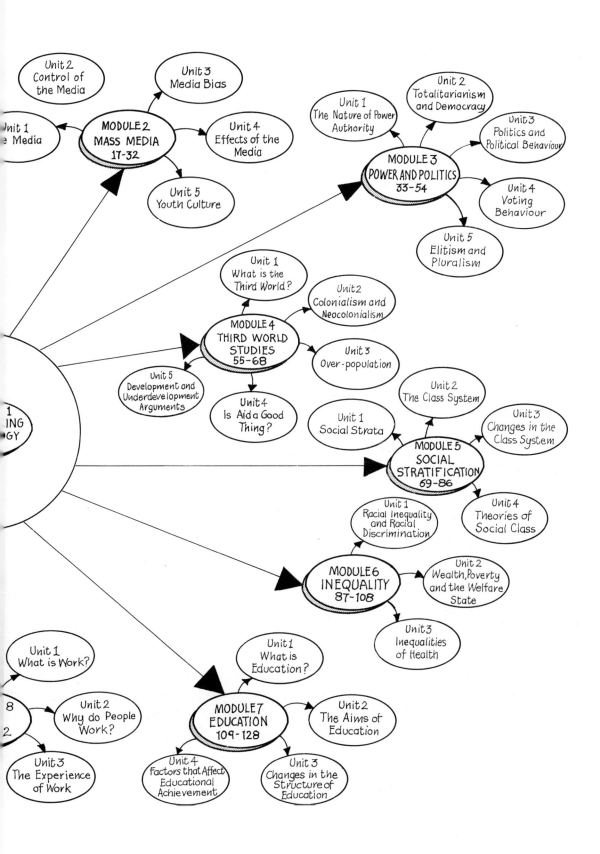

Unit 2
Control of
the Media

Unit 3
Media Bias

Unit 1
e Media

MODULE 2
MASS MEDIA
17-32

Unit 4
Effects of the
Media

Unit 5
Youth Culture

Unit 1
The Nature of Power
Authority

Unit 2
Totalitarianism
and Democracy

Unit 3
Politics and
Political Behaviour

MODULE 3
POWER AND POLITICS
33-54

Unit 4
Voting
Behaviour

Unit 5
Elitism and
Pluralism

Unit 1
What is the
Third World?

Unit 2
Colonialism and
Neocolonialism

MODULE 4
THIRD WORLD
STUDIES
55-68

Unit 3
Over-population

Unit 5
Development and
Underdevelopment
Arguments

Unit 4
Is Aid a Good
Thing?

Unit 1
Social Strata

Unit 2
The Class System

Unit 3
Changes in the
Class System

MODULE 5
SOCIAL
STRATIFICATION
69-86

Unit 4
Theories of
Social Class

1
ING
GY

Unit 1
Racial Inequality
and Racial
Discrimination

MODULE 6
INEQUALITY
87-108

Unit 2
Wealth, Poverty
and the Welfare
State

Unit 3
Inequalities
of Health

Unit 1
What is Work?

Unit 2
Why do People
Work?

8

2

Unit 3
The Experience
of Work

Unit 1
What is
Education?

MODULE 7
EDUCATION
109-128

Unit 2
The Aims of
Education

Unit 4
Factors that Affect
Educational
Achievement

Unit 3
Changes in the
Structure of
Education

MODULE · 1

INTRODUCING SOCIOLOGY

ONE

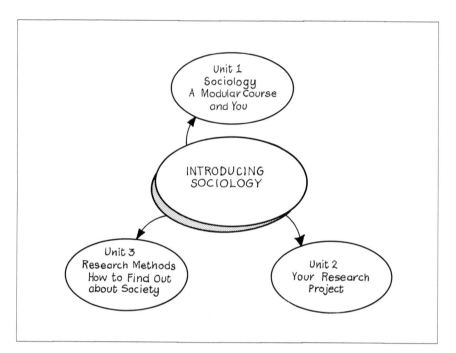

WHAT THIS MODULE IS ABOUT

This module introduces you to sociology. It encourages you to investigate society in an active and critical way and provides the research techniques that will enable you to do this.

BY THE END OF THIS MODULE YOU SHOULD BE ABLE TO:

1 Understand that sociology is about asking questions, i.e. examining society through a variety of research methods.

2 Appreciate the various strengths and weaknesses of questionnaires, interviews, observation, and experiments as methods of obtaining primary data, and also the use of secondary source material as a method of finding out about society.

3 Start to use these research methods effectively in a research project or task.

4 Appreciate how this introductory module links with the research processes to be found throughout this book.

U N I T 1 SOCIOLOGY: A MODULAR COURSE AND YOU

Sociology: A Modular Course reflects the 'active', 'learning by doing' emphasis of the GCSE examination. It allows you to enjoy the *skills* of sociology, rather than just the course content; to learn and understand by actually *doing* sociological research yourself, rather than just reading about it!

This book is specially designed to help you to learn at your own pace and encourages you to manage your own learning, in the way that is most appropriate for *you*.

Perhaps the best way of defining 'sociology' is to say, 'if you want to know what sociology is, then look at what sociologists *do*', i.e. at the kinds of questions they ask about society, the methods they adopt to gather information, the issues they look at and the arguments they use to get their message across.

You will quickly learn that sociology is about **investigating** society – because within the first two pages, you will be doing just that. As a sociologist, you will *ask questions* about all aspects of life in British Society. These might be questions about issues you had previously taken for granted, such as: why males and female behave differently; or, why most societies in the world have similar social **structures** or **systems** like the family, education, politics, religion, work and so on.

It is important to recognise that sociologists are interested in a number of key questions about the world we live in, for example:

How did society get to be the way it is?

What kind of people live in it and how do they relate to one another?

How does society change?

This book will help you to find out the 'answers' . . . You may not gain a satisfactory answer to your questions. In fact you may instead discover several *partial* answers, but one thing is certain – you will enjoy the process of attempting to *find out*! You will also be able to share your research enquiries and findings with others.

This course is arranged in **modules** or free-standing packages of learning which are sub-divided into **units**. These units are clearly laid out in a **spider diagram** at the front of each module and allows you to see at a glance the learning process involved in each module.

Following initial guidance and advice you will be able to choose your own starting point in *Sociology: A Modular Course* and to formulate your own learning pathway through the modules. Its modular structure allows you considerable flexibility and freedom.

The links and connections between the modules and the sociological issues they address are drawn out in the text, and as you progress through your course you will be making more of these links for yourself and achieving a **sociological perspective**.

You will realise gradually that each aspect or structure of society is just part of an integrated whole. As individuals living in society we are involved in, or part of, each of these structures or systems, e.g. the family structure, the education system and others shown in the diagram at the top of page 3.

BEWARE SPIDERS

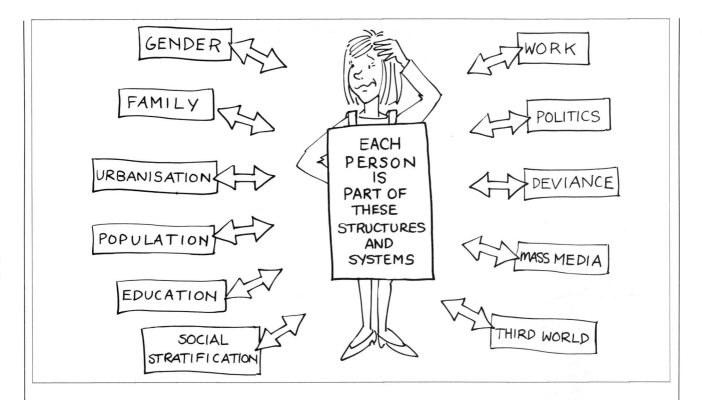

The following extract from a case history explains the way in which a person is involved in or a part of many different social structures or social systems:

'I come from a large working-class family of eight children . . . I suppose you could say that I was part of the "baby boom" since I was born, like thousands of others, twelve months after the Second World War ended, when my R.A.F. father returned home.

'There was a Labour Government in first after the war, and the Welfare State was started. I remember having free milk at school until I was 17, although my own children were only able to have milk at school until they were 9 – I wonder why? We also had free orange juice and cod liver oil – perhaps they thought we were likely to be undernourished in those days . . . Although I do think there is just as much chance of that these days with the massive unemployment and poverty in some areas of the country.

'I went to three different secondary schools, one was a Comprehensive in Leicestershire which I liked very much. The other two were grammar schools and, since I was the only one to have passed my 11+ at my primary school, I was separated from all my friends and very lonely at the time. At my last school, the headmistress walked around the corridors ringing a large handbell when it was time to change lessons!

'There were only two suitable jobs for girls leaving that sort of school in those days. You either left to go to University or College in order to teach, or you became a nurse. I must have been a deviant, as I ended up in the Civil Service, finding other people jobs . . .'

Sociologists use words that have specialist meanings, just as chemists, engineers or biologists do. The words that sociologists use are sometimes the same that people use anyway, such as class, family or deviance. This means that you must be careful to learn the sociological meanings for words and terms. As with other subjects when you learn sociology you are also learning its language, vocabulary and ways of looking at things. In this book you will find that words with **special meanings** are printed in **bold type** to remind you to take particular notice of them.

T A S K

1 Which social structures or systems are mentioned in this extract?
2 Write a brief account of your own life. How many different social structures have you been a part of or involved in?

UNIT 2 YOUR RESEARCH PROJECT

One of the main **structures** in your life at the moment is probably the education system. *Sociology: A Modular Approach* gives you the chance to investigate or **research** the power and processes of the education system and each of the other structures or systems examined through the modules.

Research investigations are not clever, difficult or new! Everyone carries out research as part of their daily lives. For example, we all study the Yellow Pages in order to find out the best place to have our hair cut, or to book a meal and so on. When we do this we are performing a simple research investigation using printed material.

Research investigations are part of the professional lives or jobs of some people. *Journalists*, for example, carry out research investigations by observing and interviewing people in order to produce newsworthy stories; *detectives* research into the backgrounds of potential criminals and also question witnesses. *Scientists* carry out research by conducting experiments in laboratories and *doctors* by asking the patient questions and by examining them are also making investigations – this time into why a person feels ill. Successful *gardeners* carry out research by observing the effects of particular soils, weather and plant food on their crops, whilst *chefs* research into . . .

You will certainly be able to add to this list of researchers and also to add examples of times when *you* have carried out investigations or research yourself, perhaps as part of other school or college course work.

Research is an everyday activity for all of us; but as a sociologist you will develop research skills to a higher degree. In this book you will learn to investigate society through a variety of activities. The main types of activities you will meet are listed below and examples of each are given on page 5.

brainstorm	This means you can throw in as many ideas as possible about the particular work or concept being examined. With a large group this produces lots of ideas.
discuss	You are invited to discuss or debate a particular issue or argument. This is a most valuable way of learning and is usually lively and enjoyable!
question	This means a quick question for you to respond to.
questions	These are set on the stimulus material used in the book, in order to give you practice in the GCSE style of questioning.
role play	You are invited to take on a role, as an actor, in order to learn more about the social situation you are studying.
task	Various tasks are suggested in the modular course work. These will enable you to learn by doing and they can also be used as **assignments** forming part of your GCSE coursework.
research ideas	These are suggestions for pieces of research or investigation for you to conduct. They can be either **mini projects** or **longer projects** that are suitable for entry as part of your GCSE examination requirements.

Sociology makes you question things that you previously took for granted as the following activities show.

BRAINSTORM

Why study sociology?

DISCUSS

Why do people take GCSE exams?

ROLE PLAY

Try being a lodger in your own home, instead of being a son, daughter, etc. Observe the effects of this role play and discuss what this tells you about your usual family roles and relationships.

T A S K

Find out why a group of students decided to take GCSE sociology.

Q Are there more males or females in your sociology group?

RESEARCH IDEA

Carry out a study into which GCSE subjects tend to be more popular with males and which with females. Try to find out the reasons for these preferences and suggest ways of obtaining a balance of sexes in each subject group.

Source: SEG Social Science GCSE, 1988

Each of these suggestions for project work are designed to be well within your capabilities and can be carried out effectively from a school or college base. These research ideas encourage you to use a whole range of methods to investigate society, such as: questionnaires, interviews, secondary source/documentary material, experiments and observation. The type of research method you choose for your project will, of course, depend on the subject you are examining.

For example, suppose you wish to investigate the area of gender inequalities in society. You might decide to:

a Use newspapers (**secondary source materials**) in order to study how females are portrayed, in what roles, and how much space is given to females in comparison to males.
b Use a **questionnaire** to ask married males and females about who should do the housework tasks and why.
c Use **observation** in order to see who actually does most housework.
d **Interview** girls and boys to see whether they have different ambitions for when they leave school.
e Conduct an **experiment** to find out whether teachers treat girls and boys differently in class according to their sex.

Each of these methods of research would give you only a *partial* answer to your questions about gender inequalities in society, and for this reason you would probably decide to use more than one approach.

Certainly, your investigations into the area of social life you have chosen to study will prove interesting and enjoyable and you will be learning by actually *doing* sociological research!

The understanding and insight you achieve into the problems of gender inequality in society will be revealed in your discussions with other people. You also will be able to share in their understandings and perceptions. The conclusion of your research will therefore reflect your own interpretations and the understanding you have gained from the invaluable process of talking to others and doing sociological research for yourself.

We now need to look at each of these research methods in more depth to discover why you should choose one technique rather than another for your project.

QUESTIONS

Here are some examples of the type of questions you may be asked in *Sociology: A Modular Approach*

a 'Boys will be boys.' Give *two* examples from picture 1 which suggest this may be true.
b Compare pictures 1 and 2. How do you think they show that our attitudes towards bringing up children have changed?
c Think of *one* example of a male stereotype and say why you think it is a good example.
d Men and women are still unequal today. Why do you think this is the case? □

1 1950s

2 1980s

RESEARCH METHODS: HOW TO FIND OUT ABOUT SOCIETY

There are many different ways that you, as a sociologist, can find things out about society. The method that you choose will depend on the problem or issue you are investigating. You will also have to take into account what is practically possible for you to achieve given the time and resources available to you. Access to information and the appropriateness of particular research topics are factors you will need to consider. It would be useless, for example, to decide to interview the Prime Minister, to study a South American tribe, or to survey teachers about their sex lives!

Each research method has advantages and disadvantages and you need to be aware of these before you can decide how you want to gain information. You can either use **primary data**, which means information that you collect yourself; or you can reuse information that someone else has obtained which is known as **secondary data**. There is a great deal of information contained within this book which will be useful to you as secondary data. You will also find ideas for primary research within each of the modules.

Primary data

Broadly speaking, sociologists collect *primary data* in two ways; by the **social survey** and by using **observation**, although occasionally they may also use **experimentation**.

The social survey

This involves using either interviews or questionnaires to collect information. An **interview** involves talking to people face to face, whereas a **questionnaire** has written questions and answers. Interviews can be either *formal*, where the sociologist has particular questions to ask, or *informal*, which is more like a conversation about a particular topic.

DISCUSS

Give some examples of topics where it would be better to use a formal interview and some where it would be better to use an informal interview. ☐

The individuals that the sociologist collects information from are called **respondents**, and they can be chosen in different ways. The group as a whole from whom the information is collected form the **sample**.

There may be problems with random sampling

TASK

Make sure you know what is meant by: primary and secondary data; a survey; formal and informal interviews; a random sample.

The national census being carried out

TASK

You can find examples of surveys throughout this book. If you turn to Module 8 on Work, Unit 3, page 134, you can read the results of a survey about what it's like to work on a car assembly line.

In order to gather information that is as objective or unbiased as possible, a **random** sample is sometimes used. This method gives everyone the same chance of being selected, it may mean picking out every tenth house on an estate to visit, or every fifth name from a register or a telephone directory. In this way, the information collected should be representative of everybody in society, so that it is then possible for the sociologist to generalise his or her findings. So, if the sociologist finds out that 70 per cent of the sample watch a particular television programme every night, then it is possible to generalise these findings and say that it is probable that 70 per cent of the whole population watch that programme. There is obviously more to sampling than this, and this topic will be examined further in the modules that follow.

Other ways of sampling include a **quota** sample, where the sociologist aims to find respondents who have particular characteristics. This may be because the sociologist wants the sample to have the same characteristics as are in the population of the country as a whole, e.g. age, sex and class. Alternatively, the sociologist may be interested in certain categories of people only, such as those with children with divorced parents for a survey on the effects of being part of a one-parent family.

Many sociologists use what is called a **convenience** sample, which means that they ask whoever is available and willing to answer questions. You will probably use a convenience sample in your research, but you must be careful that you do not bias your findings by doing so.

Q   How would these surveys be biased by the sample?

1   Interviewing shoppers when standing outside either Harrods in London, or Woolworths in Stoke-on-Trent?
2   Interviewing pupils about private education when standing outside your local state school, or outside Eton?
3   Asking a group of old people whether pensions are high enough. □

Survey methods are used to collect factual information, such as which television programmes are watched by different age groups or how often people visit their relatives. They may also be used to collect people's opinions, such as attitudes towards the police, politicians, or football fans. Many surveys use questionnaires where the questions and answers are written down. This can cause difficulties if people are illiterate, or if they do not understand the questions, because unlike an interview there is no one there to explain or to help them.

One major survey is done by the government every ten years. This is the **census**, which is a questionnaire sent to everybody living in Great Britain. The census provides the government with lots of useful information, the only people who are missed out are those who do not have a permanent address because the census is taken through households.

Q   What kinds of people may be missed off the census? Does this matter? □

DISCUSS

Why might the government need details about the population, such as their age, sex, house, wealth, etc? How might this knowledge affect government policy on spending on schools, hospitals, housing, or the Welfare State? What other reasons are there for taking a population census? □

There are advantages and disadvantages with each research method. An interview can be a quick and easy way of collecting information. Most people are prepared to be helpful, and some are flattered to be chosen as a respondent. Any misunderstandings can be quickly sorted out, and the sociologist can probe for extra information that may be useful. You will probably find that the interview will be an effective way for you to do your research.

Choose a convenient time!

The way that questions are asked may affect the answers given. Your tone of voice, the way the questions are phrased and what you look like can also affect what people say in reply to your questions.

Q What is wrong with these questions if they are being asked by a seventeen year-old girl? Why are the answers likely to be biased?

1 You do like going to school, don't you?
2 Surely you aren't going to vote Conservative?
3 What is your attitude to young people in society today?
4 Do you think there is such a thing as a generation gap?
5 How many times do you go to a pub each week?
6 Do you think a woman's place is in the home?
7 8 9 10 Now you think of some more examples of biased questions! □

Consider the following. Most interviewers are middle-aged, middle-class women, because they tend to get the least biased results. Why do you think this is so? Before answering this question decide whether you think it is 'leading' or not. If questions are leading this may affect the answers.

There are other problems with asking people questions. It may be that it is an inconvenient time, or that the questions are on topics that people are not prepared to answer honestly on.

BRAINSTORM

Sensitive topics which are difficult for sociologists to obtain accurate information about include questions about sexual behaviour, religious beliefs, ages, and earnings. Why do you think this is so? What other topics might it be difficult to get accurate information about? □

Postal questionnaires can be mailed to people but this research method can be time-consuming and expensive, especially if another reminder or follow-up form has to be sent. The major problem with postal questionnaires is that they have a very low response rate, most people put them straight in the bin! The only exception to this is government questionnaires like the census, where it is an offence not to fill them in, and so the response rate is much higher.

Q Can you think of any other types of postal questionnaire that might get a higher than average response? □

T A S K

Make a list of all the advantages and disadvantages of using survey methods from the information that you have been given in this unit. Then think of an idea for one survey which you could do, using either an interview or a questionnaire.

Try out your questions on a friend before you do the proper survey. This can help iron out any difficulties there might be with the wording of the questions. Remember that if you ask people questions on sensitive topics you are unlikely to get accurate results. Also try and look neat and non-threatening, so that people are willing to stop and talk to you!

Finally make sure you explain what you are doing and thank your respondents for their help at the end of the interview. □

What you look like can affect the results

Observation

Observation is the second method of collecting information or data. It involves the sociologist joining the group that they wish to study. Usually the group is not aware it is being studied, because sociologists have shown that people's behaviour changes when they know they are being watched. (See Elton Mayo's Hawthorne Experiment, page 134 for more about this).

This method requires the sociologist to be able to adapt to a group so that they won't suspect their real identity and is called **participant observation**. This may be difficult, if not impossible, because some groups are a particular age or sex.

Participant observation can be difficult because groups do not always accept strangers. Another difficulty with this method is that some sociologists consider it unethical or morally wrong to study people without their knowledge. However, sometimes this is the only way of collecting information, because respondents would not answer truthfully about some topics, such as whether they engage in criminal activities.

Another advantage of participant observation is that it gives the sociologist a real understanding of what someone else's life is like. Some sociologists would argue that collecting facts and figures about society does not give in-depth knowledge about other people's norms, values and life styles. Only joining a group and living their life can provide this.

One participant observation study done in the 1930s, was *Street Corner Society* by **William Foote Whyte**. This was a study of an Italian slum community in the United States. Whyte's study showed many of the advantages of this sort of research. It would have been impossible to collect all his information by the more usual survey methods of interview or questionnaire.

The following extract from *Street Corner Society* highlights some of the problems and the benefits of participant observation.

> One has to learn when to question and when not to question as well as what questions to ask.
>
> I learned this lesson one night in the early months when I was with Doc in Chichi's gambling joint. A man from another part of the city was regaling us with a tale of the organization of gambling activity. I had been told that he had once been a very big gambling operator, and he talked knowingly about many interesting matters. He did most of the talking, but the others asked questions and threw in comments, so at length I began to feel that I must say something in order to be part of the group. I said: "I suppose the cops were all paid off?"
>
> The gambler's jaw dropped. He glared at me. Then he denied vehemently that any policemen had been paid off and immediately switched the conversation to another subject. For the rest of that evening I felt very uncomfortable.
>
> The next day Doc explained the lesson of the previous evening. "Go easy on that 'who,' 'what,' 'why,' 'when,' 'where' stuff, Bill. You ask those questions, and people will clam up on you. If people accept you, you can just hang around, and you'll learn the answers in the long run without even having to ask the questions."
>
> I found that this was true. As I sat and listened, I learned the answers to questions that I would not even have had the sense to ask if I had been getting my information solely on an interviewing basis. I did not abandon questioning altogether, of course. I simply learned to judge the sensitiveness of the question and my relationship to the people so that I only asked a question in a sensitive area when I was sure that my relationship to the people involved was very solid.

DISCUSS

Could you or your friends join the following groups as a participant observer?

1 A family
2 A football crowd
3 A women's hockey team
4 A delinquent gang
5 Assistants at a fast food cafe
6 Market stall holders
7 Prisoners
8 School teachers
9 Night club goers
10 A youth club

Q Is it ethical to study people without their knowledge?

But, I'm really a sociologist.

For more on delinquency turn to Module 13 on Deviance, page 248.

For more on delinquency turn to Module 13 on Deviance, page 248.

T A S K

List the advantages and disadvantages of participant observation. One disadvantage is that the group may get angry when they realise that they have been studied without their knowledge. Make sure this does not happen to you!

You mean you've been studying us?

Another sociologist who became a participant observer was **James Patrick** who joined a violent Glasgow gang in the late 1960s. He was teaching in an approved school when he was invited by Tim, a member of the gang, to see what life in a gang was really like. However, his cover was almost blown at once, when he bought a suit with cash instead of on credit, and then fastened the middle button on the jacket instead of the top one. The gang would never behave like this! He later left the gang, because he was expected to join in with their aggressive gang warfare. He also felt that his continued avoidance of violence would result in the boys suspecting that he was not really what he appeared to be.

Patrick begins his account like this: 'I was dressed in a midnight-blue suit, with a twelve-inch middle vent, three-inch flaps over the side pockets and a light blue handkerchief with a white polka dot (to match my tie) in the top pocket. My hair, which I had allowed to grow long, was newly washed and combed into a parting just to the left of centre. My nails I had cut down as far as possible, leaving them ragged and dirty. I approached the gang of boys standing outside the pub . . .'

Source: A Glasgow Gang Observed by James Patrick, 1973

Q How do you think the Glasgow gang felt when they found out that they had been studied without their knowledge? □

DISCUSS

Could information about a gang be obtained by another method? Why was Patrick able to join the gang, and what difficulties did he find? □

There are many other examples of participant observation studies using groups that are more accessible to most people than delinquent gangs. A sociologist called *Garfinkel* asked his students to go home and pretend that they were strangers in their own homes in order to discover the unwritten rules that govern people's behaviour.

RESEARCH IDEAS

It may be possible for you to do a project using participant observation as a method. You could do some research based on Garfinkel's idea. Try going home as a stranger; you may have to knock on the door and ask if you can come in! The reactions of your family should indicate to you how much of everyday behaviour is just taken for granted. Other possibilities could include a study of your place of work (even if this is part time, such as a newspaper round or a Saturday job); a study of people shopping; a study of a magistrates court; or a study of classroom behaviour. □

Remember that people may get irate at being studied in this way, and it may be a good idea to stop and explain before things get out of hand! Most participant observers find that it is impossible to continue in their role indefinitely. William Foote Whyte says he became so involved with his new life he stopped being a participant observer and became a non-observing participant. James Patrick gave up when it became impossible for him to be non-violent and retain his credibility as a gang member.

Sometimes the sociologist observes the group being studied rather than joining it. This is called **non-participant observation**, and it is a method used by many natural scientists including biologists and zoologists, as well as psychologists and sociologists. Non-participant observational methods usually mean that the people being studied are aware that a sociologist is recording their behaviour, although sometimes the observer is hidden, perhaps behind a two-way mirror.

Many sociologists use a structured approach to observing others, perhaps by using a watch and writing down what is happening at one minute intervals. Other sociologists will write a descriptive account of what they

Descriptive account (top), Observation account (bottom).

Source: *Children into Pupils* by Mary Willes, 1983 (top); Sylva and Lunt *Child Development* (bottom)

RESEARCH IDEA

In order to discover the limitations of observation, ask two people to write an account of an event they both attended, such as a party, lesson, concert or sports event. Then compare their accounts to see whether they are the same. Have they both thought the same things were important? Did they both understand what was happening? How did both make sense of what they saw, and what are the main areas of agreement and disagreement in their accounts?

Observation is one way of discovering the unwritten rules that control people's behaviour. Try out some observation in your school/staff canteen.

have seen. Examples of both these techniques appear below; a structured approach using an observation schedule, and a descriptive account.

Teachers themselves, in my experience, assisted the learning of what a pupil is expected to do, but less directly than might be anticipated. They taught the children how to respond when the register was taken – and not without some difficulty. Making the required response on hearing one's name called was, for these newcomers to the educational system, easy enough. The demanding part of the task was in remaining silent before and after. In the initial weeks, these teachers did not require hands to be raised. They named the individual from whom they wanted a response, and this practice must have been useful to the teacher in imprinting each new name early and indelibly on her memory and useful to pupils, in impressing on them that everyone normally could expect to have a turn.

They looked at many different activities and tried to evaluate which factors were more conducive to the children's development during play. Four kinds of information were recorded: activity (what was the child doing?) language (did the target child talk to another child or adult or was he spoken to?) social setting (was the child alone or in a group?) and play themes (was there a coherent theme to a period of activity?). Here is an extract from a 20–minute recorded and coded observation.

Minute	Activity	Language	Social setting	Play theme
1	Puts hat on. Makes 'fire engine' noises	TC→ CS (about hats) TC:+ CS: 'Dor dor dor dor.' TC→ C: 'What's here?'	Small group	Pretend
1.5	TC with 2 CS on steps	C→TC: 'Here's mine.' (showing a toy)	Small group	
2	Talking and moving with the 2 CS. playing on steps.	T→ CS 'What have you there?' TC→T: 'fire engine'	Small group	
2.5	Places large cardboard box beside large steps, throws hat off. Steps carefully from top of steps onto cardboard box	TC→ C: 'Steps on it.' C→TC: 'I want to come down' [hollow | box]	Small group	Gross motor play

Observation is a much easier method to use than participant observation, where you must be accepted by the group you are studying. It is a method that sociologists can carry out without special training, but it is limited in its use, because people's answers about their feelings, attitudes or values may not be truthful and may change over time. It is mainly used to study people's behaviour and even in this field it is not always accurate, because the researcher may not really understand what is happening.

RESEARCH IDEAS

If you are part of a school you could observe behaviour in the canteen or common room. You may be interested in the unwritten rules governing people's behaviour in a situation like this. These may include rules about queuing, about who sits next to whom, or about the sex of the canteen staff.

If you wish to conduct a more formal observation, you could observe a group of primary school children at play. In this instance, it is easiest to focus on one child and record what they are doing at one minute intervals. Sometimes it is better to prepare a schedule before you start, with an agreed way of recording categories like solitary play, talking to another child, or standing alone. It is important to decide what behaviour you are interested in before you start your observation. □

TASK

Write down the advantages and disadvantages of observation as a research method, from the information given. Then add to your list when you have tried an observation yourself. □

Experimentation

Experimentation is the main research method of the natural sciences, which include physics, chemistry and biology. This method involves controlling the surroundings in which the experiment is done, so that the effects of one variable can be discovered. In a scientific experiment to discover the effect of sunlight on plants for example, the only variable must be the light, and not heat or humidity which might also affect the plants. A control group is used to make sure that the experiment is really testing the effects of just one thing; in this case the control group of plants would be kept in the same conditions of heat, humidity etc, but the amount of sunlight would remain unaltered.

In the social sciences experimentation is more problematic. It is very difficult to control the variables that affect people's behaviour, or to set up a control group. A major problem is that it would be considered unethical to experiment on humans, if it would cause them suffering. It is therefore impossible to experiment to discover the effects of factors, such as divorce on children, or wife-battering, or putting pupils into detention every week.

Further problems for the sociologist using experiments are that people react to being experimented on, and so the behaviour that is being recorded is not typical of the way people normally behave. It is also impossible to stop people talking about what is going on, so that the control group's behaviour may also be affected. If the sociologist asks for volunteers for an experiment, their behaviour will be biased in favour of helping the sociologist; if the people studied are unaware they are being experimented on, then it raises the ethical question again.

RESEARCH IDEAS

Although experiments are rarely used because of the problems highlighted above, there *are* experiments you can carry out to examine how people behave in different situations. Usually it is not possible to be very scientific when experimenting on humans, and it may be easier not to bother about control groups, or controlling all the variables. Nevertheless, if you use experiment as a research method, remember to do the experiment on a number of people so that you can see if their behaviour follows a pattern; and do remember that most people will be very annoyed when they find out they have been the victims of a sociology experiment!

You could consider the following ideas:

1   Experiments in the home researching into family attitudes (you could appear very interested in what they have been doing all day.)
2   Experiments on your friends to examine their attitudes towards you if you suddenly show eccentric behaviour or clothing style.
3   Experiments on the public to examine attitudes towards those dressed in an outrageous way or attitudes to someone in a wheelchair. □

Secondary data

Secondary data is the name given to information collected or written for another purpose, that is reused by the sociologist. Secondary data can include descriptive information, such as letters, diaries, newspaper articles, reports written by teachers or case histories written by social workers or doctors. All these can give the sociologist useful information about society, but they must be aware that this material was not written to be used by other people and may therefore be inaccurate or biased, because they only show one person's point of view.

TASK

What are the advantages and disadvantages of experiment.

A society is a group of people who have the same **culture**, that is, the same values and norms (ways of behaving). The culture of a society is passed on from parents to their children, so that each generation is socialised into the accepted values and behaviour of their society.

For more about socialisation read unit 1 from Module 11 on Family, page 191 and unit 2 from Module 7 on Education, page 113.

Source: *Human Societies* by G. Hurd, 1973

A sociologist who was interested in researching into the effects of a society's culture on individuals, might turn to secondary data for accounts of children brought up in the wild. Two accounts of children who have not been brought up as human, and so have not been socialised into the culture of a society, appear below.

In 1920 two girls were reportedly discovered in a wolf den in Bengal, India. Aged about two and eight years, they were taken to an orphanage where they were looked after by the Reverend J. A. L. Singh and his wife. The younger child, Amala died soon after she arrived at the orphanage, the elder girl, Kamala, remained in the orphanage until 1929 when she too died. Despite the fact that Amala and Kamala were called 'wolf-children' and found in a wolf's den, there is no evidence that they were actually raised by wolves. The Reverend Singh wrote the following description of their behaviour in 1926.

'At the present time Kamala can utter about forty words. She is able to form a few sentences, each sentence containing two, or at the most, three words. She never talks unless spoken to, and when spoken to she may or may not reply. She is obedient to Mrs Singh and myself only. Kamala is possessed of very acute hearing and evidences an exceedingly acute animal-like sense of smell. She can smell meat at a great distance. Never weeps or smiles but has a 'smiling appearance'. Shed a single tear when Amala died and would not leave the place where she lay dead. She is learning very slowly to imitate. Does not now play at all and does not mingle with other children. Once both Amala and Kamala somewhat liked the company of an infant by the name of Benjamin while he was crawling and learning to talk. But one day they gave him such a biting and scratching that the infant was frightened and would never approach the wolf-children again. Amala and Kamala liked the company of Mrs Singh, and Kamala, the surviving of the pair, is much attached to her. The eyes of the children possessed a peculiar glare, such as that observed in the eyes of dogs or cats in the dark. Up to the present time Kamala sees better at night than during the daytime and seldom sleeps after midnight. The children used to cry or howl in a peculiar voice neither animal nor human. Kamala still makes these noises at times. She is averse to all cleanliness, and serves the calls of nature anywhere, wherever she may happen to be at the time.'

DISCUSS

Discuss the following points: One of the problems of reusing existing information is not knowing how accurate it is.

1 What can we learn about the behaviour of children brought up as animals from the above extracts?
2 In what way is their behaviour abnormal?
3 Do you think these accounts are accurate, or is there anything in the content or style that might indicate that the authors are exaggerating the behaviour of the children? ☐

RESEARCH IDEA

Documentary sources of information, such as letters and diaries, can be a useful source of information. Case histories of patients or clients, are kept by doctors and social workers. Although you would not be able to get hold of these you may be able to use historical documents, or old school reports to use for research purposes. ☐

Q What is meant by secondary data?

Find out more about the population of British society. For example, what is the current birth rate and death rate? How have these changed in the last fifty years? Don't forget that you can use this book as a resource, the information you want may be in Module 10 on Population or in Module 11 on Family.

TASK

Turn to Module 13 on Deviance, page 230 and do the task on understanding tables.

Source: *Daily Mirror*, April 1987

TASK

Write down the advantages and disadvantages of using secondary data.

You should now have a complete list of the advantages and disadvantages of all the research methods.

For more about gender roles turn to pages 212–217.
For more ideas on research on the media see pages 18–21.

Secondary data can also include tables, graphs and charts, empirical or statistical data. Many examples of such data appear throughout this book, giving information about a wide range of topics. Statistical information is used a lot by sociologists, it is easily obtained, and is therefore cheap, quick and easy to use.

In every library there is a mass of information collected by the govenment that sociologists can use. *Social Trends* for example is published every year by the Central Statistical Office, and contains masses of information about society. Sport and leisure activities, marriage and divorce, offences and prisons are only some of the subjects covered by it. The census (see page 7) also provides sociologists with much information to use as secondary data.

In Module 13 on Deviance on page 237, there is an example of statistical information from *Social Trends* about the number of serious offences of crime recorded in the years 1961 to 1985. There is also some advice about how to make sense of statistics because many people find numbers off-putting.

TASK

Go to the nearest library and find out what information is available for your use. Is there a copy of *Social Trends* or any other government publications in the reference section? You may also find that some information is available on the computer. (The *General Household Survey* is an example of such data.) □

RESEARCH IDEA

The following cartoons are taken from the Daily Mirror in 1987. If you look at them you can see that they are all jokes about women, portraying females in a stereotypical way. Cartoons like these frequently appear in newspapers and magazines. Sociologists are interested in the way females are presented in the media, and the effects this may have on the way both sexes see the role of females in society. Do you find these cartoons amusing? It may depend on whether you are male or female; why might this be so?

You could examine jokes and cartoons in newspapers and magazines (some examples are given below) for a short period of time and record systematically how many are jokes against women. This method of finding out about society is called **content analysis**, because you are analysing, or making sense of the content of documentary sources of information. □

"I'm going to town to pump some money into the economy."

YOUR FINGERS ARE COLD

"How many of those tranquillisers have you had today"

"The wife's learning to drive!!"

Conclusion on Research Methods

The sociologist, that is *you*, has a number of different research techniques available in order to find things out about society.

Q Can you remember what all these methods mean?

Can you remember some of the advantages and disadvantages of these different techniques?

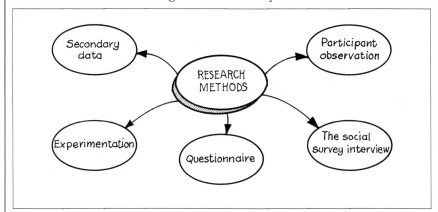

Remember the method chosen will depend on what the sociologist is trying to find out, as well as what is feasible. Often sociologists have more than one method open to them, and many will use two or three research techniques together. Paul Willis in *Learning to Labour* used interviews and asked the boys he was studying to keep diaries, so he was combining primary and secondary data. (See page 248 for more about this study.) Willmott and Young's classic study of family and community life in the East End of London combined interviews and participant observation. (See page 189 in Module 11 on Family and Unit 3 in Module 14 on Urbanisation for more about *Family and Kinship in East London*).

DISCUSS

Which method would be most appropriate to test the following hypotheses?

a Most people would like to see the reintroduction of hanging.
b The labour party will win the next election.
c The divorce rate has been steadily increasing for the last ten years.
d Most housewives find housework boring.
e If a car has broken down, members of the public are more likely to stop and help a female than a male.
f Middle-class pupils get better exam results than working-class pupils.
g Teachers pay more attention in class to boys than to girls.
h Most people will steal money from a machine (e.g. a drinks machine with money left in the change section.)
i Very few people will steal from others (e.g. from someone standing with an open purse and ten pence lying on the floor next to them.)
j Glue sniffing is common amongst young people who go around in gangs. □

RESEARCH IDEA

If you have not yet done any research, work with a friend and choose a topic that interests you both. Decide which research method will achieve the best results, and go and find something out! Remember, finding out is easy, everybody does it all the time! Sociologists usually have a practice run called a **pilot study** or **survey**, before they do the actual research, in order to test out their questions. Your first attempt can be your pilot survey or study! □

WHERE TO NOW?

You might find it interesting to start reading one of the other modules. Remember you don't have to read this book in any particular order, and there are lots of research ideas in each module.

You can read them in any order, although you will find that it is suggested that some are read together.

MODULE · 2
MASS MEDIA

TWO

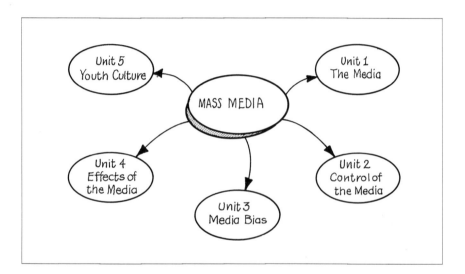

WHAT THIS MODULE IS ABOUT

The mass media is part of most people's lives in Britain today and this module examines the nature of the media and its possible effects. The final unit analyses the links between young people, their culture and the mass media.

BY THE END OF THIS MODULE YOU SHOULD BE ABLE TO:

1 Explain what is meant by the mass media and give examples of the different types of media.
2 Show an understanding of the influence of sex, age and social class in affecting newspaper readership, and on the composition of radio and television audiences.
3 Understand what is meant by soft sell and hard sell in advertising.

4 Explain what is meant by a gatekeeper, and by agenda-setting and understand the meaning of the terms propaganda and censorship.
5 Debate the question of who controls the media.
6 Outline two alternative theories about the effects of the media.
7 Demonstrate an understanding of the possible power of the media.
8 Explain the relevance of the way the media reports deviance.
9 Understand the terms moral panic and amplification spiral.
10 Examine the relationship between the mass media and youth culture.

THE MEDIA

The mass media covers all the possible ways there are of communicating to a large number of people at the same time. This means that the communication is one-way only, people cannot immediately reply.

The mass media therefore includes cinema, television, radio, newspapers, magazines and comics, books, records, and advertisements. Some mass media is visual, some printed and some aural.

Newspapers

The mass media has changed rapidly as technology has become more advanced. The newspaper was the earliest form of mass media, and people used to rely on newspapers for all their information including national and international news. The first newspaper was *The Spectator* which later became *The Times*, first published in 1785. However, newspapers were not read widely until the middle of the Nineteenth century because of the low literacy rates that existed until then.

Newspapers today tend to be classified as either quality or popular papers. The quality papers are also called 'the heavies' and these include papers, such as *The Guardian*, *The Times*, *The Daily Telegraph*, the *Financial Times* and *The Independent*. The popular press consists of papers such as the *Sun*, the *Daily Mail*, the *Daily Mirror*, and the *Daily Star*.

The Daily Telegraph has the highest circulation amongst the quality papers, with over one million readers each day. The *Sun* which was founded in 1964, is now the most widely read of the popular daily papers, with a circulation of about four million readers per day. About three quarters of all adults read a Sunday paper, but fewer read a paper every day.

In 1986 two new papers were published for the first time; *The Independent*, a quality paper, and *Today*, a popular paper.

The different papers each attract a different social class of readers, as you can see in the following graph. For an explanation of the division of social classes into A, B, C1, C2, D and E refer to Module 5 on Social Stratification, page 73.

Q Which type of communication is printed, which visual, and which spoken?

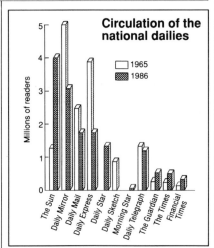

Circulation of the national dailies

☐ 1965
▨ 1986

Millions of readers

The Sun, Daily Mirror, Daily Mail, Daily Express, Daily Star, Daily Sketch, Morning Star, Daily Telegraph, The Guardian, The Times, Financial Times

Source: *New Society*, 28 November 1986

Q Which newspaper do you like best and why?

DISCUSS

Which social class group reads which newspaper? What other information is contained in the graph about the relative popularity of the papers?

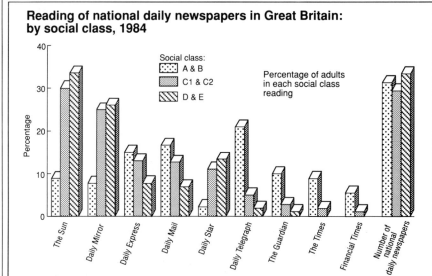

Reading of national daily newspapers in Great Britain: by social class, 1984

Social class:
▢ A & B
▨ C1 & C2
▧ D & E

Percentage of adults in each social class reading

Percentage

The Sun, Daily Mirror, Daily Express, Daily Mail, Daily Star, Daily Telegraph, The Guardian, The Times, Financial Times, Number of national daily newspapers

Source: National Readership Survey 1984, *Social Trends*

Q Do you think that people deliberately choose a newspaper which is biased in favour of the political party they support or does reading a particular paper affect a person's politics?

TASK

Find out which newspaper supports which political party, and compare newspaper stories on a particular issue to clarify their standpoints.

The major daily newspapers – apart from *The Guardian* and *The Independent* – are owned by five main proprietors: the Pergamon Press, Fleet Holdings, the Associated Newspapers Group, News International, and the Telegraph Newspaper Trust, as shown below.

Who owns what?

The big five newspaper proprietors (with foundation dates of newspapers)

Pergamon Press:
Daily Mirror (1903). *Sunday Mirror* (1963). *Sunday People* (1881).

Fleet Holdings:
Daily Express (1900). *Daily Star* (1978). *Sunday Express* (1918).

Associated Newspapers Group:
Daily Mail (1896). *Mail on Sunday* (1982).

News International:
The Sun (1964). *The Times* (1785). *News of the World* (1843). *Sunday Times* (1822).

Telegraph Newspaper Trust:
Daily Telegraph (1855). *Sunday Telegraph* (1961).

Source: *New Society*, 28 November 1986

RESEARCH IDEA

Conduct a survey on radio audiences. Does the amount of time spent listening to the radio, or in the choice of programme differ according to factors of age, sex or class?

Radio

Radio remains popular despite the amount of television that is watched. It has changed during the last thirty years, with a choice now of four national stations, and local radio stations in most regions.

DISCUSS

Look at this BBC survey on radio and then discuss the answers to the questions below.

Radio: average amount of listening per week in the UK, 1976 to 1984

Hours and minutes per head per week

	BBC National Radio								BBC		Independent					
	1		2		3		4		Local Radio		Other Local Radio		Total			
	Hrs	mins	Hrs	mins	Hrs	mins	Hrs	mins	Hrs	mins	Hrs	mins	Hrs	mins	Hrs	mins
1976	3	09	2	18	0	11	1	17	0	35	1	14	0	05	8	49
1980	3	07	2	41	0	10	1	05	0	38	1	27	0	12	9	20
1981	2	49	2	27	0	12	1	03	0	38	1	53	0	15	9	17
1982	2	53	2	20	0	10	1	07	0	47	2	29	0	15	10	01
1983	2	54	2	04	0	10	1	07	0	46	2	09	0	13	9	23
1984	2	38	1	44	0	10	1	03	0	46	1	59	0	24	8	44

Source: British Broadcasting Corporation, *Social Trends*

1 Do people listen to more or less national radio than they used to?
2 Which national radio station is the most popular, and which the least popular? □

Q The BBC is a non-profit-making organisation whose members are appointed by the government. The IBA is a commercial organisation. What does this mean?

Television

Today fewer people go to the cinema than did so thirty years ago, and television is now the most popular type of mass media. In 1985 about 94 per cent of the population watched television for some time each week.

Q Why do you think fewer people now go to the cinema? How often do you go to the pictures to see a film? □

Television is watched by all age groups all year round. However it is watched more by the elderly than the young, and is watched more in the winter than in the summer. It is also watched more by females than males, and is watched more by those in the working class than those in the middle class. (For more on social class read page 73). Make sure you know the meaning of social class groups A, B, C1, C2, D, and E.) There are therefore differences in viewing according to criteria of age, sex and social class.

BRAINSTORM

Why do you think there are these differences in viewing? Think of other relevant factors, such as leisure pursuits (see Module 8 on Work, Unit 4), or who is most likely to be at home. □

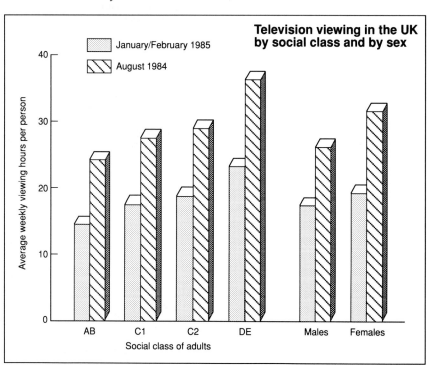

Source: Broadcasting Audience Research Board; Audits of Great Britain

QUESTIONS

Look at the graph above, and then answer the following questions.

1 Which social class watched the least television in 1984 and 1985?
2 How many average weekly hours were viewed by each person in social class C2 in August 1984? How does this compare with the amount watched by those in social class AB in January/February 1985?
3 How many more hours television were watched by females in August 1984 than by males in the same month? □

Cinema-going is a form of mass media which enjoyed a revival in the 1980s, after a period of decline.

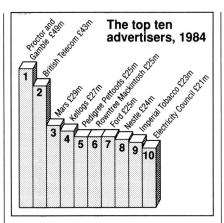

The top ten advertisers, 1984

1 Proctor and Gamble £49m
2 British Telecom £43m
3 Mars £29m
4 Kellogs £27m
5 Pedigree Petfoods £25m
6 Rowntree Mackintosh £25m
7 Ford £25m
8 Nestle £24m
9 Imperial Tobacco £23m
10 Electricity Council £21m

Source: *New Society*, 21 November 1986

Advertising

Advertisements are one form of mass media. Adverts are used to persuade people to buy a product, which could be anything from company shares to a summer holiday to tooth paste.

Q The bar chart on the left shows the top ten advertisers in 1984. What sorts of goods were they selling? □

Many adverts use a **hard sell** technique, where the consumer is offered a benefit from the product such as a free gift, or a saving on another product. Other adverts use a **soft sell** technique which links the product to an idea that it is thought will make it more attractive. Ideas of sex appeal, health and status are all frequently used in this way in advertising.

T A S K

Look at the advertisements on this page and analyse the message that is being used to sell each product. Is it a soft sell or a hard sell technique? □

What is the hidden message of these advertisements?

RESEARCH IDEAS

1 Take some examples of products specifically aimed at young people in society, and analyse the values that are being attached to the product to make it sell. (You could do this by going through a teenage magazine systematically.)
2 Make a study of television advertisements for one week, and examine their portrayal of males and females, and/or ethnic minorities. □

U N I T 2   CONTROL OF THE MEDIA

What the public hear and see in the media is the result of a number of different processes and controls. There is a lot of argument among sociologists over whether the media is free to broadcast what it likes.

Radio is one form of mass media which many people listen to for the news coverage. Making a news bulletin is one way of finding out about the workings of the media.

ROLE PLAY: RADIO FUN

ROLES: ANNOUNCER (S) one or two people
PRODUCER [and ASSISTANT PRODUCER]
DIRECTOR [and ASSISTANT DIRECTOR]
TECHNICAL ASSISTANT (S) one or two people.

Get into groups of between four and eight people. You are working for your local radio station, Radio Fun.

You have received the following ten items for a two-minute news bulletin later today. You have only enough time to include *six* of these items. You must now prepare your news programme, choosing carefully which items to include and which to leave out.

The group should next decide who is to read the news, and which order the items are to go in. You may find it helpful to appoint a Producer, to decide on the order of the news items, in conjunction with his/her Assistant Producer. It may also help if you have a Technical Assistant to organise the taping of your broadcast, and a Director who has overall responsibility for the radio programme and whose job it is to keep things running smoothly! These people may also have assistants.

By the end of the session the group must have produced a tape recording of their two-minute news bulletin. (NB You do not have to read the items out as they appear below, you can add or subtract information to fit in with your time requirements.)

TASK

It would be possible to use the news items given below for a newspaper role play. Make up a front page leaving spaces for any illustrations you might want to include on the news items covered.

News items

1 *Good news*. A funny news item about a cat found stranded on a sand bank on the River Tees. The cat was rescued by two girls who later found out that the cat's name was Robinson Crusoe!

2 *National news*. The Prime Minister has made a major speech in the House of Commons, in which s/he defended the Government's unemployment record. The latest figures showed a remarkable improvement s/he argued, especially in the light of the increasing numbers of companies in the South East forced to make large numbers of people redundant.

3 *Local news*. The star of Britain's most popular soap opera is due to open the new shopping centre in Hanley, Stoke-on-Trent today. The city centre has been affected by this development for the last eighteen months but will be reopened to traffic following today's ceremony.

4 *Local news*. In the centre of Leeds today there has been a major fire in one of the largest department stores. This is the second fire in the area within a week and police are investigating the possibility that it was started deliberately.

5 *The weather*. Overnight gales and high rainfall have led to problems locally. The damage to property is estimated to be in the region of half-a-million pounds, flooding on roads has led to a spate of minor accidents. The police are appealing to drivers to proceed with caution until conditions improve.

6 *Regional news*. Students in the Midlands today are demonstrating against the latest education cuts announced last week by the Government. It is estimated that around 50 000 students, many of whom are said to be extremely militant, are at the moment converging on Birmingham University where the Education Minister is due to give a speech this afternoon.

7 *Sport*. Port Vale are continuing their amazing run of victories this season, they are at the top of the table and stand a real chance of winning the cup this year.

8 *National news*. The latest crime statistics show a dramatic rise in the number of cases of child abuse. This follows a warning given by the NSPCC that people could expect an increase in the official figures, following their assessment of the increasing amount of both physical and psychological abuse.

9 *Traffic news*. We have just received information that there has been a motorway pile-up on the M62. Two lorries and eleven cars are thought to be involved. More on this later in the bulletin.

10 *International news*. The American President has been accused of lying about arms deals. In this latest crisis in his/her first term of office, s/he has been accused of yet another Watergate-style cover up.

DISCUSS

When you have all completed your news bulletin, discuss the similarities and differences between yours and other groups'. Which items were given priority, and which were left out? Why was this? Did some make a better story?

Which person in the group had most influence over the eventual broadcast? Why was this? □

The person who decides what is seen or heard by the public is known as the **gatekeeper**. In the role play you have done, who was the gatekeeper? Did the final choice of news items vary between the groups because of the decisions, of these people?

Arguments over the control of the media include the idea that the gatekeepers are responsible for what the public sees and hears. Journalists respond by saying that the process is not a deliberate attempt to affect the media, but merely a result of filtering news for what is most entertaining or newsworthy.

The public themselves may exercise control over the content of programmes, and the format of the news. They can do this by switching channels or by switching off! Many programmes are affected in this way, such as the extension of the late evening news into a half-hour programme by the BBC after the success of ITV's *News at Ten*. Other changes have included the news being read by two news readers instead of one and the retention of *Doctor Who* after the public dismay that followed the announcement of its supposedly last series in 1986.

However some sociologists argue that the public have very little direct effect on the content of the media, because they have very little direct access to it. Although local radio may attempt to meet the needs of the local population and give air time to local people, television generally does not. There are a few programmes, such as *Open Door* on BBC2, which allow groups to make their own programmes from their point of view, but there is very little real criticism (apart from *Right to Reply* on Channel Four) where ordinary people can make their views known.

Q How much effect has the media on public opinion? □

It is also argued that the media controls public opinion rather than being controlled by it. The content of programmes may influence people's opinions towards, for example, violence or nudity or gender roles. Public opinion may also be affected because the mass media and television in particular is where most people get their information from. This means that what is discussed in households each day, such as the crime rate or the weather forecast, depends on what has been broadcast.

This process is called **agenda-setting**, because in formal meetings it is only items on a list called an agenda that are discussed. In the same way the media also decides what is not discussed by the public. In the radio role play, for example, the audience listening would assume that the news for the day were broadcast; but the public were not given the opportunity to discuss the news items that your groups left out!

In real life there are many items of news that are not used. The selection may depend on whether there are interesting pictures to go with the item, or whether something that has just happened replaces an earlier item.

Marxist sociologists would go further and argue that the media is controlled by the ruling classes who own it. The media is seen as a tool of the ruling classes, who deliberately manipulate public opinion in a way that will be to their benefit. This causes bias within the media, which is supposed to be strictly neutral. To counteract this bias newspapers, such as the *Morning Star* and the *Socialist Worker*, are published by the Marxist press, but the circulation of these papers is small in comparison to the major newspapers.

Q What are the Open University and the Open College? What is their link with the media?

6.00pm
Right to Reply

GUS MACDONALD

Have you a point to make about Channel Four or ITV? Write to *Right to Reply*, Channel Four TV, 60 Charlotte Street, London W1P 2AZ (01-631 4444), or have a go at TV in the Video Box at Channel Four (Mon-Sat, 8am to 8pm) or at Scottish Television, Glasgow (seven days a week, 7am to 6pm) or at Central Television, Alpha Tower entrance, Birmingham (Mon-Fri, 9.30am to 6pm) or at Tyne Tees Television, United House, Piccadilly, York (Mon-Fri 9am to 5pm) or at the new Video Box at Bradford Museum of Photography, Film and Television, Princes View, Bradford, (Tues-Sun 11am to 6pm).

PRODUCER CAROLINE PICK
EDITOR GWYNN PRITCHARD

Channel Four Production

Q How much control do you think the public has over the media?

T A S K

Make sure you can explain the term agenda-setting.

Two different views on the eve of the 1987 General Election.

TASK

Imagine that you are a reporter for a popular daily paper. You have to cover the following story: In the latest opinion poll questions were asked about the popularity of the Government. The results were as follows:

Question: Do you think the Prime Minister is doing a good job?
Answers: Yes 45% No 35% Don't Know 20%

Now write two alternative headlines, one that will support the Prime Minister, and one that will appear critical of him/her. You must use the same set of figures. □

Newspapers are not expected to be neutral in the same way as television, and many newspapers openly support one political party and bias their articles accordingly. The same piece of news will be reported very differently in different papers, as in the task above.

The *Daily Mirror* and *The Guardian* are left wing, and the *Sun* and *The Daily Telegraph* right wing. (For an explanation of these terms read Module 3 on Power and Politics page 41.) The papers can be arranged from left to right as shown below.

RESEARCH IDEA

Collect all the daily papers for one day, and read their treatment of one or more news items. Is it possible to see the political bias of the papers from this, or from reading the editorial found inside? What differences do you see between the quality papers and the tabloids, i.e. the popular press? □

The Independent was launched in 1986, as a quality paper which would compete with the *Daily Telegraph*, and perhaps *The Guardian* and *The Times*. However, a survey in October 1986 showed that its readers had come mainly from the *Daily Mail* and *The Guardian*.

The newspapers in this country are owned and controlled by only a few people, sometimes called press barons or press lords. This means that a handful of rich individuals are potentially very influential because they have the power to control what is read by the public. Most newspapers in this country are right wing and they support the Conservative party.

TASK

Find out who these press barons are. How much of the media do they control both here and abroad? Which political party do they support? What affect might this have on the content of their newspapers? □

Television is bound by law to be impartial. Both the BBC and the IBA have codes of conduct which control the neutrality of their news, as well as programme content. However, the IBA said in 1978, 'The Authority is not required to secure impartiality on matters such as drug trafficking, cruelty and racial intolerance, for example, on which society, even today, is virtually unanimous.' This therefore means that the neutrality of television only extends to some areas – those about which there is agreement in society. Where there is a difference of opinion within society, about a strike for example, then television is expected to provide a balanced picture, to cover both sides of any argument in a neutral way.

The Glasgow University Media Group have made a special study of television news; and they argue that it is definitely not neutral. For example, in their first study called *Bad News* (1976), they show that a speech made by the then Prime Minister, Harold Wilson, was reported in such a way that he appeared to be blaming the workers at British Leyland in January 1976 for a series of strikes. In fact, he blamed both the workers and the management in his speech.

The media coverage of the Falklands War between Britain and Argentina which began in April 1982 has also been studied by the Glasgow University Media Group and other sociologists. They have argued that there was deliberate bias in the way the news was presented, which in some cases became propaganda. **Propaganda** means information that is slanted to mislead people on purpose.

Propaganda is used by most governments in wartime, to keep up people's morale. Examples of Argentinian propaganda from the Falklands War can be seen below, alongside cuttings from the British press of the same time.

Q Explain why these press reports can be called propaganda.

SECUNDA PARTE DE SU HISTORIA NEGRA: SU MARIDO LA ODIA, SU HIJO ES DROGADICTO, SU ABUELO ERA LADRON

LA DAMA DE LA MUERTE

USTED PUEDE AYUDAR A GANAR LA GUERRA

¡CULPABLE!

STICK THIS UP YOUR JUNTA!

H IS FOR HERO

The incredible story of Colonel H and the 600 Paras who captured 1,400 Argentinians

Headlines from the British and Argentinian Press during the Falklands War

Translations from Spanish: Second part of her black story: Her husband hates her, her son is a drug addict, her grandfather was a thief. The Woman of Death (far left). You can help to win the war. Guilty (middle left)

In wartime the government will usually control the media because it does not want the enemy to have information that may help them. The government may also censor certain items, not permitting them to be published at all. In wartime propaganda is seen to be justified, but often the government may exert this media control for another reason. Brian Hanrahan who was a BBC reporter in the Falklands, said later in *Society Today* that: 'news of the loss of the two Sea Harriers on Thursday May 6th – the day of the local elections in the UK – was delayed until after the poll had closed.'

Q Explain why this news item was deliberately delayed by the Government. □

UNIT 4 EFFECTS OF THE MEDIA

There is much discussion, by both sociologists and psychologists, over the possible effects of the media. At the very least it is agreed that the media tends to present a stereotyped view of people and society. This artificial way of presenting types of people whether in, for example, soap operas or in comedy, can affect the way people see the world. There is evidence that gender stereotyping is partly the result of the media portrayal of males and females. (See Module 12 on Gender, pages 216–217).

More immediate effects of the media were recognised in the early days of radio broadcasting, when a 1938 radio play was broadcast in the style of a documentary. The play was *The Martians Have Landed* (an adaptation of *The War of the Worlds*) by Orson Welles and many people who switched on late and therefore missed the introduction were convinced that the invasion was really happening. Many people were so frightened that they left their homes to try and escape! The documentary style of the play meant the involvement of 'interviews' with 'real' experts, such as government officials and army officers, which further convinced the audience that it was really happening.

Q Can you give any examples of TV 'spoofs', such as April Fool's Day broadcasts which had you convinced that they were real? □

The acceptance by the audience of the truthfulness of the media is worrying to many people. One argument is that the media acts like an injection does in the body – it produces an immediate effect. This model of the media is sometimes called the **hypodermic syringe model**. It argues that an injection of say, violence on the television will cause the effect of violent behaviour in the audience. An experiment on children by the psychologist *Bandura* showed some evidence for this argument.

In the experiment two groups were used, one as the control group and one as the experimental group. The experimental group were shown a film of children behaving aggressively with toys, such as a weighted 'bobo' doll, shouting things like 'zap' and 'kapow!' This experimental group behaved more aggressively with toys they were then given to play with, than the control group did who were shown a non-violent film.

'The girls . . . huddled around their radios trembling and weeping in each other's arms . . . Terror-stricken girls, hoping to escape from the Mars invaders, rushed to the basement of the dormitory' (Cantril writing in 1940 – just one of the responses to the Welles' broadcast.)

RESEARCH IDEA

Examine the way the media portrays groups, such as females and/or ethnic minorities.

The Bandura Experiment on the effects of the media

However the Bandura experiment is not conclusive, many others have been done since which do *not* show a direct relationship between what is heard or seen in the media and an audience effect of the sort described.

Q Does the Bandura experiment and *The Martians Have Landed* incident support or reject the hypodermic model of the media? □

Q Do you agree with this theory about the effects of the media? □

An alternative view on the effects of the media is given by *Katz and Lazarsfield*, who argue that the real importance of the media is that it influences the ideas of powerful people, who then spread these opinions in society. This is known as the **two step flow model** because the influence of the media is in two stages, affecting one person who then influences another. Katz and Lazarsfield's argument sees the media as only indirectly affecting people's opinions. However, it is very difficult to prove this or to estimate whether gradual cultural changes also take place because of media influence.

DISCUSS

Do you think that there is more bad language in the media than there used to be? Is this because it is more common in society, or is there more bad language in real life because it is heard more in the media? □

Q What is a pressure group? (Reread Module 3 on Power and Politics, pages 50–54 for more on pressure groups.) □

Pressure groups, such as the National Viewers' and Listeners' Association, led by Mrs Mary Whitehouse, are convinced that the media does influence human behaviour. This organisation campaigns for stricter controls on the media, and argues that there should be a lot less nudity, violence, sex, and swearing on the television.

'Adult' film warning for C4

THE TELEVISION crusader Mrs Mary Whitehouse yesterday claimed success in a campaign to get advertisers to boycott films carrying Channel 4's new "adults-only" warning symbol.

Mrs Whitehouse, president of the National Viewers and Listeners Association, wrote to every company whose advertisement appeared during the screening of the first red warning symbol film, *Themroc*, on September 19.

The film included scenes of incest and of two policemen being roasted on a spit and eaten.

Source: *The Guardian*, October 1986

It can be argued that the media itself acts as a pressure group, forcing government action on issues that are reported by the media. The new style of investigative journalism has meant that in the last few years reporters have publicised allegations of police brutality, corruption amongst officials, and new evidence pointing to the innocence of convicted criminals which have all led to official action being taken.

The style chosen for reporting on deviance, may also have serious implications for government policy, as well as affecting public reactions to a particular problem.

Q Can you name some television or radio programmes that involve investigative journalism?

Deviance and the media

The sociologist *Stan Cohen*, writing in 1972, argued that societies tend to focus on one or two social problems that are seen to epitomise all that is wrong with society at that time. He calls this **moral panic**, and comments, 'Societies appear to be subject, every now and then, to periods of moral panic. A condition, episode or group of persons emerges to become defined as a threat to society. The moral barricades are manned by editors, bishops, politicians and other right-thinking people.'

BRAINSTORM

How many issues can you think of in the last two years that might be seen as a moral panic of the sort that Cohen describes? □

This does not mean of course that the problem in question does not exist or is not important. It does mean however, that particular emphasis is given to one problem. The media then helps to draw the public's attention to this problem, to define it as a social problem, and to cause a moral panic.

In 1985, 1986, and 1987 the media treatment of issues, such as child abuse, football hooliganism, heroin addiction and AIDS was highly dramatic. This coverage coloured the way the public perceived these issues, and demanded government action on them.

There are a number of studies on deviance and the effects of the media. These include the way the media reports football hooliganism, street crime and suicide. Some sociologists argue that the media may actually encourage deviance because of the way it is reported. For more on media and crime read Module 13 on Deviance, Unit 6.

AIDS outburst police chief's amazing claim

I MAY BE GOD'S PROPHET

OUTSPOKEN police chief James Anderton claimed yesterday that he could be a prophet from God.

He declared: "I may well be used by God in this way."

The Greater Manchester chief constable said "something happened" to him moments before his AIDS outburst last month, when he accused homosexuals of "swirling around in a human cesspit of their own making."

"Something was speaking to me inside and the words that I was using in my speech just flooded into my mind," he said.

"I couldn't qualify them, I couldn't change them and I couldn't alter them. I had to say what I was compelled to say.

"If Jesus were here today He may have spoken in terms similar to the ones I used."

Mr Anderton's astonishing claims were branded "disgraceful" last night by a member of his own police committee.

Source: *Daily Mirror*, January 1987

Arson attacks on homes of Aids victims

TWO MEN in one London borough have had their homes burned after neighbours learned that they had Aids. Six others committed suicide after they were told they had the disease.

Source: *The Independent*, February 1987 (left) and *The Evening Sentinel*, February 1987

Cash for 'gays' rap over AIDS

A CHESHIRE councillor yesterday accused councils who provided cash for "gay" centres of contributing to the spread of AIDS.

The Amplification Spiral

Is the coverage of AIDS by the press an example of a moral panic?

In 1986 the AIDS epidemic led to speeches being made by a politician, a Chief Constable of the police, and by a Church of England Bishop, all condemning those with the AIDS virus as morally bad. It was seen by some as a punishment for sexual activity outside marriage, and many influential people used the media to call for a return to the more traditional and supposedly better moral values of monogamy.

Cohen also argues that the media is partly responsible for the courts' decisions on the sentencing of offenders. He argues that the relationship between courts, police, media and public opinion can result in stiffer penalties and more police resources for some crimes. He calls this *deviancy amplification*, and argues that there is frequently a spiralling effect caused by the interaction of these agencies.

The amplification spiral results in a crime being reported by the media, and public opinion demanding heavier policing in this area. The equation made is that a larger number of police means that more criminals are caught and again this will be of interest to the media. These events may lead to a moral panic and a demand for stiffer sentences, which in turn will be reported upon in the press.

UNIT 5 YOUTH CULTURE

Culture refers to the values, norms, attitudes, and way of life of people in a society. Youth culture therefore means the distinctive way of life of young people in society. Studies of youth culture may focus on the differences in dress, hair-style, language, leisure pursuits or interests of young people.

The mass media appears to be partly responsible for the development of a distinctive youth culture in modern society. After the Second World War a separation took place between the music and dress of people in their late teens and early twenties, and those who were older or younger. The term **teenager** was used for the first time.

RESEARCH IDEA

Find out about young people in the 1990s; what music do they like, what radio and television programmes are most popular? Are there differences in values between different age groups in society? ☐

By the 1950s the mass media was capable of spreading a distinctive style and value system quickly, so that young people all over the country watched or listened to the same programmes. Most sociologists think that it was the affluence of the fifties that made it possible for young people to form a distinctive group for the first time. Teenagers were free from money worries, and indeed had money to spare to buy consumer goods, such as clothes and records. They were also free from family responsibilities because of their youth.

The comparative affluence of teenagers meant that a vast industry quickly grew to cater for the needs and wants of this section of society. It is estimated that young people today spend over £1000 million on goods, such as records, clothes, magazines, cosmetics, entertainments, etc. Many advertisements are aimed specifically at this age group.

In the 1950s youth groups, such as beatniks or teddy boys, could be easily identified by their appearance, as could the Mods and Rockers of the early sixties, the Hippies of the late sixties, the Skinheads in the early 1970s and the Punks of the late 1970s.

Punk youth culture began as a working-class sub-culture of a generation that were hit by unemployment. Their slogans of: 'No wealth', and 'No future', were a reaction against the drug subculture of the hippies and the wealth of rock stars. Although punk declined sharply once it was commercialised in the late 1970s the movement still has its supporters.

DISCUSS

Look at the photograph of the punk family on the left. It was taken in 1986 at the Queen's sixtieth birthday celebrations, and seems to challenge the values of this occasion. Can you explain the contradiction in values that this picture shows? ☐

If you were the editor of a national daily paper, would you include it in the paper for that day? If so, would you run it on the front page or on an inside page?

Now decide on a caption that you think would be most appropriate for this photograph.

RESEARCH IDEA

Take some examples of products specifically aimed at young people in society, and analyse the values and ideas that are being attached to the product to make it sell.

(You could do this by carefully going through a teenage magazine.) ☐

Q What do you think this punk family feel about life in the UK today?

Most youth movements are a protest against the accepted value systems of the mainstream culture in society. The symbols used to express this protest therefore include dress and hair-style, which quickly identify that person as not accepting the norms and values of the day.

Youth Culture from the mid 1950s to the mid 1980s

The dominant value system responds by rejecting the youth culture and seeing it as a symptom of what is wrong with society. Stan Cohen in *Folk Devils and Moral Panics* even goes as far as saying that some young people are seen as devils, labelled as evil and bad because of their appearance, in the same way that our ancestors saw some old women as witches!

RESEARCH IDEA

Examine the treatment of young people by the media. Are there times that the media stereotypes young people as devils, an indication of modern evil? □

Young people have a marginal status in society, they are seen to be neither adults nor children. Legally too, their status is inconsistent. Young people can have sex at sixteen, but cannot drive until seventeen. They cannot vote, drink alcohol or marry without parental consent until eighteen. A couple cannot adopt a child, or an individual stand as a member of parliament until the age of twenty-one.

Many young offenders in front of the courts are aged between sixteen and twenty-one. It is thought by some sociologists that one explanation of this is the lack of identity many young people feel during this transitional period between childhood and being considered an adult. Some young people may therefore join a youth culture that has a delinquent value system.

WHERE TO NOW?

This module has attempted to show both the structure and the impact of the media in society today. You may now like to read Module 13 on Deviance or Module 3 on Power and Politics.

Turn to Module 13 on Deviance for more on juvenile delinquency.

MODULE · 3

POWER AND POLITICS

THREE

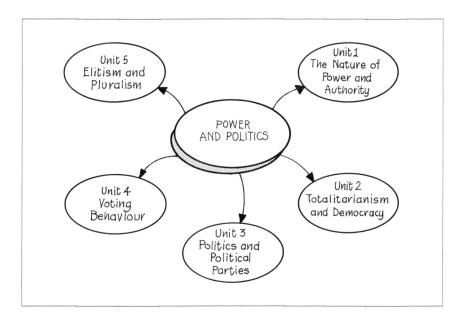

WHAT THIS MODULE IS ABOUT

Power is the ability to make decisions that affect others. Everyone has power, but some people seem to have more power than others. This module explores the unequal distribution of power in society, and examines closely the nature of political power and parliamentary democracy in Britain.

BY THE END OF THIS MODULE YOU SHOULD BE ABLE TO:

1 Define power and identify the difference between power and authority.
2 Appreciate the difference between totalitarianism and democracy.
3 Understand what is meant by 'first past the post' and proportional representation.
4 Demonstrate a knowledge of the political parties in Britain.
5 Describe what is meant by the term deviant voting.
6 Discuss the influences affecting how people vote in elections.
7 Discuss whether democracy really exists in Britain today.
8 Outline the role of pressure groups in society and describe the methods they use.
9 Appreciate the role of the media in political socialisation.

THE NATURE OF POWER AND AUTHORITY

What is power?

If every person has a degree of power to make decisions that affect others, then it follows that a **hierarchy** of power exists, i.e. where each level or position has power over the levels below, but has less power than the ones above.

Study the diagram of the hierarchical structure of a typical secondary school or college shown on the left.

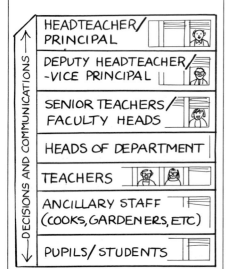

QUESTIONS

1　According to the diagram, who has most power?
2　Who has the least?
3　A Head of Department has power over whom?
4　Who has power over a Head of Department?
5　How much power does the canteen worker have?
6　Where does the caretaker fit in this hierarchy?
7　How many females are in powerful or top positions in your school or college? □

This alternative structure could be described as a **democratic** power structure. The difference lies in the fact that this sort of organisation, the head or principal does not make all the decisions and rules themselves. Instead, the power is *shared* and the school or college acts as a **community**, where everyone participates in the general running and decision-making processes.

DISCUSS

What do you think would be the advantages and disadvantages of the *democratic* power structure? Do you think it is possible for a school or college to be a community and to share the power in this way? □

Q　Which power model most accurately depicts your own particular school or college? □

Q　What sort of organisational structure do most factories and offices have? □

DISCUSS

Does the diagram above depict the power structure within most schools and colleges? Do you think that this sort of hierarchical organisation works well? Look carefully at the alternative power structure shown on the right.

TASK

Are all pupils equal? Or is there a hierarchical strucutre among pupils.

Consider prefects and sixth-formers. Draw a diagram to depict the distribution of power between pupils in school.

DISCUSS

Do you think corporal punishment gets results? Do teachers still have some physical or repressive power. Consider detentions, confiscations, etc.

The difference between power and authority

In the hierarchical model of the school, the teacher is seen to have power over the pupil. However, a more accurate description would be to say that the teacher has **authority** and that the pupil accepts this authority and behaves accordingly.

Naturally, it would be quite easy to find examples in a school, where the pupil does not accept the authority of the teacher at all! But generally, it is true to say that *order* prevails and the authority of the teacher is accepted. Pupils and students generally accept the right of the teacher or lecturer to teach them, because they want to learn. Authority is therefore attached to the role of the teacher which then allows them to make decisions that affect the student.

Weber (whose theories are examined in more detail on page 84) has called this a **legal** type of authority. Where the teacher is given authority by pupils, parents and by the government to act in the pupils' best interests.

Of course, teachers can be very powerful in terms of whether a pupil succeeds or fails in their education (as shown in Module 7 on Education pages 122–124). Their power lies more in the art of **persuasion** than in terms of physical force or **coercion**, especially since corporal punishment, such as caning, has now largely disappeared from schools.

Teachers also have an **economic** power. Examination results, certificates and reports do matter greatly to most pupils, since they can affect their future employment prospects. Teachers therefore have the power to affect pupils' economic position in society.

Weber identified two other forms of authority besides the *legal* and these are **traditional** and **charismatic**.

Using the teacher as an example again, it is possible to describe the teacher who has *traditional* authority as being one who has perhaps taught at the school for a long time; and may have even taught the parents of the pupils! This sort of teacher has traditional authority and is respected because of the number of years they have taught at school.

Q Can you think of a teacher at your school or college with traditional authority? □

A description of *charismatic* authority is given in Module 9 on Religion, page 166, when discussing the power and influence of leaders, such as Jesus, Hitler, Ayatollah Khomeini and so on. A person with charismatic authority is usually personally liked or admired to the extent that people will do whatever they say without question.

Q Can you think of any teachers or lecturers in your school or college with charismatic authority, i.e. they can influence pupils' behaviour simply because of their personality and popularity. □

Of course, pupils also have power! The power of the pupils is perhaps best described as the **non-co-operation** type. An example of this would be where a pupil refuses to work normally in class unless allowed to sit where they want. This sort of power can be quite effective as many teachers are aware.

Now look at the task on power and authority overleaf.

We have now examined the seven different types of power and authority illustrated here.

QUESTIONS

Read the following interview between Bill, a skinhead gang leader, and his social worker, and then answer the questions which follow:

Q   When did you become leader of the gang?

A   Nine months ago.

Q   How did you become leader?

A   I beat up Harry (previous leader). Now the rest of the gang do what I tell them.

Q   So, if your friends don't do as they're told, you beat them up?

A   No! We decide together what to do. It's only when someone gets heavy (aggressive) that I have to sort him out – or he leaves the gang. I like to be fair though. I'm not a bully. Some leave the gang because they chicken out.

Q   What sort of things do the gang do?

A   Well, we go fighting, nicking and smashing things. The best thing is being chased by the police.

a   Many people would consider that the activities of the gang challenge 'Authority'. Why do you think this is so?

b   Does Bill have power, or authority, or both, over the gang? Give reasons for your answer.

Source: Cambridge Board Sociology GCSE, 1984

DISCUSS

What sort of power or authority do these members of society have?

Although we have only considered how power and authority exists in the school, these of course exist in all parts of society. The cartoons below illustrate the different types of power and authority that can be seen in family life.

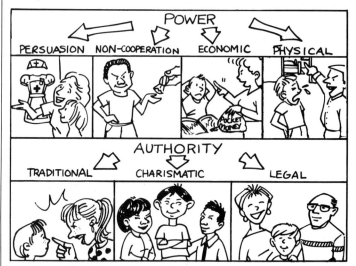

Study the examples given above. Then provide comparable examples of power and authority for school life, using the previous discussion to help you.

Similarly, give examples of how power and authority works in a group of friends, i.e. within a peer group, e.g. a member of the gang who has the power of persuasion and charismatic authority.

Doctor (top left), factory manager (top right), police woman (bottom left), Michael Jackson (bottom right)

Look back at the hierarchical model of school organisation on page 34.

Q Does the headteacher have *total* power over the people below? ☐

Most headteachers would claim that they do not have total power; that they are not in total control of their school. The reason for this is that there are other more powerful bodies who control what goes on in school.

Perhaps the most powerful body is the **Board of Governors** who are now totally responsible for the **Local management of schools (LMS)**. This means for example that the Board of Governors ensures that the National Curriculum is being followed, decides how money should be spent in the school, interviews for staff and makes appointments – including the appointment of the head or principal. The headteacher reports termly on the work of the school to the Governing Body.

One body that has had much power taken away from it by the Education Reform Act is the **County Council** or **Local Education Authority (LEA)**. Most of this power now lies with school governing bodies. However, although the governing body employs and dismisses staff, it is still the County Council who pays teachers' salaries and who decides how much a school will receive in its budget for the year. This figure is usually calculated on the number of pupils in the school. And so the greater the number of pupils, the greater the funding for the school.

Schools can opt-out of County Council control by voting for **grant-maintained status**. They are then directly funded by the **National Government**.

It is the Department of Education and Science and particularly the Secretary of State and Minister of Education who have the power to make major policy decisions affecting education, such as the recent introduction of national assessment and reporting on pupils' attainment.

RESEARCH IDEA

Attempt to find the answer to the following questions by researching in libraries, newspapers, council offices, e.g. your town hall, or interview staff, teachers, headteachers, parents and governors.

1 Who are your local County Councillors?
2 Where does the County Council gets its money from?
3 Who is the current Secretary of State for Education?
4 How much money did the Government allow for education spending in its budget this year. Was it more or less than last year?
5 By comparison, how much did the Government allow for defence? ☐

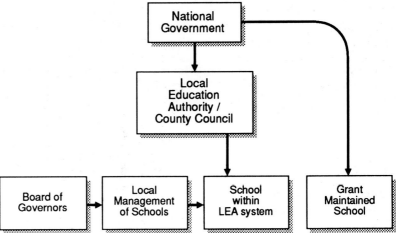

The government of schools

RESEARCH IDEA

Who makes up the Board of Governors at your school or college? Are they parents, business people, politicians, teachers or caretakers? Are they all elected or are some co-opted or invited to join the Governing Body? There are suggestions that pupils should also be part of the Governing Body. Pupils might then also be able to share in the decisions over school policy. Do you think this is a good idea? Conduct a survey to find out what most people in your school or college think.

T A S K

In conclusion to this unit, you should now be in a position to:

1 Draw up a full model of the distribution of power in your school. Is it hierarchical or democratic?
2 Demonstrate with examples the difference between power and authority.
3 Write a short essay in answer to the question 'How is power distributed in schools today?' ☐

U N I T 2 TOTALITARIANISM AND DEMOCRACY

The previous unit looked at how power is divided and used, particularly in schools. This is what **politics** is all about – looking at how society or a part of society, such as a school, is governed or run.

There are two principal ways of governing a country (or a school)

a   by totalitarianism and
b   by using democracy.

If a country is governed by **totalitarianism**, then power lies entirely in the hands of a small group of people, an **élite**. Or, if just one person runs the country then this is a **dictatorship**. In a totalitarian organisation, individual people have no way of sharing in the decision-making processes, that is, no way of sharing in the power.

T A S K

Find examples of totalitarian régimes in the world. Consider Germany in the period 1933 to 1944, Italy 1922 to 1943; Russia in the Eighteenth, Nineteenth and Twentieth centuries and Chile, Haiti and the Phillipines in the 1970s. Who were the leaders of these countries?

Stalin (left) and Papa Doc Duvalier (right), heads of later and modern-day totalitarian régimes

Some people in Western countries think that communist countries like modern Russia, China and Cuba are dictatorships, because they have only one party. However, the governments in these countries call themselves Peoples' Democracies, because they believe that all the people benefit from having a communist government and communist way of life, where everyone is regarded as equal.

In a democracy, the country is run very differently. The word democracy comes from two Greek words *demos* meaning people and *kratos* meaning power. **Democracy** means, therefore that the people share the power and make their own decisions. In the Athens of Ancient Greece, the people of the city met in an assembly to discuss and vote on what course of action the city should take. This was possible in Ancient Greece because by comparison with Western democracies today the population of Athens in 5BC was small and so everyone could meet together and take part in direct democratic government.

RESEARCH IDEA

Find out when Britain had slaves and whether they were allowed to vote. Also, women in Britain did not have any political power until quite recently. Discover when women began to gain some political power and how they gained it. See Module 12 on Gender, page 222.

Q   Do you think it would be physically possible for everyone in Britain, or even in London, to meet together and make political decisions? □

It is interesting however, that even in democratic Athens, women and slaves were not allowed any political power. They could not join in the assembly, make decisions and vote with the men.

Perhaps the most famous definition of democracy is Abraham Lincoln's, 'government of the people, for the people, by the people'. A democratic state, by this definition, is where everyone participates in the decision-making and government is thus run by the people.

Q   Do we have this sort of democracy in Britain? □

When people got the vote

% over 18 years

100
90
80
70
60
50
40
30
20
10
0

1832 1867 1884 1918 1928 1970

Middle Classes | Some working men | Almost all working men | Women over 30 | Women over 21 | All over 18

Not everyone has a vote. People who are under eighteen, insane, serving a prison sentence, or a peer of the realm, cannot vote.

DISCUSS
Why are these groups not allowed to vote.

The answer to the last question is, of course, 'No'. The sort of democracy that exists, in Britain and many other countries is called **representative democracy**. This is where individual people stand as candidates to undertake government on behalf of the people. At an election, these candidates are chosen by the people, the **electorate**, who each have one **vote**.

In a *representative democracy*, individuals can influence political decisions indirectly, by voting for the candidate or representative, whose views they agree with. These representatives or **Members of Parliament**, as they are called if elected, represent an area containing approximately 60 000 people called a **constituency**. In the **House of Commons** there are 635 elected Members of Parliament (MPs).

Besides national government, people in Britain also elect their representatives for local government. These representatives are called **councillors** and are either town councillors, district councillors, or county councillors. They are elected in the same way as the Members of Parliament.

Whilst central government deals with national and international affairs, local government deals with a range of functions and services that are vitally important to everyone. At local level, individuals have a greater chance of direct participation in political decision-making as the diagram below shows.

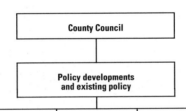

County Council
Policy developments and existing policy

Education	Libraries	Fire and Public Protection	Highways	Planning	Police	Social Services	Waste Disposal
Provision for education service/ adult education/ careers service	Museums/County Record Office	Provision of Fire Brigade/Trading Standards and Consumer Protection	Construction and maintenance of roads and bridges/ street lighting/road safety/coordination of public transport	Land use planning/ control of mineral extraction/tourism/ conservation	Maintenance of an adequate and efficient police force	Care and protection of people at risk: elderly/mentally ill/ parents/young children	Disposal of domestic/industrial waste/control of pollution/land reclamation/ recycling waste

RESEARCH IDEA

Find out
1 Who is your representative in Parliament, your MP?
2 What does local government do? Research and write a short paragraph about each function.
3 What is a parish council?
4 Where does your town or district council hold their meetings?
5 Are there any councillors on your Board of Governors at school? What sort of councillors are they? ☐

DISCUSS

You should now be in a position to discuss answers to the following:

The majority of the British people are proud to say that they live in a democratic society. Explain the difference between a parliamentary democracy and a dictatorship.

Or compare the political organisation of school with society. Is your school totalitarian or democratic? ☐

U N I T 3 POLITICS AND POLITICAL PARTIES

Politics comes from the Greek word *polis* meaning city. In Ancient Greece all the citizens of Athens were assembled to take part in a debate about the important issues and to make decisions about how the country should be run.

Direct democracy like that in Ancient Greece is of course impossible in modern Britain. It would mean assembling the whole of the *electorate*, i.e. the 41 million people eligible to vote, and then trying to hold a debate! Instead Britain has **indirect** or **representative** democracy where the people take an active part in making decisions, at the time of elections, by **voting** for their representatives.

However, not everyone who is eligible uses their vote. In fact, only three out of four people in Britain actually bother to turn out to vote in the General Election, held at least every five years.

British elections are conducted on a *first past the post* system, i.e. the parliamentary candidate who gains the largest number of votes is elected to office. Likewise, the parliamentary party which has the most MPs takes power and its leader is invited by the Queen to form a government. A party does not have to have an overall majority in the House of Commons, i.e. more than 50 per cent of the seats. It can combine with another party to form a *coalition* government instead.

RESEARCH IDEA

Try to find out when Britain last had a coalition government and which political parties decided to join together. □

The leader of the political party elected at a General Election becomes the Prime Minister and chooses 51 Ministers and 22 Cabinet Ministers as shown below.

BRAINSTORM

As a group suggest reasons why only three out of four people bother to turn out to vote in the General Election. □

T A S K

Can you name any of the present Cabinet Ministers? Remember, it is the Cabinet that makes the major government decisions.

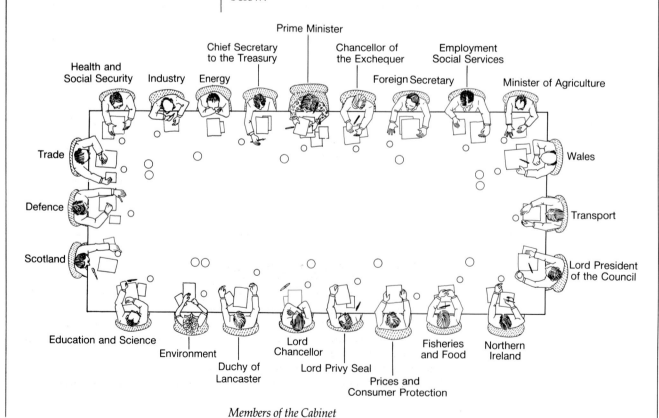

Members of the Cabinet

There are several different political parties in Britain but, the two major ones are the Conservative and the Labour Party. The **Labour Party** is politically *left wing*, or *socialist*. People who belong to the Labour Party believe in a fairer distribution of wealth and state ownership of the large industries, such as telecommunications, gas, coal, electricity, etc. The Labour Party is closely linked to the trade union movement and it is a defender of the Welfare State.

Since the last war, the Labour Party has been in power three times: 1945 to 1951, 1964 to 1970 and 1974 to 1979. In 1987, it had 225 seats in parliament.

The **Conservative Party**, or Tories as its members are also called, is politically *right wing* and people who belong to the Conservative Party believe in *free-enterprise* and little or no state control of industry. The Conservative Party is generally associated with the interests of big business and is financed by it. It is easily the richest political party in Britain and supports the existence of great inequalities of wealth.

Since the last war, the Conservative Party has been in office during the following periods: 1951 to 1964, 1979 to the present date. It had 345 seats in Parliament after the 1987 election.

QUESTIONS

1 Who are the leaders of these political parties?
2 Which political party won the 1987 election? How big was their majority over the next party, i.e. how many more seats than their rival did they have?
3 Why might the Labour Party and the Conservative Party have very different attitudes towards trade unions?
4 The Liberal Democrat Party is made up of two parties that joined together in 1989. What were the names of these? ☐

There are other political parties in Britain – in the *centre*, the *extreme left* and *extreme right* wings of the **political spectrum**, as the diagram below reveals.

> **Q**   Which major political party has been in power for the longest period since the Second World War?

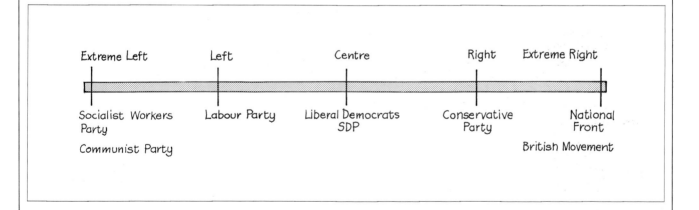

RESEARCH IDEA

a Find out what sort of society the other parties in the diagram believe in.
b Find out how many seats in parliament each party holds.
c There are other political parties such as the Scottish National Party, the Green Party and even the Raving Monster Looney Party. Try to find out more about these parties.
d Conduct a quick survey to see which political philosophy or beliefs most of your friends agree with. Which party would they vote for and why?

In June 1975, the question 'Should Britain remain a member of the EEC?' was put to the entire British people in the form of a referendum, where everyone could vote on this issue. The turn out to vote was 64 per cent of the population and just over two-thirds of those voted 'yes'. In a referendum, *direct democracy* is therefore possible, and the people make decisions themselves rather than leaving them to their elected representatives in Parliament.

Q What is the difference between an election and a referendum?

On page 40 we said that British elections are conducted on a 'first past the post' basis, where the party which has most MPs takes power. An alternative system called **proportional representation** (PR) is described below in an article from *New Society*. In PR people vote for parties and not the individual candidates.

FIRST PAST THE POST OR IS IT LAST PAST THE POST?

There is a bewildering variety of electoral systems in operation in western democracies, many of which involve some kind of proportional representation. Most European countries, including the Irish Republic, now use proportional representation in elections. Britain's first-past-the-post system has become the exception.

The perfect example of the distortions created by the British system is, of course, the 1983 general election result. The Conservatives got 13 million votes and 396 seats, Labour 8.5 million votes and 209 seats, while the Alliance polled nearly as many votes as Labour (7.8 million) but got only 23 seats. It took 33,000 votes to elect a Conservative MP, 40,000 to elect a Labour MP and 339,000 to elect an Alliance MP.

Had the election been carried out on a proportional representation basis, Mrs Thatcher would not have gained a majority at all, let alone one of 144. The Tories would have got 280 seats, Labour 182, the Alliance 170 and others 18.

Source: *New Society*, 1983

TASK

Design a bar chart revealing the relationship between the number of votes polled and the number of seats actually won by the three major parties in 1983. □

Q In 1987, Conservatives polled 43 per cent of the vote, Labour 32 per cent and the Alliance 23 per cent. How many seats did each party gain? □

RESEARCH IDEA

The Liberal Democrats support proportional representation. Why? What problems could be caused by the adoption of PR? □

Most MPs have an occupation before they get elected to serve as an MP. The table below reveals that many of our MPs have held professional jobs before becoming MPs, which might indicate that it is more difficult for manual workers to get elected to Parliament, than middle-class professional people.

Similarly, a high number of our MPs, especially in the Conservative Party, have attended public school and university compared with the rest of the population.

QUESTIONS

Study the data below and answer the questions that follow it.

The people's representatives

Occupations of MPs

	Con	Lab	Lib	Other
Barristers	54	21	—	1
Solicitors	16	10	—	1
Journalists	31	19	1	1
Publishers	5	—	—	—
Public relations	2	—	—	—
Teachers	14	53	3	4
Medical	3	5	—	—
Farmers, landowners	25	2	2	1
Company directors	82	1	2	—
Accountants	12	4	1	—
Brokers	17	—	—	—
Managers	52	33	—	2
Architects	5	1	1	—
Scientists	1	5	—	—
Economists	8	9	—	1
Banking	12	—	—	—
Diplomatic	2	1	—	—
Social workers	1	3	—	—
Civil servants	—	3	—	—
Local government	1	2	—	—
Clerical and technical	1	3	—	—
Engineers	8	30	1	—
Mineworkers	—	16	—	—
Rail workers	—	9	—	—
Other manual workers	—	7	—	2
Trade union officials	1	27	—	—
Party officials	12	5	—	—
Hoteliers	—	—	—	2
Other jobs	10	5	—	—
Ministers of religion	—	—	—	2

In the present Parliament, 67 per cent of Conservative MPs went to public school compared with 3 per cent of the population as a whole. Nearly 15 per cent had been to Britain's top public school, Eton. A total of 48 per cent of Conservative MPs went to Oxford or Cambridge, whereas only 5 per cent of the population have been to any university.

In contrast, nearly 90 per cent of Labour MPs attended state schools and only 20 per cent went to Oxford or Cambridge. 32 per cent of Labour MPs went to non-Oxbridge universities, compared with 17 per cent of Tory MPs.

Source: *New Society*, March 1980

1 What percentage of the following had been to any university: *a* Conservative MPs, *b* Labour MPs, *c* the general population?
2 List the top five occupations of: *a* Conservative MPs, *b* Labour MPs.
3 The Labour Party claims to represent the working class in Britain. How much does the educational and occupational background of Labour MPs reflect this working-class representation?
4 As well as social classes, what other social groups are under- or over-represented in Parliament?
5 What are some of the principal ways in which an individual can have an influence on the government of Britain? □

Source: AEB Sociology GCE, 1984

UNIT 4

VOTING BEHAVIOUR

Q Why would a politician be tempted to make promises or to change their policies in accordance with the results of an opinion poll?

Thursday June 11 1987   25p

Tories coasting to 7-point win, say three polls

Marplan for The Guardian, Harris for TV-am and NOP, in national projections from a poll taken for The Independent in marginal seats, all showed the Conservatives with 42 per cent of the vote, Labour with 35 and the Alliance with 21. On a uniform swing across the nation, that would produce a Conservative majority of about 40 seats.

Source: *The Guardian*

DISCUSS

Discuss with your group whether the results of your survey support the following statement that 'Many voters are poorly informed about political issues'. Give specific examples to support your view.

DISCUSS

Why do you think working-class people vote Tory when this party is known to support big business and the preservation of the inequalities between people?

Opinion polls

Opinion polls are sample surveys: where a small representative section of the population is asked about its attitudes on particular issues, e.g. how they will vote at the next election. From this small survey, researchers make assumptions about the whole population and may predict the result of a forthcoming election.

Sometimes these predictions are highly inaccurate. For example, in 1970 four out of five polls predicted a Labour victory, yet the result of the election was a substantial Conservative one.

Some people claim that opinion polls can affect election results. For instance, if the polls predict a substantial victory for one party then the supporters of that party may feel that it is not so important for them to turn out to vote. Also, people fear that political leaders are influenced by opinion polls and that they might make promises and change their policies according to the result of the polls.

Opinion polls, such as Gallup, show that many voters ae poorly informed about political issues and find it difficult to describe the policies of particular political parties, i.e. what each party says it stands for and what it will do, if elected.

RESEARCH IDEA

Test whether this is true. Conduct your own opinion poll. Select your sample (making sure that it is representative, see page 6–7) and ask the following questions:

a   Which political party has strong policies in connection with law and order?
b   Which party puts a high priority on the issue of unemployment?
c   What are the policies of the major political parties regarding nuclear weapons.
   Add any other questions on political issues that you want to.

When you have a response to each question, ask the interviewee if they can describe in detail any of the policies of a political party of their choice. □

Studies have shown that not only are voters poorly informed, but that many voters simply have a long-standing *loyalty* to a particular party; although, in Britain this tendency is now on the decline. Many writers have suggested that it is social class that lies behind this traditional party loyalty and is the explanation for the fact that the working class have remained loyal to the Labour Party and have mainly voted Labour and that the middle class have been loyal to the Conservative Party and have mainly voted Tory.

DISCUSS

Why do you think the middle and upper classes have mainly supported the Conservative Party? □

Of course, if the working class were totally loyal to the Labour Party, and always voted Labour then there would be a Labour government in power permanently, as the working class make up approximately 65 per cent of the British population.

In fact, one third of working-class voters have regularly voted for the Conservatives, not for the Labour Party.

Deviant voting

Various writers have described these working-class people who do not vote for the party of their class, i.e. the Labour Party, as being **deviant voters**.

These sociologists give the following explanations for this deviant voting behaviour:

Runciman found that if a working-class person believed themselves to be middle class, then they were more likely to vote Conservative.

Q   Is this false class consciousness? See Module 5 on Social Stratification, pages 78–81. □

See Module 5 on Social Stratification, pages 78–81.

QUESTIONS

Study this chart which shows the results of an opinion poll taken in June 1983. This asked people which issues they considered to have been the successes and failures of the 1979–1983 Conservative Government.

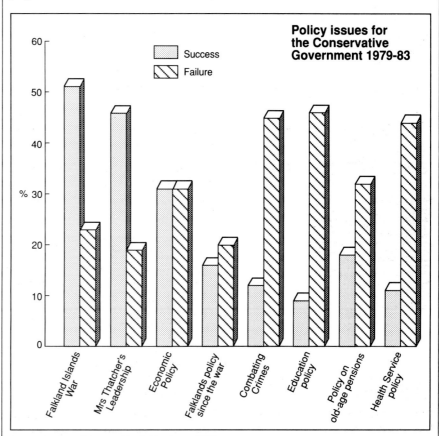

Source: Britain Observed by B Harrison, 1985

a   On which issue did people think the Government was most successful?
b   On which TWO issues did people think the Government has most clearly failed?
c   Explain why the results of the poll might not have been an absolutely accurate guide to public opinion. □

McKenzie and Silver found that many poorer working-class people believe that upper-class people are born to rule. Since the Conservative Party is made up of mostly upper-class politicians, these working-class **deferential voters** vote Tory.

Q   Why do you think some working-class people think the upper class is born to rule? □

McKenzie and Silver also found that there are **secular voters**, i.e. those working-class people who decide that the Tories are more likely to govern competently and to deliver the goods thus making everyone better off in the long run. These working-class people therefore vote Conservative.

Source: MEG Government, Politics and Law GCSE, Specimen question, 1988

Parkin, however, argued that only working-class people who live in working-class neighbourhoods and who work and mix with other working-class people are likely to vote for the working-class party, i.e. Labour. Otherwise, Parkin argues, the working-class person is exposed to the dominant values of society which are middle class and so is likely to vote for a middle-class party.

Q How are people exposed to values in society? ☐

Nordlinger suggested that well paid working-class people had a sense of being well off and therefore identified with the middle class and voted for the Conservative Party.

Butler and Rose also agreed that affluence was the cause of working-class deviant voting. This concept of the better off sections of the working class were becoming middle class in their attitudes (and thus voting Conservative) is called the **embourgeoisement** thesis and was tested by *Goldthorpe and Lockwood* in their study of the Vauxhall car workers. They concluded that there was no evidence to support the idea of embourgeiousement taking place (see Module 5 on Social Stratification page 80).

Besides working-class deviant voters, sociologists have discovered that there are middle-class deviant voters'. These individuals who might reasonably be expected to vote for the Conservative Party but who, instead vote Labour. There are about 20 per cent of the middle class who in fact vote Labour. They do so, it is claimed, because they once belonged to the working class, before gaining upward social mobility into the managerial and professional classes.

In particular these middle-class Labour voters, who Parkin calls 'Middle-class Radicals' tend to belong to the teaching profession, to be the sons or daughters of active trade unionists; or, to work in the caring professions, such as social work.

DISCUSS

Why do you think these workers tend to vote Labour? Could it have something to do with what the Labour Party stands for and its policies on education, social services, etc? ☐

DISCUSS

In the 1980 election, the affluent or highly paid workers were the ones who voted SDP and Conservative rather than for the Labour Party. Do you think that the embourgeouisement theory works in practice? Do you think that better off workers are likely to become middle class in their attitudes? Why would these affluent working-class people vote SDP or Conservative? Why do you think they might not vote Labour?

Is there a way of finding out definite or objective answers to these questions. What could you do as a social scientist?

Q How is upward social mobility achieved? (See Module 5 on Social Stratification, Unit 3).

·RESEARCH IDEA

Conduct a small survey to find out how the teachers or lecturers at your school or college voted at the last General Election, in order to see if they are 'Middle-class Radicals'. You must remember however, the condition of the secret ballot. Some teachers or lecturers may refuse to tell you how they voted. Respect their privacy.

In addition to social class, sociologists have discovered that there may be other factors affecting the way people vote. These are suggested in the table below.

Factors affecting voting behaviour

Factor	Evidence
Age	Older people are more likely to vote Conservative.
Gender	Women are more likely to vote Conservative than men, especially working-class women.
Geographical Location/ Region	The industrial North of Britain tends to vote Labour; and the richer South, Conservative. Also, the outer suburbs tend to be Tory whilst inner areas of towns and cities are often Labour.
Ethnicity	There is no clear evidence to suggest that ethnic minorities in Britain vote en masse. Many do not vote at all.
Religion	Catholics are more likely to vote Labour and Anglicans to vote Conservative.
Family	The majority of people vote as their parents do (see table at side)
Mass Media	Tends to reinforce the political views of the reader, rather than change them. Opinion polls can perhaps have an effect.

T A S K

1 Discuss in your groups whether these suggested factors are likely to affect voting behaviour.
2 Suggest reasons for each of these types of voting behaviour.
   For example, why do you think older people vote Conservative.
   Remember your ideas or theories are extremely valuable. □

In conclusion, it can be said that although some people still vote according to class, nevertheless there have been some big changes in voting patterns in recent years. These changes were especially noticeable at the 1983 election when the SDP Party took a quarter of all votes from both social classes.

There are signs that the Labour Party is losing some of its traditional working-class support, perhaps due to the decline in traditional heavy industries and the moves towards more white-collar work.

However since 27 per cent of the electorate do not vote (they **abstain**) and 15 per cent are **floating** or **volatile** voters, i.e. they regularly switch parties, it is impossible to predict how voting will go in the future.

You should now be in a position to answer the examination questions that follow on page 48 and to tackle the task that comes after them.

Non-voters or abstainers

In general elections approximately 27 per cent of the electorate do not vote. It would appear that *poorer* people, *older* people, *women*, *young* voters and the *least educated* are the groups who tend to abstain more than other groups.

Abstaining from voting is very important, because it can influence the result of an election.

New poll puts Tories

ON COURSE FOR NARROW MAJORITY

THE Conservatives are 3.5% ahead of Labour in General Election voting intentions, says a Marplan poll for the Press Association issued today.

The poll, the first ever commissioned by the national news agency and based on a massive 9,000 sample of electors in 324 constituencies, shows voting intentions in Great Britain as: Conservative 41.0%, Labour 37.5%, Alliance 19.0% and Others 2.5%.

The result represents a major boost for the Conservatives after they had been trailing in many recent polls. But it still indicates a swing to Labour of 5.8% compared with voting in mainland Britain at the last General Election in 1983.

It is estimated that such a swing at the next election would maintain a Conservative overall majority in the House of Commons, although reducing it to 22 from 144 last time.

For Labour the figures represent a major blow. Normally at this stage in the lifetime of a Parliament the leading Opposition party should have a substantial lead in the polls if they are to have a realistic chance of forming the next government.

The Liberal/SDP Alliance percentage is a drop of 7% compared with their General Election performance. But Alliance politicians will argue that opinion polls consistently understate their actual support at elections.

The national trend almost matches that in a Harris poll for TV-am on Tuesday, which gave the Conservatives a 4 per cent lead on a sample of 1,038 interviews.

This contrasts with three other polls in the past fortnight showing Labour 2% ahead (MORI in the London Standard) and 1% ahead (Marplan in the Today newspaper) and both parties neck and neck (Gallup in the Daily Telegraph). All these polls were based on representative quota samples of between 952 and 1,915 voters.

For the PA/Marplan poll, 750 electors — strictly representative of age, sex and social class — were interviewed face to face in each of the 12 standard regions of the U.K., including Northern Ireland.

Interviewing took place from October 21 to 24 after all the party conferences.

The results show marked regional variations, with the highest degree of Conservative support (49%) in the South East and the lowest (22%) in Scotland.

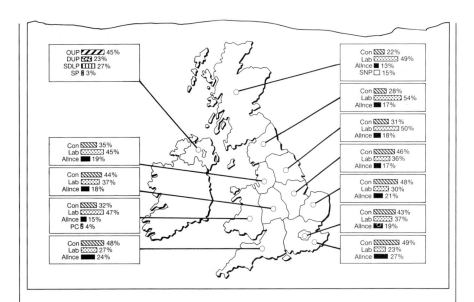

Source: *The Evening Sentinel*, 1987

|T|A|S|K| | | | | | | | |

1 Name the four opinion polls referred to in the article.
2 How did the researcher gain the information or data for this article?
3 How big was their sample?
4 In one paragraph describe the results of the Marplan opinion poll.
5 What is meant by the sentence: 'The results show marked regional variations, with the highest degree of Conservative support (48 per cent) in the South East and the lowest in Scotland.
6 Explain why the results of opinion polls like these are often inaccurate and may not reflect the actual result of an election.
7 What were the actual results of the 1987 General Election? □

Voting by class in the 1987 General Election

	A/B Professional Managerial %	C1 Clerical + Office Workers %	C2 Skilled Manual %	D/E Semi-skilled + Unskilled Manual %
Conservative	57	51	40	30
Labour	14	21	36	48
Alliance	26	26	22	20

Source: *Sunday Times/MORI Poll*, 14 June 1987

QUESTIONS

1 What percentage of professional/managerial people voted Conservative in the 1987 Election?
2 What is the traditional relationship between social class and voting behaviour?
3 According to the table this traditional relationship is breaking down. In what ways is the traditional pattern of voting changing?
4 a What percentage of skilled manual workers voted Conservative in 1987?
  b Sociologists would refer to these workers as *deviant voters*. Who are deviant voters and why do sociologists describe them as deviant?
5 Give four explanations of why working-class or manual workers are likely to vote Conservative.
6 Describe and explain the various influences that affect an individual's voting behaviour. □

UNIT 5

ÉLITISM AND PLURALISM

The élitist theory

Some writers believe that democracy is an illusion in Britain. They say that even though everyone has the right to vote in Britain and even though there are several political parties and a wide range of political opinions to choose from, nevertheless democracy does not exist. Instead, they claim that society is dominated by *élites* and that power lies in the hands of the privileged few, leaving the ordinary people powerless.

Karl Marx identified the ruling class as being the group that dominates society. They own most of the country's wealth and Marx argued that being rich allowed them to gain political power. The table on the left shows wealth distribution figures for 1976 to 1983.

QUESTIONS

1 What percentage of wealth was owned by the top 5 per cent of the population in 1983?
2 What percentage of wealth was owned by the bottom 95 per cent of the population? □

Marxist writers point out that 70 per cent of Conservative and 10 per cent of Labour MPs went to public schools. Over half of Conservative MPs are company directors and the current Prime Minister's husband, Denis Thatcher, is a millionaire. Marx argues that the rich (the **bourgeoisie**) make sure that they retain their wealth by creating a political system that will act for their benefit.

Other surveys have shown that the middle classes and those people who attended public school have the biggest share of top jobs, e.g. important positions in the civil service, the army, the Bank of England and the Church of England as the table on the left shows.

C. Wright Mills in *The Power Élite* argued that three groups of élites dominated American society:

1 the **economic élite**
2 the **military élite**
3 the **political élite**

Mills claimed that these groups tend to stick together; they share common interests in their desire to retain power and also share their special or privileged educational background. Mills argued that these élite groups manipulate the population especially through the media which they also control.

The classical Élite Theorists, *Pareto*, *Mosca* and *Michels*, argue that these élite groups gain their power either through their natural ability or by physical strength – like foxes or lions, says Pareto. Once they are in power, they stay their because of their superior **organisational** power.

Michels reveals how even political parties are undemocratic in their structure, because there are always just a few leaders or committee members running the party. This, Michels describes as an **oligarchical** structure or organisation. If this is true, then political parties cannot represent the interests of the majority of their members and democracy *is* therefore an illusion!

DISCUSS

Are our democratic political parties, such as the Labour Party, the Conservative Party, the Liberal Democrat Party and Communist Party really democratic or are they oligarchical, as Michels might claim? □

Distribution of wealth 1976–83
Total personal wealth

	1976	1979	1981
Top 1%	24%	23%	23%
Top 5%	46%	45%	45%

Source: *Sociology Update*, 1984

Percentage of posts filled by those with a public school education

	Percentage
Conservative cabinet	87
Judges	76
Conservative MPs	76
Ambassadors	70
Lieutenants general and above	70
Governors of the Bank of England	67
Bishops	66
Chief executives in 100 largest firms	64
Air marshals	60
Civil servants above assistant secretary	59
Directors of leading firms	58
Chairmen of government committees of enquiry	55
Members of the Royal Commissions	51
Civil servants above and including assistant secretary	48
All city directors	47
BBC governors	44
Members of arts and British councils	41
Labour cabinet	35
Top managers of 65 largest firms	33
Members of government research councils	31
Labour MPs	15

Source: *Understanding Sociology* by J. Andrews, 1984

The pluralist theory

Pluralists disagree with this élitist view of society; they believe that democracy does exist and that power is shared amongst the population. They claim that since the electorate actually vote and have a say in how Parliament is made up, that this system of government is democratic and that Parliament represents the interests of the majority of the people.

Pluralists believe that the existence of **Pressure Groups** or **Interest Groups** is another example of how democratic British society really is.

Pressure groups are different from political parties because they have only *one* cause or interest that they want to promote or defend; and they do this by putting pressure on the government. For example, they might pressurise an MP to introduce a Private Members Bill in Parliament on their behalf, or they might present a petition to Parliament. There are however, several other methods of exerting pressure, as the following pages will show.

There are two main types of pressure groups:
1 **Protective** or **defensive** pressure groups. These try to protect or defend the interests of their members. For example, the Automobile Association fights to protect the interests of the motorist and would pressurise the government or the car manufacturers if the need arose. Trade Unions are another example of a protective pressure group, since they were formed to protect the working conditions and rates of pay of their workers. They can put considerable pressure on the government by striking.

Q Can you name one particular strike in 1984 that put considerable pressure on the Conservative Government? □

2 **Promotional** pressure groups. These try to put forward or promote a particular viewpoint or cause which they believe in. For example CND is one of the biggest promotional pressure groups. Its members wish to have nuclear weapons abolished in Britain and if they succeed then the pressure group would be dissolved. The Friends of the Earth are another example of a promotional pressure group, they make people aware of the problems and dangers facing all forms of life on the planet – for example whales, and seals.

Q What methods do groups like Greenpeace use to put pressure on the government regarding environmental issues?

A FEW PRESSURE GROUPS

Welfare
Shelter
Child Poverty Action Group
Campaign for Nuclear Disarmament
National Society for the Prevention of Cruelty
  to Children

Animal Welfare
British Union for the Abolition of Vivisection
Anti-Blood Sports League
Save the Whale
Royal Society for the Prevention of Cruelty
  to Animals

Environmental
Anti-nuclear lobby
Ramblers' Association
Historic Buildings Preservation Trust
Friends of the Earth
Green Peace

Medical
Spastics Society
Cancer Research

Professional Organisations
British Medical Association
Bar Council
Law Society
Business and Professional Women
  (UK Federation of)

Sectional Interests
Automobile Association
Women's Institute
Confederation of British Industry
National Farmers' Union
Lords Day Observance Society
Trade Union Congress
British Field Sports Society
National Anti Fluoridisation Campaign
Anti-Apartheid Movement

T A S K

Consider the list of pressure groups above. What type of pressure groups are they? Look at one pressure group in detail. What are its aims? What method does it use to achieve those aims? Do you think this group is effective in influencing government and public opinion? □

Methods used by pressure groups

Pressure groups use various methods in order to influence government and politicians and to bring about the change they want to see.

1 The pressure group might approach an MP or a Minister, civil servant or local government officer. In some cases MPs have their secretarial or election expenses paid for by a pressure group. (This happens with Labour MPs and the trade unions.) Another way of gaining the ear of an MP is to employ one as a consultant. This happens when big business pays an MP to keep an eye on how particular laws debated in the House of Commons might affect their industry. (This sponsorship often occurs with Conservative MPs.) MPs also act as paid political agents, lobbying ministers on behalf of a particular pressure group.

DISCUSS

Do you think MPs should do this? Is it right? ☐

2 Pressure groups also use petitions and make deputations to Parliament or their local council.

A **petition** is a request signed by those people who wish to see that request put into action. Sometimes many thousands of people sign the petition which is then presented to the government.

Q Have you ever signed a petition? ☐

A **deputation** can be an individual or a small group of people who represent the rest of the pressure group and who call on a member of the government in order to make the views of their pressure group known. For example, a deputation may knock at the door of No 10 Downing Street, the home of the Prime Minister, and may also have a petition with them.

3 Pressure groups also like to educate and inform people about their beliefs and usually do this by using the media. There are many ways in which pressure groups can utilise the media; for example, leaflets can be printed and distributed in the street, articles and letters can be written and published in local and national newspapers. Radio and television interviews also provide a powerful means of gaining publicity and winning support from the general public. Greenpeace and other groups fighting against the killing of baby seals have won much support by their media campaign.

DISCUSS

Consider the Animal Rights pressure group. Do you think they have used the media well and gained much support?

What sort of disruption did the women at Greenham Common arrange in their protest against the siting of American Cruise missiles on British soil?

DISCUSS

Can you give examples of violent protests? Do you think violence helps a pressure group to gain support?

4 **Mass meetings**, **demonstrations** and **marches** are further methods of attracting publicity for the pressure group's cause. Sometimes a pressure group will gain attention for itself by causing some sort of disruption which guarantees the presence of newspaper reporters and television cameras. An example of this might be a planned sit in or some other disruption which gains media coverage.

Showbusiness personalities can greatly help to gain the attention of the Press and TV cameras at a demonstration or protest meeting. For example, Bob Geldof's high profile during the Ethiopian famine crisis.

Sometimes demonstrations and protest meetings become violent and involve confrontations with the police.

Angry parents defend village school

'We'll march'

Action Group would storm Whitehall

MILITANT Moorlands parents are prepared to march on Parliament in a bid to save their children's school.

Mr Edwin Wain, chairman of the re-formed Action Group to keep Waterhouses Middle School open, warned the county council this week that if they decided to close the school they would take their fight to Westminster.

"If those responsible go ahead we will send a deputation from Waterhouses to lobby Kenneth Baker, the Secretary of State for Education," said Mr Wain.

For the battle-weary parents the new threat is a carbon copy of the council's attempts to shut the middle school just three years ago, which they successfully defeated.

But an angry meeting in the school hall two weeks ago, Education Chairman Coun. Bob Cant told protesting parents that the falling rolls and a lack of money meant that the school, opened in 1979, would have to close.

In the wake of the meeting the Action Group which masterminded the 1983 fight for the school, was re-formed with the unanimous backing of parents.

Mr Wain said there were 138 children in the middle school and 90 in the junior school and the parents of all the children were totally behind the Action Group.

He explained that the group's tactics at the moment were to encourage parents to write to the education department and councillors to express their objections. They also planned to lobby the council when it meets to make the decision on closing the school and if that failed they would be approaching the Secretary of State.

"Our case is as strong now as it was in 1983. We will fight this on the grounds of the social damage it will do to our community, the dangers of transporting children from rural areas and the overcrowding which is inevitably going to occur in Leek schools."

TASK

1 What sort of pressure group is described in the article?
2 What are its aims?
3 What methods does it intend to use?
4 Explain the following terms: deputation, lobby.
5 Suggest possible reasons why this pressure group was successful three years ago.
6 a 'Pressure groups are the means whereby anyone in Britain can have their say and influence decisions made about life in Britain.' Discuss.
  b 'The right to form a pressure group such as the one in the article, makes Britain democratic.' Discuss the extent to which this is true?

Source: *Leek Post and Times*, November 1986

In conclusion to this unit on whether democracy really exists in Britain today, it can be said that there are two major views.

According to the *pluralist* view, pressure groups play an important role in maintaining democracy, by keeping political parties and politicians informed and in touch with the wishes of the people.

However, the *élitist* or ruling class argument is that the richer and more powerful pressure groups in society, such as the CBI, do influence the government, but that the poorer pressure groups are much less powerful. In fact the élitist view holds them to be totally ineffective.

Q You should now be able to answer the following questions. If you need to, refer back to the sections in previous units on political parties and opinion polls.

Parliamentary by-elections, May 1979–June 1983

	May 1979–June 1983	Previous* General Election May 1979
Number of by-elections	20	
Votes recorded by party (*percentages*)		
Conservative	23.8	33.7
Labour	25.7	35.2
Liberal	9.0	8.0
Social Democratic Party	14.2	
Plaid Cymru	0.5	0.4
Scottish National Party	1.7	1.4
Other	25.1	21.2
Total votes recorded (= 100%) (thousands)	715	852

*Votes recorded in the same seats in the previous General Election.

Source: adapted from *Social Trends*, 1985

1 How many by-elections were held in the United Kingdom between May 1979 and June 1983?
2 How many votes were recorded in these constituencies in the General Election May 1979?
3 What change took place in the percentage of votes recorded for:
 a the Labour Party;
 b the Liberal Party
 in the by-elections compared with the General Election May 1979?
4 Name the Nationalist parties mentioned in the chart.
5 Explain why no votes were recorded for the Social Democratic Party in the General Election May 1979.
6 Name *two* different types of pressure group. Give an example of each.
7 Give *four* methods used by pressure groups by which they hope to influence government policy and/or public opinion.
8 Identify and explain *two* reasons why the results of a poll on voting intentions taken one month before an election may not accurately reflect the actual result of the election. □

WHERE TO NOW?

Power and Politics comes into each of the modules in this book, but you can read about the power of the media by turning to Module 2 on Mass Media, page 17.

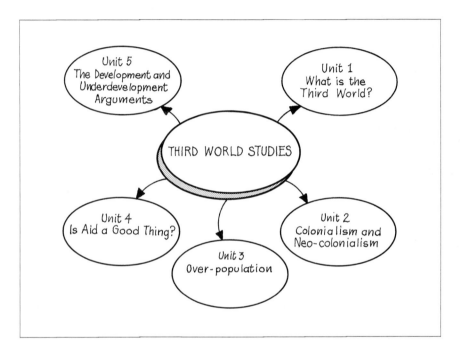

WHAT THIS MODULE IS ABOUT

Every year over 35 million people die of famine in third world countries. How this can happen, and whether it is likely to continue to happen in the future, is the central issue explored in this module. The controversial arguments surrounding over-population and aid are discussed: alongside a critical view of colonisation and its long-reaching effects.

BY THE END OF THIS MODULE YOU SHOULD BE ABLE TO:

1   Understand what is meant by the terms North–South Divide and First and Third Worlds.

2   Appreciate how the First World became richer through imperialism and colonialisation.

3   Examine the effects of colonialisation and neo-colonialism on the economies of third world nations.

4   Discuss some of the complex arguments regarding the causes of over-population, high birth rates and malnutrition.

5   Examine the effectiveness of aid agencies, such as Oxfam, War on Want and Christian Aid, in reducing third world poverty.

6   Appreciate that there are differing sociological views regarding the causes of under development in third world countries.

WHAT IS THE THIRD WORLD?

During 1985 and 1986, millions of people in Britain gave money, time and effort to several charity appeals in order to help the poor people of the Third World. For example, Bob Geldof and Midge Ure organised Live Aid, where the world's top groups and pop stars performed freely and raised £65 million, which went to the poor people of countries like Ethiopia. However, many people question whether giving money to third world charities really can stop the poverty and famine there.

This is an important and complex question for everyone, not just sociologists, to consider, but it is essential to do this to understand what sort of poverty exists in the Third World.

In *The Hunger to Come*, **John Laffin** describes the 'extreme poverty' suffered by those people living in the poorer countries of the world as the extract below shows.

Extreme poverty

Poverty means total lack of amenities. To express it starkly, millions and millions of people have never seen toilet paper or any other hygienic necessity. They have neither soap nor toothbrush. When ill, they are unlikely to see a doctor, if only because in poor countries there is only one doctor for every 50 000 or 75 000 people. No matter how willing he might be, one doctor serving an area of perhaps 15 000 square miles could not reach parts of it in under two days and in the rainy season he could not possibly reach many parts.

Poverty can also be revealingly measured by the number of dentists available. At the last count 150 million people living in African countries and territories had 250 trained dentists: five of these countries, with a population of 60 million, had 50 dentists—more than a million people to one dentist. In the United States there is a dentist to every 2000 people and in Britain one to every 2200.

Poverty results in parents watching their children die from disease or lack of food. Often the death is a long, wasting one—the worst of all.

Poverty is having an eternally bare cupboard and being in debt to the local moneylender for life.

Poverty means no heating in winter and no cooling in scorching summer, it means one ragged set of clothing, practically no furniture and almost nothing in the cupboard, which in any case does not exist.

Source: *The Hunger to Come* by John Laffin (Humanities Curriculum Project leaflet).

BRAINSTORM:

As many third world charities as you can think of.

T A S K

Compare John Laffin's description of 'extreme poverty' with that of Booth's 'very poor' or Rowntree's definition of 'primary poverty' (See Module 6, page 101)

John Laffin paints a depressing picture of what it is like to live in one of the poorer countries of the world. These poorer countries are often referred to as the **third world** or **developing countries** and they are to be found in the Southern hemisphere or the South as it is usually called: in Asia, Africa and Latin America.

Whilst the rich countries, like Britain, lie in the Northern hemisphere: in North America, Europe, USSR, Japan, Australia and New Zealand. These are usually referred to as the **first world** or **developed** countries. This distinction or division between the rich, *industrialised* countries in the North and the poorer, *agrarian* countries in the South is often referred to as the **North–South Divide**, a term used in the Brandt Report of 1980.

Definitions, however, are always difficult or problematical and this is particularly true of the terms *third world* and *first world*, *developing* and *developed*. These terms tend to mean different things to different people.

DISCUSS

What were the results of your brainstorming sessions? Was there general agreement or consensus in the whole group on what these terms mean? □

Some descriptions or definitions of third world and first world life-styles that are given in school text books can also be problematical, as the following illustration shows:

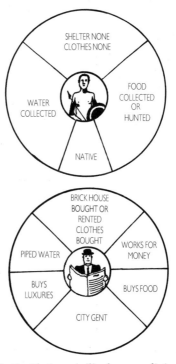

These definitions imply that being *civilised* means living in a city in a brick house, buying food, clothes and luxuries; whilst being *primitive* means collecting your own food and water and having no shelter or clothes.

Q   What do you think about these two pictures? Are they fair? Are they accurate? □

These pictures present a **stereotypical** view of two life-styles. Many people would disagree with the images of primitive and civilised ways of life as they are portrayed in these pictures as they are inaccurate and they do not illustrate the wide range of life-styles that exist in the world today.

Unfortunately, inaccurate views like these persist in society and they help to promote a narrow, stereotypical and also prejudiced view of people in third world countries. This is explored further in Module 10 on Population, Unit 4.

BRAINSTORM

What sort of images, pictures and words spring to mind when you think of a third world country? One person in the group should record them.
Now, brainstorm a first world country.

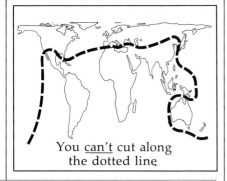

You <u>can't</u> cut along the dotted line

DISCUSS

'You can't cut along the dotted line . . .' says the Centre for World Development (CWDE). We shall return to this statement towards the end of this module see page 67. But what do *you* think CWDE might mean by this?

DISCUSS

Can you think of ways in which the person in the lower illustration might be *less* civilised or developed than the one in the upper picture?

Consider areas of social life, such as violence, crime, old age, pollution, family life . . .

U N I T 2 COLONIALISM AND NEO-COLONIALISM

DISCUSS

'Many sociologists believe that these colonies have been exploited by Britain and other capitalist countries.' What do you think? If your group tends to agree with this statement, discuss the ways in which the First World can repay the Third World for the riches taken out of these countries during colonialisation.

The idea that people in the Third World are uncivilised or lacking in development probably started in the days of **imperialism** and **colonialisation**. This was the period in the Eighteenth and Nineteenth Centuries when Britain and othert capitalist countries in the rich North, invaded and controlled some of the countries in the poor South; taking away their land and raw materials in order to run their industries at home more cheaply. During this period, they also took away the people from the South, to work as slaves in their growing industries.

Much of the improved diet that the British people have enjoyed during the last 150 years, and which has led to a fall in the mortality rate, (see Module 10 on Population, page 174), has come from the cheap food imported from these invaded colonies. Similarly, the cheap raw materials, such as cotton, sugar, tea, gold and ivory obtained from these colonies, made the first world countries richer and raised the living standards of British people during the last century.

Many writers argue that these third world nations were simply moulded into economic satellites in order to supply the needs of the imperial powers. For example, the West Indies was moulded into providing sugar for Europe, West Africa was forced into providing slaves for the West Indian sugar plantations, while in India traditional or local industries, e.g. farming and textiles, were actually destroyed by the British in favour of the British manufacturers' requirements.

In this way, the First World became rich through the cheap imported food, cheap raw materials and new merchandise provided by the 'poor' undeveloped countries of the Third World. Meanwhile the poor countries were made poorer by being milked of their natural resources and by their own traditional industries being destroyed. This ensured that these colonies were *dependent* on the First World in order to support their own local population. In this way, it is argued, the Third World has been effectively *underdeveloped* by the First World.

The effects of colonialisation are still felt today in the Third World; since, although the British Empire and several other empires have now disappeared, neo-colonialism still exists.

Neo-colonialism is a term that describes the way in which the First World continues to exploit, control and dominate the Third World, such as the way in which profit is drained away from third world countries to big multinational companies based in the Western World and Japan.

An example of how this occurs can be seen in the soap-making industry. Throughout the Third World, the small soap-making industries that previously used cheap, locally available raw materials, have now been replaced by factories owned by the first world detergent giants. These large-scale industries use expensive *imported* oil as raw material, rather than local resources, and also employ far fewer people than the small-scale soap-making works. They also make more expensive products for people to buy!

The effects of colonialism and neo-colonialism on one country, in this case Egypt, are summed up by Lord Cromer, who governed Egypt from 1883 to 1907.

'The difference is apparent to any man whose recollections go back some ten or fifteen years. Some quarters of Cairo that formerly used to be veritable centres of varied industries – spinning, weaving, ribbonmaking, dyeing, tentmaking, embroidery, shoemaking, jewellery making, spice grinding, copper work . . . etc . . . have shrunk considerably or vanished. Now there are coffee houses and European novelty shops where once there were prosperous workshops.'

Small-scale soap-making industry (left) alongside vast oil refineries in the Third World (right)

In addition to this economic colonialism, the First World also has a stranglehold over the Third World in relation to education. During colonialisation, Britain imported its own education system into its colonies, and the British curriculum with such subjects as British History continues to be taught in these countries today.

DISCUSS

What do you think are the possible effects of teaching British subjects in African or Indian schools, for example? Is a British-style education better than one designed by the country in question? □

Many sociologists believe that the result of perpetuating a British education and British way of life in these poorer third world countries is that the culture of these countries will in some way be regarded as deficient, or not as good as the British culture and way of life.

DISCUSS

In groups explain why every year thousands of students from the poorer countries come to Britain to gain a university education – and to study a variety of subjects including sociology. Is this education likely to be relevant to their own country's needs? □

UNIT 3 | OVER-POPULATION: TOO MANY MOUTHS TO FEED . . .?

Recent United Nations Food and Agriculture Organisation (FAO) figures reveal that the world's population is growing at two per cent a year and that in many countries the quantity of food available per person is decreasing. It is estimated that about one person in five, or one billion of the world's five billion people live on the verge of starvation. In fact, every year thirty-five million people in third world countries die due to famine.

Many people, including some sociologists, believe that this problem of starvation could be reduced by the use of contraception to control population growth. Other people believe that there is enough food in the world to prevent starvation, if it could only be shared out more evenly.

The problem of not enough food to feed the people is particularly acute in some African countries where the world recession of the 1980s is hitting developing countries harder than the developed ones. However, despite this shortage of food, **life expectancy**, or how long a person can expect to live, in Africa has surprisingly leapt from 39 years in 1960 to around 50 years in 1983.

TASK

Suggest reasons why this increase in life expectancy has occurred? □

As the table on page 61 reveals, there is still a wide difference in the average life expectancy of a person living in Uganda and that of a person living in the UK.

TASK

Suggest reasons why people live longer in Britain than in Africa. Refer to Module 10 on Population for further information. □

Many babies die before they reach their first birthday in third world countries, as the high infant mortality figures in the table, page 61 reveal. This high infant **mortality rate** is accompanied by a high **birth rate**, as poor families often feel the need to have several children so that some will survive to work and help support the family. There are other social norms, such as the high status or prestige that a large family brings in many third world countries and the importance attached to the extended kinship networks, all of which add to the likelihood of there being a high birth rate in these poor countries.

Family planning solutions, organised by the World Health Organisation, have proved to be largely unsuccessful in many third world countries, and the birth rate remains high. This is because the problem of reducing population growth is not simply a question of providing the means for birth control for the people. Large families have been an important part of the culture of these countries for many hundreds of years and it takes time to change long-established social norms or traditions.

Q How long did it take Britain to change its family size? Why did it change? □

Since the average life expectancy in third world countries is relatively lower than that of first world countries, this means that the average age of the whole population in Uganda, for example, will be relatively young in comparison to that of Britain. The result of this is that the level of fertility in Uganda will, therefore, be relatively higher than that in Britain, i.e. there will be a relatively higher number of women of child-bearing age per 1000 of the population in Uganda than in Britain. This factor again adds to the problem of a high birth rate and growth in the population.

Comparison of life chances in developed and developing countries

Country	Population (millions)	Birth rate	Death rate	Infant mortality	Life expectancy Males	Females
UK	55.5	11.8	11.7	14.0	67.8	73.8
USA	203.3	15.3	8.8	14.0	68.7	76.5
India	548.2	35.2	15.9	122.0	41.9	40.6
Uganda	9.5	45.2	15.9	160.0	48.3	51.7
W. Germany	60.7	9.5	11.5	15.5	68.3	74.8
Chile	8.9	23.9	7.8	55.6	60.5	66.0

Source: Adapted from *UN Statistical Yearbook*, 1980

QUESTIONS

Using the information in the table and the extract from *New Society* given here, answer these questions.
1 What do the third world countries of India and Uganda have in common in terms of
   a Birth rate
   b Infant mortality
   c Life expectancy
2 What do the first world countries of the UK, USA and W Germany have in common in terms of
   a Birth rate
   b Infant mortality
   c Life expectancy
3 Why is it that in all major regions of the Third World except Africa, the rate of population growth decreased during the 1980s?

In all the major regions of the Third World except Africa, the rate of population growth is expected to decrease in the eighties. For Africa, UN projections expect a continuing rise in the rate of growth, peaking at about 3 per cent around 1990. It is predicted that Africa will need between two and three times its present levels of food imports by the end of the decade.

Source: *New Society*, October 1982

Not all sociologists agree with the introduction of drastic birth control techniques to control population growth in the poorer Southern hemisphere. Several of the techniques used have been heavily criticised, such as the sterilisation programme introduced in India since the 1960s and the use of the dangerous injectable contraceptive drug, Depo Provera, whose effects can include upsetting the menstrual cycle, reduction of the milk supply and even permanent sterility and cancer.

Q   What do you personally feel about these birth control techniques? □

There is a further critical argument concerning over-population that needs to be considered. This is the view of sociologists, such as *Hayter*, who argues that despite the increasing population levels there is enough food in the world as a whole to feed everyone, because food production and supplies have been increasing faster than population levels.

The CWDE, agree with Hayter that there is enough food in the world to prevent starvation and point out that this food is very unevenly shared around the world.

BRAINSTORM

What is meant by the 'food mountains' held by the EEC? □

According to some estimates the first world countries consume over half of the available supply of food grains in the world, much of which is used to feed animals. This is regarded as a highly wasteful way of producing protein for humans to eat and Hayter describes the 'rich white man' as behaving 'like a cannibal' by eating too many intensively grain-fed animals and failing to give the grain to the poor people of the world.

DISCUSS

Hayter says that 'by consuming meat, which wastes the grain that could have saved them, last year we ate the children of the Sahel, Ethiopia and Bangladesh. And we continue to eat them this year with undiminished appetite'. □

Do you agree with this sociologist's view that rich white people behave like cannibals?

The FAO and other organisations believe along with Hayter that feeding grain to animals is an inefficient way of producing potein for people. In order to produce one kilo of meat, several kilos of grain must be fed to the animal; whereas, a much more productive use of the land would be to grow vegetables and potatoes and to use the grain to make bread. It has been estimated that there would be no malnutrition in the world if only 10 per cent of the cereals currently being fed to animals was instead eaten by the people directly.

The chart below reveals the daily food energy supplies around the world and shows that on average people need 2400 calories daily to stay fit.

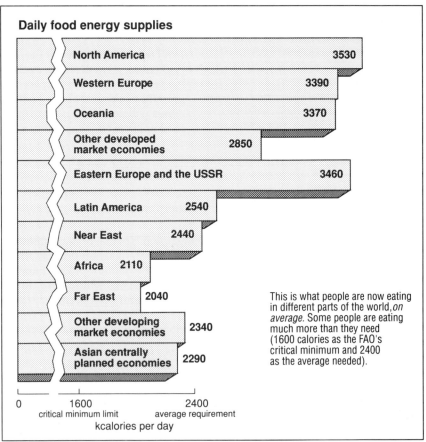

Daily food energy supplies

Region	kcalories
North America	3530
Western Europe	3390
Oceania	3370
Other developed market economies	2850
Eastern Europe and the USSR	3460
Latin America	2540
Near East	2440
Africa	2110
Far East	2040
Other developing market economies	2340
Asian centrally planned economies	2290

0   1600   2400
critical minimum limit   average requirement
kcalories per day

This is what people are now eating in different parts of the world, *on average*. Some people are eating much more than they need (1600 calories as the FAO's critical minimum and 2400 as the average needed).

Source: *South magazine* FAO figures, 1977

Many of the undernourished people in the world live in Asia. Using FAO figures about what food people need . . .

● Over a third of the people in India consume less than three-quarters of the calories they need

● Nearly 10% of the people in India eat less than half of the daily calories they need

Children, and pregnant and nursing women, suffer the most malnutrition. Between 25% and 30% of the children in poorer countries die before they are five.

Q In which countries are people not getting the average amount of calories needed to stay fit?

How many more calories than they actually need are the people of Western Europe, Australia, Japan, North America and the USSR consuming? □

Studies suggest that in many developing countries, adult women are poorly nourished in comparison to men, and that girls are often not as well nourished as boys, especially in African countries.

DISCUSS

Why do you think this inequality exists

One other inequality in the distribution of food lies within third world countries themselves where the rich or élite people in those countries enjoy far greater privileges and wealth than the poor people. Figures show that the élite eat twice as many calories as the poorest 20 per cent of the population.

The writer, *North*, has suggested that there should be fewer Mercedes Benz cars for government officials in third world countries and many more water taps for the villages, since three out of every five people in the Southern hemisphere do not have easy access to safe drinking water.

Q   Do you agree with North? ☐

However, by far the greatest inequalities between people in the world are those that exist between the people living in the North and those in the South. There are two further ways in which the rich countries of the world stay rich at the expense of the poor countries.

Firstly, the huge EEC mountains of unsold and over-produced butter and unskimmed milk are now being fed back to the European cows who initially produced it! Furthermore, in 1984 EEC officials actually destroyed 866 lbs of apples, 1648 lbs of lemons, 1388 lbs of oranges and 41 lbs of cauliflower every single minute of the year in order to keep prices artificially high for the European farmers' benefit.

DISCUSS

While millions of men, women and children are starving in the world, should the ECC destroy this food? ☐

Secondly, not only does the rich world destroy food in order to keep prices artificially high, but it also erects **tariff barriers** which effectively prevent third world countries developing a healthy export trade with the First World. Rich countries like Britain and the USA do buy a tremendous range of products from the poorer countries of the world but, in general, they pay too little for these goods, as the banana split diagram below reveals.

In these ways poor third world countries are kept poor and dependent.

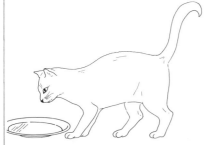

The price of a pet. *The average contented cat is a considerable eater, demanding about a third more calories, weight for weight, than its owner. A four kilogramme cat eats about 350 kilocalories of animal protein a day – twice as much as the average African, and better than a third more than the average citizen of the Third World. The money spent on its upkeep – around £170 per year – is greater than the per capita gross national product of the billion-plus people who live in the world's 15 poorest countries.*

DISCUSS

'World Food Day' is October 16 each year. What could people in richer countries do
1 to make world food problems more widely understood?
2 to help world food to be shared out fairly?
3 to help the poor to produce and afford the food they need?
4 to increase their own food production (e.g Britain imports over half its food)?

WHO PAYS THE PRICE?

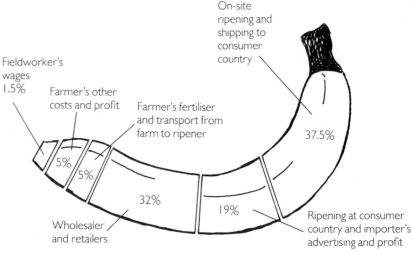

On-site ripening and shipping to consumer country

Fieldworker's wages 1.5%

Farmer's other costs and profit

Farmer's fertiliser and transport from farm to ripener

37.5%

5%

5%

32%

19%

Wholesaler and retailers

Ripening at consumer country and importer's advertising and profit

Banana split. *Throughout the poor world, the growers of cash crops (those grown for sale rather than subsistence) usually get very little for their work. Many (coffee and cotton, for example) are in chronic over-supply, which forces prices down. It is common for poor countries – capitalist and socialist alike – to have voracious bureaucracies designed to help farmers and to market their produce. In reality they tend to absorb money which should go to the growers, and they often delay it so long that crops go unpicked because the farmers can't afford the labour to gather them*

U|N|I|T 4

IS AID A GOOD THING?

Most people in the rich world do, of course, want to share their food and wealth with the poor people of the world. Hence, people and governments give money to help the Third World and charities like Oxfam, War on Want and Christian Aid exist to organise and distribute the aid.

Unfortunately, however, all of these organisations also know that most food aid is ineffective and often damaging to the poor country itself. The reason for this is that the food aid brought to the country competes with the local economy and stems its people's incentive to grow crops. It does not encourage the poor to support themselves, and so it increases the dependence of the Third World on the First World, rather than encouraging development.

DISCUSS

How can the poorer countries be encouraged to support themselves? What should the rich world do? □

The extract on the left from a book published by War on Want, exploring 225 years of British involvement in Bangledesh, highlights this problem of the way in which aid creates dependence.

The extract refers to the profit that Britain makes from its involvement in Bangledesh and the way in which the rich élite in Bangledesh is helped by the aid while the poor people actually get poorer.

Some writers claim that many governments only give aid on the condition that it is spent on the products of companies in the rich First World. This **tied-aid** does nothing to help develop the poor countries and often the projects built with such aid have been irrelevant to the needs of the majority of the poor people, such as new roads in countries where most people cannot afford cars, and prestige airports where most people do not ever leave the country, let alone fly abroad. The following cartoon illustrates this point well.

Bangladesh is a beautiful, green country. It has the most fertile soil, and potentially the largest inland fish resources in the world. It could produce enough food for everyone, yet most of its people are malnourished. £500 million worth of aid pours in every year, but it only worsens the situation. While the poor get poorer, aid helps the rich consolidate their power. Britain makes a profit from its involvement in Bangladesh, and has done since the early days of Empire.

Source: War on Want Power Pack

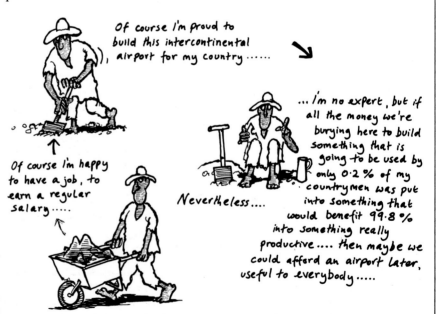

DISCUSS

What first world products would be used in building and running an airport? In what ways would only the first world benefit from projects like this? Would these developments also help the Third World? □

RESEARCH IDEA

Find out how much Britain spent on overseas aid to poorer countries last year.

How much did Britain spend on arms during the same period?

Sources of information to investigate include: Oxfam, War on Want, One World, etc.

Source: CWDE leaflet

The money required to provide adequate food, water, education, health and housing for everyone in the world has been estimated at $17 billion a year. It is a huge sum of money

...about as much as the world spends on arms every two weeks.

Q In what ways would better water supplies and sanitation affect the life of people in third world countries?

Some Aid programmes are more positive and do help poorer countries to establish and support themselves.

For example, the United Nations declared 1981 to 1990, as International Drinking Water Supply and Sanitation Decade and has introduced a 30 billion dollar programme of aid to provide 'clean water and safe toilet for all by 1990'. Poorer countries will meet 80 per cent of the costs themselves.

About half of the world's people still do not have access to a safe supply of drinking water and the solution is often made much worse by natural disasters, such as the drought and flooding suffered by third world countries like Sudan in 1988. Between 20 and 25 million children below the age of five die every year in developing countries, and a third of these deaths are from diarrhoea caused by polluted water.

> **There are...**
> ● **water-borne diseases** (such as diarrhoea, cholera, polio, typhoid) which are spread by drinking or washing hands, food or utensils in contaminated water.
> ● **water-washed diseases** (such as leprosy, yaws, scabies, and roundworm) which are spread by poor personal hygiene, insufficient water for washing, and lack of facilities for proper disposal of human wastes.
> ● **water-based diseases** (such as bilharzia) which are transmitted by a vector which spends part of its life cycle in water. Contact with infected water allows the parasite to enter humans through the skin or mouth.
> ● **diseases with water-related vectors** (such as malaria, African sleeping sickness, and river blindness) which are passed through infection-carrying insects breeding in stagnant water and biting near it.
> ● **fecal disposal diseases** (such as hookworm) which are caused by organisms breeding in excreta when sanitation is inadequate.

Through the official overseas aid programme, Britain has helped to develop 44 different water and sanitation schemes in 28 poorer countries, at a cost of about £80 million. These schemes involve low-cost simple technology that is easy to operate and Britain provides training in the skills necessary for the installation, operation and maintenance of these water and sanitation schemes. In this way, aid is helping the poorer countries to help themselves.

Tube Wells or *boreholes* are simple to operate and maintain. All that is needed is ground water, a suction hand-pump and a water-lifting device.

Other schemes for the provision of water and sanitation are also being implemented in the Third World. For example, systems of solar panels are currently being tested in India, the Sudan and the Philippines.

There are many varieties of simple water pumps used around the world. Some are operated by hand, some by foot

Another example of aid being used to introduce low-cost technology that helps poorer countries to help themselves can be seen in the area of health. Primary Health Care is a programme based on simple preventative health education, using appropriate and inexpensive technology instead of expensive sophisticated equipment. The programme concentrates on building practical and easily maintained buildings instead of large hospitals, and provides basic training for community health workers, rather than spending the limited amount of money available on highly specialised staff and technicians as we have in Britain.

UNIT 5 THE DEVELOPMENT AND UNDERDEVELOPMENT ARGUMENTS

The evidence produced in this module so far makes it clear that the problem of poverty in the Third World is a complex one. Sociologists themselves are divided in their views about the causes of and solutions to this problem of poverty or lack of development.

For example, there are those sociologists, often called **modernisation theorists**, who place great emphasis on the backwardness and immaturity of the third world countries as being a prime cause of poverty. They, therefore, stress the need for progress towards the kind of industrialised society to be found in Western Europe, USA or Japan. They emphasise the need for birth control and a nuclear form of family life, instead of the traditional extended kinship system which is seen as less efficient in a modern society.

Q At which stage of development is Britain?

DISCUSS

Is the sort of development described by Rostow necessarily desirable?

ROSTOW'S FIVE STAGES OF DEVELOPMENT

1 **Traditional society** Mainly agricultural. No science or technology and low social mobility.

2  **Preconditions for take off** This occurred in Europe in the late Seventeenth century and early Eighteenth century. There is an expansion of economic production caused by science and technology.

3  **Take off** Development of industry and agriculture; build up of capital and profits: increasing urbanisation and greater influence for all.

4 **Drive to maturity** Period of sustained progress with the extension of modern technology. Extensive provision of welfare facilities for all.

5 **Age of high mass consumption** Where the majority of the population have access to a large number and a great variety of consumer products and services.

In their recipe for development, the modernisation theorists stress the importance of formal education, adequate health and medical services, and the valuable role of the media in spreading up-to-date knowledge and new attitudes. They also emphasise the need to develop towns and cities and to introduce modern techniques of industrial production – both through aid and by multinational companies establishing factories in the third world countries.

DISCUSS

This modernisation theory has been criticised because of the way in which it infers that the culture of third world societies are inadequate or deprived and suggests that western culture, knowledge, attitudes and social structures are better than those of the third world countries. What do you think? Do you agree that third world countries need to progress or develop along first world lines? Is there a better alternative? □

Another group of sociologists with a different view about the causes of the poverty in the Third World are the **marxist** or **dependency theorists**. They stress the way in which the rich capitalist countries in the North have exploited the poorer countries of the South, both as colonies and then afterwards for the cheap raw materials, cheap labour and new markets they provide for first world industries.

According to this perspective, the rich have grown richer at the expense of the poor, and the third world countries are seen to be in a state of permanently arrested development or **underdevelopment**, as it is called, i.e. always being sapped dry by the capitalists based in the rich North.

DISCUSS

Critics claim that the flaw in the dependency theorists' view is that it does not readily suggest ways of helping to develop the Third World. Do you agree? ☐

T A S K

Using the evidence and arguments provided in the previous units, write a short essay revealing the ways in which the First World underdevelops the Third World. ☐

Finally, there is one other group of theorists who believe that further industrialisation and urbanisation in the world would be a disaster. The radical writer, *Ivan Illich*, and many in the Green movement point out that the earth's resources are finite or limited and unable to support a population of five billion two-car families in semi-detached houses with freezers and televisions.

These theorists believe that the development problem does not lie with the poor countries, but with the rich ones, who squander the earth's resources. As remedies they suggest small-scale development projects in the poorer countries, such as the clean water and primary health care schemes described on page 65 and the Tanzanian programme of rural socialism, with its emphasis on the production of food for local consumption, rather than the exploitative cash crop farming or the production of industrial goods for export.

Q In what ways does the rich world 'squander the earth's resources'? ☐

When CWDE says that 'you cannot cut along the dotted line', as discussed on page 57, they are stressing how inextricably linked the rich North and poor South parts of the world really are.

Whether the Third World will continue to be underdeveloped and dependent on the First World in the future or will become fully developed and interdependent with the rest of the world, lies in the hands of the individuals of the First World as much as with their governments.

There are many benefits to creating just one world instead of the present one which is divided into three or four unequal worlds.

RESEARCH IDEA

Find out more about 'One World Week'. What does it mean? ☐

WHERE TO NOW?

Reading this module may have aroused your interest in politics, it may also make you interested in reading more about poverty in Britain. You could go on to read Module 3 on Power and Politics, Module 6 on Inequality or Module 5 on Social Stratification next.

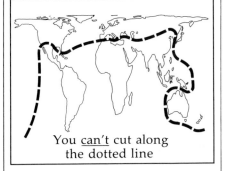
You <u>can't</u> cut along the dotted line

DISCUSS

What do you think Britain's role should be in helping third world countries?

MODULE · 5

SOCIAL STRATIFICATION

FIVE

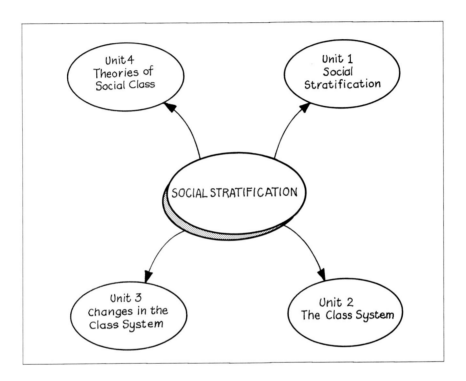

WHAT THIS MODULE IS ABOUT

This module explains what is meant by stratification, analyses the characteristics of the class system, and examines some major theories about the reasons for the existence of social class.

BY THE END OF THIS MODULE YOU SHOULD BE ABLE TO:

1 Define stratification, and give examples of different types of stratification systems.
2 Have an understanding of how social class is objectively measured, and the criticisms made of scales of social class.
3 Be able to explain what is meant by status, and explain the difference between achieved and ascribed status.
4 Discuss why stratification exists, and the importance of power relationships.
5 Explain the difference between sponsored and contest mobility.
6 Understand in what ways our class system is open or closed.
7 Know the findings of mobility studies.
8 Discuss Marxist theories of class, the bourgeoisie (those who have) and the proletariat (those who have not).
9 Explain Weber's theory of class, including his ideas about status and life-chances.

UNIT 1   SOCIAL STRATA

ROLE PLAY 'BOMB SHELTER'

The worst has happened! A nuclear war is imminent! You are in the local council's bomb shelter with fourteen other people who were nearby when the alarm went off. In the shelter there is only enough food for eight (whatever their age), and so seven people must go outside to face an uncertain future. You have been chosen to make the decision about who is to leave and who is to stay!

Get into small groups and try to reach a unanimous verdict on who is allowed to remain in the bomb shelter and later form part of a new society. Choose one of your group to write down your decisions and on what basis you made them.

Here are the occupants of your shelter. The table below contains all the information you have about them.

Occupation	Sex	Age
1 Computer programmer	male	37
2 Baby	female	6 months
3 Agricultural labourer	male	45
4 MP	male	40
5 Teenager still at school	male	14
6 Minister of religion	male	67
7 IRA suspected terrorist	female	28
8 Teacher	female	30
9 International footballer	male	22
10 Housewife	female	25
11 Her husband	male	27
12 Laboratory technician	male	50
13 Schoolgirl	female	8
14 Famous author	male	56

When you have reached your decision discuss your results with the other groups. ☐

DISCUSS

What sort of new society did you create? Who would be the most important people, and who the least important?

Did you keep both the husband and the wife, so that our existing type of family would continue, or did you envisage a new sort of family coming into existence?

Did you decide that females were more important than males, or that people over a certain age were useless? ☐

Stratification means dividing people into strata or layers, with the most important at the top and the least important at the bottom. When you did the 'bomb shelter' role play, you were stratifying people into layers according to factors you thought were important, such as age, sex, education, or occupation. All societies appear to have some type of stratification system.

Sociologists argue that some form of social stratification occurs in every society in the world, despite the fact that people have always dreamt of a society where everyone is equal. All societies appear to distinguish between people and they become more, or less important than others. The strata may be separated by man-made differences, such as education or wealth; or by

Q Did you discuss factors, such as age, sex and education? Would these be important in a new society? Did you argue the relevance of people's occupation in this new world? What else did you think was relevant?

Q Why is it usually assumed that men are more important than women? For more on this debate turn to Module 12 on Gender, Units 2, 3 and 4.

Rich and poor housing in Hong Kong

Q   How do you see your life in ten years' time? Now imagine that you are an Untouchable in India; what would your life be like in ten years' time? How and why are your two estimates different?

TASK

There are other stratification systems not mentioned here. Find out about the **feudal system**. You could ask a history teacher for some information on this.

RESEARCH IDEA

Find out about the bar mitzvah ceremony and other celebrations associated with age in the Jewish culture.

physical differences, such as sex, race, age or health. There does not appear to be any society past or present where everyone is really equal.

In all countries some people are better educated, more powerful, or have a higher status job than others. In most countries males are more important than females, and white-collar (non-manual) workers more important than peasants working the land. Stratification systems do change over time. As China opens up to the West for example, a new system of stratification will almost certainly develop in its society as it allows more private enterprise, and takes over Hong Kong in 1997.

The 'bomb shelter' game demonstrated that stratification depends on the needs of each society, and may be affected by factors, such as population, religion, economy or gender. If physical strength is needed for hunting, men may have more power than women; if learning is passed on by word of mouth, the old may be more important than the young. Stratification systems include the caste system, the age-set system and the class system, each of which will be examined in the following pages.

The caste system

The **caste system** is found in India and elsewhere in Asia where people are typically divided into five main strata. In India there are four main *caste groups* and an *outcaste group* called the Untouchables. The Untouchables are thought to be unclean and impure, and they do jobs like dealing with sewage, cutting up dead animals, and washing dirty clothes.

The four caste groups are subdivided into occupational groups called **jatis** which determine the kind of work each individual can do. The Brahmins at the top of the caste system are priests, and professionals, e.g. lawyers. The caste a person is born into therefore determines all aspects of your life. It affects individuals' life-styles, who they can marry, eat with, or visit, as well as the job they can do.

The caste system is a very rigid system of stratification. This means that there is little chance of social mobility up or down. Status is **ascribed**, i.e. it is given at birth, unlike **achieved** status which can be altered by success or failure.

Although the caste system was officially abolished in 1949 when India became independent, it continues to exist. It is still very strong because it is based on the teachings of the Hindu religion. It is therefore part of the economic system, the social system and the religious system of the country and very difficult to break down.

The age-set system

The age-set system is a stratification system where the older the person is, the more important he is. This is known as a **gerontocracy**. It is a system found in parts of Africa, and was also the stratification system of the Australian Aborigines.

Children of about the same age form the first age-set, and they usually stay together as they age and become more important. Often rituals mark the movement of the group through the age-sets, particularly when the group reach puberty.

Each age-set has rights and duties associated with it. Ownership of property, such as cattle, or the right to marry, are dependent on reaching a certain age and so having a certain status within the society. The age-set system is very different from the stratification system found in Western Europe.

UNIT 2 THE CLASS SYSTEM

The stratification system in British society is known as the class system. Most people think that we have three social class groups, the working class, the middle class, and the upper class. The differences between these are often stereotyped, but as other modules show there are obvious differences between classes in terms of educational success, family size and structure, and voting behaviour.

DISCUSS

Do you have definite ideas about people from different class groups? Describe the sort of person that would choose the following drink at a pub; what is their age, sex, and class?

1   A champagne cocktail.
2   A pint of bitter.
3   A gin and tonic.
4   Half a lager and lime.
5   A double whisky.
6   A Mackeson.
7   Perrier Water.
8   A glass of white wine.
9   Half of cider.
10 A dry martini – shaken not stirred!

Did most members of your group come up with similar answers? Sociologists argue that people do fit into patterns, including their patterns of drinking! □

RESEARCH IDEA

Find out whether there really are class differences in preferred drinks. □

Social class is a way of describing similar groups of people; people with similar houses, leisure activities, or jobs. Social class is also used to distinguish between people who dress, speak and live differently from others. The media too, make use of recognisable 'types' of people, whether in soap operas like *Coronation Street* or *EastEnders*, or in cartoons.

Q   What picture does this cartoon give us of the relationship between the husband and wife? What jobs do you think they do? What about their education? What sort of house might they live in? □

TASK

Draw a similar cartoon using stereotypes of upper-, middle-, and working-class couples.

Source: The Gambols by Brian Appleby in *The Daily Express*, 1986

Class scales

A person's occupation is frequently used as a way of assessing their importance. Often the first question asked of someone met for the first time is, 'what do you do?' Occupation is used as a way of classifying people, it indicates how much they might earn, their probable education, and their life-style.

T A S K

Reorder the following occupations into a hierarchy, i.e. a ladder with the most important person at the top and the least important at the bottom.

1	Minister of religion	9	Road sweeper
2	Cleaner	10	Shop assistant
3	Plumber	11	Secretary
4	Bank manager	12	MP
5	Agricultural worker	13	Accountant
6	Bus driver	14	Nurse
7	Doctor	15	Police officer
8	Window cleaner	16	Lawyer

Now compare your list with that of others in your group. Did you have a measure of agreement, or were there fundamental differences in the way you ranked the occupations? □

Most people rank occupations which are well paid and require education and training above poorly paid manual work. This means that doctors have more prestige or status than road sweepers. The government classifies occupations in this way, using the Registrar-General's scale of social class. In this scale there are five social class groups, from class one at the top down to class five at the bottom as the table below shows.

This scale has been criticised for not clearly defining occupational groups, so that a 'farmer' (social class B or 2) could be someone with a smallholding who keeps a few goats, or someone with thousands of acres of land.

It has been criticised for being 'top heavy', with more middle-class than working-class occupations. Similar criticisms are aimed at the Hall-Jones scale, but sociologists often prefer it, because it offers seven categories.

The Registrar-General's scale

Class	Definition	Example
A or I	Higher Professional & Higher Managerial	lawyer, accountant, doctor, minister, bank manager.
B or 2	Lower Professional & Lower Managerial	nurse, teacher, farmer, school teacher, MP, police officer
C or 3	Skilled Manual and remainder of Non-manual Workers	plumber, shop assistant, typist, mechanic
D or 4	Semi-skilled Worker	lorry driver, assembly line worker, postmen, bus conductor, agricultural worker
E or 5	Unskilled Worker	window cleaner, labourer, messenger, road sweeper, cleaner

C is often sub-divided into two, known as C1 and C2.

Classes **I, 2 and 3**, are middle class; classes **4** and **5** are working class.

You will find the Hall-Jones scale on page 76.

What is the social class of the following people? □

Vicar (top left), factory worker (top right), nurse (bottom left), refuse collector (bottom right)

Q   Can you think of any other factor that could be used to determine someone's social class? In what ways would it be a better or worse means of assessing class?

Should there be more, or less, than five or seven social class groups used to classify occupations?

Can you think of any other criticisms of these objective social class scales?

Occupation is used to measure social class because a person's job, or the likelihood of unemployment relates to their educational success or failure. A person's occupation also affects how much they earn, and this determines their life-style. It is used because unlike other possible indicators of class, it affects all aspects of someone's life.

Some other criticisms that are levelled against these scales include firstly, that they ignore inherited wealth. Somone at the bottom of the class system according to their occupation might be very wealthy, but they would still be in the same category as everyone else with the same job.

Secondly, the scales ignore **status**, meaning the social honour or prestige that other people give you. This can be important in everyday life in how we think of others and how we treat them. It affects the system of relationships we have with other people and groups, i.e. our social interaction. The phrase 'keeping up with the Jones's' shows that status as well as class is important in affecting what we do, say, or wear.

For most people, *class* and *status* are the same thing, because class is defined primarily in terms of occupation, which creates economic inequalities of wealth or poverty, which in turn give prestige.

Status may be *achieved status*, that the person has worked for, perhaps becoming a surgeon or a big name in the music business. Status can also be *ascribed status*, status that is inherited from your parents, like being a member of the royal family.

For a few people (mainly those with *ascribed status*) their social *class* position, based on their occupation, is not the same as their position in terms of *status*, based on the social position others give to them.

What social class do the following belong to? Is their status position the same as their class position?

1	Prince Andrew – helicopter pilot	**5**	A film star
2	A footballer earning £50 000 a year	**6**	A vicar
		7	A punk rocker
3	A cleaning lady who wins the pools	**8**	An Asian shop keeper
		9	You
4	An unemployed man of fifty	**10**	A nurse

For more on status see Unit 4, page 85 □

A third problem with the class scales is that many people would not agree with the rankings! A study by *Willmott and Young* found that many people rank according to the **social contribution** of a job, meaning the good it does for society. These respondents ranked people with occupations like nursing, mining and agricultural work above accountants or company directors.

Many of the people who rank according to the social contribution of a job are from working-class backgrounds, or are politically left wing. Willmott and Young called this group's response a 'deviant' response, because they did not agree with the accepted way of ranking occupations.

RESEARCH IDEA

Find out the class and political sympathies of a group of respondents and also ask them to rank a list of occupations you present them with. Include occupations from each class on the Registrar General's scale. Also ask respondents which party they would vote for, or their attitude to topics, such as defence, race relations, private education or any other topic you think relevant in assessing whether someone is left wing (see Module 3 on Power and Politics, page 41). □

A final criticism of the Registrar General's scale and the Hall-Jones scale is that they do not take into account people's feelings about social class. Many people feel **subjectively** that there is a difference between the social class they think they are, and the way they would be assessed **objectively** by these scales. This may be important in affecting various aspects of

Q Explain the difference between someone's objective social class, and their subjective social class.

someone's life, such as their voting behaviour, their leisure pursuits, their aspirations for their children, or their type of housing. Sociologists are especially interested in an individual's subjective social class because it affects their behaviour, or as the American sociologist *W.I. Thomas* put it, their belief is 'real in its consequences'.

Social class is used widely by sociologists as a way of differentiating between people despite the criticisms made against the objective scales. However, sociologists would use the term class to indicate not only a person's occupation, but also differences in life-style, chance of educational success, or family life.

Belonging to a social strata in a system of stratification affects what Weber terms a person's **life-chances**. These are the opportunities open to an individual throughout their life, and include the chance to be born healthy and to live a long life, the chance to be successful in education, and the chance of keeping out of trouble with the law (see Unit 4 on Theories of Social Class, page 84). It is therefore not sociologists who create systems of stratification, they merely use terms, such as social class to point out the differences between people that already exist.

BRAINSTORM

Some of you probably ranked occupations according to their social contribution in the task on page 74. Discuss or recap on your reasons for this. □

T A S K

Go through the other modules and make a list of class differences that are discussed there. For example, in comparison to working-class people, middle-class people generally: have fewer children; live longer; work shorter hours. What other distinguishing features can you think of between these two class groups? □

DISCUSS

What does the Hall Jones table tell us about class differences? □

The Hall–Jones scale

Class	Definition
1	Professional and high administrative
2	Managerial and executive
3	Inspectional, supervisory and other non-manual, higher grade
4	Inspectional, supervisory and other non-manual, lower grade
5	Skilled manual and routine grades of non-manual
6	Semi-skilled manual
7	Unskilled manual

Q   Sociologists often use the Hall-Jones scale when using a class scale based on occupation. In what ways is it different to the Registrar-General's scale on page 73? □

Why do societies stratify?

It has been argued that stratification systems exist to ensure that the jobs which are needed most by a society are done by people who will do them well, and to the best of their ability.

This is the reason given for doctors or lawyers being paid more than typists or cleaners; the jobs that are at the top of the class system are those that require ability, and educational success. In order to make sure that these jobs will be done by able people, who have spent extra years in the education system, society gives these occupations high rewards, such as high status and high pay. A stratification system is therefore created, because the highly rewarded people become more important than the others, who are seen as less important.

Not all sociologists would agree with this argument. It is very difficult to decide which jobs are the most important; is the company director more important than the workers who produce the goods? Or the job of a bank manager more important than that of the refuse collector?

BRAINSTORM

Which jobs do you think are most necessary for the well-being of our society? Do you all agree? Are they the occupations that involve a long period of training? Are they the best paid? □

Many jobs that appear to be necessary to society are not very well paid, even when they require educational success; perhaps nurses, teachers and social workers might come into this category. Their reward is often thought to be job satisfaction, but many of these workers have recently been on strike for more money!

Another explanation of stratification is that it reflects the power held by certain groups in society: powerful groups ask for and get more money. But sometimes it appears that both individuals and groups can move up or down the class system, i.e. they become **socially mobile**.

DISCUSS

1 Which groups are powerful in British society? Why?
2 Do other stratification systems, e.g. the caste system, have the most able people doing the most important jobs? □

UNIT 3 CHANGES IN THE CLASS SYSTEM

Social mobility

Social mobility means moving up or down a stratification system. In the caste system mobility is unlikely, because status is ascribed and because a person's choice of occupation depends on their caste. In the age-set system social mobility is dependent on age, and a whole group are mobile at the same time (see Unit 1, page 71).

In a class stratified society mobility is possible, and many people have a class position that is different from that of their parents.

Q How many different ways can you think of for someone to be socially mobile? □

A sociologist called *Turner* distinguishes between two different sorts of mobility: sponsored mobility and contest mobility. **Sponsored mobility** means being helped up the class system, perhaps by being born into a wealthy family who can afford to pay for private education. Sponsored mobility is therefore often linked to ascribed status. **Contest mobility** on the other hand, is a result of an individual's own efforts. In this case a person may be mobile due to being successful in education, or perhaps due to working hard and being promoted.

Turner argues that the American system of education fosters contest mobility, and the British system with its public school element gives rise to a sponsored system of mobility.

T A S K

1 Read page 117 in Module 7 on Education to assess the importance of public schools in sponsoring individuals up the class system. Discuss the chances of mobility through the state schooling system; or through an individual's hard work.
2 What does this extract from a television interview tell us about social class and public schools? [A Wykehamist is a past or present student from the English public school, Winchester College.) □

> A young Wykehamist speaking frankly about class—in this case, the prospects of any young lad, not quite quite, who ended up at the school: 'If anyone did have a particularly, um, fringe accent—who was right on the borders—he would first of all be sort of persuaded gradually to conform with everybody else. And if he didn't he would be ostracised—put out—and people would go out of their way to be unpleasant to him.'

Mobility can be measured by comparing the occupations of father and son; this is known as **intergenerational mobility**, meaning a comparison between generations. Alternatively a study can be made of the career of an individual throughout his life, which is known as **intragenerational mobility**.

T A S K

Look at the table on page 43 in Module 3 on Power and Politics and assess how important ascribed status is in Great Britain today.

Source: *The Story of English*

T A S K

Read Module 7 on Education and discuss whether Britain has a meritocratic society.

Q Explain the message of this car-sticker.

> **Designed by a computer, built by a robot, driven by a moron!**

The main avenues of social mobility in British society are by hard work, educational success, or through marriage. It has been said that if middle-class people have fewer children than working-class people, this may give opportunities for mobility. Another suggestion is that in times of full employment there may be middle-class occupations available for the upwardly mobile because of differential fertility rates, however this is debatable.

Further opportunities for mobility in society may arise if those with ability are able to move up the class system. This would create a **meritocratic** society where those with merit, i.e. talent and ability, are at the top of the stratification system.

Changes in the structure of occupations may also lead to social mobility. British society is becoming increasingly mechanised. Consequently there are an increasing number of professional and other non-manual occupations, and a decreasing number of unskilled manual jobs. This may mean that the class system is changing in a way that gives more chance of upwards mobility, but class is more than just a person's occupation.

Q Explain in your own words three possible reasons for upwards mobility in this society. What difference does a high rate of unemployment make to the chance of mobility? □

T A S K

Who's who? Match the face to the description. Which of these people have been socially mobile? □

1 Fashion designer – once a 'Barnado's boy'.   2 Agha Khan's nephew turned newspaper proprietor.   3 Aristocratic lady who became a royal.   4 Grocer's daughter gets to be number one.

Surveys on social mobility

1 *The Affluent Worker*   In the 1950s some manual workers were earning high wages for jobs, such as assembly-line work. The increasing affluence of these groups led to media headlines like: 'We're all middle class now!' and 'You've never had it so good!' In order to discover whether affluence had really changed the class of this group of workers some sociologists decided to study car assemblers at Vauxhall Motors in Luton near London. As these were highly paid, *Lockwood and Goldthorpe* reasoned that if any workers would show a change in social class because of affluence it would be this group. Their study is called *The Affluent Worker*.

Assembly-line workers at the Vauxhall Motors factory in Luton

Lockwood and Goldthorpe found that although the assemblers got high wages, they were not really middle class in attitudes. The workers were paid in cash at the end of the week, not on a salary like most middle-class occupations. They did not have job security, and many did not have bank accounts.

The affluent workers showed working-class attitudes towards unions and politics; most were union members and voted Labour. Their family life too was working class, although their leisure was spent at home like the privatised middle-class family.

Lockwood and Goldthorpe concluded that only two of the eighty workers studied had become middle class and were accepted as such by other middle-class people. The others had become a 'new middle class', affluent and perhaps owning their own homes; but not middle class in outlook, values norms, sociability, etc.

Q   What would make someone middle class? Why did Lockwood and Goldthorpe conclude that affluence alone is not enough to change someone's social class? □

2 *The Black Coated Worker*   While some groups appeared to be showing signs of upwards mobility, others were moving down the class system. Lockwood's study of the clerical worker, *The Black Coated Worker*, 1958, was so called because clerical workers used to wear black coats that wouldn't show ink stains!

This group of workers used to be seen by themselves and by others as middle class. A clerk was often to be found in a room next to the manager, and clerical work was seen as a high-status job which might lead on to management.

However, as educational qualifications became more important and management trainees were introduced, there was little opportunity for the clerk to become upwardly mobile. Even worse, the position of clerk was itself changing. The clerical workers were not unionised, because they had always seen themselves as part of the management, rather than the workers. This meant that their pay and working conditions were not protected, and they suffered downwards mobility as aspects of their job changed and became mechanised.

BRAINSTORM

How many reasons can you think of for the downwards mobility of the clerical worker? As well as the reasons discussed above you could also consider: the sex of the clerical worker today and the impact of the new technology, such as VDUs and word processors. □

T A S K

There is more about changes in the class system and the way jobs are changing in Module 8 on Work, Units 3 and 4. What sort of changes in work have taken place in the last fifty years? □

RESEARCH IDEA

Interview some elderly people about the occupations that were highly regarded when they were young. Then take the list to a younger age group of respondents and assess which occupations have changed their class position. □

The most recent study of social mobility is the *Oxford Mobility Study*, 1980 by Goldthorpe et al. An earlier study done in the 1930s by *Glass* had found about equal numbers going up and down the class system; but this has now changed. It now appears that more people than ever before are upwardly mobile mainly due to changes in the structure of the class system.

The increasing number of middle-class occupations, such as professional jobs, has meant that there is now a large number of objectively middle-class people. However, this Goldthorpe called a 'class of low classness', meaning that it is made up of many dissimilar people. These 'new middle-class' people come from a variety of backgrounds and they may not see themselves as middle class. They may have different values and attitudes, and different voting patterns from those traditionally associated with the middle classes, see Module 3 on Power and Politics.

Q Explain in your own words what is meant by a 'new middle class'.

THEORIES OF SOCIAL CLASS

At the end of Unit 2 it was argued that stratification was needed by society. A stratification system meant that the most able people took the functionally more important jobs. This meant that everyone was rewarded according to their abilities, and the system was therefore fair and just. There are many criticisms of the idea that societies need stratifying and one of the most significant of these comes from Karl Marx.

Karl Marx

Marx lived from 1818 to 1883, and his writings have been an important influence all over the world. He was a German but spent time in other countries including here in Britain where he is buried. He spent some time in the industrial North, and his ideas about stratification and social class were partly a result of what he saw there.

Marx argues that in all societies there has always been two main groups, one in power over the other. He believed that these two groups were caused by the economic system of the society. You might have, for example, a feudal system, a slave society or a class system; each of these systems having two main antagonistic groups: those who have, and those who have not.

In British society the economic system is a **capitalist** one, meaning that it is dependent on profit making. The two classes that result from this capitalist system are the workers who sell their labour, and the owners of the factories who employ them. Marx therefore sees the difference between the two groups as their relationship to the economic system, in this case owners or workers.

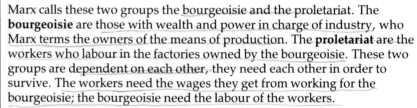

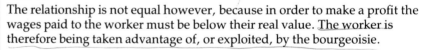

Marx calls these two groups the bourgeoisie and the proletariat. The **bourgeoisie** are those with wealth and power in charge of industry, who Marx terms the owners of the means of production. The **proletariat** are the workers who labour in the factories owned by the bourgeoisie. These two groups are dependent on each other, they need each other in order to survive. The workers need the wages they get from working for the bourgeoisie; the bourgeoisie need the labour of the workers.

The relationship is not equal however, because in order to make a profit the wages paid to the worker must be below their real value. The worker is therefore being taken advantage of, or exploited, by the bourgeoisie.

Marx believed that society is in a state of conflict between the two social class groups. The proletariat are struggling to achieve a better life-style, and the bourgeoisie are struggling to stay in power at the top of society. Changes come about because of this conflict, and Marx believed that eventually the classes would get further apart as the proletariat got poorer and the bourgeoisie got richer. Then the workers would feel a sense of common identity, or **class consciousness**. The proletariat would then be prepared to fight as a whole group, and to try to overthrow the bourgeoisie, by force if necessary.

The armed struggle predicted by Marx actually took place in Russia in 1917, with the Communist Revolution when the workers took control of the state and set up a society in which everyone was theoretically equal – a communist state. In such a society there would be no private property, and no inherited wealth. The society would be classless.

Is Russia a classless society today?

These theories of Marx have been responsible for the political systems of both Russia and China, as well as affecting many other societies that have communist parties.

Q   Is it possible to have a classless society? □

DISCUSS

Is it likely that there could be a revolution in Britain? Consider the following points when debating this question:

1   What happens when one group of workers goes on strike, do other groups join in to show class consciousness?
2   What has prevented the mass poverty among workers foretold by Marx?
3   Why don't the proletariat take control of society by voting working-class people in as Members of Parliament? □

TASK

Read the following extract written by a student of Marx, then answer the following questions.

> 'The wage-worker sells to the capitalist his labour-force for a certain daily sum. After a few hours work he has reproduced the value of that sum, but the substance of his contract is, that he has to work another series of hours to complete his working day; and the value he produces during those additional hours as surplus (extra) labour is surplus value, which costs the capitalist nothing, but yet goes into his pocket.'
>
> (Engels)

1   What terms does Marx give to
    a   a wage-worker group
    b   a capitalist group
2   What does capitalism mean?
3   Explain in your own words the meaning of the passage.
4   Give two criticisms made against Marxist theory. □

Max Weber

Max Weber lived from 1864 to 1920. He has also been an important influence on sociological ideas about social class. Whereas Marx defines class as the relationship of the person to the economic system, Weber argues a class group is a group of individuals who share a similar position in the economic system and get similar rewards for the work they do.

Weber believed that if people have a similar class position they share similar **life chances**. These are the chances a person has to obtain desirable things, whether a house, a foreign holiday, good health or educational success.

Weber sees class as separate from status. Status or social honour is the way other people rank an individual, and this is not necessarily linked to the job that person does. People may form status groups because of their religion, ethnic group, or life-style.

Q Is Weber right about status groups being different from class groups? Consider the class and status of the following:

a A teacher who is taking industrial action.
b A minister of religion.
c An Asian doctor.
d A nurse.
e A homosexual MP.
f A black lawyer.
g An unmarried mother.
h Give your own example of a person whose status may be different from their class position. □

Weber argues that there were four main class groups in society. These are:

1 The propertied upper class, e.g. the Duke of Westminster.
2 The propertyless white-collar worker, e.g. a computer programmer, a solicitor or a nurse.
3 The petty bourgeoisie, e.g. the owner of a corner shop.
4 The manual working class, e.g. a fitter.

Unlike Marx, Weber did not think that there are two main classes always in conflict, or that there will be a revolution. He argued instead that the middle classes would expand as the society needs more bureaucrats, administrators and professional people. This means that the working class may express their dissatisfaction with their wages or conditions by striking, but are unlikely to come together as one group as Marx suggested.

The two theories of Marx and Weber are very different, but each gives an important contribution to an understanding of social class.

Q Which theory do you think best explains the class system in Britain today? Are the classes getting further apart, as Marx suggests or are there more middle-class groups, as in Weber's theory? □

Despite theories of social class, the ordinary man or woman in the street still sees three main class groups; the upper, middle and working classes. Most people feel subjectively that they belong to one of these three groups, even if their occupation would classify them differently.

However, it would also appear that people's perception of class may be changing. A new class group that the media call 'the winners' seem to be appearing. These are an increasingly large group of successful people, who don't fit into the usual categories. They are both men and women, black and white, from a variety of occupations.

Read the extract below and then answer the following questions.

Wogan 'winners' break class mould

TERRY WOGAN, Joan Collins and Bob Geldof emerge as members of "the winners", a new social group identified in a survey of public opinion commissioned for a new television series.

Leading sportsmen such as Henry Cooper are also among members of the group which appears to transcend the division with upper middle and working classes. Mr Chris Riley, producer, explained yesterday: "Structurally, little has changed in society over the past 20 years, except for this special, almost classless class.

The opinion poll, part of a Gallup Survey of Britain and said to be the biggest yet conducted by the company forms the basis of "20 Years On", from Television South which compares the optimism of the 1960s with the realities of today.

The first of four new programmes, due to be shown next weekend looks at changes in class, status and style.

Distinctions blurred

Mr Lucian Hudson, series researcher, said: "The divisions between rich and poor have not altered much, but class distinctions have become blurred by this class of "winners" who are seen crossing classes and spanning a whole range of taste.

"What they have is the nous to carry things off with style. They don't have to shop in Harrods or speak with posh accents to achieve credibility."

Mr Rice said: "They include celebrities like Terry Wogan and Bob Geldof and sportsmen. They are seen on television mixing with royalty and people from all walks of life, and this tends to confuse how people perceive them in terms of social class."

Politicians are not included in the group. Mr Wedgwood Benn and Mr Norman Tebbit were perceived as upper class. So was Mrs Thatcher, except amongst the well-educated, who considered her as middle class as Mr Steel and Dr. Owen. Mr Kinnock dwelt in both middle and working classes.

Mr Arthur Scargill, Mr Ken Livingstone and Lenny Henry the comedian were cited as working class heroes, while Joan Collins was "almost regal" to some.

Half the population now consider themselves middle class, compared to 38 per cent. a few decades ago, when Britain saw itself predominantly as a working class society.

Only 40 per cent. of those questioned in the latest survey said they were working class. No-one in a sample of 879 people, chosen to represent every socio-economic group in Britain, admitted to being upper class.

The survey report concluded: "Given the negative connotations of the concept of "upper class" in British mentality, the image of top businessmen emerges as selfish, uncaring people indulging in an easy life and riding around in a Rolls Royce remote from the people around them."

Middle class attributes were found to include "helping others," having few or no money worries, holding white-collar jobs, attending dinner parties, going to the theatre, playing golf and driving Volvos.

"The image of the working class was classically Coronation Street," said the survey. Apart from admiration for their values of determination and honesty and a close family tie, the "cloth-cap" image of trade unions, working men's clubs, terraced houses and "the workers" predominated.

The working class were found to be much prouder (75 per cent.) of their class than the middle class (61 per cent.) The middle classes thought the working classes were much more likeable than themselves.

Education was much more important than household income as a class indicator.

Just over half those with an annual income of £20,000 or more classify themselves as middle class, yet 41 per cent with the same income see themselves as working class.

Only 12 per cent of those questioned who had some form of higher education regarded themselves as working class, compared with 53 per cent who had left school at 16 or earlier.

Source: *The Daily Telegraph*, July 1986

1 Who are the 'winners'? Why are they being called a new class group?
2 Give some examples of people that you think fit into this new group and explain why.
3 Why do you think that some people may be muddled about the class position of individuals, such as politicians, e.g. Mrs Thatcher or Mr Kinnock, or union leaders like Arthur Scargill?
4 How does Britain see itself now compared to thirty years ago?
5 What sort of image do upper-, middle- and working-class people have according to the respondents of this survey?
6 Why do 41 per cent of people with an income of over £20 000 feel that they are working class? What according to this extract do people think is the most important indicator of class?
7 Do the 'winners' fit into either Marx's theory of class, or Weber's theory of class? □

This module has explained why stratification systems exist, and has examined the class system closely. The next module focuses on specific factors that affect a person's class position, in particular factors of race, poverty and health. Another important factor is that of gender, and this is dealt with separately in Module 12, page 209.

QUESTIONS

Britain is often referred to as a class-bound society. But does the British public share that impression? According to this survey, the majority do. Class prejudice or discrimination is still seen as important.

Importance of social class by class and party identification

	Total	Social class						Party identification			
		I/II	III Non-manual	III Manual	IV/V	Looks after home	Other	Conservative	Alliance	Labour	Non-aligned
Affects opportunities in Britain today	%	%	%	%	%	%	%	%	%	%	%
A great deal	25	23	17	30	33	18	34	19	24	33	22
Quite a lot	45	44	51	44	38	47	44	48	51	41	39
Not very much	25	28	29	22	22	27	12	28	22	21	27
Not at all	3	3	1	2	2	5	5	3	1	3	6
Other/Don't know	2	1	1	1	4	4	3	2	2	2	4
Not answered	*	*	*	–	1	–	2	*	*	*	1

* = Negligible

(Adapted from: *British Social Attitudes* edited by R Jowell and C Airey)

Using the information given above, answer these questions. Refer back to earlier parts of this module if necessary.

1 What percentage of social class III manual workers believe that social class affects opportunities a great deal?
2 What is the percentage of people who believe that class affects opportunities quite a lot?
3 Which party supporters are most likely to believe that class affects opportunities:
   a a great deal;
   b not very much?
4 What is meant by the term social mobility? Give two examples of the ways it may be achieved.
5 The lower the social class the higher the infant mortality rate. Identify and explain two reasons for this.
6 We usually determine an individual's social class by finding out what occupation they have. Identify and explain two problems associated with determining social class in this way.
7 Identify and explain two differences between caste and class. □

Source: SEG Sociology GCSE, specimen paper, 1988

WHERE TO NOW?

Next read Module 6 on Inequality which follows this module. You may also be interested to then read the modules on Gender, Education, or Work.

MODULE · 6

INEQUALITY

SIX

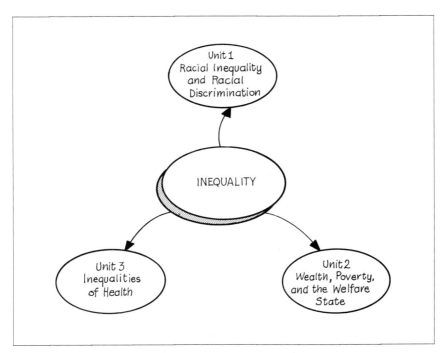

Unit 1
Racial Inequality
and Racial
Discrimination

INEQUALITY

Unit 3
Inequalities
of Health

Unit 2
Wealth, Poverty,
and the Welfare
State

WHAT THIS MODULE IS ABOUT

This module analyses the importance of factors of race, poverty and health in society today; and the causes and consequences of these inequalities are debated.

BY THE END OF THIS MODULE YOU SHOULD BE ABLE TO:

1 Explain what is meant by the terms racial discrimination, racial prejudice and underclass.
2 Cite the evidence for the view that racial prejudice does exist.
3 Give three possible explanations for racial prejudice.
4 Explain the difference in meaning between wealth and income and understand why Britain is called 'two nations'.

5 Explain the difference between absolute and relative poverty, primary and secondary poverty, poverty line and poverty trap.
6 Suggest which groups of people are most likely to be suffering from poverty, and the reasons for this including the theory of the culture of poverty.
7 Explain what Rowntree and Booth found out about poverty at the turn of the century.
8 Understand why the Welfare State was set up.
9 Know how and why the expectation of life has improved this century.
10 Explain why inequalities of health still exist in different class groups, and offer alternative suggestions for the persistence of these inequalities.

RACIAL INEQUALITY AND RACIAL DISCRIMINATION

There are some groups in society whose social class position is dependent not only on their occupation or wealth, but also on their age, sex or race. Women and ethnic minorities are more likely to be at the bottom of the class system than white men. If we ignore arguments about the possible inferiority of these groups, then this in effect strengthens them, i.e. it indicates that the low class position of these groups is due to discrimination against them.

To assess whether racial inequality actually exists, it is necessary to find out what jobs are done by minority groups. Obviously other factors, such as status, are also important in deciding someone's class position, particularly for people from a different ethnic group.

|T|A|S|K|

Look at the following table showing figures for men in employment by ethnic group and occupation, between 1984 and 1986.

1 Which occupational group do most white men belong to, e.g. managerial, craft or clerical?
2 Which single occupational group do most West Indian or Guyanese men belong to?
3 Which two occupational groups do most Indian, Pakistani or Bangladeshi men belong to?
4 Suggest some factors to explain the differences between the occupations of various ethnic groups shown by this table. □

Men in employment: by sex, ethnic group and occupation in Great Britain, 1984–86

	Ethnic group			
	White	West Indian or Guyanese	Indian/ Pakistani/ Bangladeshi	Other[1]
Occupation	%	%	%	%
Non-manual				
Managerial and professional	34	10	38	42
Clerical and related	5	—	6	8
Other	6	—	5	—
Total	46	21	48	57
Manual				
Craft and similar	26	34	19	13
General labourers	2	—	—	—
Other	26	40	30	29
Total	54	78	51	43
All occupations[2] (= 100%) (thousands)	12,911	107	253	133

1 Includes African, Arab, Chinese, other stated and mixed.
2 Excludes occupation inadequately described or not stated.

Source: *Social Trends* 18, 1988

Sociologists have suggested that Blacks form a separate group stuck at the bottom of society. **Rex and Tomlinson** used the term **underclass** to signify a disadvantaged group which does not share the same privileges or experiences as the white working class. (The term was first used in the United States to refer to the section of the population which appeared to be permanently trapped in a situation of poverty and unemployment). A study done by Rex and Tomlinson in 1979 on Handsworth in Birmingham showed a clear structural break between the white working class and the coloured underclass in a range of market situations, such as education, employment and housing.

In a study of the position of Blacks in America, *Warner* argues that there are two different kinds of stratification system operating there; a class system for Whites, and a caste system for Blacks. By this he means that Blacks are given a low social status (their ascribed status), which is inescapable and that there is no real chance of social mobility. This is therefore very similar to the caste system of India, which has a rigid system of mobility, and where caste position affects all aspects of a person's social life. (For more information on the caste system turn to page 71 in Module 5).

Warner suggests that there is a barrier that Blacks cannot cross between the white class system and the black caste system as shown in the diagram below.

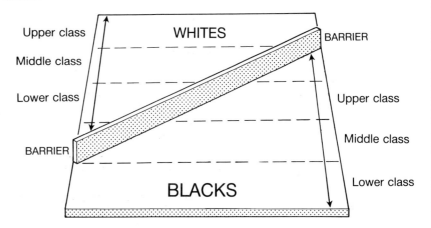

Q   According to this diagram, how far up and down the white class system can Blacks move?
What evidence is there that the situation of Blacks in this country is similar to the caste society described by Warner? Do people from ethnic minority groups reach the top of our class system? □

RESEARCH IDEAS

In your area find out what jobs are done by Asians, West Indians or other minority groups. Do they work anti-social hours? It may be difficult to collect such information using a survey. Why? Instead a visit to a local community group, or a branch of the Race Relations Council may provide an alternative way of finding data. □

An underclass?

What is meant in reality by a group being in an underclass? It means that the people in this group are severely disadvantaged. They are more likely to be living in poverty, to be ill, to be unemployed. They have fewer life-chances than the rest of the population. They are unlikely to be successful in education and so opportunities for social mobility are limited.

People from ethnic minority groups frequently live in poor housing but pay higher rents than the white population, and many are unaware of the benefits available through the Welfare State. Asian families, for example, also suffer from a poor diet. This may be partly due to economic reasons, but also because their religion imposes restrictions on what they can eat and preferred food may not be available, or may be very expensive in this country.

The table below shows that the Asian diet is frequently lower in certain important nutrients than the diet of low income groups in Britain.

Percentage recommended intake

	Average British diet	Low income British diet*	Asian diet
Energy	104	100	81
Protein	124	117	91
Calcium	193	175	137
Iron	118	112	95
Vitamin D	89	91	51
Vitamin C	189	154	216

* Low income British diet is drawn from income group D wage earners.

Source: *National Food Survey, 1973*

Q   What does this table show about the differences in the diets of Asians, an average British diet, and a low income British diet?

DISCUSS

Ethnic minority groups living in poverty experience a way of life that is often made worse because of discrimination against Blacks. This extract is from a conversation with a recently widowed black woman aged thirty-nine. Why does this woman feel that her life is without hope?

The Cost of Hope

A conversation with a woman, recently widowed, living in a poor black community of London, reveals the difficulty in merely surviving that she, her family and families like her own presently are experiencing. Her concerns are with housing, schools, health care for herself and her children, ageing when one lives in poverty and, perhaps most significantly, her gradual loss of hope that anything can be done to improve her circumstances. The study reported has been done on one single family; it is not a composite of several families, although clearly, the life of this one woman is most representative of families living where she lives.

A few financial benefits are still being received, but the two-room flat is wholly inadequate for Dionne and her children, especially in the winter when she is cold all the time, and her joints ache from the coldness and dampness. The building, in which she and seven other families live, has never had sufficient hot water. All sorts of workers have come to solve the problem, but no one is willing to put in a whole new hot water system which is the only and obvious solution.

David's death, the reduction in the hot water and heating supplies, the steady rise in rent, the day-by-day decay of the building: there have been many changes in the life of 39 year old Dionne Stapleton.

'I don't feel any more hope, like I used to. I can live with the bad weather, I can live with the knowledge I can't get my share of food or hot water. But now, you see, it's all beginning to get to me. I've lost the heart for living, and that's a mighty horrible condition to be in. I'm old, I can't say I'm young any more. But I'm not done with my life. I was reading the papers this morning how women in Britain can expect to live until they're 75 years old. That gives me a lot of time, a lot of time, I thought when I read that. Maybe I'm not so old after all. But then I thought, how do I know those numbers are meant for me, for women like me, I mean. How do I know that women with warm flats, who get to take hot baths whenever they want, and have their children fed properly, aren't the women living until 75. Maybe women like me who are always cold, who get pains in their fingers and their toes before they're even 40 years old are the ones who die at 50, or 60.

Source: 'The Cost of Hope' by Thomas J. Cotlle in *British Journal of Social Work,* Vol 7

These tables compare the different types of housing that West Indians and Asians live in with those that the white population live in. Minority groups may be more likely to live in their own homes, but their houses are also more likely to be small and lacking in basic amenities.

DISCUSS

What other information do these three tables give about racial disadvantage in housing?

Housing: West Indians, Asians and the general population

	West Indians	Asians	General population
	%	%	%
Owner-occupied	50	76	50
Rented from council	26	4	28
Privately rented	23	19	22
Not stated	1	1	—

Type and age of dwelling: comparison between minorities and whites

	Minorities	Whites
Type of dwelling:	%	%
Detached	1	21
Semi-detached	15	36
Terraced	66	30
Flat/rooms/maisonette	15	12
Not stated	3	1
Age of dwelling:		
Built before 1914	46	24
Built before 1940	86	48

Basic amenities: households not having exclusive use of bath, hot water and inside WC

West Indians	Pakistanis/ Bangladeshis	Indians	African Asians	General population
%	%	%	%	%
33	57	35	31	17.9

Source: adapted from *Racial Disadvantage in Britain*, by D J Smith, 1977

Racial discrimination

Many people in society today have strong feelings about those from a different ethnic group to themselves. Racial prejudice means having negative attitudes towards members of another ethnic group. It seems that most people are **ethnocentric** to some degree, meaning that they believe their own group to be superior to anyone else's. Most races for example have jokes against those from a different race, religion or country.

Racial prejudice turns into racial discrimination when people behave in a prejudiced way. Most discrimination in British society is against black immigrants. (For more information on immigration see Module 10 on Population, page 179–181.) Despite legislation against racial discrimination it remains a serious social problem.

In the last twenty years there have been a number of surveys trying to assess the amount of racial discrimination that exists despite laws against it. Three of these surveys are by Daniel, 1968, Smith, 1977, and the Swann Report, 1985.

In the *Daniel* survey it was decided to test the amount of discrimination by using situation tests. In these tests three actors would apply for the same

TASK

The tests used by Daniel are a type of experiment. For more about the method of experimentation turn to page 12 in Module 1.

job, type of council or private housing, or the same commercial service, such as a mortgage. The actors were a black immigrant, either Asian or West Indian; a white immigrant, such as a Pole or Hungarian; and lastly a white native Briton. They were all given the same qualifications, and matched for age and appearance. This meant that discrimination could then be defined as a case in which one tester was made an offer or a better offer than another.

The survey found that there was widespread evidence of discrimination based on colour. The darker the skin colour the greater the amount of discrimination.

White gang stab black youths

Three young black youths were in hospital with knife wounds last night after they were set upon early yesterday by 30 to 40 white youths as they left a club following a party at Mitcham, South London.

Two of the men, Jamie Mumuni, 20, and Ian Henry, 18, were stabbed as they left the hall. The third, Adrian Bennett, 17, was confronted by a gang as he walked away to find a minicab and he was forced back to the hall, and also stabbed outside. Police believe the attack was racially motivated.

Bradford mayor rebukes judge

Britain's first Asian Lord Mayor yesterday called for an inquiry by the Lord Chancellor, Lord Hailsham, into illegal immigration remarks allegedly made last week by an Old Bailey judge.

Mr Mohammed Ajeeb, Mayor of Bradford, is seeking a transcript of the speech made by Judge Michael Argyle to students at the Law Society in Trent Polytechnic, Nottingham, when he reportedly claimed there were five million illegal immigrants in Britain, remarking, "I don't have the figures but just go to Bradford."

Mr Ajeeb said yesterday: "Saying there are five million illegal immigrants when there are only three million non-whites in the country is a stupid statement. It's irresponsible to say the least coming from an Old Bailey judge."

Source: *The Daily Telegraph* (left) and *The Independent*, March 1987 (right)

DISCUSS

1 Situation tests are not a usual method of collecting data. Most surveys use interviews and/or questionnaires.
2 Why do you think situation tests were used in this survey, rather than other research methods?
3 Can you see any reasons why these tests might also lead to biased results? □

The 1968 Race Relations Act outlawed discrimination in housing, employment, and commercial services. Racial discrimination is very difficult to prove because it is rarely open, and so very few prosecutions take place. When *Smith* tested the strength of the Act in a survey conducted in 1973 to 1974, he found that discrimination on the grounds of colour was still widespread. He stated that there were about '6000 cases a year of discrimination against Asian and West Indian job applicants in the non-skilled field alone'.

Evidence of racial discrimination from Smith's survey, 1973–1974

Q According to this table which group experiences the most discrimination, and which the least?

	West Indians		Indians		Pakistanis		Greeks	
No of cases	104		111		109		84	
	No	%	No	%	No	%	No	%
Discrimination	28	27	31	28	25	23	9	11

Source: *Racial Disadvantage in Britain* by D J Smith, 1977

Smith also used letters to test for discrimination in granting job interviews to black immingrants, and again found clear evidence that it existed. This technique had been used in a survey by *Jowell and Prescott-Clarke* in 1970, an example from their survey can be seen below.

Reply to British applicant:

Dear Mr Robinson,
Thank you for your letter of 31st July in response to our advertisement for an electronics engineer.
We should like you to attend for interview so that we can discuss the position further, and would ask you to telephone . . . as soon as possible so that we can arrange this . . .

Yours sincerely,

Reply to Indian applicant:

Dear Mr Singh,
Thank you very much for your letter of 31st July in connection with an advertisement for an electronics engineer. There was a big response to this advertisement and we have studied all letters carefully before making our final short list of candidates. It seemed to us that you were really a little well-qualified for the type of job we were offering and therefore regret to inform you that we decided against including your name on the short list.
We would like to wish you every success in obtaining the type of position for which your qualifications fit you.
Once again, our thanks for your interest.

Yours sincerely,

Source: *Race Relations in Britain* by A Pilkington, 1984

T A S K

Read the letters above received in response to two 'matched' applications for a white-collar job.
1 What job were the two men applying for?
2 What excuse does the company make for not offering an interview to Mr Singh?
3 Would someone receiving a letter like that of Mr Singh's be likely to suspect that he was the victim of racial discrimination? How could he prove that he was?
4 Why would sociologists use a correspondence test like this as a way of gathering data on discrimination? □

People from ethnic minority groups are more likely to be unemployed than whites. For more about this turn to Module 8 on Work, page 151.

Explanations of racial discrimination

1 *The self-fulfilling prophecy* If people are expected to behave in a particular way, it seems that they are indeed more likely to behave in that way. Sociologists call this effect a **self-fulfilling prophecy**, and it has important implications for the streaming of pupils at school, and for the deviance of certain groups in society (see Module 7 on Education, page 122–124 and Module 13 on Deviance, page 244).

Turn to Module 14 on Urbanisation, Unit 5 for more about inner-city policing.

The urban riots of 1980 to 1986 between the police and ethnic minority groups in the inner-city areas of Bristol, Liverpool, Manchester and London can partly be explained in this way. Many white people felt that the riots confirmed their stereotype of black youths being aggressive and violent.

Q How many examples of a self-fulfilling prophecy causing a change in behaviour can you think of?

The police saw the rioters as a delinquent minority whose behaviour must be stopped. The rioters on the other hand felt that they were being provoked by aggressive policing (see Module 13 on Deviance, page 235).

The self-fulfilling prophecy is explained by *Desmond Morris* as the result of a sub-group having an easily identifiable physical badge, such as skin colour. He writes:

A vicious circle soon develops. If the physical badge-wearers are treated, through no fault of their own, as a hostile sub-group, they will all too soon begin to behave like one . . . Let me illustrate what happens, using an imaginary example. These are the stages:

1   Look at that green-haired man hitting a child.
2   That green-haired man is vicious.
3   All green-haired men are vicious.
4   Green-haired men will attack anyone.
5   There's another green-haired man – hit him before he hits you. The green-haired man, who has done nothing to provoke aggression, hits back to defend himself.
6   There you are – that proves it: green-haired men *are* vicious.
7   Hit all green-haired men.

It is, of course ridiculous, but nevertheless it represents a very real way of thinking . . . After the green-haired men have been hit for no reason for long enough, they do, rather naturally, become vicious. The original false prophecy has fulfilled itself and become a true prophecy.

Source: *The Human Zoo* by Desmond Morris, 1969

2 *Scapegoating or misplaced aggression* (A psychological explanation) Psychologists have other explanations for racial discrimination. They argue that if people feel angry, frustrated, or aggressive, they normally express their feelings either verbally or physically. If someone you know is rude to you, for example, you will probably respond by being rude back.

Sometimes, however, this is not possible and you may feel angry but be unable to hit back at the cause of that anger. You may not even be sure what is making you cross, or you may not be in a position to, or want to blame the other person. This could happen if, for example, you were told off for being late for work when it wasn't your fault; or had an argument with a close friend. In a situation like this your anger might be **displaced** or expressed against someone else instead, so making them your **scapegoat**.

Scapegoating means blaming an innocent victim for your troubles, making that person the target for your anger or frustration. Some people's racial prejudice against minority groups can be explained as partly a result of displaced aggression or scapegoating. Minority groups are often blamed for the problems of the society in which they live. At times of high unemployment for example, they may be unfairly blamed for 'taking all the jobs', as suggested in the extract below, when in fact minority groups are usually the first to lose their jobs.

Q One example of scapegoating would be the teacher who has an argument with her husband at breakfast, and shouts at her class at school. Can you think of any times that you have shown displaced aggression? Why were you angry, and who became your scapegoat? □

3 *Unintentional racism* *The Swann report*, 1985, found that racism was the key factor in explaining the relatively low achievement of ethnic minority pupils. Most of this is unintentional, such as 'colour blindness', where all the pupils are treated as if they are of one colour and belong to one ethnic group. Teachers may do this with the mistaken impression that it avoids rascism. In fact it ignores the educational needs of different groups and as this may result in less success at school for minority groups, it is still a form of racial discrimination.

For more on the underachievement of ethnic minority pupils turn to Module 7 on Education, page 120–124.

Racial stereotypes, according to the report, were often used by teachers, and they would expect West Indian pupils, for example, to be good at dance, music and sport.

Fact or stereotype?

The school curriculum is in most cases *ethnocentric*, and assumes that the white, Christian view of things is the most important. The point of view of other cultures is rarely considered.

4 *Stereotyping* This means exaggerating certain characteristics until they become the dominant feature. For ethnic minorities, stereotyped characteristics can be either cultural or physical. *Lyon*, 1972 distinguishes between an ethnic and a racial group in this way. An *ethnic* group is defined culturally by differences in language, dress, values, or religion; a *racial* group is physically defined, for example, by skin colour, hair type, or facial features.

T A S K

One effect of beliefs about racial inequality has been government controls on immigration. There is more about this in Module 10 on Population, page 180. Find out what percentage of the population of Britain are of white ethnic origin and how many ae of West Indian, Guyanese, Indian or Pakistani ethnic origin.

T A S K

Make a list of groups that are commonly stereotyped, e.g. Scots, Irish, Welsh. How many have nicknames that come from cultural or physical features, e.g. 'skinhead'. How many of your groups have stereotyped behaviour attached to them, such as West Indians being good at music and dance? How many of your groups are from ethnic minorities? What do these stereotypes tell us about the way people from ethnic minority groups are regarded in our society? □

It should now be clear from working on this unit that one of the major reasons for inequality is racial discrimination. Poverty and poor health are two other factors in Inequality that will be considered in the following units.

WEALTH, POVERTY, AND THE WELFARE STATE

Q The problem of poverty is often called the problem of wealth, why?

Wealth

Wealth includes everything that has a value, such as money, land, houses, cars, and stocks and shares. Wealth is therefore separate from income, and those who are wealthy are not only those in highly paid jobs, but also those who inherit wealth from their family.

The objective scales of social class, such as the Registrar General's scale, see Module 5 on Stratification, page 73, do not include those with inherited wealth. Those at the top of society and those at the bottom who are unemployed are invisible when the class system is examined by such scales, as this breakdown of the Registrar General's scale shows.

In 1985 the wealthiest 1 per cent of the population owned 20 per cent of the country's wealth, so a few people in society are still extremely rich. The wealthier half of the population own 93 per cent of the wealth, so the less wealthy half have only 7 per cent between them! This is why Britain is sometimes called a country of two nations – the rich and the poor, or the haves and have-nots.

The Registrar-General's scale of social class

Class	Definition	Example	% workforce in 1970
A or 1	Professional	Doctors, Lawyers	5
B or 2	Managerial and Lower Professional	Teachers, Sales Managers	18
C or 3 C1	Non-manual Skilled	Clerks, Computer Operators	12
C2	Skilled Manual	Bricklayers, Underground Coal Miners	38
D or 4	Semi-Skilled	Bus Conductors, Postmen	18
E or 5	Unskilled	Porters, Ticket Collectors, General Labourers	9

T A S K

Look at the table below and then answer the following questions:

Distribution of wealth in the UK, 1971, 1976, 1981 and 1985

				Percentages and £s billion
	1971	1976	1981	1985
Marketable wealth *Percentage of wealth owned by:*				
Most wealthy 1%	31	24	21	20
Most wealthy 5%	52	45	40	40
Most wealthy 10%	65	60	54	54
Most wealthy 25%	86	84	77	76
Most wealthy 50%	97	95	94	93
Total marketable wealth (£s billion)	140	263	546	863
Marketable wealth plus occupational and state pension rights *Percentage of wealth owned by:*				
Most wealthy 1%	21	14	12	11
Most wealthy 5%	37	27	24	25
Most wealthy 10%	49	37	34	36
Most wealthy 25%	69–72	58–61	55–58	57–60
Most wealthy 50%	85–89	80–85	78–82	81–85

Source: *Social Trends* 18, 1988

1 Do the most wealthy 1 per cent of the population own more or less of the wealth in 1985 than they did in 1971?
2 How many billion pounds was the total marketable wealth in 1971 and in 1985?

RESEARCH IDEA

Find out which taxes remove money from the wealthy, e.g. capital gains tax. How much money is taken each year in this way?

(You may find some relevant information in *Social Trends*, a good resource for secondary data.)

3 What percentage of wealth was owned by the most wealthy 10 per cent in 1981?

4 What percentage of wealth was owned by the most wealthy 50 per cent in 1971 and in 1981?

5 What changes in the distribution of wealth are shown by this table? □

The government redistributes wealth by taking money from the rich in the form of taxes, and giving it to the poor in the form of benefits. The government taxes the wealthy and those in work using income tax, death duties, and capital gains tax. Benefits, such as free education, welfare and health services, are then made available to everyone.

However, this redistribution has been criticised especially by Marxists, who argue that those at the top of society benefit most because they keep most of their wealth while at the same time taking the free benefits if they choose to do so. The middle classes make more use of the education system as their children stay on longer than do those of the working class. On the other hand, those less well off, especially the elderly, make more use of the health and welfare benefits, available. It may therefore seem surprising that in a wealthy society, such as Britain's, there are still people living in poverty.

DISCUSS

If you were members of the Cabinet how would you redistribute wealth? You need to discuss whether to keep or revise existing taxes, such as income tax, which is a progressive system; the more you earn, the more you pay in tax. You also need to discuss the effects of removing money from people who have earned or inherited it. □

Poverty

Poverty can be defined in absolute or relative terms. **Absolute** poverty means not having enough to live on. There is absolute poverty in many parts of the world today, as described in Module 4 on Third World Studies. In this country the subsistence level is measured by the State in terms of the amount a person or family has. Below this level, often called the **poverty line**, Income Support can be claimed. Absolute poverty in British society is caused either by low income, by low benefits, or by people not claiming benefits that they are entitled to.

RESEARCH IDEA

Find out what benefits are currently available. How many people receive Income Support?

The Child Poverty Action Group criticises the Government for not increasing benefits in line with inflation. Which benefits have kept up with the current rate of inflation in the last year? □

Poverty can also be measured in relative terms, **relative poverty** means a comparison between those who are well off and those who are less well off in the same society or class. People may therefore feel that they are in poverty, even if they are living at above subsistence level, because they are much worse off than others in that society. It is obvious that those in poverty in Britain are relatively wealthy if they are compared to people starving in third world countries. Therefore sociologists say that poverty is a relative concept.

Q   What is the difference between relative and absolute poverty? Which definition tends to be used by the State and which by sociologists?

For other ideas and more information about extreme poverty go to page 56 of Module 4 on Third World Studies.

The people living in poverty in our society are shown in the chart below.

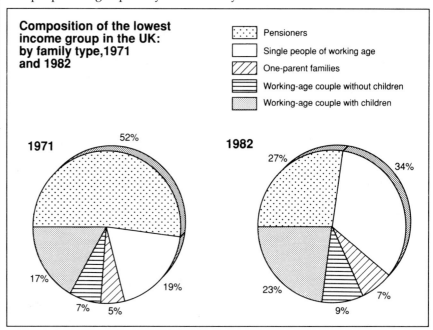

Composition of the lowest income group in the UK: by family type, 1971 and 1982

Pensioners
Single people of working age
One-parent families
Working-age couple without children
Working-age couple with children

1971
52%
17%
7%
5%
19%

1982
27%
34%
23%
9%
7%

Source: *Social Trends 14*, 1984

Q Do you know how many people are unemployed and how many one-parent families there are today in Britain? You can find some figures for this in Module 11, page 189. This information is also available in publications by voluntary organisations, as well as in government publications, such as *Social Trends* which is published every year.

Q See if you can explain in your own words what is meant by the poverty line.

THE POVERTY LINE

Those 20 per cent of families with the lowest income has changed in composition between 1971 and 1982. The shifts reflect the increased numbers of unemployed, and the increased numbers of one-parent families. It does not mean that pensioners are now well off, merely that other groups are now forming a larger proportion of those in poverty.

Q Which groups form those with the lowest income? What changes have taken place in the relative size of these groups between 1971 and 1982? □

Those in poverty in this society include the elderly, one-parent families, the disabled, large families, widows, low earners, and the unemployed. Although benefits are available for these groups, many people die each year through poverty, the elderly in particular.

Current estimates show that the number of people living in poverty is rising each year. The 1983 government figures show 16 million people living in poverty, and of these 2.8 million were living below the basic supplementary benefit level – the poverty line. This is an increase of 33 per cent between 1979 and 1983, according to the Child Poverty Action Group (CPAG).

The CPAG say that the new poor includes low-paid workers who are taxed comparatively heavily; people of working age who are unable to find work; or those unable to work because of home commitments or because they are disabled or ill.

Unclaimed benefits

Many benefits available are unclaimed by those most in need.

BRAINSTORM

How many reasons can you think of for different groups of people not claiming benefits that they are entitled to? □

It is estimated that about half the people eligible to claim benefits, such as Family Credit, do not in fact claim them. Some benefits are unclaimed because people do not know they exist; this might apply particularly to recent immigrants, especially those coming from countries that do not have a welfare state.

The fact that forms have to be filled in correctly may discourage people, especially if their written English and spelling is poor because they have not been highly educated. This red-tape and the impersonality of bureaucratic organisations also makes many feel so uncomfortable that they feel unable to apply for their benefits.

For many elderly people in this society, there is a stigma attached to claiming benefits. This is because it was felt until recently that the poor should help themselves, and only those without pride would depend on charity. Many old people claim their pensions (which were first introduced in 1908) but would not dream of asking for more, such as help with heating bills.

The poverty trap

Some people are trapped into poverty. If they are low earners they can in some cases get more money from benefits than they can get from working. Therefore it pays some people not to work.

This type of poverty trap is not new. In 1930 the dole (unemployment benefit) was £1.50 for a man and wife with two children, but if any member of the family had money coming in, it was reduced because of the **Means Test** – an absolute measure of poverty. This is described below in an extract from *The Road to Wigan Pier* by George Orwell.

The Means Test is very strictly enforced, and you are liable to be refused relief at the slightest hint that you are getting money from another source. Dock-labourers, for instance, who are generally hired by the half day, have to sign on at a Labour Exchange twice daily; if they fail to do so it is assumed that they have been working and their dole is reduced correspondingly. I have seen cases of evasion of the Means Test, but I should say that in the industrial towns, where there is still a certain amount of communal life and everyone has neighbours who know him, it is much harder than it would be in London. The usual method is for a young man who is actually living with his parents to get an accommodation address , so that supposedly he has a separate establishment and draws a separate allowance. But there is much spying and tale-bearing. One man I knew, for instance, was seen feeding his neighbour's chickens while the neighbour was away. It was reported to the authorities that he "had a job feeding chickens" and he had great difficulty in refuting this. The favourite joke in Wigan was about a man who was refused relief on the ground that he "had a job carting firewood". He had been seen, it was said, carting firewood at night. He had to explain that he was not carting firewood but doing a moonlight flit. The "firewood" was his furniture.

The most cruel and evil effect of the Means Test is the way in which it breaks up families. Old people, sometimes bedridden, are driven out of their homes by it. An old age pensioner, for instance, if a widower, would normally live with one or other of his children; his weekly ten shillings goes towards the household expenses, and probably he is not badly cared for. Under the Means Test, however, he counts as a "lodger" and if he stays at home his children's dole will be docked. So, perhaps at seventy or seventy-five years of age, he has to turn out into lodgings, handing his pension over to the lodging-house keeper and existing on the verge of starvation. I have seen several cases of this myself, It is happening all over England at this moment, thanks to the Means Test.

Q What does this extract tell us about the way many working class people lived in the 1930s?

Why does Orwell criticise the Means Test?

What was Britain like in the 1930s? □

Q   Explain in your own words the meaning of a cycle of poverty.

The poverty cycle

The amount of money people have, often varies at different stages of their lives, and for part of their life they may be in poverty. The stages of early childhood and old age often put a family in poverty. This **cycle of poverty** was first discovered by *Seebohm Rowntree*, who studied poverty in York in 1899, and whose work is discussed later in this unit.

The graph below shows a similar pattern of comparative wealth and poverty, despite the system of taxes and benefits we now have.

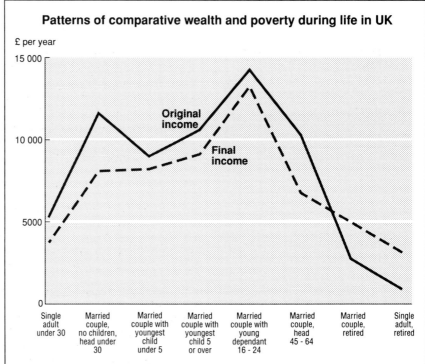

Patterns of comparative wealth and poverty during life in UK

Source: Social Trends, 1986

Discuss why single adults under 30 earn less than a married couple; why parents with a young child bring in less money; why the highest income belongs to a married couple with a young dependant aged 16 to 24; and why the single retired adult is the least well off.

DISCUSS

Discuss the changes in wealth and poverty in an individual's life shown in the graph.

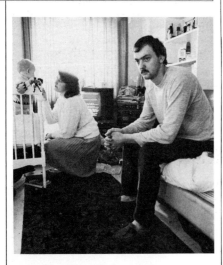

DISCUSS

Debate whether the culture of poverty theory means that there is little point in spending money on the poor, or whether it means that more benefits should be made available to those in need.

The culture of poverty

Some sociologists argue that one of the main reasons that people remain in poverty is their culture, i.e. their values norms and beliefs. *Oscar Lewis* studied the lives of those living in poverty and suggested that values of hopelessness, apathy, disorganisation, and fatalism, characterise the day-to-day existence of the poor. These values and attitudes are passed on from one generation to the next, and prevent those in poverty from taking advantage of the chances for improvement offered by their society. This is also known as a **cycle of deprivation**, because a poor standard of living is continually repeated.

However a study done in Nottingham by *Coates and Silburn* in 1970, suggests that the values of those in poverty are in essence no different from anyone else's, their hopelessness comes from a realistic assessment of their situation.

Q   Do you agree with the theory of a culture of poverty? What do you think could be done to prevent the culture of poverty being transmitted to the next generation? □

Political acceptance for the culture of poverty theory, has led some politicians to suggest that better housing and nursery provision would help to counteract the effects of poverty. In reality, however, little has been done to help those at the bottom of society. This may be, as other politicians argue, because the poor do not take advantage of many of the benefits already available to them, so that it would be pointless to give them more.

The stigma of poverty

In British society there is still a stigma attached to being poor, with those in poverty being stereotyped as being lazy and useless. The idea that the poor are in some way undeserving comes from the way that those in poverty were thought of historically. Until studies, such as **Charles Booth**'s, in 1886 on the poor in London, it was felt that the poor should help themselves and that it was a person's own fault if they were in poverty. Booth's study examined all aspects of the lives of those in poverty through statistics, and suggested for the first time a link between unemployment, health and housing. It was at Booth's suggestion that Old Age Pensions were introduced in 1908, because he felt that this age group was most in need.

A study of poverty by **Rowntree** in 1899 was also influential in changing attitudes to poverty. Rowntree introduced the ideas of primary and secondary poverty. **Primary poverty** means that a peson's income is not enough to cover subsistence, whilst **secondary poverty** means that the income is spent on non-essential items, such as beer and cigarettes.

Rowntree found that 10 per cent of the population of York were in primary poverty, and 18 per cent were in secondary poverty. Rowntree also established the idea of a poverty line at subsistence level. However, he later changed his ideas on poverty to a relative definition because he felt that it was necessary for people in this position to have items, such as holidays and tobacco, even if they are not essential.

The attitude to those in poverty gradually changed this century to the idea that people were not always themselves responsible for being poor. This change in attitude paved the way for the introduction of the Welfare State.

RESEARCH IDEA

Conduct a survey on the attitudes of people towards those in poverty. Do they believe that there is work for those that try to find it?

Do your respondents believe that many in poverty misspend their money by buying non-essential items like alcohol and cigarettes? Do your respondents understand the difference between primary and secondary poverty?

(For more information about survey methods turn to Unit 3 on research methods in Module 1, page 6.) □

BRAINSTORM

How many different ways can you think of to eradicate poverty from British society? □

Should there be positive discrimination in favour of the poorer sections of the community? This might help to compensate for their poor home environment, their lower achievement in education, and their difficulty in gaining employment.

RESEARCH IDEA

Find out how the poor survived before the introduction of state benefits this century.

Q   Can you explain the difference between **primary** and **secondary** poverty?

The Welfare State

The Welfare State that we have today has gradually evolved this century, but it was the *Beveridge Report* of 1942 that first proposed welfare for everyone whatever their occupation or income.

Up to 1942 statutory social services were restricted to particular groups, such as the elderly or unemployed. The new proposals meant that the principle of welfare 'from the cradle to the grave' became a reality. The introduction of The National Health Service and the 1945 Family Allowance Act, provided for all age groups whether rich or poor. By 1948 it was generally accepted that the State was responsible for all those who were ill, homeless or in poverty.

It was hoped that the need for welfare would gradually disappear as post-war Britain became more affluent, and for a time in the 1950s it was thought that this was happening (see the Affluent Worker study by Lockwood and Goldthorpe, page 80). However, it soon became obvious that poverty was not disappearing as had been hoped, and that the problem might even be getting worse.

Q What has been happening to the economy in the last twenty years? How might this have had an effect on the numbers in poverty? □

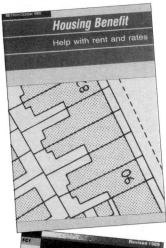
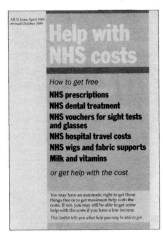

RESEARCH IDEA

Find out which areas of Britain are the most deprived. (Refer to Unit 6 in Module 14 on Urbanisation).

The Welfare State today provides financial help to all families, and supplies the services of professional workers, such as doctors and social workers. It provides benefits that include unemployment benefit, housing benefits, free school meals, etc. Some benefits are given to everyone even if they are wealthy, such as child benefit and medical care; others are only given to those who qualify on financial grounds.

Q What is the attitude of the State to different groups suffering from poverty? For example, which groups receive a Christmas bonus?

Is there a difference in the ways widows are treated compared to one-parent families? Why do you think this is so?

T A S K

Many voluntary organisations have been set up to help with the social problems in our society. These include rape-crisis centres, women's refuges, and national pressure groups, such as SHELTER and the NSPCC.

Find out about one of these pressure groups, when and why it was set up, and what it actually does to alleviate problems.

(For more on pressure or interest groups turn to Module 3 on Power and Politics, page 51.)

DISCUSS

Debate these Marxist ideas. Do you think that this was why the Welfare State was set up?

RESEARCH IDEA

Find out what benefits the following families are entitled to.

a   An unemployed man and wife with three children.
b   A family where the man earns £50 a week, and his wife stays at home with their two children.
c   A homeless single-parent family, consisting of a mother and her child. Would it make a difference if the mother's boy-friend moved in with them?
d   A middle-aged working couple, where the wife has to give up her job to look after her disabled mother.
e   A young couple who have role-swapped, the wife goes out to work earning £150 a week, and the husband stays at home to look after their two young children. □

There is still disagreement over whether Britain is really a Welfare State. Marxist sociologists would argue that the continued poverty in this society is a symptom of the vast inequalities that exist. They would argue that it is useless to give out a few cash benefits in order to get rid of poverty; instead the whole of society needs restructuring. The official treatment of the disadvantaged, serves to hide the real problems in society, so that the wealthy can hold on to their positions at the top of society.

UNIT 3 INEQUALITIES OF HEALTH

Expectation of life means the age a person can expect to live to, given the prevailing conditions of the time they were born.

The health of the population as a whole has steadily improved during the last two hundred years. The decline in infectious diseases, such as tuberculosis has increased everyone's expectation of life. Other killer diseases of the last century, such as pneumonia and whooping cough, are now also much less serious, although some people still die from them.

The changes in society that have been responsible for the improvement in health, include improved living and working conditions for most of the population. Improvements in public hygiene, a better diet, smaller family size, and medical advances, such as the use of antibiotics have also made a significant difference to health. The table below shows how the expectation of life has steadily risen in the UK this century.

Expectation of life in the UK: from birth and from specific ages

	Males							Females						
	1901	1931	1951	1961	1971	1981	1983	1901	1931	1951	1961	1971	1981	1983
Expectation of life From birth	48.0	58.4	66.2	67.9	68.8	69.8	71.4	51.6	62.4	71.2	73.8	75.0	76.2	77.2
From age 1 year	55.0	62.1	67.5	68.6	69.2	69.6	71.2	57.4	65.1	72.1	74.2	75.2	76.1	76.9
10 years	51.4	55.6	59.1	60.0	60.5	60.8	62.4	53.9	58.6	63.6	65.6	66.5	67.2	68.1
15 years	46.9	51.1	54.3	55.1	55.6	55.9	57.5	49.5	54.0	58.7	60.6	61.6	62.3	63.2
20 years	42.7	46.7	49.5	50.4	50.9	51.2	52.7	45.2	49.6	53.9	55.7	56.7	57.4	58.3
30 years	34.6	38.1	40.2	40.9	41.3	41.6	43.1	36.9	41.0	44.4	46.0	47.0	47.6	48.5
40 years	26.8	29.5	30.9	31.5	31.9	32.0	33.5	29.1	32.4	35.1	36.5	37.3	38.0	38.8
45 years	23.2	25.5	26.4	26.9	27.3	27.5	28.9	25.3	28.2	30.6	31.9	32.7	33.3	34.1
50 years	19.7	21.6	22.2	22.6	23.0	23.1	24.5	21.6	24.1	26.2	27.4	28.3	29.0	29.5
60 years	13.4	14.4	14.8	15.0	15.3	15.6	16.5	14.9	16.4	17.9	19.0	19.8	20.6	21.0
65 years	10.8	11.3	11.7	11.9	12.1	12.4	13.2	11.9	13.0	14.2	15.1	16.0	16.7	17.1
70 years	8.4	8.6	9.0	9.3	9.5	9.5	10.3	9.2	10.0	10.9	11.7	12.5	13.2	13.5
75 years	6.4	6.4	6.7	7.0	7.3	7.4	7.8	7.1	7.4	8.0	8.7	9.4	10.0	10.3
80 years	4.9	4.8	4.8	5.2	5.5	5.5	5.9	5.4	5.4	5.8	6.3	6.9	7.3	7.6

Source: *Social Trends* 17, 1987

DISCUSS

Did you know that a hundred years ago a person was more likely to survive an illness if they were *not* taken into hospital! Many people in hospital died from a different disease than the one they were admitted for! Why do you think this was so?

Although health has steadily improved for everyone in society there has always been significant differences in the health of those at the top of society compared to those at the bottom. The introduction of the National Health Service (NHS) by the post-war Labour government in 1948, was intended to give equal health care to everyone, and thereby also to give all social groups equal health.

However, the inequalities in health have not improved since 1948, in fact they appear to have worsened! Today, manual workers and their families are likely to suffer worse health than the family of a professional worker, and the death rate for manual workers is still far higher than that for professional workers (see table on next page). These inequalities cannot be entirely due to poor health care, there must be other factors affecting the health of those at the bottom of society.

Q   What reasons can you suggest for the continuing inequalities of health between different social classes? □

Q   What do most people die of? Which diseases continue to threaten life today? □

For more on birth and death rates see Module 10, Unit 2.

TASK

Learn the definition of **infant mortality rate**.

It means the number of children who die in their first year of life per thousand live births.

Q It has also been suggested that middle-class people live longer and are healthier than working-class people, because middle-class people say they still feel young at an older age than working-class people. Middle-class people also take more care to preserve a youthful appearance, and to remain fit and active.

Why might these factors affect their health?

TASK

Explain in your own words what this table shows about the different death rates for social classes and about the difference in death rates between males and females. □

Death rates by sex and social class

Social class	Males	Females	Ratio male to female
I	3.98	2.15	1.85
II	5.54	2.85	1.94
IIIN	5.80	2.76	1.96
IIIM	6.08	3.41	1.78
IV	7.96	4.27	1.87
V	9.88	5.31	1.86
	2.5	2.5	

Females = Married women classified by their husband's occupation. Death rates per 1000 population
Source: Adapted from *Occupational Mortality, 1970–72*

Q Can you define the term **death rate**? □

The Black Report published by the DHSS in 1980 showed that there are still class differences in both health, and in the access to health services. There are regional differences in the health provision available, in terms of the numbers of doctors and dentists; waiting times for hospital appointments, and the facilities in each area. Those people who live in deprived areas have the worst provision, although the NHS is now attempting to reallocate its resources more equally over the country.

However, although this may aid equality in health care, it may not completely solve the problem. Studies of the behaviour of doctors in their consulting rooms by *Cartwright and O'Brian* in 1976, show that doctors spend more time with their middle-class patients, and know them better than their working-class patients.

There are also differences between the social classes in infant mortality rates, life expectancy, the amount of illness experienced, the chance of having an accident, and the likelihood of the person going for regular check-ups. Although the actual health of all families has improved in the last forty years, the gap between the health of unskilled manual workers and professional workers has widened.

The reasons for inequalities of health are therefore many and include social and cultural factors, such as the effects of the culture of poverty (see Unit 2 in this Module), sub-standard housing, a poor diet, large families, and the effects of long-term unemployment. All of these factors are likely to contribute to the continuing poor health of the lowest socio-economic groups.

TASK

Write a case study for a fictitious family who are in poor health due to social and economic reasons. □

For example, the father could be unemployed and the mother working part time in a factory to bring in some extra money. They could live in a damp council house with their five children.

TASK

Consider other health hazards, such as drinking heavily or using drugs, that may be linked to particular social class groups?

How do health issues, such as AIDS, affect other aspects of people's life-styles?

RESEARCH IDEA

Examine the way cigarettes are advertised, what is the hidden message used to persuade people to smoke? What controls are there on the advertising of cigarettes?

For more on advertising turn to Module 2 on the Mass Media, page 21.

RESEARCH IDEA

Find out what proportion of young people smoke cigarettes regularly. Find out whether they are aware of the possible health risks, and why they first started smoking.

Does smoking appear to be part of youth culture? (See Module 2 on Mass Media, Unit 5 for more on youth culture.)

Discover whether there are any possible links between smoking, gender, or social class.

Factors related to health, such as smoking cigarettes, also vary between the social classes, and smoking is a good illustration of the complex social and economic factors that affect health.

Although fewer people now smoke, cigarette smoking is done more amongst manual than non-manual men and women. It appears that professional groups that used to smoke, have stopped quicker than other groups. This change in behaviour could be due to the increased publicity about the health risks taken by smokers; but it could also be because cigarettes are used by both males and females as a symbol of being an adult. For a working-class person who leaves school as soon as possible in the hope of getting a job, the symbolic importance of smoking may be more important than possible health risks. Indeed a recent survey in 1982 found that 19 per cent of pupils aged between eleven and sixteen smoked.

TASK

Look at the following pictures. What hidden or overt messages are contained in them? What effect do images like these actually have? □

In 1983 the Royal College of Physicians estimated that 90 per cent of deaths from lung cancer, chronic bronchitis and obstructive lung diseases were attributable to smoking, and perhaps 20 per cent of deaths due to the obstruction of the arteries to the heart were related to smoking.

However, those people that actually smoke are much more unlikely to believe that smoking causes ill-health than those who don't smoke. Why?

In the last unit it was suggested that Marxist sociologists saw the introduction of the Welfare State as an attempt by the ruling classes to appear concerned about poverty without having to redistribute the wealth of society.

TASK

Explain how Marxist sociologists would see the introduction of the NHS. What evidence could they give for this view? What evidence would you use against this view?

It is possible to pay privately for hospital treatment in hospitals like this one. This means that if you are wealthy, or can afford private medical insurance cover, it is possible to jump the queues that exist in NHS hospitals. Often it is the same surgeons who carry out the operations privately and for the NHS.

DISCUSS

Why do people pay for private health care?

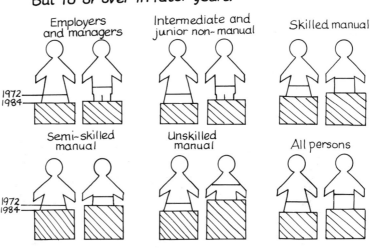

Source: *New Society*, 7 March 1986

TASK

Look at the above information and answer the following questions.
1 Which sex smokes more, males or females?
2 Which social class group smoked the most in 1972?
3 Which social class group or groups smoked the most in 1984?
4 Why can you criticise this diagram for not giving us an accurate picture of everyone who smokes in Britain?
5 What reasons can you give for the class differences in cigarette smoking? □

The health inequalities that still exist in society today may therefore be the result of regional inequalities in health care, but are also due to important differences in the life-styles of the social class groups. Material, cultural, social and economic differences between the classes are all responsible for the inequalities in health that still exist.

BRAINSTORM

What are all the possible factors that are responsible for the health differences between the social classes? □

Factors, such as gender, race, health and poverty, all affect a person's life-chances, their chance of a good job, a well paid job, and a long life. All these factors make people in society unequal, and contribute to the system of social stratification.

WHERE TO NOW?

You may now want to look at some of the other modules that relate to this one, such as Module 10 on Population, Module 11 on Family, and Module 14 on Urbanisation.

M O D U L E · 7

EDUCATION

SEVEN

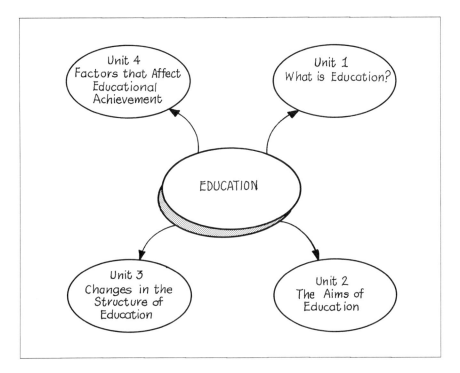

WHAT THIS MODULE IS ABOUT

Education is an important part of everyone's life. The structure of the education system has changed since the Second World War, but despite these changes certain groups of pupils still tend to underachieve. This module focuses on the home background, school interaction and the demands of capitalist society, as partial explanations for some pupils' failure at school.

BY THE END OF THIS MODULE YOU SHOULD BE ABLE TO:

1 Define formal and informal education.
2 Explain the aims or function of education.
3 Outline the major changes and developments in education, particularly since 1944.
4 Understand the importance of social class factors on a pupil's achievement in school.
5 Define a policy of positive discrimination.
6 Explain the importance of the teacher and organisation of the school on a pupil's achievement.
7 Demonstrate an awareness of the effects of the hidden curriculum, ethos and labelling on achievement.
8 Have a basic understanding of the critical Marxist view of schooling.

WHAT IS EDUCATION?

Education is a process of learning. It is the way that each society passes on the skills, knowledge and values which are important for the next generation.

The skills that are relevant to *one* society may not be relevant to another. For example in the Arctic the daily process of learning for the young Eskimo would include being taught how to catch and skin a seal. This knowledge is vital for the survival of Eskimo society in terms of providing the basic human needs of warmth, clothing and food. This knowledge is therefore highly valued and a good hunter is given high status.

A young Inuit is taught traditional stitching in the waterproofing of a kayak

BRAINSTORM
What sort of things do parents teach children?

T A S K

What sort of skills and knowledge are valued highly in British society? Make a list of these in order of importance. ☐

Informal education

There are different ways of passing on, or transmitting, these skills, knowledge and values. We use books but in a **preliterate** society, i.e. one where the people do not read or write, learning takes place by imitating others or by word of mouth. It is the family that is the most important source of learning in these simple societies. Sociologists would call this process of learning **informal education** in order to distinguish it from the **formal education** that goes on in schools.
Learning by word of mouth is called an **oral tradition**

T A S K

Make sure that you can explain what is meant by informal education.

There are other informal agencies of education that act on an individual, such as the mass media and the peer group. A **peer group** is a group of friends who share similar likes and interests. In our **literate** society informal education processes are also important. The family is where **primary socialisation** takes place i.e. where children first start to learn. Psychologists have shown that children learn fastest from birth to three years old, although learning is a life-long process.

Q   Who is in your peer group? In what ways do you influence each other?

French pupils in the classroom

Raising of the school leaving-age (ROSLA)

1880	Ten years
1899	Twelve years
1918	Fourteen years
1944	Fifteen years
1971	Sixteen years

Formal education

In Britain there is compulsory education for everyone between the ages of five and sixteen. Most people have to go to a particular building at a particular time where there are specially trained people to educate them.

DISCUSS

Did you know that in other European countries school times vary? In France and Germany for example school hours are from 8am till 2pm.

1 What do you think the advantages and disadvantages are of these times for
  a the pupils
  b the parents
  c the school staff.
2 Can you see any particular problems for certain groups in society, for example, one-parent families? □

The formal education system in Britain is said to have begun in 1870, with Forster's Education Act. This set up elementary schools for all children up to the age of ten who were taught mainly reading, writing, arithmetic and religion.

Since then various governments have introduced new measures affecting education, such as by raising the school leaving-age (ROSLA) and by changing the content of the curriculum.

Q Why do you think the school leaving-age has been raised? □

RESEARCH IDEA

Interview people of different age groups, for example your parents and grandparents about their school leaving-age and the subjects they studied as part of their school curriculum. □

A classroom in the late Nineteenth century

UNIT 2 THE AIMS OF EDUCATION

The functions of education

Ask some of the people in your group 'Why do you go to school?' You will probably get some interesting answers. □

Sociologists often refer to the purposes of education as being *the functions of education*. Take a look at the functions outlined on these two pages and see whether the answers you received from your question about why people go to school match these functions. Remember many examination questions are framed with these aims of education in mind.

The Functions

Social Control Pupils at school learn that they are meant to respect and obey teachers. Many schools emphasise the importance of order and discipline, so that pupils, when they leave, will respect authority and obey the rules of society.

Skills A hundred years ago the main skills taught at school were the three R's: reading, writing and arithmetic. Today other skills are also felt to be important, so pupils may learn anything from word processing to orienteering.

Conduct a survey among adults asking whether the education they received at school is relevant to their lives. ☐

DISCUSS

Do you think that because of the changes in society today, such as the growth in unemployment, that our form of education is still relevant. What changes would you like to make to the current education system? ☐

Q What sorts of schools are the most successful in attracting pupils and in helping their pupils achieve most from life? ☐

You will note that the functions of skills, qualifications, socialisation and social control shown here, are factors that society regards as valuable for its young people to have gained when they leave school. The value of education appears to lie in the pupil's future and the world of work.

# of Education

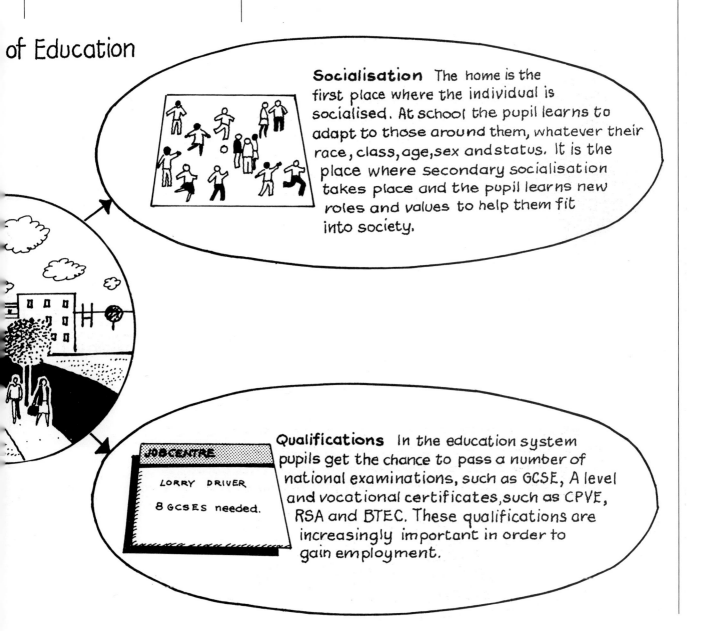

Socialisation The home is the first place where the individual is socialised. At school the pupil learns to adapt to those around them, whatever their race, class, age, sex and status. It is the place where secondary socialisation takes place and the pupil learns new roles and values to help them fit into society.

JOBCENTRE

LORRY DRIVER

8 GCSES needed.

Qualifications In the education system pupils get the chance to pass a number of national examinations, such as GCSE, A level and vocational certificates, such as CPVE, RSA and BTEC. These qualifications are increasingly important in order to gain employment.

CHANGES IN THE STRUCTURE OF EDUCATION

Developments in education since 1944

T A S K

When interviewing your parents and others about their school days you may have found that they attended secondary modern or grammar schools. Their schools were part of the **tripartite system**. This contrasts with many schools today which are part of the **comprehensive system**, although there are still grammar schools in existence along with public and independent schools. What is meant by the comprehensive system? Look at the description of tripartite and comprehensive schools below and decide which of these two systems you prefer.

The Tripartite System

* The *tripartite* system was introduced by the 1944 Education Act. It made secondary education free and set out to provide equality of educational opportunity for all, regardless of class, colour or gender.
* The belief was that at 11 years of age it was possible to measure a child's intelligence or ability and on the basis of this to decide the type of job, or career they would be most suited to.
* Children sat the 11+ examination which was made up of English, Maths and IQ tests. Those who passed were believed to be more academic. These children were selected to go to **grammar** schools and went on to take O- and A-levels. Those who failed the 11+ exam were believed to be less academic and to have more manual skills. These children were selected for **modern** or **technical** schools and took a more practical curriculum.
* Grammar schools and secondary modern schools were supposed to have 'parity of esteem' or equal status. But this turned out to be unrealistic. Society valued the academic examination successes of the grammar school, rather than the practical abilities learnt in the secondary modern schools.
* Only 1 in 5 children passed the 11+ exam and went on to grammar schools

The Comprehensive System

* In the late 1950s **comprehensive** schools started their development. This was because the 11+ exam and tripartite system was unpopular with some education authorities, e.g. Angelesey, London and Leicestershire.
* By 1964 the Labour Government decided that all authorities should have comprehensive schools, i.e. all children should go to one **comprehensive school** as opposed to three different types of secondary school.
* The 11+ exam was abolished which took away a great strain from teachers and pupils.
* Large comprehensives can be more economical and can provide better facilities than small secondary schools can.
* There should be less wastage of talent particularly among working-class children and and late developers. Comprehensives should be fairer to all.

Criticisms of the Tripartite System	*Criticisms of the Comprehensive System*
* It is very difficult if not impossible to measure intelligence. * 11 years of age is far too early to decide about a child's future. * Some pupils who might be quite bright could suffer from exam nerves and perform badly. * There were big differences in the number of grammar school places available throughout the country. Children in Wales had the highest chance of a grammar school place with 1 out of 3 passing the 11+, and children in the South of England the lowest chance, only 1 in 8 going to grammar school. * Local Education Authorities often provided better facilities for their grammar schools than for the secondary modern schools in their area. * About 1 in 10 children were probably sent to the wrong school. Few late developers were switched to grammar schools later on. * Mainly middle-class children passed the 11+ exam and obtained grammar school places. They also stayed at school longer and gained more qualifications there. * This system did not therefore produce **equality of opportunity** for all.	* In a large school it is perhaps possible for a pupil to lose their identity, to become just a name and number. * It is argued that where pupils are taught in mixed ability groups, the brightest are held back by the slowest learners and their achievements are affected. * There are big differences between individual comprehensive schools according to their particular catchment area. Some comprehensives have mainly middle-class pupils and others mainly working-class. Some comprehensives have excellent facilities and others are run down. * Many comprehensive schools put their pupils into **streams** according to their ability. This can damage a pupil's self-esteem and also prevents equality of opportunity. * Many comprehensives retain tripartism under one roof.

DISCUSS

Which of these two systems of education do you prefer and why? There has been some talk of bringing back the tripartite system. Explain why you think this would be a good or bad idea. Do the 1988 Education Act and the National Curriculum look back to and reflect the values of the tripartite system in their thinking? ☐

RESEARCH IDEA

Recent research carried out by Mori Poll and quoted in the *Reader's Digest* showed that two-thirds of all parents preferred a selective system of schooling rather than a comprehensive one.

Check the results of this research by conducting your own survey of parents' opinions. Find out *why* parents prefer one system to the other. ☐

Read the extract below. Then using the information you have gathered, attempt to answer the exam questions that follow it. □

The Tripartite System At the time, the 1944 Act was welcomed as a new beginning. Although the Act recognised the principle of 'equality of educational opportunity' it assumed that there were different types of children, with different types of ability, who could be best catered for in different types of schools. It was thought that this ability could be measured by special intelligence tests which should be taken at eleven years old. On the basis of children's results in this '11-plus examination' they were allowed to one of three types of schools. The number of places varied in different areas, but in general the top 15–20 per cent of children passing the 11-plus went to *grammar schools* to follow a highly academic curriculum in preparation for GCE O-levels and A-levels. The 'less academic' 11-plus passes were sent to *technical schools*, to follow a more practically biased curriculum, based on technical and vocational subjects. The large majority which remained, between 60 and 70 per cent of the population who failed their 11-plus, was sent to *secondary modern schools*, to follow a watered-down version of the grammar-school curriculum, geared to the needs of so-called 'less able' and 'non-academic' children, destined for unskilled and menial employment.

1 Explain what is meant by the phrase 'equality of educational opportunity'.
2 What are the main criticisms of the tripartite system?
3 To what extent have comprehensive schools overcome the social divisions associated with the tripartite system?

Source: UCLES Sociology GCE, 1984

Recent developments in education

Attention has now been focused on what goes on inside schools rather than the structure of the education system itself. There are now moves to make the curriculum more **practical** and **vocational**, i.e. related to the world of work.

For example, GCSE is considered to be a more **active** way of learning and developing new skills. This is seen as quite different from the old style CSE and O-levels where knowledge was often just memorised in order to pass exams.

TASK

Define these other recent developments in education: TVEI and CPVE. Try to interview a TVEI and/or a CPVE student about their course; or, invite them to speak to the group about this new kind of learning. Is their course full of active, practical and vocational learning? □

RESEARCH IDEA

What are modular courses? Why have they become popular. What are the advantages and disadvantages of modular schemes? □

Q What are Records of Achievement? Who are they for? □

RESEARCH IDEA

The 1988 Education Act introduced a National Curriculum for all primary and secondary pupils in British schools.

a What are the national foundation subjects that each pupil must study in primary schools and in secondary schools?
b Discover which subjects are not included in the national curriculum foundation subjects?
c The Conservative Government has introduced testing at the ages of 7, 11, 14 and 16. What are the purposes of the tests? Interview teachers, educational advisors, governors, etc. to find out what they feel about these tests.

'There is a poor match between education and the world of work. We are less 'efficient' than our competitors overseas. Only 5.5% of the labour force in the U.K. are graduates compared with 7.1% in West Germany. Only 30% of British people have intermediate vocational qualifications (including apprenticeships) compared with about 60% in West Germany.'

Source: *Society Today*, February 1982

Q What are the advantages and disadvantages of being educated at home?

Degree for 13-year-old at Oxford

Ruth Lawrence aged 13, the mathematics prodigy from Huddersfield who won a scholarship to St Hugh's College, Oxford when she was 10 has been awarded a first class degree. It took her two years, instead of the usual three and her results were posted yesterday at the Examination Schools in Oxford.

Source: *The Times*, July 1985
© Times Newspapers Ltd, 1985

Q Is it **ethical**, i.e. morally right to have a private education system that only the rich people in society can use?

TASK

Read this extract and with the details you have collected, answer the questions below.

1 According to the extract, what percentage of the work-force in Britain are graduates?
2 According to the extract, what percentage of West Germans have intermediate vocational qualifications?
3 Identity and explain two ways in which a British government might improve the 'efficiency' of education as a preparation for work?
4 Identify and explain the *other* functions of education apart from the preparation of young people for the world of work. □

Source: UCLES Sociology GCE, 1982

The state education system

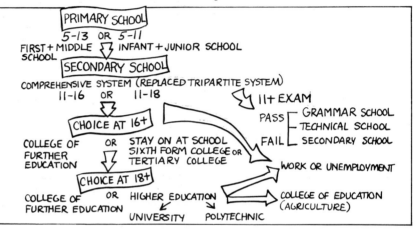

Most people's education follows the path indicated above, through state primary and secondary schools to a choice of provision at sixteen and eighteen for those who choose to stay on past the minimum leaving-age.

There are exceptions to this pattern. In some areas there are state nursery schools for children aged three to five, but in fact you don't *have* to go to school at all, provided you can show you are being properly educated at home. You can also enter higher education at an earlier age. In 1986 Ruth Lawrence, who had been educated at home by her father, achieved a first class degree in mathematics from Oxford University at the age of thirteen!

The private education system

Some parents prefer to buy private education for their children, and send them to fee-paying schools. These schools are also called **independent** or **public schools**. Some of the best known public schools are the boys' schools Eton, Harrow and Gordonstoun, and the girls' school Roedean. Public schools usually have smaller classes and better facilities than state schools, and place emphasis on academic achievement that leads many pupils on to a university education.

The importance of the private education system is out of proportion to the numbers of pupils who attend. In 1985 for example, only 6 per cent of pupils attended independent schools. They are given such importance because so many ex-public school pupils get the top jobs in society, as the table in Module 3 on Power and Politics, page 43 shows. It is due to this bias that some people feel private education should be abolished, so that it is impossible to buy a better education. Others argue that there should be freedom of choice, and parents should have the right to pay for schooling.

FACTORS THAT AFFECT EDUCATIONAL ACHIEVEMENT

Q   Why do some pupils do better at school than others?   □

It seems obvious that the clever pupils usually achieve the best examination results, but 'cleverness' or intelligence is a result of *genetic* factors that you inherit from your parents, and *environmental* factors, such as where you live.

Sociologists are particularly interested in the environmental factors that affect educational success. They have found that three groups in particular do not do as well as they should, they *underachieve*. These underachievers are girls, blacks, and the working class. Factors of gender, race, and social class therefore affect chances of success in education.

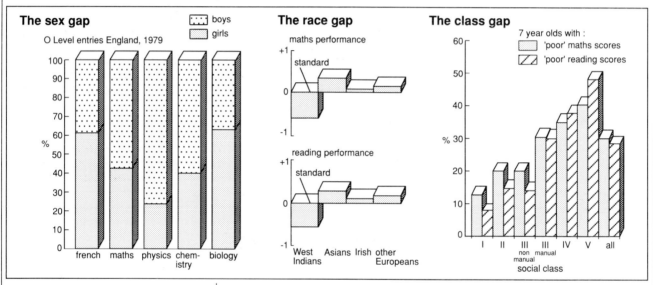

Source: DES

T A S K
Look at the information given in the charts above. What do they show about the differential in the education of:
a boys and girls.
b pupils from different racial backgrounds.
c pupils from different social class backgrounds.
How many factors can you think of that may explain these differences?

For the last thirty years sociologists have been finding out why certain groups do better in education than others. They began by focusing on social class, and discovered environmental factors, such as poor housing that made working-class pupils less successful.

In the 1970s the emphasis changed to examine what went on in schools, for example the effect of teaching styles, or classroom organisation.

Recently the differences in achievement between these groups have been explained by Marxist sociologists as the way ruling class groups prevent changes that would threaten their position at the top of society.

Social class factors

Home environment

Sociologists often examine differential achievement by studying the same group of children for a number of years. This method is called a **longitudinal survey**. An example of a longitudinal survey is the National Child Development Study which followed the progress of all children born in the week of 3 to 9 March 1958.

A clear link has been found between factors, such as low income, poor housing and family size and educational success. Working-class children disadvantaged by these factors, are less likely to do well at school. Disadvantaged children may be sharing a bedroom or even a bed. They are also more likely to be ill and so miss school.

Class values

Other class factors resulting in underachievement may be less obvious than being overcrowded, or having to do homework with the television on. Class values are also important. Working-class parents are more likely to urge their children to leave school as soon as they can and find a steady job.

Middle-class parents are more likely to socialise their children into wanting to stay on in education in the hope of getting a better job when they do leave. This middle-class value is called **deferred gratification**, and it is one reason why middle-class pupils stay on at school and get better examination results than working-class pupils.

Parental interest

Although factors like family size and income affect educational success, the single most important factor is the interest shown by parents in their child's education. In *The Home and The School*, 1964, *JWB Douglas* found that middle-class parents tended to visit the school more, encouraged their children to stay on at school, and were generally more interested in their child's education. He found that an upper middle-class child was five times more likely to get into a grammar school than a child from the lower working class.
Other research such as *Education and the Working Class* by *Jackson and Marsden*, found that most of the working-class pupils who were successful came from homes that were similar to middle-class homes. The mothers of these pupils were often 'sunken middle class' (i.e. they had been middle class) and they wanted their child to do well.

RESEARCH IDEA

Carry out a survey on parental attitudes to education. Parental interest could be assessed by how often homework is checked on, or how often Parent Teachers' Association meetings are attended. You may find a *correlation* or link between parental interest and the child's wish to leave or stay on at school. □

Language

Another key factor affecting educational achievement is the way language is used and spoken. *Professor Basil Bernstein* has shown that there are different patterns of speech used by the middle class and the working class. He calls these speech patterns **linguistic codes**. The middle-class way of talking he calls the *elaborated code*, and the working-class speech the *restricted code*. The elaborated code is made up of longer, more complex sentences in which words are used to convey meanings. The restricted code is more like shorthand speech, with gestures and tone of voice replacing some words. Bernstein argues that the working-class restricted code is not a worse way of speaking, it is just different from the way middle-class people speak, because the sentences are shorter and simpler.

Bernstein's theory of linguistic codes has been criticised by some sociologists who say he is stereotyping language differences and that really there is a wide variety of speech patterns in each social class. He has also been criticised for being biased because he seems to be assuming that the elaborated code is superior to the restricted code.

Q   Do you agree with Bernstein's theory of linguistic codes? □

DISCUSS

More recently Bernstein's work has been criticised by *Labov*, an American sociologist. Labov argues that a person's ability to speak fluently may well depend on the social situation they are in, e.g. whether they feel frightened, uncomfortable or happy.

Are you more or less articulate in certain social situations, e.g. a party, on a date, in an interview?

Does this mean Bernstein's theory is invalid?

Children and helpers involved in Operation Headstart

Positive discrimination

Research done in the 1960s focused on the underachievement of working-class pupils. This was also highlighted in government reports. The 1963 Newsom Report drew attention to the importance of language development, whilst the 1967 Plowden Report, *Children and their Primary School*, stressed home background as a major factor affecting educational success.

A poor home background is one in which children do not have interested parents and where they are culturally deprived. Theories of cultural deprivation led to the introduction of measures, both here and in America, to compensate for a poor home environment. This **compensatory education** often took the form of nursery schools for children aged three upwards.

In the late 1960s 'Operation Headstart' in America gave pre-school education to many children from deprived areas. In Britain Educational Priority Areas (EPAs) were introduced. These areas were given extra money for buildings, nursery schools and teachers. Compensatory education aimed for **positive discrimination**, by giving more to those most in need.

Most compensatory education schemes had no long-lasting effects on the educational performance of the children involved, so most have been discontinued. Many sociologists now believe that this is because by three years old a child has already been effectively socialised. A three year old has learnt to speak in a particular way and has learnt values, such as only playing with sex-typed toys, e.g. dolls for girls, cars for boys. Therefore it is too late to change their chances of success.

It has recently been suggested that there should be positive discrimination in favour of girls and blacks. There could be extra language lessons for ethnic minority groups, such as West Indian children, who do less well than Asians in our schools. This is thought to be partly because it is obvious that Asian children often speak a different language at home, so they get extra English lessons at school. West Indians may also speak a different language at home – creole – but because it sounds like English, they do not get extra help at school, in fact many teachers just think their speech is sloppy.

DISCUSS

What sorts of class factors would compensatory education schemes help to overcome? Should society introduce new measures of positive discrimination? Can you suggest alternative ways in which underachievers could be helped?

T A S K

Write a short essay giving reasons why this statement may or may not be correct.
'Many studies have shown that children from working-class homes are less successful at school than those from middle-class homes.'

QUESTIONS

Using the information you have gained from this unit so far and from reading the extract below, attempt the following examination questions.

> If you ask any teacher they will tell you that the home has an important part to play in a child's education.
>
> With plenty of help from home, students can make the most of their abilities in school.
>
> Of course, it is not just the family itself, but also the physical features and facilities that it provides. For example, plenty of stimulating toys.
>
> To be a success at school, it helps to have parents who think education is important. But we must not forget that the school and the teachers also make a difference to a child's progress in learning.

Source: Comprehensive School Headteacher

1 Suggest *two* ways in which a sociologist could measure success and failure of students in education.
2 Name *two* groups which tend to underachieve in the education system.
3 Describe the physical features and facilities of the home which can help a child's education in school.
4 Explain how parents' values and attitudes can influence a child's achievement in school.
5 How can schools and teachers affect the educational achievement of students? □

Source: MEG Sociology GCSE, 1988

School interaction: what goes on in schools

In recent years the emphasis on home background has been increasingly criticised by sociologists and more attention paid instead to the effects of the school itself in influencing the pupil's achievement. Sociologists have concentrated on what goes on in the classroom, on the role of the teacher and the content of the curriculum.

The hidden curriculum

Pupils in school learn many things that are not actually taught to them.

For instance, pupils learn to size up their teachers and to behave in different ways with different teachers. They know, for example, that they can ask a personal or even silly question of some teachers without being made fun of and, know that other teachers only let them talk in class if it is about work, whilst other teachers do not allow them to speak at all! This knowledge about how to behave in different classroom situations, which pupils and teachers learn through experience, is called **unofficial** or **informal** knowledge and is very important to pupils if they are to survive and succeed in school. Sociologists refer to this type of knowledge as being part of the **hidden curriculum**. (For more on this see Module 12 on Gender, page 215.)

Q Can you give examples of how pupils' behaviour changes with different teachers? Can you give examples of how a teacher's behaviour changes with different pupils? □

There are other hidden messages that schools send to pupils, such as how girls are expected to be quieter in class than boys, how middle-class pupils are expected to achieve more and how some subjects are regarded as more important than others. These *unofficial* or *informal* messages are transmitted to pupils every day of their lives in school through their face-to-face interactions with others. These **relationships** between teachers and pupils, pupils and pupils and also between teachers and teachers are very important for the sociologist to study in attempting to understand more about the causes of pupils' success and failure in schools.

The **overt curriculum** which is part of the **formal** organization of the school is made up of the subjects on your timetable, such as Art & Design, Biology, Sociology, French, Geography, History. Music, Drama, English, Maths, etc.

DISCUSS

Are relationships in school important to you? Which relationships matter most to you, relationships with your peer group (friends), or relationships with your teacher(s)?

T A S K

Imagine that you are recommending options for a third form pupil

1 Which three of the subjects on your curriculum do you think most people in society would consider to be the most important?
2 Which three subjects do you consider to be most useful? Explain your choices. □

Some of these pupils even think this school exists for their benefit..

RESEARCH IDEA

Neville Bennett's research in 1976 entitled *Teaching Styles and Pupil Progress* investigated the teaching methods of 37 teachers in Cumbria and Lancaster. Their styles of teaching were placed in the categories of 'formal' 'mixed' and 'informal' and the research findings showed that the pupils achieved most progress in the formal teaching situation, least progress in the informal, while the mixed situation came in between the two.

Bennett's research has been criticised for bias in the tests that were used (see Module 1 on Research Methods) and may not therefore be accurate.
Which do you think is likely to be the most effective teaching style? Interview your friends about which teaching style they prefer and also try to observe different teachers in action, in terms of the categories formal, informal and mixed. Do most teachers adopt a mixed approach? Does your research show that some teachers are more formal with some classes and less formal with others? Would simply interviewing teachers about their teaching styles give you accurate information or do you need to observe them in action.

Teacher-Pupil relations and the effects of teaching styles

Schools contain a variety of teachers who have very different beliefs about how pupils should behave in the classroom. They also have different styles of teaching. Some teachers are very **traditional** or **formal** and might see some pupil behaviour as being cheeky or deviant; whilst other more **progressive** or **informal** teachers would probably see the same pupil behaviour as being natural, open or even friendly.

Q Can you think of any teachers you have known who have traditional/formal *or* informal teaching styles.

There are strong disagreements among teachers about the way schools should be run and about what the relationship between teachers and pupils should be. There are those like *Rhodes Boyson*, Conservative MP and ex-headmaster, who advocate strict, formal schooling with a return to traditional values and others following the Plowden Report of 1967 who feel that informal teaching particularly in the primary and middle schools is most effective. There are also some people who like *Ivan Illich* believe that schools (and teachers) are harmful because they are oppressive. He advocates **deschooling**, i.e. abolishing schools and finding other ways of teaching and learning.

DISCUSS

Teachers vary in their expectations of pupil behaviour. In groups discuss and give definitions of pupil behaviour that is cheeky as opposed to behaviour that is informal, friendly or open. □

QUESTIONS

'Teachers try to impose their view of the situation ('I'm in charge here') by doing most of the talking and by trying to catch and keep pupils' attention, mostly by asking questions and insisting on answers. While talking, teachers make clear, directly or indirectly, what counts as good work, an intelligent answer, silliness and so on. Pupils are controlled largely through reward and punishment, especially the threat of public shame. Pupils try to find out what the teacher wants and deliver it. But if nothing is gained, disruption is likely. Pupils seek approval from their friends and equals as much as from teachers. If what friends approve of is very different from what the teacher wants, there is likely to be a good deal of classroom conflict and what the teacher would regard as deviance.'

Source: *Fundamentals of Sociology* by P McNeill and C Townley, 1981

1 What is likely to happen to a pupil who repeatedly fails in their attempts to gain the teacher's approval?
2 Why might disruptive classroom behaviour be described as deviant by a teacher but not by a pupil?
3 a Explain what is meant by the term 'hidden curriculum'.
  b Why might there be a clash between the values of teachers and some of their pupils? □

Source: UCLES Sociology GCE, 1984

School leavers in England with higher grade passes at 'O' level or CSE, 1986–1987

Subject	1986–1987		
	Boys	Girls	Total
Any subject	51.3	57.9	54.5
English	34.3	45.5	39.7
Mathematics	32.6	27.7	30.2
Physics	21.9	9.2	15.7
Chemistry	15.8	11.5	13.7
Biology	12.3	18.6	15.4
Design/Technology	17.1	4.5	10.9
French	10.9	18.2	14.5
History	13.3	14.9	14.1
Geography	18.1	14.2	16.2
Creative Arts	11.0	18.1	14.5
Commercial & Domestic Studies	4.1	17.4	10.6
General Studies	2.6	2.6	2.6

Q Are these figures representative of your own experiences of boys and girls at school?

DISCUSS

What are the likely effects of fewer girls passing physics, maths and CDT exams at sixteen and at higher levels. How might this affect their lives? Will the National Curriculum bring any change?

Teacher expectations and the effects of teacher labelling

Ervin Goffman, an American sociologist, argues that people tend to be **labelled** by those in authority over them (see Module 13 on Deviance). He says that people conform to these labels or descriptions which have been imposed on them. Labelling can be seen to operate quite clearly in schools. Many studies have shown that teachers tend to label working-class children as less academic, lacking in motivation and in extreme cases as failures. Teachers do this according to their subjective expectations of a pupil according to their home background.

T A S K

From your reading of Unit 4, explain why some teachers expect working-class pupils to be less academic and to have poor motivation. □

Similarly in terms of the sex or gender differences in achievement there is evidence to show that teachers tend to see girls as more passive, compliant, polite and non-aggressive. These sorts of labels are enforced by the teacher's behaviour, such as expecting girls to talk less in class. By the time that many girls have reached the middle of their secondary school career they may well have been socialised to act in a submissive way towards males and to underachieve.

This socialisation process begins long before secondary school. At birth girls and boys are dressed differently, given different toys, treated differently by their parents. When they reach school, their gender identity is firmly established and the school instead of breaking down these gender differences tends to intensify them. Girls choose arts subjects rather than science or technology at the age of thirteen or fourteen (as the table above reveals) and therefore fewer girls obtain passes in these science subjects at sixteen and beyond. (See Module 12 on Gender, page 213 for further discussion of this sex role socialisation)

Research has also shown that the children from some ethnic minorities become labelled not only as failures, but also as deviants (see Module 13 on Deviance and Module 6 on Inequality). The chart on page 118 reveals how some ethnic groups, particularly West Indian boys, lag badly behind other pupils in terms of maths and reading. This poor achievement could be due to the cultural disadvantages they suffer in a predominantly white, society. But these ethnic groups may also suffer from the same social class handicap that affects some working-class white children, i.e. poverty. Low paid jobs and life in the poor inner-city housing areas are disadvantageous to both white and black people.

Children from some ethnic minorities arrive at school with considerable disadvantages, especially if their first language is not English. Despite this the teacher and the school system itself often make these initial disadvantages even worse. The teacher may, for example, underestimate a child's difficulty in speaking and writing English which is a second language for them.

In The Rampton Report, 1981, and in The Swann Report, 1985, showed that besides these language difficulties, black children suffered at school from poor relations with teachers and also from racial discrimination. It has been argued that Britain is a racist society and that teachers are therefore racist perhaps without even realising it – i.e. **unconsciously** racist. The effects of this vary. For instance, if the teacher is unconsciously racist and treats all pupils alike, irrespective of their colour, then the teacher would be ignoring the special difficulties that some black pupils can suffer. If the teacher is **overtly** racist and thinks that blacks are inferior, then in accordance with the self-fulfilling prophecy, this will cause low self-esteem and great learning problems for these black pupils.

Q What are the special difficulties that some black pupils can suffer?

Q What is meant by low self-esteem?

DISCUSS

One feminist sociologist named *Dale Spender* wrote a book about females in education entitled *Invisible Women*. Why do you think it was given this title?

DISCUSS

JWB Douglas wrote that if the teacher encourages you and gives you the impression that you can really do well, you are more likely to try, than if the teacher makes it plain to you that he thinks you are a complete failure.

Do you agree with Douglas? Have you any experience of the labelling and/or self-fulfilling prophecy theories from your own relationships with teachers? □

DISCUSS

Saturday morning schools. Are they a good idea? Will they help to overcome the problem of low self-esteem and underachievement among some ethnic minorities?

Sociologists argue therefore that **positive discrimination**, in the form of extra help for ethnic minorities, is still needed in order to achieve social justice. They argue for the provision of multi-cultural learning materials in schools instead of books full of white, Christian images. Specialist language teaching is also recommended to help pupils to overcome their language difficulties; and, even supplementary or Saturday morning schools to help the children to cope with the rest of the curriculum.

Organisation of the school – the effects of streaming and 'ethos' on achievement

Perhaps the best known studies of the way in which teachers label some pupils as less academic or lacking in motivation, are those on **streaming** by *D. Hargreaves* (1967) and *C Lacey* (1970). Both Hargreaves in his study of Lumley High, a boys' secondary modern school and Lacey in his research at Hightown Grammar found that boys allocated to the lower streams quickly developed an anti-school subculture. They did not conform to the rules and were troublemakers in class. The reason for this behaviour, the writers suggest, is that these pupils, who were mainly working-class had been labelled as failures by the school by being placed in the bottom form. 'The education system had rejected them and so the pupils rejected education'.

DISCUSS

Is it fair for schools to stream pupils? Do you think that streaming labels some pupils as failures? Is mixed ability teaching fairer for all pupils? ☐

RESEARCH IDEA

Which school do you think most pupils and teachers would prefer to work in, one that mixes the pupils for lessons *or* one that streams pupils according to ability? Interview several teachers and pupils in order to obtain your data. ☐

Schools vary in the way they are organised and in the way they expect their pupils to behave. For example, some schools are more traditional. They push their pupils hard and expect them to achieve good academic examination results. Other schools are more 'liberal' or progressive and are concerned with developing broader educational aims. These ideas and expectations about what is important in education permeate through a school and are sometimes referred to as its **ethos**. Some sociologists suggest that a school's ethos is probably as important as any social class, ethnic or gender differences the pupils bring to school with them.

In 1978, *Michael Rutter* (a psychiatrist, not a sociologist) and his team found that twelve London comprehensives, all in similar areas with similar types of pupils, had very different results when it came to the attitudes and achievement of their pupils. School ethos, Rutter decided, was the key. Those schools which expected hard work and good behaviour were more likely to get it. Teachers' 'low expectations' are, it is claimed, the main problem in comprehensive schools.

Children spend around 15 000 hours in school. Rutter suggests that during that time teachers should expect *more* of their pupils.

> For almost a dozen years children spend almost as much of their waking life at school as at home. Altogether this works out at some 15 000 hours (from the age of five until school leaving) during which schools and teachers may have an impact on the development of children in their care. Do a child's experiences at school have any effect; does it matter which school he goes to. . .? The research findings provide a clear 'yes' in response to these questions. Schools do indeed have an effect on children's development and it does matter which school a child attends.

Source: *Fifteen Thousand Hours* by M Rutter, 1979

DISCUSS

What is the ethos of your school or college? Describe it to a friend. How important do you think the ethos of a school is in terms of the success of all of the pupils?

DISCUSS

Which is more important and why?
a The ethos of the school *or*
b The physical state of the school?

Q According to this extract why does it matter which school a child attends? Do you agree?

The critical Marxist view of schooling

In the previous two sections the effects of the pupil's home background and of what goes on inside schools were discussed as possible reasons why certain groups of pupils tend to underachieve in education. These groups are: working-class pupils, girls and ethnic minorities.

This last section on educational achievement, discusses the Marxist argument that most working-class pupils are bound to fail in school, because they are destined to have the least desirable jobs in society. The school's function is simply to teach them obedience, punctuality, and the willingness to work.

Three Neo-marxist writers, *Herbert Bowles* and *Samuel Gintis* in the United States and *Pierre Bourdieu* in France, have criticised schools for carrying out the wishes of the dominant class, i.e. the bourgeois or capitalist class. They see schools as being places where 'appropriate' attitudes and knowledge are taught to certain groups. For the working class these attitudes include, respect for authority, punctuality, and the willingness to tolerate boring, repetitive work in unpleasant surroundings. These sociologists argue that the kind of knowledge given to those destined to have low status in society is the sort which, for example, enables factory hands to do a useful day's work for their employer.

DISCUSS

Is there really such a close link between education and work as these writers suggest? Is a school simply preparing its pupils for their future positions in a capitalist society? □

The theory or argument just outlined, is often referred to as a **correspondence theory**, i.e. the education system with its unequal organisation of pupils into streams and its emphasis on rules and respect for authority, can be said to mirror or correspond closely to capitalist society. Our society is also organised into social classes in terms of an unequal distribution of wealth and power; and, is maintained through rules or laws and by those in authority. (See Module 4 on Social Stratification and Module 3 on Power and Politics.)

TASK

List those groups in society that maintain law and order. Then list those people in the education system who also maintain order. How do these groups operate? Are there any similarities? □

These Neo-marxist sociologists argue that the school hierarchy and the teacher socialise pupils to accept the **status quo**, i.e. society the way it is. This is done by placing a child in a particular stream, e.g. a low stream, labelling or expecting them, in this case to underachieve, giving them only a particular type of knowledge, e.g. low-status knowledge so that at the end of the course they have few or no qualifications. The pupils learn to accept this state of affairs and come to believe that they deserve their low position in the school. They tend to think that they are not as intelligent or able as other pupils in the top stream. These 'C' stream pupils usually go on to accept a low paid, low-status job and the life-style that goes with it.

Earlier research by *Nel Keddie* showed that the 'A' streams in British schools were dominated by middle-class children, who tended to fit the teacher's image of the ideal pupil. They were seen as capable of learning as having the correct attitude to education. The 'C' stream was composed of mainly working-class children and it was assumed by the teacher that they had little capacity for learning.

According to the critical Marxist argument, the school acts as a **social controlling** agency. It helps to control or maintain order in society by its hierarchical organisation (see Module 3 on Power and Politics), and by its rules, by the way in which pupils are streamed, and by teacher labelling of some pupils as less able than others. In this way, the education system reproduces or perpetuates the inequalities that exist between people in our capitalist society.

These critical sociologists argue that attempts to produce equality of opportunity within school are destined to fail. Instead of tinkering about with mixed ability teaching, positive discrimination and massive social changes are needed in society to remove the social class inequalities that exist. Only in this way, can equality of opportunity be achieved in schools.

TASK

How does the hierarchical organisation of the school or college, its streaming, rules and the attitude of teachers, act as a means of controlling the pupils, and of fitting them for capitalist society? Discuss the issue in groups and then write a short answer to this important question. ☐

QUESTIONS

Study this photograph and then answer the following questions. Try to discuss your points of view on these questions with others in your group.
1   What school occasion do you think is shown in the photograph?
2   Choose *two* details from the photograph which support your answer to 1.
3   Mention *two* things which you think the photograph tells us about the attitude to discipline in this school.
4   Choose *two* examples of rules in your own school which you believe help prepare you for the world of work. Give the reasons for your choice.
5   Briefly describe *three* benefits which pupils might gain from their education.
6   The pupil who leaves school at 16 without any GCSE examinations may be seen as a 'failure', yet in their future lives prove 'successful'. How would you account for this failure and success? ☐

Source: SEG Social Science GCSE, 1988

WHERE TO NEXT?

It would be useful to read Module 12 on Gender next, in order to learn more about females and underachievement in education. You could also find out more about racial disadvantage in education through Module 6 on Inequality.

MODULE · 8
WORK

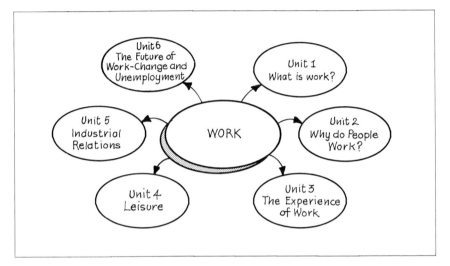

EIGHT

WORK

- Unit 6 The Future of Work – Change and Unemployment
- Unit 1 What is work?
- Unit 5 Industrial Relations
- Unit 2 Why do People Work?
- Unit 4 Leisure
- Unit 3 The Experience of Work

WHAT THIS MODULE IS ABOUT

Patterns of work and leisure are rapidly changing in today's society; but, work remains one of the most important features of our lives, affecting everything we do.

BY THE END OF THIS MODULE YOU SHOULD BE ABLE TO:

1 Define work and non-work. Appreciate why people work.
2 Discuss the cause and effects of job satisfaction and alienation.
3 Describe the advantages and disadvantages of industrialisation, division of labour, assembly-line production and automation.
4 Discuss the differences between work, leisure and unemployment.
5 Appreciate that leisure patterns are changing and that they vary according to social class, age gender, and occupation.
6 Demonstrate an awareness of the changes in ownership and control.

7 Give a balanced view of the role of strikes, trade unions, professional associations and employers' associations.
8 Discuss the effects of unemployment on the individual, the family and the community.
9 Identify new patterns of working for the future.

Work

WHAT IS WORK?

Consider the following statements and decide for yourself whether the activity referred to is really work. Discuss your decisions with the rest of your group.

a   Putting handles on cups in a pottery factory.
b   Painting and decorating your own home.
c   Packing butter into boxes in a butter factory.
d   Painting and decorating a customer's house.
e   Gardening.
f   A pupil doing homework.
g   Housework.
h   Teachers preparing the next day's lessons at home in the evenings.
i   Delivering meals on wheels to the elderly.
j   The Queen and Prince Philip's visit to China. □

Sociologists have spent several years discussing the differences between what is **work** and what is **non-work**. They have suggested that *work* is an *activity* that is usually carried out for a specific period of *time*, in a place away from home. This time is usually *paid* for by an employer.

DISCUSS

What about the person who stays at home to care for the children and do the housework? This person is not usually paid a wage and the activities, i.e. looking after children and doing housework, take place in the home. Is this person really doing work? Or is it *non-work*? What do you think? □

TASK

How much time do you spend on work and non-work activities during the course of one typical day? Make a list of the activities, calculate the amount of time and then construct a pie-chart to illustrate the distribution of time. You could also construct a pie-chart of work/non-work time for a parent and grandparent and then compare all three charts. Who spends the most time engaged in work activities? □

Evidently, there are great problems in defining what work is exactly, since it need not be paid labour (like painting and decorating a customer's house) but, could instead be simply a useful activity (like painting and decorating your own house – which is obviously unpaid).

Q   Is this last activity really a pastime or leisure pursuit? □

Also, sociologists have shown that work need not take place away from home, it can also take place inside the home. Indeed there has been a big increase in **home-working** or **tele-commuting** as it is called, by professional workers like computer programmers, who work on their computers in their own homes instead of in the office. In fact, in Britain there are now seven million home-workers, not all professionals of course, who account for seven per cent of the total work-force.

Q   What is the total work-force in Britain? □

The sort of home-workers just described are working as paid labour and are part of the **formal economy**. There is however also an **informal economy**, which is made up of:

a the *black economy*, i.e. work that is hidden and illegal, such as work that is done for cash on the side or off the books, without the taxman or social security office knowing about it and

b the *grey economy*, i.e. work that is quite legal and which is done for free, such as housework and work done voluntarily in the community, like delivering meals on wheels to pensioners, which is unpaid. Do-it-Yourself, wine- and beer-making at home are other examples of the grey economy.

T A S K

Look back at the activities listed in the task on page 130. Which ones could be described as being part of the grey economy? Does your own work form part of the formal or informal economy? □

DISCUSS

As more people become unemployed and retire early, do you think the grey economy, i.e. doing jobs for yourself and others freely, will increase? □

RESEARCH IDEA

According to the research of two sociologists the amount of time spent doing housework has *not* declined in the past fifty years!

Conduct your own research to find out whether this is likely to be true. Find out how many hours are spent in your family on housework. Interview your grandparents or neighbours of that generation to see what they think.

Surely, having atuomatic washing machines, vacuum cleaners, freezers etc. means *less* time spent on work in the house. Or does it . . .?

One writer has pointed out that because people are tending to own their own washing machines, microwaves, hovermowers, videos and so on these days, they do not use the launderette, pop into cafés, hire gardeners or go to the cinema, as much as they used to. He says that this trend is important because it affects the future of paid employment in these service industries. There are three types of **industry** in Britain:

1　**Primary** – such as mining or agriculture which involves using the country's natural resources.
2　**Secondary** or **Manufacturing** – where the goods are produced to be sold.
3　**Tertiary** or **Service** industry – which involves providing a service of some kind, such as banking or transport.

T A S K

Consider the following list of industries and categorise or group them according to the three types of industry described above.
a　Miss Selfridge Stores
b　A glass-making factory
c　The Post Office
d　A poultry producers
e　Wedgwood Fine China Ltd.
f　A car factory
g　The Macdonalds Chain of Burger Bars.
h　An iron smelting works
i　A corner shop.
j　Schools and colleges
k　Stoke City FC
l　A pig farm □

WHY DO PEOPLE WORK?

Work affects all areas of a person's life in society. It can affect the food they eat, the clothes they wear, the house they live in, their health, wealth and happiness.

Work is also a vital part of the socialisation or learning process. For example, when a person takes a job, they learn to take on a **role** or **identity** which has certain **expectations** about behaviour attached to it. For instance a judge is expected to be serious and sober, a pilot is expected to be cool and in control, a bookkeeper to be accurate and neat, etc.

A job not only gives a person their identity, but also gives them their **social class** and **social status**. As already discussed in Module 5 on Social Stratification, a person's social class position is defined in Britain mainly by their occupation, which is either **manual** or **non-manual**. (See pages 73 and 76 for the Registrar General's scale and Hall-Jones scale of occupations.) Some jobs are of a higher **status**, or regarded as more important than others, and the people who have these jobs are therefore higher up the social class scale and enjoy many advantages in society.

Sociologists argue that manual workers (Registrar General's classes 4 and 5) suffer many disadvantages compared to non-manual workers. For example, in terms of promotion and pay, a road digger and a trainee hospital doctor might earn the same pay, but as the doctor becomes more experienced he gets promoted and earns more pay; the road digger, however, stays on approximately the same rate of pay all his life, with the additional worry of not being able to do the job when he is not fit.

Another disadvantage is the lack of job security offered to manual workers. Although some white-collar (non-manual) workers were made redundant during the recent economic recession, nevertheless it was still manual workers who were hardest hit by lay-offs, mass sackings and short-time working. At the present time about a third of unemployed men are general labourers; and in fact manual workers can expect to be made redundant several times in their working life.

Manual workers are also worse off in terms of working conditions, e.g. the number of hours they work. The average working week for a manual worker was 46 hours (because of the need to do overtime) compared with 38 hours for the white-collar worker.

Economic factors

In developing countries people work mainly to satisfy the basic human needs of food, clothing and shelter. This is also true in our developed society, but instead people work in order to gain *money* or wages so that they can buy the food, clothing and shelter they need.

Q Are there any other basic human needs besides food, clothing and shelter that people must satisfy in order to survive? □

When *Goldthorpe and Lockwood* studied the Luton car workers, in 1968, they described those people who work mainly for their pay packet as having an **instrumental** attitude to their job. Since these workers did not gain any real satisfaction from the job itself, they were described as gaining only **extrinsic** satisfaction, i.e. they used their high wages to buy some satisfaction or happiness outside their workplace either with their families or perhaps in leisure activities. Goldthorpe and Lockwood called them **privatised** workers.

TASK

Give one example of a high status and one example of a low status occupation. Are there any differences in pay and working conditions between these occupations? What are these differences?

RESEARCH IDEA

Interview one manual worker and one non-manual worker. Find out whether there is a difference in the number of hours they work each week or any difference in the amount of holiday and sickness pay each is entitled to receive. You could choose to start your interviews with a teacher (non-manual) and a school canteen worker (manual).

DISCUSS

How can high wages give workers extrinsic satisfaction or pleasure outside their job? Do you think that working just for the wages, i.e. having an economic motive is a good enough reason for doing a job that is not enjoyable or satisfying?

Other people gain **intrinsic** satisfaction from their job. Their work is enjoyable, stimulating, a source of achievement, pride and interest. They do not work just for the money; and in some cases the pay could be quite low, but the job is intrinsically satisfying to them.

BRAINSTORM

Make a list of jobs in society that you think are intrinsically satisfying. ☐

DISCUSS

Would people do the jobs you have listed even if the pay was very low? Why? ☐

Nurses tend to be low-paid workers. Why do people want to become nurses? What do they gain from such a job?

ANGELS ANGUISH

B RITAIN'S nurses are underpaid and undervalued by the Government. And under physical attack by patients.

These are the shock findings of two reports that reveal the anguish of the angels who look after the sick with total dedication and poor reward.

First, a report published on Friday showed that one in three of our 500,000 nurses have taken home pay of less than £70-a-week.

About 3,00 of them earn so little that their pay has to be boosted by social security.

Skilled

The report—based on interviews with nurses throughout the country—was carried out for NUPE and the Low Pay Unit by the Kingston Polytechnic School of Industrial Relations.

It found that many hospitals are so under-staffed that untrained auxiliaries are taking responsibility for skilled jobs, such as giving injections and checking drip feeds. And for no extra pay.

The second report, on the same day revealed that four out of five nurses have suffered violent attacks from patients in the past 12 months.

This survey was carried out by Nursing Standard, the newspaper of the Royal College of Nursing.

Nurses complained that less than a quarter of hospitals provided security systems, such as panic buttons, night lights in hospital grounds or 24-hour security personnel.

Labour health spokesman Frank Dobson said yesterday that 27,000 nurses left the Health Service last year, but only 21,000 students had started training.

"We will all suffer unless this process is reversed" he said.

Overtime

"But nurses are being abused, subjected to disparaging remarks about their efficiency and given little credit for the work they are doing."

NUPE official Bob Jones said recent Common Market figures showed that, compared with their counterparts on the Continent, Britain's nurses were the most poorly paid.

The low pay report, entitled Nursing A Grievance showed that 44 per cent of nurses work overtime—but only four per cent are given extra pay.

The survey's findings have been sent to the Nurses Pay Review Body, which is to recommend the size of the next pay rise due in April.

Comments from individual nurses included in the survey show the extend to which the angels are suffering.

A second-year student nurse at a Sunderland hospital (take-home pay £62.30), said: "Students are just treated as a pair of hands. We are not paid for the work we do. I could earn more working in a supermarket."

And a third-year student in an Inner-London hospital (take home pay £76.15) summed up the frustration. "We are used as slave labour," she said.

Source: *Sunday Mirror*, January 1987

DISCUSS

Do you feel that social factors are important to you in your work role as a student in school or college? Do you gain satisfaction from working with others?

Q Does a person spend more time during their life with their work mates than with their close relatives, such as wife, husband, parents, brothers, sisters?

Social factors

Sociologists have suggested that another reason why people work is to fulfil their need to meet and work alongside others, in short, to enjoy the company of others. This is a **social** reason for working. Many people who retire or who are made unemployed miss this aspect of work the most.

DISCUSS

What are the possible implications of such a change in time spent with family or work mates? What might this lead to? ☐

Jobs that are boring, repetitive or dangerous can be made bearable and even enjoyable by the friendship and support of colleagues at work.

RESEARCH IDEA

Discover whether this idea could be true. Interview workers whose jobs could be described as boring, repetitive or difficult. Ask them what it is they enjoy most about their work and see whether they mention the social contacts or friendships they gain at work. ☐

THE EXPERIENCE OF WORK

Job satisfaction

The reasons why people work have been described in the previous unit as being:

1 economic
2 intrinsic
3 social.

It is argued that workers can gain **satisfaction** through high wages, or by doing an interesting challenging job, or through the social contacts or friends they make at work. The status or importance of a job can also give a person satisfaction.

Lack of job satisfaction – alienation

However, many people are very **dissatisfied** with their jobs, particularly, those people working on assembly lines in factories, where the machines control how fast you must work and where the work is repetitive and requires little skill.

The comments on the left from men working on the car assembly line at Ford's highlight this job dissatisfaction.

The feelings of the workers expressed in these quotations could be described as feelings of:

Powerlessness – they could not stop the line or slow down the piece of work if they wanted to;
Meaninglessness – in that the work was boring, it could be done by a robot and required no thought, in fact the men just 'blanked out their minds.'
Isolation – because even though the men were working close to their mates on the line, nevertheless the level of noise was such that conversation was impossible and the men therefore felt isolated;
Self-Estrangement – in that these car workers did not seem able to take any pride or interest in their work.
The job therefore became simply a way of making money to spend on things they really wanted to do outside the workplace.

A sociologist named *Blauner* referred to this lack of job satisfaction and the feelings of powerlessness, meaninglessness, isolation and self-estrangement as **alienation**.

Ways of making work more satisfying

Elton Mayo's famous studies of the Hawthorne works in Chicago in the 1920s showed that people worked better when they were treated as *individuals* rather than cogs in a machine. This idea is known as the **human relations** approach to workers.

Recently, there have been attempts to make industrial work more satisfying through the use of: teamwork, job rotation schemes, a four day week, flexitime and increased worker participation in decision-making.

They wouldn't stop that f..... line. You could be dying and they wouldn't stop it. If someone was hurt the first thing the supervisor thought about was filling the job. He'd start doing the work before he made sure the bloke was all right . . .

They 'blanked out their minds'; they made great efforts to communicate with their mates, but there was the problem of the noise.

. . . he collapsed again. Y'know – flat on the floor. His face was an awful grey colour. We all rushed round him and the buzzer went. The line started. The foreman came across shouting ` get to work – get on the line ´. And there we were sticking things on the cars and he was lying there. He must have been lying there ten minutes . . . dead. In front of us.

Source: *Working For Ford* by H Beynon

TASK

Taking each of these suggestions for how to make industrial work more satisfying, consider the advantages and disadvantages of each idea.

> '. . . it was terrible . . .
> I was working on the
> headlinings and I never
> thought I'd survive. I used to
> come home from work and fall
> straight asleep . . . I knew
> hard work. I'd been on the
> buildings but this place was a
> b . . . . . . then. I didn't have
> any relations with my wife for
> months . . .'

Source: *Working for Ford* by H Beynon

DISCUSS

1 Do you think people are more likely to be sick, absent, have an accident or go on strike in a job that is alienating than in a job that is satisfying? Consider reasons why.
2 Do you think people in professional and managerial occupations are more likely to be satisfied with their jobs than people in unskilled manual occupations? Use the information and discussions in this and the previous units to support your arguments.

Alienation is a concept which came from Karl Marx. He believed that working with machines in factories within a capitalist society was likely to be a hostile activity that was out of the worker's own control and which would produce feelings of alienation in them.

This alienation or hostility can be seen in the previous extracts and in this comment from a Ford car worker.

DISCUSS

What might be the long-term effects of doing this sort of job on the man's family life? □

Such alienating work can even be physically damaging to health. A study by the Stress Research Unit at Nottingham University has shown that routine, boring jobs can cause backache, neckache, changes in mood and even changes in heart activity. □

Q   Why should routine jobs that are easy to do produce stress? Consider housework in relation to this. □

Finally, some writers argue that this dissatisfaction with boring, meaningless work leads to high rates of absenteeism, sickness, accidents and strikes.

T A S K | | | | | | |

A number of different occupations are given in the table below. First, copy out the table. Then on the basis of the information above and what your have read in newspapers or what you have seen on television try to assess the jobs listed in the table. For each of the four aspects of alienation outlined on page 134 score four marks if you think a job is extremely alienating, three if you think it is very alienating, two if you think it is quite alienating, and one if you think it is only a little alienating. If you think the job would have no disadvantages at all then put a zero in that column. Do this for each of the jobs and then calculate the alienation total. □

Alienation factors in selected jobs

Occupation	Power-lessness	Isolation	Meaning-lessness	Lack of pride	Total score
Example Production line worker in car factory	2	1	2	1	6
Waitress					
Dinner lady in school					
Miner (face worker)					
Computer programmer					
Secretary					
Housewife					
Nurse					
Garage mechanic					
Teacher					

Q   What sort of jobs from your assessment prove to be more alienating than others? Discuss your findings with others in your group. □

Technology and the changes in employment

Back in 1830, 70 per cent of the British work-force were employed in agriculture. Today, only 3 per cent of all workers are employed on the land! Britain was the first country in the world to **industrialise**, that is to change from being based on agriculture to being based on large-scale industry. The first factories of the Industrial Revolution were built in the 1750s and 1760s. Today most countries of the western world including Europe, the USA, USSR, and parts of South East Asia, such as Japan, have industrialised.

T A S K

Name three countries that have not industrialised. Turn to Module 4 on Third World Studies for any help you may need. □

Industrialisation brought factories and the use of *machines* to do the work that previously had been done by hand. The use of machines is called **mechanisation** and work that was done by hand is called **craft**. One of the main features of industrialisation is **division of labour**, which is the way that goods are produced in the factories by dividing the work into small, simple, repetitive tasks using machines or mechanisation.

The most famous example of division of labour was given by Adam Smith in the Eighteenth century when he described the production of pins. If each worker made a whole pin each, then in one day they would only be able to make two pins each. If ten people worked in the pin factory, they would therefore produce 20 pins a day. But, by dividing the labour, i.e. dividing the job of making one pin between the 10 workers, then these ten people actually made 48 000 pins a day!

Assembly-line production, as described by the car workers on pages 80, was the next technological advance to take place. This is where the product moves along a conveyor belt from one worker to the next, each adding another part to the product. When it reaches the end of the line it is complete. This assembly-line method is the way most *mass-produced* items are made.

Division of labour, mechanisation and assembly-line production, provide several *advantages*, such as producing goods at a lower price, giving employment to more people and earning greater profits for the owners of the factories. They also have several *disadvantages* for the workers. Pride in their craft and traditional skills are lost and lack of pride can lead to a poorer quality product being made. The workers lose control over their work and the pace at which they work. The resulting boredom, dissatisfaction and alienation can, it is claimed, cause industrial disputes (see Unit 6 in this module).

Where very high levels of technology are used in industry, **automation** is likely to take place, i.e. where the machines begin to run themselves. They become automatic and computers take over many jobs previously held by workers. Automation can be seen in the Fiat car factory in Italy, for example, where computer-controlled machines manufacture the cars almost entirely unaided by people.

Automation and the use of microchip technology has not only affected manufacturing industries. Service industries have also been affected. For example, banks now have cash dispensers, office staff use word processors, pocket calculators and computer information terminals.

Automation and the use of microchip technology has been described as the Second Industrial Revolution and has brought with it several advantages. Many alienating and dangerous jobs can now be done by machines. Goods can be produced more quickly and the working week could be shortened to give the workers more leisure time. Jobs could become more interesting and

DISCUSS

Craft technology or mechanisation? Which method of production is better and why? Which method of working is likely to give most job satisfaction to the worker?

responsible, with the presence of these complex machines, and automation could lead to management and workers working better together as a team. People can now work from home using computers and can even do their shopping from their armchairs, using the Prestel Communication system.

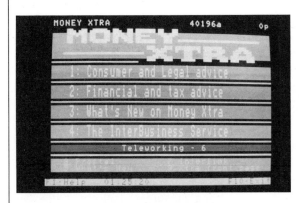

A Prestel screen

RESEARCH IDEA

Find out how the Prestel system works. You will find one in your library. Besides shopping, what other services can you obtain by Prestel? ☐

There are however major disadvantages associated with the increased use of automation in industry. The biggest disadvantage is the rise in unemployment, as machines take over the jobs previously done by skilled, semi-skilled and unskilled workers. Computers can now perform very complex tasks: e.g. in the printing industry where it once took five years to learn how to set the type. Now, the job can be learned in a day with the help of a word processor. *Henry Braverman* called this process **deskilling**, whereby workers lose their skills to machines.

DISCUSS

Henry Braverman claims that employers use deskilling as an opportunity to cut the work-force and decrease wages. What do you think? ☐

Only fifty years ago, more than 50 per cent of the work-force in Britain were employed in the secondary or manufacturing industries (see table on page 149 for more details). In the 1980s the figure went down to 25 per cent. The service industry will soon employ 70 per cent of the work force – the same number of people who worked on the land only 150 years ago.

Q Why do you think there has been a huge drop in the number of people employed in manufacturing in this country? ☐

(see table on page 149 for more details)

TASK

How many service industries does the average person or family use in one week? List as many as you can. ☐

DISCUSS

a 'New technology means higher productivity (more goods made) which in turn means greater wealth for the country and therefore means more jobs and prosperity for everyone in the long run.'
b 'The microchip will have a devastating effect on employment in this country. There will be mass joblessness as the jobs will be taken over by computers on a huge scale.'

Which of these views do you support and why?
Do you have an alternative view about unemployment? ☐

TASK

Explain the difference between assembly-line and automated technology.
What are the possible consequences of an increase in automation?

UNIT 4

LEISURE

In 1940, The Holidays with Pay Act stated that employers had to give one day's paid holiday for each month worked. Before this time, there had been no paid holidays and Christmas Day and other Bank Holidays were the only days off work – but without pay!

RESEARCH IDEA

How many days paid holiday do your parents, friends and relatives get? How many do teachers get?

TASK

Are the following activities work or leisure?
1   Choosing a birthday card.
2   Cooking a meal for friends.
3   Attending a union meeting.
4   Keep fit training at night.
5   Visiting the hairdressers.

Unemployment, work and leisure

Unit 3 described how rapid technological change taking place in industry has altered the nature of many jobs and also reduced the need for as many workers in primary, manufacturing and even service industries. The result has been redundancy and unemployment for some of these workers.

It could be argued that unemployment and leisure are experiences that have a common denominator, i.e. that people who are unemployed or enjoying leisure hours both have time away from work. However, it would of course be quite wrong to suggest that unemployment and leisure are the same thing. **Leisure** is a concept or idea that suggests people not only have time, but also enough money and the opportunity to enjoy themselves. Whilst most long-term unemployed are relatively poor and often miserable, and unable to afford leisure.

One sociologist who tried to describe the differences between work and leisure is *SR Parker*, who defines leisure as both a period of time and also as an activity.

TASK

Consider the definitions below and add or subtract to them as you see fit. ☐

work is . . .	whilst . . .	**leisure is . . .**
paid		unpaid
means following orders		means having the
means a person is not free		freedom of choice
to do as they please		of what to do
is not very pleasurable		not needing to
		follow orders
		is enjoyable

Changing leisure patterns in Britain

People now have more time and money to spend on leisure than ever before.

RESEARCH IDEA

It has been suggested that about 14 per cent of a family's income is spent on leisure activities, find out if this is accurate. Find out how much money is spent on leisure activities by your own family during one week. Remember to include the costs of all the things we take for granted, such as television (is it rented?) the electricity to run the TV , radio, stereo etc. ☐

Young and Willmott in their research, found that the most popular leisure activity in the home was watching television, although radio listening has increased greatly during the last ten years. They suggest that on average people spend just over two and half hours a day watching television, i.e. about eighteen hours each week, and roughly ten hours per week listening to the radio.

RESEARCH IDEA

Conduct a small-scale survey to find out if these figures are fairly accurate. What questions will you need to cover your questionnaire? □

Research has shown that the type of leisure activities people take part in tend to vary according to *social class*. For example, as the table below shows, professional or managerial workers tend to garden more often than other employees; and that semi- and unskilled groups decorate or make repairs to their property the least of all. These are referred to as differences in leisure patterns.

Differences in leisure patterns by social class

		Professional and Managerial %	Clerical %	Skilled %	Semi- and Unskilled %
Proportion in class doing activity 12 times or more in the previous years	(All)				
Watching television	(97%)	95	99	98	95
Gardening	(64%)	70	62	66	50
Playing with children	(62%)	59	63	66	59
Listening to music	(57%)	65	70	52	44
Home decorations or repairs	(53%)	52	55	56	45
Car cleaning	(48%)	55	44	51	35
Reading (books)	(46%)	67	63	33	28

Source: *The Symmetrical Family* by Young and Willmott, 1972

QUESTIONS

1 Suggest possible reasons why professional or managerials garden and read more often than most other economic groups.
2 Suggest possible reasons why unskilled workers do the least amount of home decorating.
   Consider factors, such as educational background, income, amount of free time available for leisure and so on.
3 Name two other differences in leisure patterns revealed in the table above and suggest possible reasons for the differences between these social class groups. □

The leisure activities discussed above are all *home-based* activities; but there are also *outdoor* leisure activities. Many people spend a lot of time outside the home with their friends, engaging in leisure pursuits, such as going to the cinema, concerts, pubs, shows, dances as well as attending evening classes and taking part in a whole range of spectator and participatory sports.

T A S K

Give one example of a spectator sport and one example of a participatory sport. □

BRAINSTORM

A list of *outdoor* leisure activities. How many different types are there?

T A S K

a Categorise or group the activities on your list according to who is most likely to take part in them.
b Give a rough idea of their costs, i.e. in terms of time, equipment, etc.
c Do more males play sports or take part in these outdoor leisure activites? If the answer is yes, suggest possible reasons why this happens.

The rate or amount of time people spend on leisure activities outside the home also differs by social class. For example, professional or managerial workers are more likely to go out for their entertainment and to take part in squash, jogging or horse-riding.

RESEARCH IDEA

1 Investigate where and how professional or managerial workers tend to spend their leisure time outside the home. Interview teachers, headteachers and any other professional or managerial workers you know. Which leisure pursuits are most popular for this social class?
2 Interview semi- and unskilled or manual workers in order to discover their dominant leisure patterns. Where do these workers tend to spend their leisure time? □

The amount of time people spend on leisure activities outside the home, not only varies according to their social class, but also according to their *age*. For example, school-leavers in their first jobs, have money to spend for the first time in their lives and spend a lot of time outside the home with their friends. It is suggested that discos, pubs and the cinema are the most popular leisure activities for young people.

RESEARCH IDEA

Conduct a small-scale survey amongst the young people you know in order to check whether:

a Young people do spend a lot of time outside the home with their friends.
b Discos, pubs and the cinema are the most popular leisure activities with this age group. Which single activity proves to be the most popular? □

A sociologist named *Abrams* has suggested that types of leisure patterns are closely related to age. He identifies five periods of age and leisure:

1 Youth Culture: Money to spend on luxury items, e.g. records, clothes. The young are searching for excitement in leisure.
2 Young Marrieds: Spending on the house and the children.
3 35 to 45 Years: Increase in spending on family and group activities.
4 45 to 64 Years: The most affluent (richest) period, the children have left home and there is spending on luxury items.
5 Over 65 Years: Decline in income, little cash for leisure activities. Television, and inexpensive leisure activity becomes very important.

RESEARCH IDEA

How could you check out this theory from Abrams? □

Leisure patterns also differ according to *gender* as well as age and social class. Women have been discouraged from taking part in some leisure activities, such as football; and men do not usually take part in others, such as netball. Sociologists argue that leisure activities are often **sex stereotyped** in this way. Other examples of this include: yoga, keep fit classes and horseriding which tend to be regarded as female leisure pursuits, and darts, going to the pub for a quick drink and motor cycle racing which are often regarded as male activities.

Q   Can you think of other sex stereotyped leisure activities? □

All in all, women are far *less* active in leisure than men as the table in the margin shows.

Participation in the most popular sporting activities for 1983

Sport	Males	Females	Total
Walking – 2 miles or more	24	21	23
Swimming	19	16	17
Snooker/Billiards/Pool	18	3	10
Darts	14	5	9
Fishing	7	1	4
Keep Fit/Yoga	1	6	3
Football	6	–	3
Squash	5	2	3
Golf	5	1	3
Cycling	3	2	3
Tennis	3	2	3

Source: *Social Trends* 17, 1987

QUESTIONS

1 What trend is evident from this table?
2 Suggest three reasons why fewer women take part in sporting activities than men.

DISCUSS

How are females and males discouraged from participating in certain sports and leisure activities? Where does this socialisation first take place? (See Module 12 on Gender, Unit 2 for more ideas on this)

Lastly, leisure patterns also vary according to a person's *occupation*. **Stanley Parker** has suggested three possible relationships between the job a person does and the way in which they spend their leisure time.

The extension pattern: when a person's leisure activities are a direct extension of their job. For example a doctor who gives talks on health matters in his spare time; or, a teacher who runs a youth club in the evenings. Leisure and work overlap in the extension pattern; and this usually occurs when people have satisfying, rewarding and responsible occupations.

Q   Can you give other examples of the extension leisure pattern?   □

The opposition pattern: when a person who has a tough, alienating or exhausting job chooses leisure activities that are completely different from their work, i.e. the reverse of the extension pattern. For example a miner who does a difficult and dangerous job might choose to relax in the pub in the company of others and forget about his work; or an assembly-line worker might enjoy skilled leisure activities, such as gardening or model-making where calmness helps to soothe away the pressure of work.

Q   Can you give other examples of the opposition leisure pattern?   □

The neutrality pattern: when there is no clear pattern or relationship between a person's occupation and the way they spend their leisure time. An example of this would be the clerical worker who is not particularly interested in their work and who perhaps plays squash. There is no clear link between their job and the way they spend their leisure time. In the neutrality pattern, unlike the extension and opposition patterns, there is no relationship between occupation and leisure.

T A S K

Identify the leisure patterns of the people listed below.
a   A deep-sea fisherman who spends much of his on-shore leave in the pub.
b   A teacher who enjoys reading books on her subject in her spare time.
c   A typist who goes to keep fit classes.
d   A company director who plays golf with his business colleagues.   □

A leisure society?

With the increasing use of technology and automation, there could be less work for people to do in society in the future and more leisure time available. The working week has been gradually reduced this century and leisure is no longer only for the rich to enjoy, as it was a hundred years ago. Instead, leisure time is available to all social classes.

DISCUSS

As we move towards a leisure society, what sort of leisure activities will become the most popular? Will work become more interesting and more like leisure, as automation takes over production-like jobs? Will people spend more time on education and learning new skills? Will women enjoy the same type of leisure activities and the same amount of time in leisure as men? Will there be fewer social class differences in this new leisure society? Or, will the unemployed workers still be poorer and unable to afford some leisure pursuits? What do you think? □

Household expenditure on selected leisure items in the UK by household income, 1982

£s and percentages

	Gross normal weekly income of household					
	Under £60	£60 and under £120	£120 and under £180	£180 and under £240	£240 or more	All house-holds
Average weekly household expenditure on (£s):						
Alcoholic drink	1.46	3.06	5.75	7.73	11.15	6.13
Books, newspapers, magazines, etc	1.04	1.59	2.05	2.43	3.23	2.14
Television, radio, and musical instruments	1.34	2.01	3.06	4.56	6.05	3.55
Purchase of materials for home repairs, etc.	0.29	0.86	1.65	3.11	3.51	1.97
Holidays	0.41	1.12	2.57	3.17	10.62	3.99
Hobbies	0.01	0.04	0.07	0.13	0.15	0.08
Cinema admissions	0.02	0.05	0.08	0.10	0.21	0.10
Dance admissions	0.02	0.06	0.08	0.13	0.25	0.12
Theatre, concert, etc admissions	0.03	0.05	0.12	0.15	0.44	0.18
Subscriptions and admission charges to participant sports	0.03	0.12	0.35	0.54	0.89	0.41
Football match admissions	–	0.01	0.08	0.07	0.10	0.06
Admissions to other spectator sports	–	–	0.02	0.02	0.05	0.02
Sports goods (excluding clothes)	0.01	0.07	0.18	0.53	0.40	0.24
Other entertainment	0.04	0.10	0.23	0.31	0.51	0.25
Total weekly expenditure on above	4.69	9.13	16.30	22.99	37.56	19.23

Source: *Social Trends*, 1984

QUESTIONS

You should now be able to attempt the following questions.

1 According to the above information, on which leisure item did all households spend the largest amount of money?

2 According to the above information, on which leisure items was the second largest amount of money spent by families with a weekly income of:

a under £60;

b £240 or more?

3 Give three reasons why it is sometimes difficult to distinguish between work and leisure.

4 Identify and explain three ways in which leisure has changed over the past 50 years.

5 Examine the extent to which it is possible to relate a person's job to their leisure activities.

Source: AEB Sociology GCE, 1985

UNIT 5 INDUSTRIAL RELATIONS

Changes in Ownership and Control

At the beginning of the Industrial Revolution, it was easy to identify the *owners* of the factories, mines and banks, i.e. the bourgeoisie or capitalists. They were the entrepreneurs or businessmen who actually set up the factory, probably worked on the site themselves and who *controlled* their workers. An example of this would be the potter, Josiah Wedgwood, who was actively involved in his first factory, which he both owned and controlled himself.

However since those early days, there has been a separation of ownership and control. No longer is there one owner who also manages or controls the factory, nowadays there are several owners of the large factories. These owners are called *shareholders* and they may never even set foot inside the works. These shareholders were introduced with the development of joint-stock companies and they simply invest money in a particular factory and receive shares in the company, i.e. they become part-owners. It is the *managers* who actually control the day-to-day running of the business. At Josiah Wedgwood, which is now a limited company, there is a huge number of shareholders instead of just one owner and a whole army of production managers, sales and export managers who run the company.

DISCUSS

Some writers claim that this separation between ownership and control can lead to a conflict of interests. They suggest that the shareholders are only interested in receiving profit on their investments, whilst the managers are concerned with the company as a whole. Do you think that owners or shareholders should be actively involved in the business they own? What possible benefits would this bring? □

Recently there has been a major development in shareholding. The Conservative Government has sold off what were *publicly-owned* or nationalised industries, such as British Telecom, British Gas and British Airways. These industries are now owned by people who bought shares in them and they are therefore *privately owned*, instead of being owned by the nation. In the case of British Gas the number of small shareholders is considerable as the advertisement on the right shows. □

THANKS A MILLION

...or, more accurately, thank you to each of around five million people who bought shares in British Gas. We gas people appreciate the confidence you've shown in us. And aim to justify that confidence by building on our success of the last twenty years or so.

Now, a word to our customers. You'll be glad to know that we intend to go on providing you with a comprehensive, first-class gas service. And to work even harder at improving it. Because we believe that by keeping our customers happy, we'll keep our shareholders happy, too.

So, if you're both a customer and a shareholder, you'll have *two* reasons for thinking gas is wonderfuel!

British Gas
ENERGY IS OUR BUSINESS

DISCUSS

Is it better for British Telecom, British Gas, British Airways, etc. to be owned by all of the nation or public, i.e. to be nationalised, or to be owned by private shareholders? Which ownership method is best and why? □

Industrial conflict

There are three different types of **conflict** in industry.

Working to rule – where workers go-slow or do no extra voluntary work at all. An example of this is the Teachers' Dispute of 1985 to 1988.

Industrial sabotage – where workers deliberately damage the machinery in order to publicise their grievances. An example of this would be the Luddites of the textile industry in the early Nineteenth century.

Striking – where workers stop working in protest against low pay and long hours. In 1986 2.3 million working days were lost through strikes in Britain. This marks a rapid decline in the number of days lost through striking in comparison to two years before when 27.1 million days were lost.

Strikes can be both *official* and *unofficial* and in fact only 5 to 10 per cent of all strikes are officially recognised by the trade union involved. Most strikes are therefore unofficial and are often on-the-spot strikes by workers with a problem that is then sorted out by the local trade union representative, i.e. the shop steward. Sometimes a union cannot afford to make a strike official, because it has not got the funds to pay the striking workers. At other times, a trade union wants to see whether the unofficial strike is successful or popular before supporting it and making it official.

Britain does not have as many strikes as several other countries, although most people would probably be surprised to hear this. The popular impression that Britain is a strike-torn country is a myth. On average, 97.8 per cent of manufacturing industries are free of stoppages in any one year, and 81.1 per cent of employees work in strike-free industries.

The government produces the statistics revealing the main causes of the strikes that do take place. They say that the main cause of the strikes and stoppages is wage-disputes, i.e. workers demanding higher wages. For example, teachers went on strike in 1985 to 1986 for more pay.

Other causes of strikes include disputes over the number of hours of work, redundancies, working conditions and disciplinary matters. Until recently, a trade union could support the strike action of a group of workers in another union. However the Conservative Government made this sort of *solidarity* action illegal in 1982.

DISCUSS

It is suggested that the number of strikes decline during a period of high unemployment. Why do you think there are less strikes when unemployment is high?

Q Why do you think most people believe that Britain has a lot of strikes?
Where do you get this impression from? Does the media help to give this impression?

Samuelson states that the number of days lost from work as a result of the common cold is much greater than from disputes in work.

Q Do you think that government statistics on strikes are likely to be unbiased?

QUESTIONS

1 Give a brief description in your own words of the image of workers which the illustration wishes to present?
2 What dangers are there in using stereotyped images of any group of people, such as 'workers'?
3 What explanations might there be for the use of such a stereotype by the media?

Source: UCLES Sociology GCE, 1981

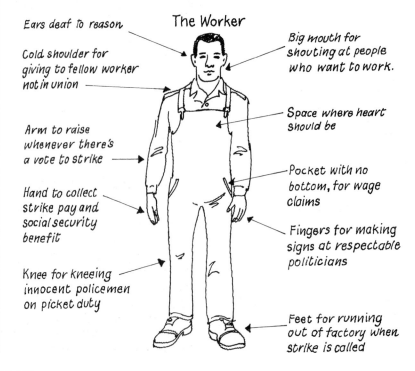

The Worker

Ears deaf to reason

Cold shoulder for giving to fellow worker not in union

Arm to raise whenever there's a vote to strike

Hand to collect strike pay and social security benefit

Knee for kneeing innocent policemen on picket duty

Big mouth for shouting at people who want to work.

Space where heart should be

Pocket with no bottom, for wage claims

Fingers for making signs at respectable politicians

Feet for running out of factory when strike is called

Trade unions

A **trade union** is a group of workers that have joined together to protect their common interests. In this union, the workers elect representatives who negotiate with employers over pay, hours and working conditions.

In Britain, there are four main *types* of trade union.

1. *General unions*: These are large and powerful unions that were originally formed to protect the interests of unskilled workers, but they now have skilled workers as members also. People join a general union, such as the Transport and General Workers' Union (TGWU) and the General and Municipal Workers' Union from a whole range of different occupations.

2. *Industrial unions*: These are unions that usually recruit their members from only one industry. They take both skilled and unskilled workers. Examples of Industrial Unions include the National Union of Mineworkers (NUM) and the Union of Post Office Workers.

3. *Craft unions*: These are the oldest trade unions in Britain; and represent the skilled workers. They often control the number of workers allowed into the craft, by having a long apprenticeship scheme. The workers in these craft unions are increasingly under the threat of *deskilling* (as explained in an earlier unit). This is where modern technology, such as microchip-based machines are taking over much skilled work. An example of this can be found in the printing union, the National Graphical Association (NGA) where many of the skilled print-workers are having their jobs taken over by computer typesetting machines.

RESEARCH IDEA

In 1986 to 1987 there was a long-running print-workers dispute at Wapping between Rupert Murdoch, the Newspaper Baron, and his print-workers. Find out what this dispute was about. What sources will you use? Interviews? Newspaper reports? Is there any problem with bias in reports? What was the result of this dispute? □

4. *White-collar unions*: These unions cover people working in clerical, administrative and professional occupations, i.e. the non-manual workers. They are the fastest growing unions in Britain and examples include the National Local Government Officers' Association (NALGO), the National Union of Teachers (NUT).

Q   Name three occupations where the worker is likely to join the Transport and General Workers Union.

Q   Give two other examples of Industrial unions.

For more on industrial disputes see Module 14 on Urbanisation, page 270.

TASK

Consider the following unions.
a   State who are the present leaders of these unions.
b   Which of these unions could be called craft unions? Which of them would be industrial unions? And which of them white-collar unions?

The Amalgamated Union of Engineering Workers (AUEW)
The National Union of Railwaymen. (NUR)
The National Association of Schoolmasters/Union of Women Teachers. (NAS/UWT)
Equity – the Actors' Union.
The Amalgamated Society of Locomotive Engineers and Firemen (ASLEF)
The First Division – the top civil servants' union.
The Society of Graphical and Allied Trades '82 (SOGAT '82)

Q   Name two other white-collar unions? Which union does your teacher or lecturer belong to?

Q What other white-collar trade unions have been on strike or in dispute? Are there *any* trade unions that are not allowed to go on strike?

Trade Unions grew up at the time of the Industrial Revolution, when the first factories were built and workers suffered long hours, low wages and poor conditions. On their own the working man or woman had little chance to bring about any improvement in their working lives, so they joined together in order to have more power.

The government (and the employers) were opposed to workers forming unions, and even had six Dorchester farm labourers transported to Australia in 1834 as a punishment for forming a farm workers' union. These early trade unionists were called the Tolpuddle Martyrs.

There have been many government attempts to **limit the power** of unions over the years. The Taff Vale Judgement of 1900, the General Strike of 1926 and the Industrial Relations Act of 1971 came as major landmarks along the route to these restrictions. Of course, it would be wrong to assume that all governments are opposed to trade union power. The Labour Party has had a special relationship with the trade union movement since the party was originally formed by trade unionists wishing to have some parliamentary power. In fact, a person cannot become a member of the Labour Party unless they are already a member of a trade union, unemployed or retired.

DISCUSS

It has been said that the Conservative and Labour Parties have very different attitudes towards the role of trade unions in society. Explain why. □

There have been considerable changes in trade union membership over the years. For example, membership increased overall from 2 million in 1900 to over 12 million in 1979. However, since 1979, trade union membership has declined to an overall figure of 11 million in 1985. The period of economic recession and high unemployment in Britain since 1979 is closely linked to this decline.

There have also been moves towards creating fewer and therefore bigger unions. For example the Transport and General Workers' Union now has a membership of 1.4 million.

Almost 40 per cent of all trade union members are **non-manual** or white-collar workers. The white-collar unions are not only the fastest growing trade unions today they are also becoming more militant or aggressive in defending their members' rights. An example of this is the way in which the teachers' unions organised their strike during 1986.

Professional associations

Q Which trade union do doctors or solicitors belong to? □

The answer to this question is that doctors and solicitors do not belong to any trade union. Instead they join **professional associations.** For example doctors belong to the British Medical Association and solicitors and lawyers to the Law Society.

These professional associations are different from trade unions in certain respects: they **recommend** their own rates of **pay**, **hours** and **conditions** of work. They also have their own **code of ethics** and can discipline any member who disobeys this code of behaviour. For example, professional associations can strike-off a doctor, or debar a lawyer for any misconduct and this would then prevent them from working or practising within their profession.

Q Do you know of any trade union who disciplines its members in this way? □

Some professional associations also control the **standards** of work and restrict the numbers of people admitted into the profession. Often they do this by demanding high standards of educational qualifications and long periods of training. For example, if the requirement to become an accountant is for a person to have a degree and to study for professional exams for several years, then only a few people can hope to become accountants.

Q Do you know of any trade union that also restricts the entry to its ranks by imposing a long period of training?

DISCUSS

Critical sociologists would say that the reason why these professions control and restrict the number of people entering the profession, is so that they can demand higher rates of pay. Do you agree? ☐

DISCUSS

No one can join a profession unless accepted by its particular professional body or association. Are there any jobs where you have to belong to a particular union before you are allowed to start work? Are there any trade unions who actually decide whether to accept a member or not? Consider the actor's union, Equity, for example. What does an actor need to do before earning their Equity card? ☐

RESEARCH IDEA

Do teachers belong to a profession? Interview several teachers about whether they think they belong to a profession. Do teachers discipline their own members for any misconduct? Do teachers' unions control entry to the teaching profession, i.e. say who can become a teacher? Does the NUT have as much power and control as the Law Society, for example? ☐

Employers' associations

Trade unions join together into a Trade Union Congress (TUC), and in the same way, employers join together into an organisation called the CBI or Confederation of British Industry. The CBI is Britain's largest organization for employers. It represents 250 000 firms and offers advice to the Government on a wide range of business, industrial and economic matters.

DISCUSS

Are professional associations really middle-class trade unions?

RESEARCH IDEA

Interview any employer you know and find out if they belong to the CBI and what they feel about its importance and role in the economy. ☐

UNIT 6 — THE FUTURE OF WORK – CHANGE AND UNEMPLOYMENT

Changes in work patterns in Britain

Today, non-manual or white-collar workers represent 62 per cent of all employees and so outnumber blue-collar workers. This change towards the service industries and a non-manual type of society, discussed in Unit 3, is not only the fundamental change taking place in the British work place at present. There are now new ways of working (and not working) that could lead to different patterns of employment for many more people in the future.

1 Self-employment Since 1979, there has been a 32 per cent increase in the number of self-employed people in Britain and in 1984, the total reached 2.5 million. One in ten people are actually self-employed and it is becoming more popular nowadays for women and young people to be self-employed.

Q Why do you think it is becoming more popular for women and young people to be self-employed? What advantages are there is working for yourself? What sort of help can a person get, e.g. from the government in order to set up their business?

2 Part-time working At present one in five of the British work-force work part-time and the figure is expected to reach one in four by 1990. In fact the number of people working part time has actually *doubled* in the past 20 years and is now around 4.5 million. Two out of three of these part-timers are women.

Q Why are the majority of part-time workers female? □

DISCUSS

What are the disadvantages of part-time working? Consider holidays, sickness benefit and pension schemes.

3 Flexi-Working This new working pattern includes shorter working weeks and flexible working hours, where the workers can choose whether to start at an earlier time and therefore finish earlier, or vice-versa. According to the Department of Employment's statistics, flexi-working is on the increase.

DISCUSS

Why should flexi-working be a good idea for many women, men and their families? Why is flexi-working impossible in some occupations? □

4 Home-working There has been a large increase in home-working recently, both in the telecommuting professionals, as discussed in this Module, and also by semi- and unskilled workers doing factory work at home. In Britain there are now 1.7 million home-workers, which represents 7 per cent of the work-force; whereas in the US the figure is more than 10 per cent with 240 companies running homework schemes.

BRAINSTORM

Make lists of the advantages and disadvantages of home-working for the employee *and* the employer. □

Q Why is it mainly females who do unskilled home-working where the pay can be as low as 40 pence an hour?

5 Temporary workers Many jobs for young people and the long-term unemployed are provided at present by the Government's Training Agency and its Youth Training and Employment Training schemes. These jobs are temporary, lasting for one year or less and do not necessarily lead to permanent employment. Temporary work includes seasonal work, such as Post Office workers at Christmas and building-site work, where a building subcontractor employs people on a short or temporary contract and then lays the worker off when the work is finished or the weather is too bad for outdoor working.

Changes in employment 1951–1981 (thousands)

	Inner cities	Outer cities	Smaller cities and larger towns	Small towns and rural areas	Great Britain
Manufacturing					
1951–1961	−143	+84	−21	+453	+374
1961–1971	−428	−217	−93	+489	−255
1971–1981	−447	−480	−311	−717	−1929
Private services					
1951–1961	+192	−110	+128	+514	+944
1961–1971	−297	+92	−7	+535	+318
1971–1981	−105	+170	+91	+805	+958
Public services					
1951–1961	+13	+54	+38	+200	+302
1961–1971	+25	+170	+110	+502	+807
1971–1981	−78	+102	+53	+456	+488
Total employment					
1951–1961	+43	+231	+140	+1060	+1490
1961–1971	−643	+19	+54	+1022	+320
1971–1981	−538	−236	−150	+404	−590

Source: Economic and Social Research Council, 1981

Q Give one example of a private service.

Give one example of a public service.

Which employment sector shows the greatest rise in the period 1971 to 1981?

During the period 1971 to 1981 what was the overall trend in employment?

Two researchers, *Nick Bosanquet* and *John Atkinson* suggest that there is a two-tier job system in Britain, and that this is likely to become more common in the future. The diagram below illustrates this.

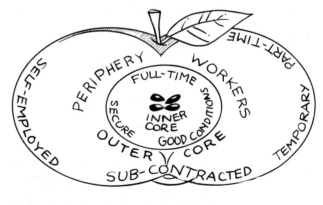

TASK

Bosanquet and Atkinson argue that the periphery workers are less secure than the inner-core workers. Explain why this is the case. ☐

Unemployment

In the mid 1980s unemployment in Britain reached record levels. This was due at least in part to automation and deskilling. It makes some people question their basic attitudes towards work and its importance in society and their lives. For example, should schools still socialise pupils into the **work ethic** and prepare them to be good workers in society when there may not be a job for them to do? Should people be classified according to their occupation, as in the Registrar General's Classification, when through no fault of their own there is not a job for them to do?

Q What social class are the unemployed in?

In future it may even become necessary to ration work, whereas in the past holidays or free time were rationed.

This turnabout will mean a complete change of attitude for most people towards work and towards the unemployed. Some politicians, who still appear to link unemployment with scrounging and immorality and who believe that unemployment benefit or social security payments should be as low as possible will also be forced to think again.

TASK

What is the weekly rate for unemployment benefit? How is this amount usually spent? Work out a typical weekly budget for someone on the dole to cover rent, rates, food, clothing, transport, etc. Is the amount the unemployed receive enough? Should people only have the bare essentials if they are unemployed? □

The effects of unemployment on a person's self-confidence and personality can be severely damaging. This is because work is such an important part of everyone's life, giving them status, satisfaction, purpose and a means of earning a living and supporting a family, as we discussed in Unit 00. When work is taken away from someone it has far reaching effects on that person and their family.

DISCUSS

Using the article on Arthur in *EastEnders* as a source, discuss and describe the effects of unemployment on the individual and on the relationships within the family. Why might unemployed people lose self-esteem and believe that others despise them? □

MILLIONS WHO SHARE TRAGEDY OF ARTHUR

THE anguish of jobless Arthur has been watched, and felt, by EastEnders fans. We have seen him sink from a hardworking, cheerful Cockney family man to the depths of despair.

Seldom shaving, scarcely able to get dressed, he no longer even wants to communicate with the outside world.

Solid, reliable Arthur, played by actor Bill Treacher, has stolen from his friends, staged a burglary at his own home and finally, when he could take no more, cracked up completely on Christmas Day.

When he fell to his knees whimpering in his little front room after wrecking the Christmas tree and smashing everything he once held dear, it was the end of a long painful road.

Filming the scene moved actor Bill to tears.

"I get hundreds of letters from people unemployed like Arthur. I went home and wept," he said.

Arthur's breakdown started when he, as tens of thousands have in real life, lost his job as a skilled factory worker.

Arthur is a proud man and being out of work came as a bitter blow.

JUST as it does to the thousands of real-life Arthurs who are forced on the dole in their 40s with little hope of finding another job.

Again and again — like countless others — Arthur tried to get another job.

His efforts were in vain.

This loss of income and self esteem could not have come at a worse time.

Arthur and wife Pauline, with two teenage children, had a late baby. Their only daughter Michelle had a baby of her own then decided to get married.

Arthur was determined to give Michelle a dream wedding. But he didn't have the cash.

That's when honour to his family took over and he stole from his Christmas Club.

It was the little things that gnawed away at Arthur's pride. Like not being able to stand his round in the local pub, the Queen Vic.

All he had left was his allotment. And there he retreated from the real world more and more.

A spokesman for Charter for Jobs — a campaigning organisation trying to bring down unemployment — said: "I think EastEnders has portrayed Arthur and the problems of unemployment brilliantly.

"It has shown what it really means to be rejected, to be under your family's feet all day.

"I think it's probably helped the three million plus other unemployed not feel quite so alone."

Source: *The Sunday Mirror*, January 1987

Whole communities can become **depressed areas** when, due to an economic recession, there is mass unemployment in the industries that supported those communities. For example, the decline of the staple industries in Tyneside i.e. shipbuilding and mining, has produced an unemployment rate of 23 per cent; which means that one in four people are out of work.

BRAINSTORM

Pool ideas on what it would be or is like to live in a depressed area. □

Certain groups are more likely to become unemployed than others. Firstly, **manual** workers are hit by lay-offs, mass sackings and short-time working far more than white-collar workers; indeed a manual worker can still expect to be made redundant several times in their lifetime. Similarly, those in the periphery jobs doing **temporary** or **part-time** work are often the first to be made unemployed; temporary workers often being **young** and part-time workers often being **female**, these are the groups who suffer.

Q   What is being done to help the unemployed school-leaver? □

Part-time workers who are usually female and married, are ineligible to claim unemployment benefit. In 1983, the Conservative Government stopped counting these women as part of the unemployment figure and so the figure of 3 million unemployed in 1986 was really inaccurate. The Government also stopped counting men over sixty years of age and young people on training schemes. The TUC says that there is a job shortage in this country of 4.5 million, and one church action group puts the figure of unemployed at over 9 million!

One other major group likely to be unemployed more than others are the **ethnic minorities**, particularly the Asians and Afro-Caribbeans.

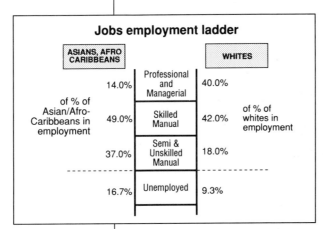

Jobs employment ladder

ASIANS, AFRO CARIBBEANS			WHITES	
14.0%	of % of Asian/Afro-Caribbeans in employment	Professional and Managerial	40.0%	of % of whites in employment
49.0%		Skilled Manual	42.0%	
37.0%		Semi & Unskilled Manual	18.0%	
16.7%		Unemployed	9.3%	

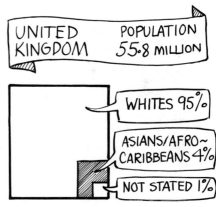

UNITED KINGDOM   POPULATION 55·8 MILLION

WHITES 95%

ASIANS/AFRO~ CARIBBEANS 4%

NOT STATED 1%

T A S K

As the diagrams above reveal, in 1982 16.7 per cent of Asian and Afro-Caribbean people were unemployed in comparison to 9.3 per cent of whites. What percentage of the population are Asian or Afro-Caribbean? Suggest reasons why this group may suffer more unemployment than whites. □

The future of work is uncertain. Will the technological revolution continue to create more unemployment and deskilling? Or will it create new types of higher skilled jobs and different patterns of employment? Has Britain already started to climb out of economic recession?

The answers to the above questions are of course open to debate and discussion and your view is as important as the next economist's. However, whatever the future holds in store for work, at present it is still unarguable that work or the lack of work play a crucial role in everyone's lives.

Unemployment: annual averages

	United Kingdom					
	Registered unemployed (thousands)					Unemployment rate %
	Females				Total males and females	
	Married	Non-married	Total	Males		
1961	—	—	95	251	346	1.5
1966	—	—	80	282	361	1.5
1971	46	81	126	666	792	3.5
1976	116	220	336	1023	1359	5.7
1977	151	263	414	1069	1484	6.2
1978	170	265	435	1040	1475	6.1
1979	181	246	427	964	1390	5.7
1980	236	325	561	1234	1795	7.4
1981	337	452	789	1944	2734	11.4
1982	363	496	859	2126	2985	12.5

Source: adapted from *Social Trends*, 1983

QUESTIONS

1   According to the table above, how many married females were registered as unemployed in 1977?
2   a   According to the table, what was the *overall* trend of unemployment between 1961 and 1982?
    b   According to the table in which *two* years did the unemployment rate go down?
3   Identify *three* ways in which unemployment may affect an individual.
4   Some groups in society are more likely to be unemployed than others. Identify *three* such groups, and explain why they are more likely to be unemployed.
5   Examine the effects of automation on those continuing to work.   □

Source: AEB Sociology GCE, 1985

T A S K | | | | | | |

Finally write an essay on 'The work we do affects many parts of our non-working lives'. Don't forget to include areas, such as family life, leisure, status and so on. Remember to include the effects of alienation and job satisfaction and of course the lack of work, i.e. unemployment.   □

WHERE TO NOW . . .

If you have not already done so, read Module 5 on Social Stratification next. You will also find more about women and work in Module 12 on Gender.

MODULE · 9
RELIGION

NINE

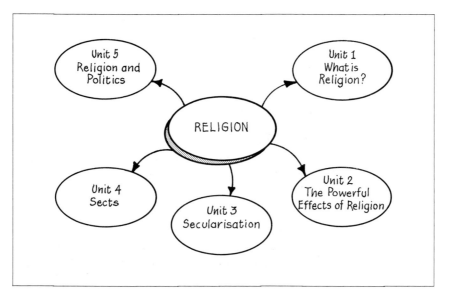

WHAT THIS MODULE IS ABOUT

This module explores the power of religion in society. It examines the view that religion is declining in importance by investigating the secularisation argument, the growth of sects and the relationship between religion and politics.

BY THE END OF THIS MODULE YOU SHOULD BE ABLE TO:

1. Explain what is meant by the term religion.
2. Discuss why religion exists and its importance in people's lives.
3. Explain what is meant by the term secularisation.
4. Discuss the importance of sects.
5. Demonstrate an understanding of the relationship between religion and politics using comparative evidence.
6. Discuss how powerful the influence of religion is in society today.

WHAT IS RELIGION?

There is little agreement among sociologists about what religion is! However, at its simplest **religion** can be described as a belief in the supernatural, and the **supernatural** can be defined as 'things beyond earthly experience'. Sociologists think that supernatural beliefs are present in every society. Some examples of these are shown below.

BRAINSTORM

As a group, try to add to these examples of supernatural belief.

DISCUSS

Is astrology really a religion?

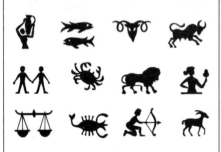

Q Which societies believe in one god?

In preliterate societies, magic and religion are closely connected. For example, in the South Pacific before the Second World War, the Trobrian Islanders always performed several important magic rituals before going out fishing in the sea. The anthropologist, *Malinowski*, noticed that the islanders did not perform any rituals before fishing in the calm lagoon. He argued, therefore, that these magic rituals gave the fishermen a feeling that they were more in control of the dangerous weather and currents at sea.

RESEARCH IDEA

Malinowski was an anthropologist. What is an anthropologist?

DISCUSS

How could you argue that magic and religion share certain similarities? What sorts of practices do they have in common? □

DISCUSS

It could be said that we now live in a scientific society since natural phenomena, such as weather, can be explained and predicted. Do you think this means that magic is no longer needed by people? Can you think of any superstitious rituals that still exist?
Do you think there is a real difference between magic and religion? If so, what is it? □

Why does religion exist?

Sometimes people are faced with experiences which they cannot explain. For example, when good fortune arrives or death comes close to them. Sociologists argue that in order to explain or to accept these events, people have developed supernatural belief systems or **religions.**

DISCUSS

This sociological view that *people* develop religions themselves is perhaps different from your own view of religion. What differences are there in the two views? Where did you learn about religion – was it from your family, school or church? □

These belief systems not only help to explain the inexplicable, but also provide a ready made set of rules or **moral code of behaviour** for people to follow. In following these rules, the believers feel united. They are part of a **community** or body of people who all believe in the same ideas and who behave in much the same way.

For example, in 1978 over 900 people living in a religious community in Guyana, called the People's Temple apparently committed suicide by drinking fruit juice mixed with cyanide. They shared the same beliefs and wanted to prove their faith to the outside world. As a result, when their community and its leader came under attack, they all decided to die together.

TASK

Consider other examples of people who are united in religious communities and who all follow the same code of behaviour. Your examples will probably be less extreme than the People's Temple. You may think of the Orthodox Jews, for example, who are easily identified as belonging to one religious community by their black dress, bearded appearances and black hats. Think of other religious groups that you know of. Describe their 'code of behaviour', i.e. how they dress, act, worship, etc. Try starting with the Salvation Army or the Sikh religion. □

The evolution of religion

In the earliest forms of religion called **animism** and **naturism** people attempted to make sense of death, dreams, visions, the power of thunder, lightning, wind and the sun, etc, by inventing the idea of spirits. In **animism**, the belief was held that the soul or the spirit left the body during dreams and permanently at death. In **naturism**, the power of the wind became the spirit of the wind, the power of the sun became the spirit of the sun, etc.

In these ways, people could explain death and the terrors and marvels they faced in life, in terms of the supernatural spirit world. People organised ceremonies, rituals and prayers so as to please the spirits. The early cave paintings show how ancient people worshipped the spirit of the wind and the spirit of the sun.

RESEARCH IDEA

Investigate one of these early religions. For example, the Aztecs. Discover what rituals and ceremonies they practised. Write down something about them and be prepared to tell the rest of the group about your research findings. □

THE POWERFUL EFFECTS OF RELIGION

Q Do you think Durkheim's description is true of British society?

Q Do you know of any society where *total* social unity exists?

The function of religion

One sociologist who believed that religion does unite people together into a 'single moral community' is *Emile Durkheim*. He described religion as being like 'moral glue', helping to keep people and society stuck together living in harmony, without any real conflict or divisions.

This is a **functionalist** view which sees religion as being the centre or basis of social life, helping people to understand their world. Religion is seen as good for society. It has a positive function and helps society to run smoothly. It also provides a set of guidelines for people to follow in their daily lives and so helps society to run efficiently.

If everyone followed the same set of rules or religion, then everybody would be united and would agree on what is 'right' or 'wrong', 'good' or 'bad' behaviour. Social order, social solidarity and social unity would prevail.

TASK

Working in small groups, take one particular religion and see how it provides the rules or codes which guide the behaviour of those who believe in that religion.

You could consider, for example, the Christian religion and in particular the Church of England denomination.

Within the Church of England, the Bible is the Holy Book which provides the standards or rules for Christians to live by.

In your group, examine the parables in the New Testament; for example, the Good Samaritan (*Luke*: Chapter 10, verses 30–35). In this parable, you can see how the story provides a code of behaviour for people to follow.

The parable of the Good Samaritan stresses that 'helping your neighbour' is desirable for good behaviour. Durkheim showed that if everyone followed this rule and helped their neighbour no matter whether they were enemies or not, then there would be no conflict or trouble in society.

This is the way that Durkheim looked at religion. He saw how sharing the same beliefs creates **consensus** or agreement in society.

Now, consider other parables and stories from the Bible, such as The Prodigal Son. Discuss the code of behaviour that each one is suggesting to the reader, listener or believer. Be prepared to explain your theories or ideas to other groups. □

RESEARCH IDEA

How is Durkheim's interpretation of the Good Samaritan different from that a Christian would give?

Interview a practising Christian to find out, e.g. a local vicar.

THOU SHALT HAVE
NO OTHER GODS
BEFORE ME.

THOU SHALT NOT
WORSHIP FALSE
GODS.

THOU SHALT NOT MISUSE
THE NAME OF THE
LORD YOUR GOD.

REMEMBER THE
SABBATH DAY BY
KEEPING IT HOLY.

HONOUR YOUR FATHER
AND MOTHER.

THOU SHALT NOT
MURDER.

THOU SHALT NOT
COMMIT ADULTERY.

THOU SHALT NOT
STEAL.

THOU SHALT NOT
GIVE FALSE TESTIMONY
AGAINST YOUR
NEIGHBOUR.

THOU SHALT NOT
COVET YOUR
NEIGHBOUR'S HOUSE
OR WIFE.

Sociologists like Durkheim and **Talcott Parsons** have not only considered the way in which parables help to create social unity, but have also examined the Ten Commandments. Here you can see quite clearly the 'rules' laid down in the Bible for Christians to live by.

Consider the commandment: 'Thou shalt not kill'. You can see how this *religious* rule is a most important rule for everyone in *society*, whether they are Christian or not. This religious commandment adds weight to the civil law for murder. Sociologists call the punishments or rewards incurred by breaking or keeping either law **sanctions**, ie in this case the fear of going to hell or long-term imprisonment.

DISCUSS

Consider each Commandment and see if there is a civil law that matches it. What are the sanctions for both obeying and disobeying each particular religious law? What are the sanctions against it in the civil law? □

The assignment above concentrates on one religion, i.e. the Christian religion, and the way that the beliefs and practices, communicated through the Bible, help to maintain a stable ordered society. You could, instead, consider any of the religions of the world, such as the Islamic religion, and examine the writings of the Koran in the same way as those of the Bible.

RESEARCH IDEA

Try to find our more about the Islamic or Muslim religion and its rules or moral codes. You could also find out more about the caste system that is part of Hindu culture by referring to Module 5, page 71. □

T A S K

You should now be able to answer the question 'What are the main functions of religion?' Alternatively answer the following question: Durkheim revealed that religion performs several important functions in society. The most important being in holding society together, like moral glue. In what ways does religion help to keep society together? □

T A S K

Write a short essay in response to the following question. 'Marxists see religion as a form of *social control*, keeping the working class in their place as a docile work-force. How does religion perform this role?'

RESEARCH IDEA

Many industrial entrepreneurs of the Eighteenth and Nineteenth centuries were religious people, often Protestants. Attempt to find out the names and a little of the background of local industrialists who started factories in your area. You could start to gain your data by interviewing staff in the History department at school, or by doing some research in the local history section of your library. Were these factory owners religious? Which church did they attend?

Q Why did the Calvinists have the capital to invest in industry?

Religion as a social control

Although agreeing with Durkheim that religion is an important and powerful force in society, other writers such as Karl Marx disagree about the nature and effects of religion.

Rather than seeing the beneficial or functional way in which religion acts in society, Marx had a very critical view and described the harmful way in which religion acts like a drug. He called it 'the opiate of the people', because like a drug, religion prevents the oppressed and poor workers from rising in revolt against the ruling class.

Unlike Durkheim therefore **Karl Marx** did not see religion as a good influence in society. He viewed it instead as a social control by which the ruling class ensured that there would be no change in the unequal distribution of wealth in a capitalist society.

DISCUSS

The poor of the Nineteenth century, when Marx was writing, were, it is argued, kept in their place by a religion that taught them to accept their 'lot' in life as being God-given. The promise of finding 'treasure in heaven', if they obeyed the rules of their religion, i.e. the Ten Commandments, was often the only source of hope for poor people in Victorian Britain, who had little or no chance of 'finding treasure on earth'. In the Victorian hymn 'All things bright and beautiful' the following verse used to be sung:

The rich man in his castle,
The poor man at his gate,
God made them high and lowly,
And ordered their estate.

The message in this verse is that the people should accept their low position or estate in society as being God-given.

Do you agree with Marxist writers that religion and its accessories could prevent people from trying to create a society where everyone is equal? □

Religion and the rise of capitalism

Another sociologist who wrote about the powerful relationship between religion and society is **Max Weber**. He studied the way in which religion, in particular the Protestant religion, helped to support capitalism.

In his book *The Protestant Ethic and the Spirit of Capitalism*, Weber looked at the role of a strict brand of protestantism, called Calvinism, in bringing about industrialisation. Calvinist beliefs stressed working hard, saving money, achieving success and not engaging in frivolous pursuits. When new mechanical inventions were introduced in the Eighteenth century, the Calvinists were able to buy the new machines for their factories. In time, they built bigger factories and bought even better machines, because they had followed the Calvinist teaching and therefore had the spare *capital* or savings available.

As a result of Calvinist thrift and capital investment Britain became the 'Workshop of the World' and was the first country to industrialise. This industrialisation was thus based on *capitalism* supported by religion. Weber's work, like that of Durkheim and Marx, stresses how religion is an important force in society.

Weber argues that if this spare capital had not been available for investment in the new machines and factories, industrialisation may not have occurred in Britain in the Eighteenth century.

UNIT 3

SECULARISATION

Durkheim, Marx and Weber – three quite different socia[l]
religion as a powerful influence in society, affecting peop[le]
creating an ordered society. Durkheim stressed the power
in creating consensus and *social unity*. Marx stressed the po[wer]
effect of religion, especially on the lives of the poor; and how
socialises them to accept a lowly position in an unequal society [la]st
Weber pointed to the way religion can bring about *social and economic change*.
It must be remembered however, that Durkheim, Marx and Weber were all
writing about religion in the Nineteenth century.

Q   How powerful or influential is religion in our lives today? Is religion
declining in importance? □

Today, it is usually taken for granted that British society is less religious
than it was during the last century. It is believed that religion is gradually
being abandoned by people. Perhaps the number of churches that have
been demolished or converted into shops or housing in towns and cities
might be an indication of this abandonment of religion. The process of
rejecting religion is called **secularisation.**

However, it is difficult to judge just how much *secularisation* is taking place
in society. Just as it has proved problematical to define what religion is; so
too it proves difficult to judge just how religious people are nowadays.

DISCUSS

Go back to the two cartoons at the beginning of the module and discuss each
of them in groups. Do the cartoons provide you with any evidence that
enables you to judge whether the people in them are religious or not? What
sort of evidence do we need in order to decide whether religion is declining
in society. □

Church attendance

Some writers have suggested that church attendance statistics, i.e. counting
the number of people who go to church, would provide evidence about
whether secularisation is taking place in society.

For instance: 'The 1851 *Census of Religion* showed that just under 40 per cent
of the adult population attended church each week. By 1900, this figure had
dropped to 35 per cent; by 1950, it had dropped to 20 per cent and by 1981
on average, only 11 per cent of the population of England and Wales
attended church on Sunday.

TASK

Organise and display this secondary data in a simple bar chart or line graph.
Discuss your results with your group. Do they reveal that religion is
declining in society? □

Certainly, these figures for church attendance are low, and reveal that few
people from the population as a whole go to church. Sociologists suggest
that one reason for such a low percentage attendance is because going to
church has always been a largely middle-class activity.

DISCUSS

Why do you think the middle classes tend to go to church more often than
the working classes? □

This building, once a church, is now a café

TASK

Make sure that you can explain
what is meant by secularisation.

RESEARCH IDEA

Check the results of the 1981
survey. Collect your own data on
church attendance. Take care
how you choose your sample of
adults to survey. See Module 1 on
research methods.

...y do you think that the ...ey may not have been carried ...ut in a reliable manner in 1851? Consider factors, such as road transport at this time.

Q What reasons can you give for the fact that nearly 100 per cent of all funerals take place in either church or chapel?

Q Can you add other possible reasons why these Victorian church attendance statistics are higher than today's?

T A S K

Write a short essay on why more people went to church in Victorian times. In your conclusion, state whether you believe that the higher church attendance *statistics* mean that the Victorians were more religious than people are today.

Source: *Social Trends*, 1982

Statistics are, of course, not always reliable or valid (see Module 1 on research methods) and special care needs to be taken when considering the results of a mid-nineteenth century survey.

Although few people attend church on a Sunday nowadays, nevertheless, there are other times when going to church is very popular. For example, **baptisms** or **christenings** in church are still extremely popular. In fact 90 per cent of all babies are christened. Why do you think this is so?

There has also been a recent rise in the number of **weddings** taking place in church. In 1981, 70 per cent of all weddings were church ceremonies.

Q Where would the other 30 per cent of weddings have taken place? ☐

Funerals are also very popular church ceremonies! In fact, practically all funerals take place in church and are religious ceremonies as opposed to civil ceremonies.

The church attendance statistics in the table below are interesting starting points for discussion. It is obvious that more people attended church on a Sunday, a hundred years ago, than attend today. There are several other reasons why people went to church regularly in Victorian times, apart from their need to carry out their religious beliefs. For example, going to church was more of a habit or tradition in the Victorian era. It provided a social outing for the whole family at a time when entertainments and transport were more limited. Victorian families did not have television, radio, tapes, records, or videos. Perhaps people went to church because of family pressures. It was the 'expected' thing to do, i.e. a **social norm**.

QUESTIONS

Answer the following questions using the information in the table below.

Attendance at Christian churches in England, 1975 and 1979

Attendances of those aged 15 and over	1975	1979	% change
	(thousands)*		1975–1979*
Protestant churches			
Episcopal	1301	1256	− 3.5
Methodist	454	447	− 1.5
Baptist	193	203	+ 5.2
United Reformed and Congregational	150	139	− 7.3
Independent	167	206	+23.4
African and West Indian	55	66	+20.0
Pentecostal and Holiness	78	88	+12.8
Other	122	128	+ 4.9
All Protestant churches	2520	2533	+ 0.5
Roman Catholic	1418	1310	− 7.6
Orthodox	6	7	+16.7
All churches (total)	3945	3850	− 2.4

1 What was the estimated total attendance at Christian churches in both 1975 and in 1979?
2 How had this attendance changed over the period?
3 Study the figures in the table and identify two significant changes in the pattern of church going.
4 Why has attendance at some churches increased and declined at others? Suggest explanations.
5 What is the role of religion in society?
6 Why are church attendance statistics not always a good indicator of how important religion is in society? ☐

Asking about religion

Looking at church attendance statistics alone is not enough to help the sociologist decide whether religion is declining in society or not, i.e. whether secularisation is taking place. It is impossible to judge whether a person is religious merely by counting the number of times they go to church. Another method of gaining this information might be to ask people if they are religious or not!

Many people in society feel that they are religious, that is, they believe there is a god or supernatural being, even though they do not belong to a church or worship publicly. Some people prefer 'private worship' at home, even at work, or the occasional prayer in times of need. These people who think of themselves as being religious, but who hardly ever take part in any church activities, do not appear in any church attendance statistics.

One survey in 1965, suggested that the number of people who believe in a god and who will call themselves Christians could be as high as 85 per cent to 90 per cent of the British population.

DISCUSS

From your *own* small-scale survey conducted in the task above, do you think these research findings are likely to be accurate? □

David Martin, a sociologist concerned with religion, points out that many people think that being a Christian is about the same as being respectable.

It is clear that there are considerable problems over evidence when examining whether religion is in decline in Britain today.
Looking at church attendance statistics does not necessarily indicate whether people were more religious in the Victorian era, since there could have been several motives for going to church, apart from religious ones.

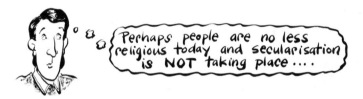

Similarly, although birth, marriage and death ceremonies in church are very popular today, this need not indicate that people are religious at all. These ceremonies might simply be a matter of tradition.

Judging just how religious a person or society is proves difficult, because 'being religious' means different things to almost every individual.

The next unit on the growth of religious sects continues this discussion on the importance of religion in society and reveals how complex this issue is.

SECTS

One development in religion that might indicate that secularisation is not taking place and that religion is still a vitally important part of people's lives, is the way in which **sects** have become more popular in recent years.

One example of such a *sect* would be 'The Exclusive Brethren'. People who join this sect believe that only they follow the true path to salvation. They keep themselves apart from society as much as possible and have very strict rules that forbid going to discos or to the cinema and any other entertainments outside family life and the sect.

Q   In which countries is the Brethren to be found? □

There are many other sects, such as the Jehovah's Witnesses, the Moonies, the Black Muslims and the Church of Jesus Christ of Latter Day Saints (the Mormons), etc. All of these sects have strict rules about who can join the group and they each believe that their behaviour or moral code is the only way to find salvation.

Q   What is salvation? Try brainstorming this idea as a group. □

These strict rules about entry to the group, and the belief that they have found the true way to heaven, are what distinguishes a sect from a **denomination**. For example, the Methodists have 'open' membership. Anyone can join, and they also accept that they are just *one* branch of the Christian church.

T A S K

Give one example of each of these.

sect

denomination

church

Q   What are the two main differences between a sect and a denomination? □

A sect can be small, such as the Plymouth Brethren, but they can also be large, such as the Jehovah's Witnesses with over 70 000 members. Jehovah's believe that at Armageddon only the saved will inherit the Kingdom of God. The Church of the Latter Day Saints or Mormons are another example of a large sect. The Mormons originally cut themselves off from the rest of America by migrating to Utah and believe that America is the home of the New Millenium or New World.

RESEARCH IDEA

Using your library or other resources, investigate terms, such as Armageddon and Millenium. Research into one particular sect or religion in depth. Collect as much information as possible on its beliefs and practices. Try to interview a member of the religion you have chosen to study. □

Mormonism has been described as the religion of young men. Why? Find out more about the roles of men and women in the Mormon religion.

DISCUSS

Bryan Wilson has attempted to classify sects into particular *types*, as you can see from the table below.

TYPOLOGY OF SECT

1. **Conversionist**	Change the self; salvation	Early Methodist; Holiness; Salvation Army; Pentecostal
2. **Revolutionist**	Overthrow the world (Armageddon)	Jehovah's Witnesses, Christaoeionians; Early 7th Day Adv.
3. **Introversionist**	Withdrawal from the world	18th cent. Quakers; Exclusive Brethren
4. **Manipulationist**	Special teaching to transcend the world	Christian Science: New Thought Movement
5. **Thaumaturigal**	Wonder-working cult (giving sp. dispensation from op. of evil)	Spiritualists: "Possession" Cults
6. **Reformist**	Change the world piecemeal	20th cent. Quakers.
7. **Utopian**	Rebuild society; communistic communities	Tolstoytans

Q Where do you think Mormons and Moonies fit in to Bryan Wilson's typology of sects?

Source: *Fundamentals of Sociology* by P McNeill & C Townley, 1981

Mormonism is the religion of young men. That it also should be governed by an old man of 96 is merely the introduction to its paradoxes; at any rate, its most usual countenance is a young man's. Joseph Smith, when the angel first appeared to him, was only 14. From tablets to which the angels directed him, he translated chronicles of immigration by Holy Land peoples to ancient America; he then was still only in his teens and, indeed, parts of the Book of Mormon seem touched with adolescence. Nor could anyone but an enraptured young man have convinced so many, as Smith did, that a lost prophet named Mormon now spoke through him; nor could Smith's successors have forced his Church to its Zion, through burning and pestilence, without young hearts and lungs as well as the Lord on their side.

A century and a half later, Mormonism has still a young man's ambition: to convert the whole world. Fast. Every day, somewhere, a new chapel is dedicated. Smith no sooner found adherents than he scattered them as missionaries. There is no professional clergy. Every Mormon boy is eligible to be ordained at 12, in a somewhat sinister pressing-down of hands, and, at 19, to be flung out in the steps of those first Apostles. He serves in a mission for two years.

...A Mormon chapel may arise in the wealthiest, most susceptible neighbourhood — it is still called a 'stake', just a foothold, with armies of darkness beaten back all around. Mormonism is a man's life – a white man's life. Women, as well as Negroes, are excluded from the priesthood, although they may preach or work in the relief organisations, one of which Brigham Young founded to occupy his own polygamously-acquired daughters. For devout Mormon females, however, the emphasis remains on needlepoint and production of the great numbers of children for which the Church was always held in awe. © Times Newspapers Ltd, 1971

Read the description of the Oneida Community given below and decide what type of sect the Oneida is.

The Oneida community was . . . founded in 1848 in New York State, by a charismatic preacher, John Humphrey-Noyes.
He taught that it was possible to achieve a perfect Christian life on earth if people loved each other and shared their worldly possessions. The life of Oneida was designed to promote common bonds, while closing the community off from the corrupting influence of the outside world.

Group marriage was practised. Any adult could have sexual relations with any other adult. Sexual approaches were made through a third party, often an older woman, and such an advance could be declined without fuss. A strong distinction was drawn between sexual activity for recreation and sexual activity for reproduction. Oneida also developed a eugenically based programme of controlled breeding, with only selected adults being chosen as suitable for parenthood.

The children who were born into the community were brought up in nursery run by the women. Parents did see their children, but there was deliberate effort to play down these strong bonds of affection. All adults were encouraged to treat all children as if they were their own.

DISCUSS

In what ways is the Oneida family form different from the nuclear family in Britain? What do you feel about the fact that, 'any adult could have sexual relations with any other adult'. Also, discuss whether it is a good idea for, 'all adults ... to treat all children as if they were their own'. Do you think it would work in practice? □

DISCUSS

What does the Black Muslim religion give to these Black Americans. Why do you think they join this sect?

RESEARCH IDEA

The world champion boxer Cassius Clay changed his name to Mohammed Ali. Try to discover why he did this.

Weber argues that sects grow up where people feel deprived or on the edge of society. An example of this could be the Black Muslim Sect in America, whose followers tend to be poor unemployed black Americans who have a *negative self image* (for more on this see Module 6, Unit 1). The Black Muslim sect believe that Blacks are by nature 'divine' and that Whites are inferior and evil by nature. They prophecy that Whites and their religion will be destroyed in the year 2000 and that Blacks will rule the New World. When black people join the sect, they replace their slave name, given by Western Culture, with a muslim name and they are told, 'You are not a negro from this day on. You are now a Muslim. You are now free'.

Despite arguments from some writers that the growth in the number of sects reveals that religion is still an important part of people's lives, other writers suggest the opposite is true. They argue that because society is becoming less religious, people feel they need to join together in small-knit communities on the margins of society, away from the disbelievers in the main body of society. They therefore use the increased number of sects as evidence that secularisation *is* taking place. According to them, the sect is like a 'refuge' where those who believe in the supernatural can believe 'in peace'.

DISCUSS

The statement that 'the growth in the number of sects indicates that secularisation is taking place in Britain'. Argue both for and against the statement.

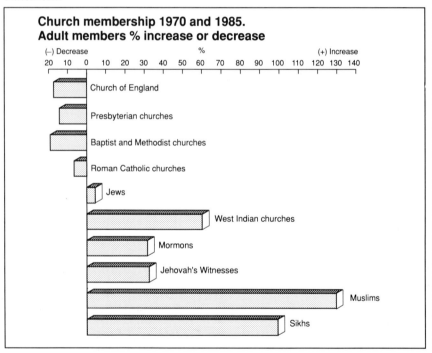

Church membership 1970 and 1985. Adult members % increase or decrease

Source: Social Trends, 1987

QUESTIONS

You should now be able to attempt the examination questions below.

1 Which religious group shows the biggest growth in membership.
2 Why do you think this religious group has grown in Britain?
3 What is a religious sect?
4 Give two examples of sects from the chart.
5 Why do people join sects?
6 Give a short definition of secularisation.
7 **a** 'Is secularisation taking place in society today?' Write a short essay giving arguments both for and against this view.
   b 'Is religion a powerful influence in society today?' Give arguments for and against this statement in your answer. □

UNIT 5 | RELIGION AND POLITICS

In Britain, the Church of England can be said to have considerable political power. It is still an extremely wealthy church and owns a great deal of land and property in the country. It is also closely connected with the government, as its Bishops sit in the House of Lords and influence political decisions.

RESEARCH IDEA

Investigate the House of Lords. Who is allowed to sit there. What powers do they have? □

There are some writers, however, who claim that religion does not have much political or decision-making power over people's lives. They reveal how the authority of the church has declined. For example, they point to the fact that a hundred years ago, the Christian religion was a central part of the school curriculum, through the 3 Rs (see Module 7 on Education, page 124). Although religion is still a compulsory subject in schools today, teachers no longer instruct pupils solely in *Christian* beliefs as they used to, but instead teach pupils about the *world religions* and show that Christianity is but *one* of several religions.

DISCUSS

Which method of teaching is fairer to instruct a pupil in a particular set of religious beliefs, e.g. Christianity, *or* to teach in comparative way about important world religions? Explain your reasons to the group. □

Q How is religion taught in your school? □

RESEARCH IDEA

Identify these religious symbols or images. Which religion does each belong to? □

In America, religion can be seen to be very powerful by the support it gives to the government and its close relationship to the 'American way of life'. Both Christianity and Judaism, the major religions of the USA, support the American values of achievement, free enterprise and motivation.

Many past presidents of the USA have been religious men. Ronald Reagan, for example, is a born-again Christian, who has fundamentalist beliefs. He is closely supported by a religious pressure group called the 'Moral Majority', who literally guaranteed Mr Reagan millions of votes in Presidential elections.

It is a fact that 40 per cent of all Americans go to church regularly.

DISCUSS

Why do you think more Americans go to church than British people. □

One sociologist, named *Herberg*, believes that these high church attendance statistics do *not* mean that Americans are particularly religious. He suggests that Americans go to church for a number of reasons that are not necessarily connected with believing in God. For example, it might be just a way of 'belonging' or proving that they are 'true Americans'.

BRAINSTORM

What is meant by a 'true American'? □

America is not the only country where fundamentalist religious beliefs are popular. In Iran, there has been a revolution based on a revival of fundamentalist Islamic beliefs. The Shah of Iran was overthrown and the Ayatollah Khomeini, a religious leader, was brought to power. There have been many deep changes in Iranian society since the revolution and the Islamic religion is a very powerful political force in the land affecting everyone's lives. For example, criminals are now treated very severely and the role of women has changed considerably.

The Ayatollah Khomeini in Iran was described as a **charistmatic leader**. He was old, but when he spoke, millions listened to his every world. He had charismatic religious authority. There are or have been other charismatic religious leaders or figures with much authority or power, Jesus, for example.

T A S K

Describe the charisma or power that Jesus had over people who listened to him. Give examples of charismatic leaders, both religious and political. □

Relationships between religion and politics can be seen in most countries of the world; but such relationships vary.

Attempt to find out why the Socialist Party and the Catholic Church in France are often in conflict with one another.

Lech Walesa addressing a meeting of Solidarity in Warsaw

DISCUSS

What degree of political power do the vicars and priests in Britain have? How much status does a vicar have in our society? Can the church affect or change politcal decisions made by the British Government?

Source: Christian Aid

In France, the relationship between the Socialist political party and the Catholic Church is often antagonistic. In Nazi Germany the Jehovah's Witnesses refused to accept the Fascist ideology and suffered as a result in the concentration camps.

In South Africa, the Christian church is heavily involved with political parties, such as the United Democratic Front (UDF)who are fighting against apartheid and campaigning for more equality for the Blacks. On the other hand, part of the Dutch Reform church, another Christian denomination, supports the Afrikaaner led government who pursue harsh racist policies which causes great suffering and hardships to the Black, Coloured and Asian people in South Africa.

In Poland, the Catholic Church has long been an outspoken critic of marxist ideology. It has supported rebellions against the government in the past and supports 'Solidarity', the modern trade union movement. The relationship between the Catholic Church and Communist state power is often difficult. Since most Poles are Catholic and nearly 80 per cent are church goers, the Roman Catholic Church has considerable power and influence over the people.

RESEARCH IDEA

Monseigneur Bruce Kent is not only a religious leader, but was also a leader of a political pressure group known as CND. Investigate what CND stands for, its aims and practices. Consider the similarities and differences between the beliefs and practices of this political pressure group and the Christian religion. ☐

TASK

Study this poster. Who has produced it? Which religion does Bishop Desmond Tutu belong to? What is his nationality? Why do you think he is puzzled? What are his views about religion and politics and why does he hold these views? ☐

'I am puzzled about which Bible people are reading when they suggest religion and politics don't mix.'
Bishop Desmond Tutu

Christian Aid

RESEARCH IDEA

Investigate other countries and discover the role of and relationship between politics and religion in a particular country. Look at India, for example, and one of the Latin American countries. ☐

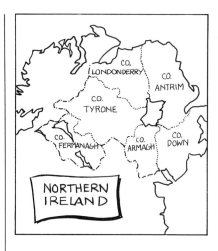

NORTHERN IRELAND

Another example of the often close relationship between religion and politics can be seen in *Northern Ireland*.

'N. Ireland is a small community of 1.5 million people, consisting of six counties. Of these one and a half million, a third are *Catholic* and two thirds are *Protestant*. The protestant two-thirds represent a quarter of the total population of Ireland.'

QUESTIONS

1 What is the total population of Northern Ireland?
2 How many people are Catholics?
3 How many people are Protestants?
4 What percentage of people in Ireland as a whole are Protestant?
5 What percentage of people in Ireland as a whole are Catholic? □

The 'struggle' in Northern Ireland between Catholics and Protestants has continued on and off since the Seventeenth century. It started when English and Scottish Protestants settled in Ireland causing a Catholic uprising which Cromwell brutally put down. In 1921, Ireland was divided in two and Northern Ireland set up as a separate state of six counties governed by Britain. A civil war followed this separation which the Unionists won, i.e. those wishing to remain united with Britain.

From 1967, there have been many civil rights marches and protests for the Catholics who, it is claimed, suffer from political and social discrimination in the Province. There have also been many sectarian killings or murders on one side or the other. During this period the Catholic denomination has been associated with the Nationalist movement, who are opposed to the British presence in Ireland and who want a united Ireland. Similarly the Protestants have become closely associated with the Unionist view to continue union with Britain.

In Northern Ireland no one can escape from the Catholic or Protestant label. Religion appears to affect every aspect of a person's life, including the area they live in, the school their children attend, where they can or cannot get a job and even the pub they drink in. Religion in Northern Ireland is an extremely powerful force in the country and has close connections with political movements.

DISCUSS

Why do you think the Nationalists want a united Ireland? Why do the Unionists want to continue close links with Britain? □

RESEARCH IDEA

Find out as much as you can about the conflict in Northern Ireland. Read and collect as many media reports as you can about it. Interview parents, teachers, friends about their views of the struggle in Northern Ireland. Ask them why the Protestant and Catholic communities are on opposite sides. Is the struggle really a political and economic conflict? What part does religion really play? □

WHERE TO NOW

Research methods or ways of finding out about religion in society have formed an important part of this module. You can learn more about the advantages and disadvantages of surveys, interviews, observation and experimental techniques in Module 1 on research methods.

TASK

It seems that religion still has great power today when we consider the fact that many wars are fought in the name of religion; that religious musicals and films are very popular, and that religion is still a compulsory part of the school curriculum. But is this really true? Write an essay or organise a debate giving both sides of the argument concerning whether religion is a powerful force in society today? □

MODULE · 10

POPULATION

T E N

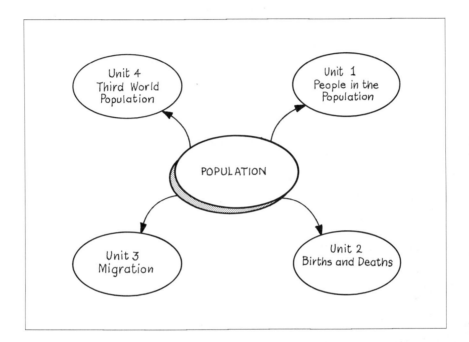

WHAT THIS MODULE IS ABOUT

Demography is part of the study of population and in particular concerns the size and structure of the population. Birth and death are two important aspects of population. Other factors include the age and sex distribution of the population, immigration, emigration and world population issues. This module studies the ways in which these factors affect everyone's life. The study of population isn't, therefore, primarily concerned with facts and figures, but with some of their longer term effects on everyday life, including education, social services, pensions, employment, housing and other issues.

BY THE END OF THIS MODULE YOU SHOULD BE ABLE TO:

1 Explain the main factors influencing population change over the past hundred years, and be able to interpret graphs and figures relating to this.
2 Discuss the links between population size and growth and age structure.
3 Describe the effects of change in population on family life, housing, education, health and welfare.
4 Identify the main patterns of migration, including patterns of immigration and emigration.
5 Outline some of the main differences in population between affluent and developing countries.
6 Understand and explain basic terms, such as rate, ratio, mortality, fertility, migration.

UNIT 1

PEOPLE IN THE POPULATION

No one is, of course, just a number or statistic. We are all individuals who interact with others in groups. As previous modules in this book demonstrate, a person's age, where they live and went to school, their gender, race and class all have a bearing on their **life chances**. The same issues are also the subject of population studies. Take, for example, the **sex structure** of the population, i.e. the ratio between men and women in society, which has important consequences for all of us.

The sex structure of the population

This is not simply a matter of calculating the obvious, i.e. the number of women and men there are to go round! Clearly the number of women of child-bearing age in the population, taken to be those aged between 14 and 44, will affect the number of births nationally. Sociologists refer to this as the **fertility rate**. However, there is also the question of the 'balance between the sexes'; an imbalance in the number of men and women in society, may affect the balance of power between the sexes. The statistics indicate, for example, that there are more women in the population and that they live longer than men. There is, however, more to the balance of power than that! Consider the following article from *New Society*.

Official information regarding the population of Britain as a whole is derived from the following sources:
– The Census.
– The Registrar General's Returns.
– The General Household Survey.
– Home Office Migration Statistics.
– The Department of Employment (Employment Statistics).
– The Department of Education and Science (Education Statistics).

Figures drawn from these sources are considered in this and other Modules of this book.

Balance of the sexes

Ever since the first census in 1851, our women have outnumbered our men. Then, there were only 960 men for every 1,000 women. But the imbalance was to get worse: by 1921, after the carnage of world war one, there were only 921 males left for every 1,000 females.

Since then, the men have started to catch up. According to the Office of Population Censuses and Surveys, the 1986 ratio—951 men to every 1,000 women—is the highest since 1851 ("The changing balance of the sexes in England and Wales, 1851-2001," Population Trends 46, HMSO, £5). By 2001, the OPCS expects there to be 968 men for every 1,000 women.

What's going on? Every year, more boys are born than girls—1,054 of them per 1,000 girls in 1985. But they tended more often to die in childhood. Thereafter, emigration and war took a further disproportionate toll of the male of the species. In the early 1900s,

women outnumbered men in every age group from 25 upwards.

Things have changed, thanks to lower infant mortality and the long peace. The contours of our population now look very different. Today, *men* are in the majority among all age groups under 55. Only thereafter, because women live longer and because more men were killed in the second world war, does the balance change. In 1981, there were only 304 men for every 1,000 women aged 85 and over.

Will more men mean a more male-dominated society? It seems unlikely that in this field mere predominance in numbers will be the settling factor; more depends on how much power each sex has. So matters might turn out precisely the opposite, with women, in short supply, able to dictate the terms of social relations. That is, unless AIDS or conventional war once more cuts off males in their prime, and tips the balance of the sexes back where it came from. ■

New Society, December 1986

A question which arises from this article is, why do women live longer than men? Women are described as both the 'gentler sex' and as the 'hardier of the species'. The fact is that in all Western Societies women have a lower death rate than men. According to one sociologist the gap between male and female death rates has been linked to three main diseases which kill more men than women; heart disease, lung cancer and bronchitis or lung disease.

Q What do you understand by the phrase 'balance between the sexes'? What are the main factors which affect the balance between the sexes? How might such factors influence the *power* relations between men and women in society?

DISCUSS

Why do you think women live longer than men? What possible explanations can you put forward to explain why this is so? What illnesses do women die of than men don't?

A number of explanations have been put forward to explain sex differences in mortality, i.e. death, although none of them are very satisfactory. One view, for example, suggests the differences are **biological** and **genetic**, i.e. hormone differences, explaining the low rate of heart disease among women. But with women tending to smoke and drink more this may no longer hold true. At one time it was socially acceptable for men to smoke more than women, but is this still the case today?

Women in society are often socialised to be more cautious and to take fewer risks – this may make them safer drivers for instance. It is certainly a view which insurance companies agree with. The statistics show that more men die in road accidents than women. But this may simply reflect the fact that more men drive cars and motorcycles, often as part of their occupations, e.g. salesmen, delivery men, lorry drivers and dispatch riders. For further discussion of such occupational differences, see Module 12 on Gender.

Some researchers argue that mortality and jobs are related, with a predominance of men in dangerous or stressful occupations, such as mining, shipbuilding or stockbroking, steelworking, building and construction, fishing, etc. It is important to recognise that the mortality differences discussed here are **social**, rather than biologically innate or hormonal.

Q   Since most accidents occur in the home, is being a housewife a dangerous occupation?

RESEARCH IDEA

In small groups, discuss and make notes about the types of work men and women do. Find out how types of work are linked with various types of illness and disease. What occupations in your locality might be connected with particular types of illness?

As gender roles become less fixed and women move into occupations traditionally associated with men's roles, namely manual and executive positions, then sex differences in mortality may narrow. Greater awareness about safety at work and the risks of stress, the dangers of smoking and drinking and the importance of diet and exercise may also reduce mortality rates, particularly among men. There is little evidence that this awareness has begun to grow among either women or men. Women, for example, increasingly occupy high-profile, pressurised jobs traditionally associated with men.

The purpose of this introductory unit has been to explain that demography is not just concerned with facts, figures and statistics. Although the demographer's method is to gain information about the size and structure of the population, there is more to it than that. We have considered one key element associated with the sex structure and examined more specifically the 'balance between the sexes' and its social effects on men and women. The units which follow, particularly the next on births and deaths, are linked with the sex structure of the population.

Sociologists and demographers are interested in three basic elements which make up the population size of any society: **births, deaths** and **migration** (which includes immigration, emigration and population movement within a society). As we shall see the 'knock-on effect' of births, deaths and migration have important consequences elsewhere in society.

BIRTHS AND DEATHS

Before looking at the birth rate it is important to say something about the overall size of the population in the UK.

The population in the UK, i.e. England, Northern Ireland, Scotland and Wales is approximately 56 million. Since the so called 'baby boom' (1955 to 1956) the rate of population growth has slowed down. In the period between 1971 and 1983 the real rate of growth has been less than one per cent.

UK Population (000s), 1971 and 1983

	UK	England	Wales	Scotland	N. Ireland
1971	55 515	46 019	2731	5229	1536
1983	56 377	46 846	2731	5150	1573

Source: *Annual Abstract of Statistics*, 1985

In contrast with various third world countries, (see Unit 4 in this module), where the population 'explosion' is a major issue, the rate of population increase in the UK has been small. This is not to say that problems do not exist. Two such problems:
a   the age structure of the population – the growth of an **ageing** population, and
b   internal migration – the drift from North to South,
are currently attracting attention. (For further discussion of these issues see Unit 3 in this module.) Before looking at these factors in more detail, we will examine two related factors, the birth rate and the death rate.

The birth rate

Q   What are the main factors which explain the decline in birth rate since the early 1870s?

Demographers tend to refer to the birth rate in terms of the number of live births per 1000 of the population. What is noticeable in the UK is that the birth rate has been going down since the early 1870s. It has fallen from 35 per 1000 in 1871 to 13 per 1000 in 1983. Apart from the increase to 19 per 1000 in the 1950s, already referred to as the 'baby boom', the rate has steadily fallen.

T A S K

A number of factors are responsible for the decline in the birth rate. Compare your answers with the following points and see how well you have done:
a   Higher standards of living and income, including improved health, welfare, pensions and social facilities, mean the elderly are less dependent on their children than in the past (either for a source of income or for support in their old age). This is seen as an incentive to parents to restrict family size to ensure independence, and better living standards and opportunities for their children.
b   Historical factors associated with Factory and Education Acts in the Nineteenth century removed young people from the labour market. This has reduced the incentive to parents of having more children as a source of income. Child allowances and family income benefits have also had an effect.

c The emancipation of women linked with their social and economic independence via education and work mean that women are less inclined to accept their traditional role as wife, mother and homemaker. More is asked of both men and women in family life today, in terms of shared social roles, work patterns, etc. On this basis, parents are more enlightened and better able to plan family size.

d Improved knowledge and methods of contraception, notably 'the pill', have also influenced family size. (Changes in family size and family size itself is sometimes referred to as **fertility**.) □

DISCUSS

The birth rate and the fertility rate are influenced by three related factors
a how many women of child-bearing age there are.
b how many women have how many babies.
c the sex structure or balance between the sexes, (ratio of men to women).
How do these factors affect birth rate, fertility rate and population size. □

The following graph provides some basic information regarding population size and projections for the UK. When you have studied the graph, complete the task below. But first look back through this module and use any information you have collected so far on population to help with this task.

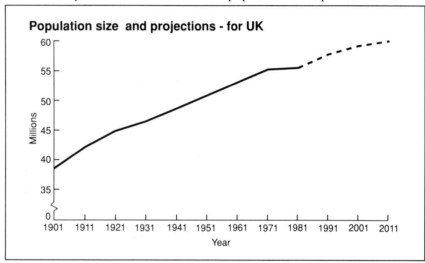

Population size and projections - for UK

T A S K

a According to the graph above, in approximately what year did the population reach 50 million in the UK?
b By approximately how much did the UK population increase between 1901 and 1981?
c What *four* factors influence the size of population in any country?
d Why has the rate of population growth slowed down since 1900? □

The death rate

Demographers tend to view the death rate (or mortality rate) in terms of deaths per 1000 of the population. As previous units have shown, expansion of the total population is *not* simply explained by the numbers of babies born. In fact the increase in the UK's population has also been caused by an overall decline in the death rate and this explains why the total population has continued to expand, despite the falling birth rate. Essentially, there are two main factors which account for this. The first is the number of babies surviving at birth, i.e within the first year of life. The second is that life expectancy for the adults of today has increased over and above that of their parents and grandparents.

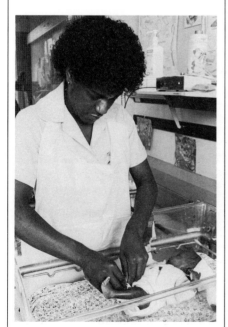

A premature baby being cared for in a special care baby unit

Visit an old cemetery or graveyard. Look at some of the headstones and compare the life span of those born in different periods, e.g. those born in the early to late 1800s and those born in the early to mid 1900s etc. In particular, look at the mortality rates of children, differences between men and women, and the effects of war in different periods. Make notes and compare your observations with other members of your class. □

The death rate (or mortality rate) is sub-divided between two main areas. The first, **infant mortality**, refers to the number of deaths per 1000 babies who die before their first birthday in any one year. The second, **life expectancy**, refers to the average life span a person can expect to live out beyond a certain age, e.g. beyond six months, one year, five, forty, sixty-five, etc.

The 'good news' about death

Major improvements in the death rate or life expectancy have taken place since the 1850s. A number of factors explain this and some of these are little different from those which explain changes in the birth rate. Much improved medical and health care for the very young, including ante- and post-natal services, has had an important effect. Similarly, improved care of the elderly has increased life expectancy which, overall, is related to better diet and an emphasis on healthy living. It is also important to recognise that improved economic prosperity has led to higher standards of sanitation, public health, housing, education and social service provision, and is also linked with improved medical technology, drugs and surgical techniques. The creation of the National Health Service has ensured that essential medical services are available to most people. Health education programmes for innoculations, eating and drinking habits, working conditions, sexual behaviour, etc., have also raised public awareness about health and safety. Such factors do not, however, hold true to all societies: contrast for example, the issues raised here with those in the Module 4 on Third World Studies, page 65.

Q What issues and problems arise for both the aged and society when people live to a ripe old age'? □

Experts reject lecturer's plan for longer life

Claims that babies could soon expect to live to the ripe old age of 130 were dismissed today as "most implausible".

Professor Malcolm Johnson, of the department of health and social welfare at the Open University, believes that by the middle of next century such life expectancy could become commonplace.

He told the International Association of Gerontology conference in Brighton that babies born today will live longer because of better diets, less smoking and drinking, a healthier environment and medical breakthroughs.

But Oxford University medical statistician Mr Richard Peto said that while many more people would in future live into middle and old age, the great majority would still die before the age of 100.

Clock

"There is no real prospect of keeping old people alive indefinitely," he said.

He said that if everyone stopped smoking and cut out fatty foods many more people would live into their seventies, but there would be little effect on lifespan from then on.

Professor Sir Richard Doll, another leading medical statistician at Oxford, has also said that humans seem to have an in-built biological clock that ensures few survive past 100.

The Office of Population Censuses and Surveys predicts that by 2025 men are likely to live until an average age of 75, three years more than now. Women, who now live an average of 78 years, can expect an average of only two extra years.

Source: *The Shropshire Star*, September 1987

'So, I'll have the baby by the 10th and be back to work by the end of the month'

'We'd like to time the baby to coincide with John's thirtieth birthday'

The 'bad news' about death!

In Britain the overall death rate (or crude death rate) is approximately 11.8 per 1000. The **crude death rate** combines both infant and adult mortality rates together, and represents an average across age, class and gender lines. Despite improvement in the death rate for all groups the general pattern of statistics hides some important differences across age, gender and class groups. When these statistics are broken down to particular groups of people by gender, class and age some interesting trends emerge.

Despite the noticeable decline in infant mortality since the 1850s, twice as many children from unskilled working-class backgrounds die in their first year of life, than children from middle-class backgrounds. This can be explained by a number of factors. Low income families are more likely to have poor home conditions and diet, which affects the health of parents and children. Repeated cycles of poverty influenced by unemployment are likely to further affect the health of future generations. The Registrar General's Scale indicates that mothers in Group E or 5 (see the Module 5 on Social Stratification, page 73) are more likely than middle-class mothers in Group A or 1 to have larger families closer together. This increases the risk of premature births, which is linked with infant mortality. For financial reasons working-class mothers are also more likely to work longer during pregnancy before their babies are born. It is also the case that hospital and health facilities are likely to be overstretched and underresourced in low income areas which will decrease service and increase impersonality.

In general, women continue to live longer than men. However, the elderly in low income groups, of which a high proportion are women, are more likely to die prematurely of hypothermia linked with malnutrition. Thus, a longer life may not be a healthy or enjoyable one. The life expectancy of men has not significantly improved since the early 1950s. Again, middle-class men tend to have a higher life expectancy than working-class men. Lower-level income groups, for example, are more likely than middle-class income groups to suffer from fatal occupational injuries or accidents at work, or illness associated with smoking, diet or poor housing.

BRAINSTORM

Examine the links between age, class, gender and mortality in explaining population trends. Give examples. ☐

So far in this unit we have considered two factors – birth and death – which influence population trends. In order to explain more about the relationship between the two we will conclude this unit with a discussion of the **ageing population**.

The ageing population

If you look back at the graph on page 173 of this unit, you will see that the increase in population between 1971 and 1983 has been small, and that the overall size of the UK population did not significantly change in this period. However, with the decrease in infant mortality and an increase in life expectancy certain 'new problems' have been created. Increasingly people are now living beyond retirement age, resulting in an expansion of the numbers of elderly people in society. In many ways extended life expectancy improves the quality of life of the elderly, but it also requires new policy responses connected with the care of the elderly, e.g. extra resources for social services and health care facilities. This is particularly the case with the over 75s, a group whose rapid increase in size is reflected by their 14 per cent growth betwen 1978 and 1983 compared with an average 0.5 per cent growth for the population as a whole. Families still play a vital role in the care of elderly relatives but nearly half the over 75s live alone, thus placing further demands on existing social services.

Some elderly people receive care from friends or relatives (top) while others receive help in their own homes from health and social services (bottom)

Q   What do you understand by the term 'ageing population'?   □

Despite their numbers, the elderly in society are not a powerful group. They are not unionised, are often very poor and their fragility makes them the victims of crime and vulnerable to illness. In other respects, the elderly, like the young, are viewed as a **marginal** or dependent group, which reduces their status to that of a second-class citizens. The *General Household Survey* data indicates that the aged make up a sizeable proportion of the *poor* in society. In this respect, three related factors are important:

a Of all those in poverty 36 per cent are elderly.
b Of all elderly people 20 per cent are in poverty.
c A further 44 per cent of elderly people are on the margin of poverty.

The following figures provide some indication of the age, sex, marital and household circumstances of elderly people, i.e. persons over 65, in the UK in 1980.

Status of elderly people in UK, 1980

Age and sex	Males 65 and over	41%
	Females 65 and over	59%
	Males 85 and over } as a % of persons {	1%
	Females 85 and over } aged 65 and over {	5%
Marital status	Married	53%
	Single	9%
	Widowed	36%
	Divorced or separated	2%
Household circumstances	Lives alone	34%
	Lives with:	
	elderly spouse only	36%
	spouse under 65 only	9%
	elderly spouse and others	5%
	spouse under 65 and others	3%
	brother(s) or sister(s)	3%
	son or daughter (including in-laws)	8%
	Other	2%

(Size of sample 4516)

Source: *General Household Survey, 1980*, updated 1985

QUESTIONS

1 What do the above figures tell you about elderly people in the UK?
2 How would you explain the fact that so many live alone or with other elderly people?
3 Describe and explain the particular problems which the elderly have to overcome in society.
4 In your own words explain the policy issues which an ageing population presents to society in terms of pensions, health care, social services and housing. □

Source: UCLES Sociology GCE 1983

If your answers to these questions provide you with some insight into the **policy issues** linked with population studies, they should also draw your attention to the relationship between births and deaths. At the moment a low birth rate coupled with a low death rate (including infant and adult mortality) have combined to increase life expectancy. Unit 3 on Migration examines another statistical relationship, namely, the link between immigration and emigration.

MIGRATION

Before looking at the central issues of immigration and emigration, it is important to know something about **internal migration**, i.e. the movement of the population within society. This is relevant for two reasons. Where people live and where they work provides information about the *geographical* and *occupational* distribution of people in society. The internal mobility of people in and around the UK, e.g. from North to South, has a number of policy implications in relation to employment, housing, health, schools, social services, etc. Currently, information from the Family Practitioners' Committee (FPC) indicates three main migratory trends:

1   Population movement away from economically depressed regions and areas of high unemployment, e.g. from North to South (linked with a decline in manufacturing, coal, steel and shipbuilding industries).
2   Population movement away from inner-city areas to smaller towns and suburban areas.
3   Population movement is mainly accounted for among the 25 to 45 year age group, (this affects population size both in the area where more people arrive and in the area they have left). Some regions are, as a consequence, depopulating and others are becoming overcrowded.

Q   How might these three migratory trends be explained? □

BRAINSTORM

Explain why some regions are depopulating and others are expanding. What effect does the population drift from North to South have on the fertility and birth rate in those areas? Explain some of the social and economic effects of this, in relation to housing, education, social services, leisure, recreation, etc.

Norman Tebbit, ex-Conservative Employment Minister, explained that when his father became unemployed he 'got on his bike' and went in search of work. So should everyone else, argued Tebbit.

Q   What major problems do the unemployed face in taking Mr Tebbit's advice?

In your answer you have probably identified one major factor associated with migration: **work**. Other possible explanations include the perceived lack of employment, facilities or amenities in inner-city, rural or depressed areas. For example, the North, West, Midlands, Scotland and Northern Ireland have lost population to regions less affected by unemployment, such as the South East and East Anglia. A major factor is the desire on the part of younger people to seek social and occupational opportunities for themselves and their families in more prosperous areas. (For more on the population shift and the North-South Divide, see Module 14 on Urbanisation, page 275.)

Using the Family Tree below draw your own family tree on similar lines.

Write down where your grandparents, parents or guardians were born. Were they born locally? If not, where did they originate from? Find out why them came to the area. Are they or were they employed, and in which occupations? Similarly, do your brothers, sisters, cousins live in the area? Are they employed? If they have moved, where have they moved to and why? □

How 'local' to your area or neighbourhood are you? How many of you are sons, daughters or grandchildren of migrants? Will you still be living in your area in ten years' time?

MY FAMILY TREE

Immigration and emigration

Contrary to popular belief, the UK is a major exporter rather than importer of people. While much political and media attention has been given over to immigration in recent years, there has been more emigration from the UK than immigration to it. Over the past 150 years there has been major emigration to the USA, Canada and Australia. This net export of people has continued since 1880 to the present day, with three possible exceptions. The first concerns the period 1931 to 1951, which witnessed the net immigration of 460 000 European refugees dislocated by war and oppression. The second concerns the period 1961 to 1962, which was influenced largely by the desire of Commonwealth citizens to enter Britain before the first Immigration Act restricted their entry. The third net inflow concerns the period 1972 to 1973, when Idi Amin, then President of Uganda, expelled Asians holding British passports.

Since 1980 there has been a net annual emigration of 440 000 people. A major factor influencing the balance between net immigration and net emigration has been the effect of the Immigration Laws (1962 to 1985) in reducing the number of new Commonwealth and Pakistani immigrants.

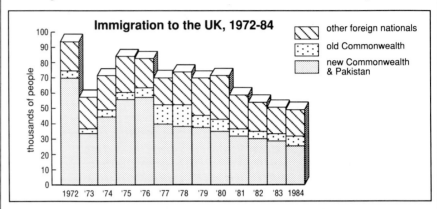

Source: HO Statistical Bulletin, 5/85, showing figures for Acceptances for settlement

QUESTIONS

1 What do you understand by the term immigration?
2 From the bar chart above name the main sources of immigration into Britain in recent years. From which countries do the immigrants in each of these groups come from?
3 Suggest *four* reasons why people from less economically developed countries wish to live in Britain.
4 Describe the various ways in which ethnic minorities experience discrimination in Britain. (For more see Module 6 on Inequality.) □

Immigration and racial prejudice

Except where people have been expelled from a country, e.g. Jewish Refugees from pre-war Germany or Asians from Uganda, the reasons why people leave a country like Britain are no different from those which bring others here. According to *Williams*, hopes of making a better living,

BRAINSTORM

What factors might encourage you to emigrate from the UK? Which country would you choose to emigrate to? Explain some of the difficulties which you might encounter as an 'outsider'.

Q Despite the fact that Black and Brown (Asian, West Indian and African) migrants have not outnumbered White migrants to any particular neighbourhood, the focus of attention has been on coloured immigration. Why do you think this has happened?

Black or brown migrants to this country are, of course, more visible than others. This does not necessarily mean that they outnumber white immigrants to any particular neighbourhood. In 1983, about 94 per cent of the population in Great Britain were of White ethnic origin. About half of the rest were known to be of West Indian, Guyanese, Indian or Pakistani ethnic origin.

Within the coloured section of the community the Asians – both those who have come directly from the Indian subcontinent and those who have come via Africa – are steadily outdistancing those of West Indian descent. In the five years from 1971–76 there was a small net emigration to the West Indies from Britain, and the main inflow was from the Indian subcontinent. In 1983 there were half a million people of West Indian origin here, compared with rather more from the Indian subcontinent.

Source: *Society Today* by M Williams, 1986

Powell out of Shadow Cabinet
HEATH ATTACKS 'RACIALIST' SPEECH

Mr. Heath, Leader of the Opposition, said he had told Mr. Powell that he considered the speech to have been racialist in tone, and liable to exacerbate racial tensions.

DISCUSS

How might adverse publicity and racism erect barriers and 'self-fulfilling prophecies'?

family ties and a feeling of restlessness and dissatisfaction with their own societies, are all important factors.

Outsiders present a threat in many societies, but patterns of discrimination against immigrants into Britain have been selective. In the 1970s, for example, political and media attention ignored two important factors:
a   Net emigration of 400 000 from Britain.
b   White immigration into Britain from the USA, Canada, Australia and elsewhere.

Politicians, such as Enoch Powell, have emphasised the threat which Black immigration poses to British society while White immigrants received little attention.

According to the psychologist, *Allport*, certain key elements of prejudice can be identified. Essentially **prejudice** consists of negative 'attitudes' or 'beliefs' which are directed toward an **out** group. Anything which can mark off an out group as 'different' can make it a target for disapproval and stereotyping. (For further discussion on this, see the Module 6 on Inequality, page 95.)

Three racist stereotypes have been used to mark out immigrants as 'outsiders':
a   They take away jobs and housing from 'British' people.
b   Their numbers, religion and beliefs undermine British traditions and culture.
c   They don't fit in and are therefore likely to cause trouble.

Taking each of these points briefly, it is important to recognise that immigration in the 1960s was encouraged by politicians and employers. At the time there was a labour shortage in the UK, and immigrants were encouraged to work in manual occupations, e.g. in public transport, hospitals and factories. As Minister for Health in the 1950s, Enoch Powell actively supported the use of immigrant labour in the National Health Service. In terms of jobs and housing, immigrants have generally been offered employment and accommodation which Whites have rejected.

Coloured immigrants and their children constitute around 5 per cent of the total UK population. In these terms the claim that ethnic minorities have taken over is suspect. (For more on this issue, see Module 14, on Urbanisation, page 266.) Adverse publicity and racism erects barriers which may prevent immigrants from 'fitting in'. In these circumstances the barriers of discrimination are erected by society and not by ethnic minorities. This can, of course, generate conflict and make people defensive, but for different reasons than Powell suggests.

In this unit, as in the previous one on births and deaths, we have looked at how two factors are interrelated. We have also seen how these factors, immigration and emigration, have various social consequences, e.g. in relation to age, race, gender and in relation to policy issues, such as education, housing, social services, etc. Unit 4 considers some of the global implications associated with population change in third world countries. Before starting the next unit, first try the assignment below.

DISCUSS

In groups, discuss the various ways in which births, deaths and migration (including immigration and emigration) are all interlinked. When you have done this, write a short account of 250 words of all the points which your group has raised. Compare your answers with other groups and collect them all together in a file marked 'population studies.' □

THIRD WORLD POPULATION

Over the years the third world countries have been described in various ways; as 'backward', 'undeveloped', 'underdeveloped', 'less developed' and 'developing'. Despite the different titles the Third World has become the main term used to described the poorer countries of the world. However, the term also describes the political status of the Third World in global terms. The first two major powers (North America and Europe – including Russia and other Eastern European Countries) are often referred to as advanced and developed countries.

So far in this module we have looked at some of the issues which interlink two sets of variables, births and deaths, and migration, immigration and emigration. One observation is that there is a relationship between economic and social development and lowering birth and death rates. This trend is not linked to Britain alone, but is a pattern now commonly associated with advanced industrial societies. The situation regarding birth and death rates is almost reversed when demographic trends in less economically developed countries is considered. This Unit turns our attention to such societies and uses two interchangeable terms to describe them – third world or developing countries. (See Module 4 on Third World Studies, Unit 1).

The situation regarding poor countries is perhaps best summarised on the left in Bob Geldof's account of the Ethiopian Crisis.

In various ways Bob Geldof's initiative brought the plight of third world countries, such as Ethiopia, into the public eye, via Band Aid and Live Aid. The first point to note is that population in developing countries is growing faster than in the highly developed ones. According to **W A Bradford** one billion people are added to the world's population every fifteen years at a rate that is thirty times the average rate of growth between the first century AD and 1650. In poor countries the rate is forty times as high.

Before looking at some of these issues in more detail, first read the extract below which looks at poverty as a relative concept and at some of the problems of living in a poor country.

The news report was of famine in Ethiopia. From the first seconds it was clear that this was a horror on a monumental scale...

There was an emaciated woman too weak to do anything but limply hold her dying child. There was a skeletal man holding out a bundle wrapped in sacking so that it could be counted; it looked like a tightly wrapped package of old sticks, but it was the desiccated body of his child.

Source: *Is That It?* by Bob Geldof, 1986

In many ways, the 'poor' people in Africa, Asia and South America are 'rich' – rich in cultural tradition, arts and community life. There are even élite groups who are rich in material wealth, but for 80% of the world's people who live in the poorer nations, life is a struggle to stay alive, a struggle much harder than that known to most people in the world's richer countries. A worker in Britain may have many difficulties with which to cope but he would appear to be rich to many peasants in poor countries. POVERTY IS ONLY RELATIVE. Some people may be considered as poor if they have only one car or have a black and white television. This person will be considered as rich by a homeless person without these material goods. Your are only poor or rich when you compare yourself with someone else.

Problems affecting the chances of people in poor countries

Food: Because you live in a poor country you are far more likely to be poorly fed than if you lived in one of the richer industrialised countries. There is less food available per person and besides not getting enough food, you may well be lacking essential proteins and vitamins your body needs.

Education: It is likely that you are unable to read or write or have even a chance to learn. This would mean that you would be illiterate. Because your country is poor, they cannot afford money for schools and teachers. They also need homes, hospitals, roads etc. Because you are not educated, you will be unlikely to find a well paid job.

Work and employment: Because you live in a poor country, you are likely to work in agriculture. It is likely that you are a subsistence farmer, i.e. just growing enough for your needs. It is likely that you will not even achieve this. You are never sure from one year to the next if you will produce enough for your family. If you do grow more than your needs, it is unlikely that you could get to the town to sell it as there are few roads and you may live in a remote part of the country.

Source: *World Population and Poverty*, ITEM 225, Resource Exchange

1 What do you understand by the term third world?
2 What is meant by the phrase 'poverty is only relative?
3 Explain some of the main differences in life chances between those living in the Third World and those living in developed countries.
4 The poverty of the Third World and the comfort of the developed countries are linked. How would you explain this? □

At the present time there are approximately 4.25 billion people in the world, and, at the current rates of growth, there will be about 7 billion by the beginning of the next century.

Of the world's population 30 per cent live in countries referred to as the developed countries, with an average rate of growth of 1 per cent per annum, whereas 70 per cent live in countries referred to as the developing countries, with a rate of growth of 2.5 per cent per annum. This suggests that most population growth occurs in those areas of the world least able to cope with it.

The character of population growth and of demographic structure in both developing and developed countries can be seen from examining the following statistics.

Birth and death rate statistics for some first and third world countries

Country	Birth Rate	Death Rate	Infant mortality rate (per 1000)	Percentage population under 15	Percentage population over 64
Egypt	38	12	108	41	3
Nigeria	49	21	157	45	2
Tanzania	47	22	167	47	2
Angola	47	23	203	42	3
India	34	14	129	40	3
China	22	8	65	33	6
Mexico	42	8	66	46	3
USA	15	9	15	24	11
UK	12	12	14	23	14

Source: *Development* by W A Bradford, 1986

Q How would you explain the main differences between countries in birth, death and infant mortality rates, shown in the above figures? □

According to *Geoffrey Hurd* in his book *Human Societies*, developing or poorer countries have experienced much faster declines in death rates than European countries ever experienced, and these declines have occurred without a corresponding rise in economic growth and increase in standard of living. Despite relatively higher infant mortality and death rates than in affluent societies, the overall death rate in developing countries has been dramatically reduced. This has been influenced by health, medical and other forms of aid from the industrialised countries, including innoculation projects, food aid programmes, agricultural investment and irrigation projects. But if developing countries have, therefore, inherited certain benefits from the developed countries which have led to a decline in the death rate, then other problems still remain. Low levels of economic growth, for example, have increased the burden of how to feed, clothe,

Q What do you understand by the remark that developing countries face a Catch 22 situation?

house, educate and employ expanding populations. In this respect, developing countries face a Catch 22 or 'poverty trap' which the developed countries do not face. Affluent societies can, for example, afford to carry increased numbers of dependents, young and old, and, at the same time, expand their economic growth rates and standard of living. This is reflected in increased expenditure on nutrition, education, housing, welfare, medical care, etc.

The following table further explains the population characteristics of societies at different levels of their social and economic development.

Population characteristics in three levels of society

Level of social and economic development	Major population characteristics	Examples
1 Societies with low national income and wealth. High percentage of labour force in agriculture. Low levels of urbanisation.	HIGH birth-rates, HIGH death-rates. HIGH infant mortality-rates. LOW expectation of life at birth. LOW rate of natural increase. HIGH percentage of children. LOW percentage of old people. LOW percentage of persons 15-64.	All societies before 1700. Contemporary modernising societies (e.g. India, Egypt, tropical Africa, most of Latin America and Asia before 1950).
2 Societies undergoing the early stages of industrialisation. National income and wealth increasing. Percentage of labour force in agriculture declining. Rising levels of urbanisation.	HIGH birth-rates at first, gradual decline in later stages. DECLINING death-rates. DECLINING infant mortality-rates. RISING expectation of life at birth. VERY HIGH rate of natural increase at first, gradual decline as birth-rates fall in later stages. VERY HIGH percentage of children at first, declining later.	Britain, 1780–1880 USA, 1870–1910 W. Europe, 1830–1900 USSR, 1910–40 Japan, 1920–50
3 Societies with high national income and health. Low percentage of labour force in agriculture. High levels of urbanisation.	LOW birth-rates. LOW death-rates. LOW infant mortality-rates. HIGH expectation of life at birth. LOW rate of natural increase. LOW percentage of children. HIGH percentage of old people. HIGH percentage of persons 15-64.	Contemporary Britain, W. Europe, USA, USSR, Japan, Australia, New Zealand, Canada.

Source: *Human Societies* by G Hurd

T A S K

In your own words, explain the population characteristics given in the above table. □

A number of myths or stereotypes have been put forward about why the Third World is poor, for example:

a   People in third world countries are poor because they breed like rabbits. It's their own fault they are poor.
b   They are lazy. We give them aid, but they don't help themselves.
c   If only people in the third world used contraceptives they could reduce family size and the birth rate and so help themselves.

DISCUSS

Discuss the above points. Present three arguments which explain the links between population and poverty in third world countries. (In your answers make reference to the table above.)

Reducing high levels of poverty and population in third world countries is not simply a matter of the West providing aid, important as this is. Introducing food and health projects, for example, have had an important effect on mortality rates and in alleviating human suffering as shown in Module 4 on Third World Studies, page 000. However, improving life expectancy and quality of life alone is not enough. Indeed, this can be a burden to those societies without the industrial and agricultural means to support expanding numbers living longer. One obvious need is to provide investment in the industrial and agricultural base of third world countries. In order to achieve independence *Julius Nyrere*, in his book *Education for Self Reliance*, argues that social, economic and agricultural developments in Third World Countries need to be home grown. By simply accommodating the developed world's factories on their territories, which tend to use cheap labour, poor countries are likely to gain little. Similarly, by importing goods and borrowing capital from abroad, third world countries place themselves in a subservient position to developed countries. According to Nyrere the challenge is for third world countries to establish their institutions and industries, and to trade with the rest of the world on equal terms. To date this has proved difficult, not least because:

a high borrowing for capital projects has increased the dependency of the Third World on the First.

b The First World (i.e. the developed world) views the Third World as a market for its goods. As a consequence poorer countries often find themselves consumers rather than producers of goods.

Yet, despite these constraints, third world countries do seek alternative solutions to their problems, including joint self-financed capital projects, for example, in agriculture, industry, business and commerce. Conflict between third world and first world countries arises mainly because third world ideas about what they see as an ideal society do not necessarily match up with first world ideas. It may be, for example, that third world countries do not wish to buy the type of product depicted in the following newspaper cartoon.

Never mind the beads, they want a compact disc

T A S K

1 How does the image above convey a stereotyped view of people in the Third World? Do you think this is a racist cartoon?
2 Describe the ways in which economic and social development in third world countries may affect population figures.
3 What according to Nyrere are the main priorities facing third world countries?
4 Why is a solution to the problems of the Third World a matter of vital importance to other nations which do not seem to be directly involved? □

WHERE TO NOW?

Reading this module may make you interested in reading more about urbanisation and change. You could progress, therefore, by reading Module 14 on Urbanisation, Module 8 on Work and Module 4 on Third World Studies.

M O D U L E · 11

THE FAMILY

ELEVEN

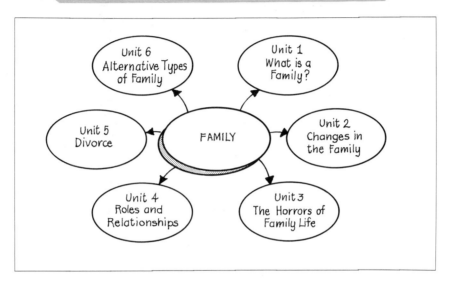

Unit 6
Alternative Types
of Family

Unit 1
What is a
Family?

Unit 5
Divorce

FAMILY

Unit 2
Changes in
the Family

Unit 4
Roles and
Relationships

Unit 3
The Horrors of
Family Life

WHAT THIS MODULE IS ABOUT

This module asks you to question why people live in families, and examines the structure, roles and relationships in families in British society and in other societies.

BY THE END OF THIS MODULE YOU SHOULD BE ABLE TO:

1 Discuss different forms of marriage.
2 Debate whether there is such a unit as a 'typical' British family.
3 Outline Bott's theory of conjugal roles.
4 Explain how the family has changed as a result of industrialisation.
5 Know the meaning of terms, such as extended, nuclear and symmetrical family.
6 Give six reasons for the increasing divorce rate.
7 Discuss the problem of abuse within the family.
8 Give three alternatives to the monogamous nuclear family.

U N I T 1

WHAT IS A FAMILY?

The family is the most basic human group. Each person in society belongs to some type of family although the form this takes varies between societies. There is no known society where people do not live in families.

Sociologists give a rather vague definition of a **family** as a group of people, consisting of adults of both sexes, with their children (siblings), who live together and look after each other. Any further attempt to define the family is difficult because there are so many different types of family found in different societies throughout the world.

In British society, marriage is **monogamous**, a term meaning that one man is married to one woman. In other places marriage is **polygamous**, meaning one person is married to more than one person of the opposite sex. There are two types of polygamy, **polygyny** where one man is married to more than one woman, and **polyandry** where one woman is married to more than one man. **Polygyny** is found in many places in Africa and Asia, whereas **polyandry** is found in only a few places, such as in the foothills of the Himalayas.

BRAINSTORM

How many different explanations can you think of for these different types of marriage? You could consider factors of gender, religion, economy, population and underdevelopment.

Family structure

If the family group consists of just parents and children living together it is called a **nuclear** family. If the family also includes relatives who live close by, such as grandparents (vertical additions), or aunts or uncles (horizontal additions) this turns a nuclear family into an **extended** family.

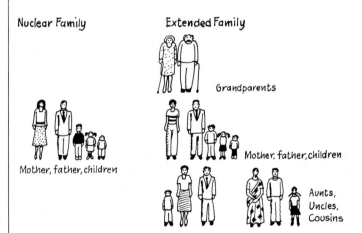

Nuclear Family

Mother, father, children

Extended Family

Grandparents

Mother, father, children

Aunts, Uncles, Cousins

T A S K

Do a quick survey to discover whether most people in your class are from a *nuclear* or an *extended* family. □

Most people think of a typical British family as being two adults and two children living together – a nuclear family. But is this really so? The picture given in the past by many sociologists is that the family was extended before the Industrial Revolution, and nuclear afterwards. It was commonly agreed that as people moved into towns in search of work, relatives were left behind to make moving easier, and so the family became nuclear.

Q What is a typical British family? How many adults and how many children does it have? Does it include grandparents?

Men and women at work in the Potteries

Recently this picture has been considered misleading. It now appears that there are, and always have been, many different types of family existing in Britain at any one time. In some areas, such as the Potteries (Stoke-on-Trent), extended families have existed for over a hundred years, because relatives have been able to offer support to working parents. The Pottery industry has always employed a large number of women, so relatives often help to look after the children of working mothers.

In other areas, as in parts of London in the early 1950s (described in *Family and Kinship in East London* by Willmott and Young) extended families were broken up as old housing was replaced by new housing estates a few miles away, and nuclear families became the norm. (See page 260–261 for more on this survey.)

In the last twenty years it has also become obvious that many British families do not consist of *two* parents living together with their children. The rising divorce rate has meant that there are now about one million single-parent families, three-quarters of them headed by women.

QUESTIONS

Look at the chart and answer the following questions:

1 Which is the commonest type of household?
2 What proportions of people lived alone in 1983? How much has this increased since 1961?
3 One other category has doubled between 1961 and 1981. Which is it?
4 What factors can you suggest for the increasing numbers of people living alone? Which two age groups are they most likely to be in?
5 Who are 'lone parents'?
6 This chart would exclude people who were in hospital, who else would it exclude?

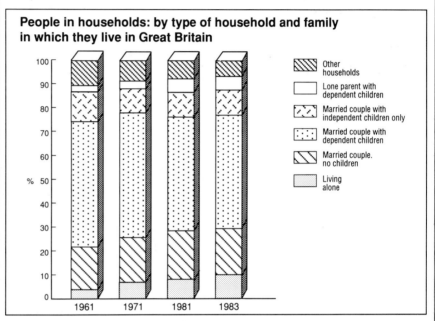

People in households: by type of household and family in which they live in Great Britain

Legend:
- Other households
- Lone parent with dependent children
- Married couple with independent children only
- Married couple with dependent children
- Married couple, no children
- Living alone

Source: Social Trends, 1986

There are many ethnic minority families now living in Britain, making up about 5 per cent of the population. Many of these families come from cultures which consider large families as economically and socially desirable. This means that many have an extended structure, and more than two children, so that they do not fit the typical pattern of two adults and two children living together as a nuclear family.

Some West Indian families for example, may not have a typical family structure. Many are single-parent families headed by the mother, i.e. **matrifocal**. (The opposite, where a father heads the family, is **patrifocal**.) In a matrifocal family the mother may look to her extended family for support, rather than to her husband or to the father of her children. The culture of the West Indies often gives a marginal role to the husband or father, perhaps because of the historical conditions of slavery which separated a man from his wife and children, leaving them as the family unit. The matrifocal family may also have originated because the original West Indian polygynous family gave the women the economic independence to support herself and her children. Certainly the high rate of unemployment in the 1980s, coupled with increasing racial discrimination against Blacks, means that the man of the household is more likely to be out of work. (See Module 6, Unit 1 for

A matrifocal family

more about racial discrimination.) This emphasis on female independence has been suggested as one reason why West Indian girls may do better than West Indian boys at school.

T A S K

Read the account below of a West Indian family living in the West Midlands. The family comprises Paulette Campbell, the mother, Gilmour Campbell, the father, and eight children. One of the children, a boy called Alric, was brought up by his grandmother in the West Indies until he was six, when he and his brother joined the family in Britain. □

```
Paulette, by now Mrs Campbell, having left her mother's home,
initially got a job in a factory to augment their income. The
arrival of more children subsequently meant her contribution was
curtailed. Nevertheless sufficient money was available to bring over
the elder children (two boys, one of whom was Alric) in 1963 to join
three others born in the UK by that date. A further three children
were born after that date - altogether making a very crowded
household for the Campbells in their Victorian terrace house.
Further problems arose for the Campbells when Gilmour's job was lost
due to recession. After 1970 he took little interest in work.
Paulette, virtually without help in looking after the children, was
obliged at the same time to go back to work, relying on whatever
help she could get in the form of childminders and nurseries to look
after the younger children, though rarely able to rely on her
unemployed husband or elder sons to care for them on a day-to-day
basis - nor was she able to call upon the wives of her husband's two
brothers, who lived close by; these women, in any case facing
similar problems, were so remote that at fourteen Alric did not know
their names. By contrast, Alric knew all his mother's siblings,
despite the fact that all lived far away - in Canada, Jamaica and
southern England. He also remembered fondly his grandmother, who had
been responsible for his upbringing until the age of six when he
came to Britain.
This portrays clearly the isolation of his mother from her
supportive kin, i.e. her mother, sisters and brothers. It also
indicates by implication the role being forced upon her of
housekeeper and childrearer to her husband and children while at the
same time being the family's only source of earned income. The
result is for her a position of both personal stress and of
increased social power while her husband is unable to act as
provider and does not take on a larger domestic or social role.
Their situation is one in which, despite the superficial appearance
of a nuclear family system, Paulette is carrying out virtually
singlehanded the major functions of the head of the Campbell
household. Perhaps because of the immediate requirements of finding
a home at the time of family migration, Gilmour acquired certain
formal and legal responsibilities which are normal to a husband in
English society, e.g. rent-book holder, but it does appear that in
day-to-day terms Paulette has been the executor of such formal
responsibilities.
```

Source: *West Indian Families: an Anthropological Perspective* by G Driver, 1982

QUESTIONS

1 Why did Paulette go back to work?
2 Who looked after the children while she was at work?
3 What *two* reasons are given for the fact that she didn't ask the wives of her husband's two brothers for help?
4 Which of Alric's relatives did he feel close to?
5 What roles did Paulette have?
6 What was Gilmour's role in the household?
7 Is the Campbell family a nuclear family, an extended family or a one-parent family? Give reasons for your answer.

T A S K

Write a short essay in answer to the question, 'Is there a typical British family?'

It should now be clear that the stereotypical picture of two adults and two children being the typical British family is oversimplified. Although the average family size was 1.9 in 1983, there are many different types of family in existence: extended, nuclear and one-parent families; with varying numbers of children. Factors of social class, housing, geographical area, and ethnicity may all affect family size and structure.

RESEARCH IDEA

Investigate the following issues:
1 Are most families in your area extended or nuclear?
2 Do ethnic minority groups tend to have an extended or a nuclear family structure?
3 What sort of family size and structure do teenagers today want in future when they are parents? □

The functions of the family

Q People all over the world live in families. What do you think are the advantages and disadvantages of living in families, both for the individual and for society? □

In every society whether simple or complex, some type of family exists. Sociologists argue that families are necessary both to the individual and to society as a whole. The family is therefore **functional**, meaning that it helps to keep society stable. However, some sociologists suggest that the functions may be changing, perhaps even that the family is no longer functional and so will cease to exist.

Sexual function
In the past marriage enabled couples to have a socially approved sexual relationship. But is this still true? Today it is estimated that about one third of both males and females have had a pre-marital sexual relationship before they are twenty. A significant minority of couples also now live together without marrying, so it would appear that the sexual function is changing. However *Schofield* found in 1978 that most pre-marital sexual relationships were just that – between couples who intended to marry.

Reproductive function
Most couples have children, but family size has fallen continuously this century. The main reason for this is due to the increased availability and efficiency of contraception. Also the proportion of illegitimate births has risen in the last twenty years from 6 per cent in 1961 to 17 per cent in 1984. Although this would appear to indicate a change in this function of the family, most of these illegitimate babies are registered by both parents suggesting that they are the result of a stable relationship.

Economic function
Parents are legally responsible for their children until they are eighteen, and are therefore responsible for clothing, feeding and looking after their offspring. This function changed especially after the introduction of the Welfare State in 1948, when the State began to aid all families who were in financial hardship. It is debatable whether the State has taken over the economic function of the family or whether as *Fletcher* argues it acts as a support, not as a replacement.

THE FUNCTIONS OF THE FAMILY

Social control function
Parents act as agents of social control. They enforce a certain behaviour pattern on their children, according to what their society considers socially acceptable behaviour. It has been argued that this function is changing as schools also control children's behaviour.

Socialisation function
The first place a child learns the culture of society is within the family; culture being the values and norms, i.e. normal ways of behaving which make each society unique. The family gives the **primary socialisation** which is so important, although it may include a young child learning gender roles, or racial prejudice as well as learning skills, such as language.

Education function
It is the parents who in pre-industrial societies pass on relevant skills to the next generation. In industrial societies the State has taken over this function by introducing a state education system. This means that the family is no longer the main agent for educating the child, although it may still pass on skills and knowledge.

DISCUSS

1 Which of the functions given on page 191 are still relevant to our society today, and which have changed, or been replaced by other agencies?
2 Why might studies done on sexual behaviour be inaccurate?
3 Who is responsible for the behaviour of young people today: the family, or schools and teachers?
4 Are there more functions of the family than those discussed above? □

Most religions support the family unit. In British society religious leaders frequently speak out in support of marriage, and family life.

T A S K

Read the following extract from the Church of England marriage service. Which functions of the family are mentioned?
'It was ordained for the procreation of children to be brought up in the nurture and fear of the Lord . . . Secondly it was ordained for a remedy against sin and to avoid fornication . . . Thirdly it was ordained for the mutual society, help and comfort, that the one ought to have of the other, both in prosperity and adversity . . .'

What does this tell us about the relationship between religion and the family? Most societies have religious values that support their family unit. □

The family in Russia in the 1930s – an example that shows the functional importance of the family.

In the 1930s Stalin was the powerful head of the Russian government. He wanted to speed up the socialisation of the people into the beliefs and values of communism (see page 82 for more details). He felt that the family in Russia was hindering this by socialising children into the old traditional values. He therefore decided to reduce the influence of the family by introducing easy, cheap divorce, and abortion on demand. Marriage was devalued, the ceremony became a civil service, and the marriage certificate was printed on cheap brown paper.

BRAINSTORM

Who is invited to weddings, christenings and funerals? What explanations might sociologists give for this?

Stalin pictured with his children (previously unheard of) in 1937, once the family became valued again in Russian society

The result was dramatic. There was a sharp fall in the birth rate and a sharp rise in delinquency, especially in the cities. Women's feeling of insecurity, caused by their husbands being encouraged to divorce them if they could get a job elsewhere led to the drop in the birth rate. The breakdown in law and order was caused by children being encouraged to inform on their parents if they were not being good communists. Parents who held old values were no longer respected.

This example demonstrates the **social control** function, the **socialisation** function, and the **reproductive** function of the family.

The government had to reverse the policy because its results had been so catastrophic! Suddenly abortion was forbidden again, divorce was difficult to obtain and marriage highly valued. Stalin suddenly appeared with his wife and children who no one knew had existed before.

T A S K

1   Explain in your own words how this example of deliberate family change in Russia shows the functional importance of the family.
2   This in an example of a real life experiment. There are few examples of experiments being implemented by sociologists, but they can make use of changes deliberately introduced into a society where these occur naturally, without their intervention. Read page 12 to find out more about experiments, then explain why this Russian example can be called an experiment. What is acting as the control? What are the variables? □

Some people argue that living in families is harmful because far from being useful it actually makes individuals unhappy and society unstable. Psychologists, such as *R D Laing*, believe that the family is a place where many people feel lonely, isolated and often suffer from emotional distress.

Here is a typical 'problem page' letter written by a fourteen-year-old boy.

> I am 14 and have a problem. I think I am old enough to make my own choices but my mother does not agree and doesn't understand what she and my dad are doing to me.
>
> They keep me away from parties and recently they embarrased me terribly by busting in when I was at a friends' party and ordering me home, because it was after 10.30pm. All the others laughed at me and I felt like crying. I will never live that incident down.

Q   Which function of the family does this letter relate to? How would you advise this teenage boy? □

DISCUSS

Is the family functional or dysfunctional? Give some examples of how the family may be **dysfunctional** for its members, and for society. □

DISCUSS

An alternative view of the functions of the family is given by Marxists. They argue that the social control function is really to produce obedient, unthinking citizens who will work for low wages in our capitalist system. They also argue that women work for free in the home, and are therefore the cheap labour that society depends on to carry out many of the functions of the family that keep society stable. Women and children also suffer in the family because the man who has had a bad day at work will come home and take out his frustrations on his family.

Do you agree with these views? (There is more on these ideas in Module 12 on Gender on page 221.) □

UNIT 2 | CHANGES IN THE FAMILY

The effects of the Industrial Revolution on the family

Before the Industrial Revolution, the family consisted of a kin group, living, working and producing goods together. It was a nuclear family with some additions. The low expectation of life meant that there were fewer old people than in society today. As society began to change from an economy based on agriculture to one based on industry, families too appeared to change.

There was a shift of population from rural areas to urban areas. Often the family moved into towns to find work, especially in areas such as Lancashire where cotton and other textiles were being produced in the mills. This meant that between about 1750 and 1840 many women worked outside the home for the first time, as well as having large families and traditional roles in the home. Conditions in the factories were often extremely bad and many working mothers relied on mixtures like 'Mothers' Blessing', a combination of drugs, such as opium, and treacle to keep their children quiet while they worked. It was not surprising that mortality rates especially for children were high. From the 1840s onwards there was a growing belief that the woman's place was in the home, to be solely responsible for both housework and children.

There were obvious differences between the family life of middle- and working-class families. The wife and children of a middle-class businessman could lead a life of leisure. In 1857, for example, an income of £1000 per annum would support a family and at least five servants. By 1881 one in seven of the working population were in domestic service. A working-class family on the other hand might have been living in overcrowded, damp, unhygienic conditions near to starvation.

The family: 1900 to 1950

The class differences between families became less between 1900 and 1950, partly as a result of the two world wars. The First World War led many women to work outside the home because their labour was needed in the factories while the men were away fighting. The Suffragette movement also demanded a better deal for women in society, and led to women getting the vote in 1919. (See Module 12 on Gender, page 222 for more details on this.) However, life was still hard for many working-class women, who remained tied to the home by their children, as until the 1930s most adults did not use reliable forms of contraception.

T A S K

One way to examine changes in family size is to draw your own family tree. Go back at least three generations if you can. Look at the family tree on the left. Which person is famous? ☐

For an example of a standard family tree turn to Module 10 on Population, page 179.

Q Did you know that we still drug our children? Gripe water is used by many mothers and is one per cent pure alcohol!

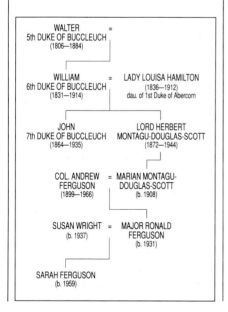

WALTER
5th DUKE OF BUCCLEUCH
(1806—1884)

WILLIAM = LADY LOUISA HAMILTON
6th DUKE OF BUCCLEUCH (1836—1912)
(1831—1914) dau. of 1st Duke of Abercorn

JOHN LORD HERBERT
7th DUKE OF BUCCLEUCH MONTAGU-DOUGLAS-SCOTT
(1864—1935) (1872—1944)

COL. ANDREW = MARIAN MONTAGU-
FERGUSON DOUGLAS-SCOTT
(1899—1966) (b. 1908)

SUSAN WRIGHT = MAJOR RONALD
(b. 1937) FERGUSON
(b. 1931)

SARAH FERGUSON
(b. 1959)

The following extract is from a survey of working-class women in the 1930s. What does it tell us about family size, family structure and living conditions? □

Mrs A. of Battersea is 48 and has had twenty children and one stillbirth in 30 years. She gets up at 6.30 and goes to bed at midnight. The Health Visitor says, "One of the children (in addition to the still-birth) died when young and one daughter at the age of 20 on the birth of *her* second child. This daughter was the mother of a boy now aged 11 and a girl aged 9, included in the lot of children living at home.

"Four children are married and living away so that the household now consists of the mother and father and sixteen children of whom two are grandchildren! The mother's own youngest child is 4 (i.e. many years younger than her grandchildren!). One of the difficulties mentioned by the mother is 'seating at mealtimes'! There is 'no bathroom, and the kitchen is too small'. She suffers from debility which came on after the last pregnancy (four years ago), and is due she says to 'multiple pregnancies'."

Source: *Working-class Wives* by M Spring Rice, 1981

The family after the 1950s

The Second World War effectively eliminated many of the inequalities of class and gender. After the introduction of the Welfare State in 1948, the differences between the middle and working classes were reduced still further (see page 102 for more on the Welfare State). However, even today there are still significant differences between families in the main social class groups. For example middle-class people still live longer, healthier lives; and their babies are less likely to die in their first year or to be born handicapped. (For more on social class difference see Module 5 on Social Stratification, Unit 2.)

The family has continued to change since the 1950s, especially in terms of its roles and relationships. The numbers of one-parent families have also increased. It has been argued by some sociologists, such as **Fletcher**, that the family we have today has developed because it is most suited to an industrial society. The modern nuclear family structure means that the family is small and geographically mobile, it can be moved around the country in search of work without being hampered by lots of relations.

Although the family has changed and continues to change with society, recent evidence about the pre-industrial family is contradictory. **Peter Laslett** found in his research that most families in this period were nuclear, only 10 per cent also had relatives living in one household. Another sociologist, **Michael Anderson**, studied the 1851 census for Preston, a cotton town in Lancashire, and found that 23 per cent of the families were extended. As was made clear in Unit 1, there has obviously always been many different types of family size and structure in existence in Britain. Today only about 30 per cent of families are nuclear.

U N I T 3 THE HORRORS OF FAMILY LIFE

As well as people being lonely and isolated living in families, they may also be victims of violent attacks. The extent of family violence is only just becoming known, although crimes, such as murder (which cannot be covered up), have already been recognised as frequently occurring in families.

Problems, such as wife-battering, child abuse, and incest, must always have existed in a minority of families, but the large amount of these offences in society today has been ignored until recently. Society's refusal to admit the existence of these problems and victims' inability to talk about them, are part of the **taboo** placed on such subjects. Official agencies, such as the police and social workers, have in the past been unwilling to intervene in family disputes, because many wives have refused to prosecute their husbands. Many victims have also been disbelieved, particularly when they have been children accusing adults.

The causes of family violence are complex, but appear to be related to factors of stress, such as unemployment, poverty, and poor housing. As most violence within the home is done by men against women and children, feminist sociologists argue it is a symptom of male power within our society, and will only disappear when there are more equal relationships between men and women.

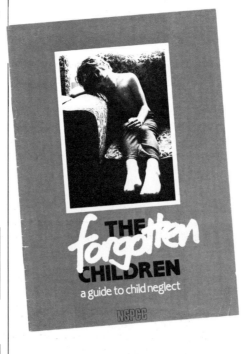

In March 1985 Jasmine Beckford's father was given a 10 year jail sentence for manslaughter. Her body when she died was covered in ulcers, burns, bruises and scars – a clear case of child abuse.

The NSPCC say this – Each year 150 to 200 children die following child abuse and neglect.
Two in every ten neglected children are less than one year old. Seven in ten are under five years old.

Q The number of cases of neglect and child abuse being reported to the NSPCC is rising.
Why do you think that this is so?

DISCUSS

Do parents own their children? In what sorts of ways are parents expected to control their children?

Child abuse

Left in squalor

Three-year-old Billy and his 15-month-old brother Paul were found by an NSPCC officer frightened and damp with urine, alone in a filthy sixth-floor flat – in a building where most of the flats were empty.

The toilet wasn't working, the bath was full of dirty clothing, soaking in fetid water, and the floor was covered in rubbish. The boys looked quite well-nourished but the only food in the flat was a single slice of bread.

No one knew where the parents were. The boys couldn't be left alone so they spent the night in hospital.

The NSPCC found that the mother's husband had left her with huge debts – rent, gas and electricity. When she discovered that her husband had a girlfriend, she walked out on everything in despair.

The NSPCC helped this mother to regain her confidence and to learn the basics of household budgeting. She now feels that her children are important and that her family does have a future.

BRAINSTORM

In what ways could society attempt to reduce the amount of child abuse that exists?

It has recently been estimated that as many as one child in ten is the victim of abuse, either physical, psychological or sexual. Statistics are unreliable because children are seen to belong to their parents, and people are reluctant to interfere in what is seen as a private matter. Nevertheless it is known that child abuse goes on in all social classes and ethnic groups.

After the change in law to allow video recordings of children as evidence in court, there may well be a rise in the statistics for child abuse. This may also be affected by increased public awareness of the problem, and the training now being given to police, social workers, teachers and health visitors.

Estimates of national incidence of physical abuse by year 1977–1982

Estimates and breakdowns 1977	1978	1979	1980	1981	1982	
Estimated number of children 0 to 14 physically abused in England and Wales	4699	4803	4493	5152	5723	6388
Severity breakdowns: fatal & seriously injured	822	749	553	606	646	647
Moderately injured	3877	4054	3940	4546	5077	5741

Source: *Trends in Child Abuse*, NSPCC

Q   What does the table above indicate about the amount and severity of physical abuse between 1977 and 1982? Why are these figures likely to be inaccurate? □

Child abuse is getting increasing amounts of coverage in the media, as it becomes more acceptable to discuss problems of neglect, physical violence, sexual abuse and incest. However, child abuse is is only one kind of violence found within the family, women and the elderly are also physically and psychologically abused in the family unit today.

Battered wives

This is again an area where statistics are likely to severely underestimate the extent of the problem. Not all cases of battering cause serious injury, but it is thought that thousands of women are regularly assaulted by their husbands each year. Violence is often triggered by sexual jealousy over real or imagined incidents, arguments over money, the house or meals, and more frequently occurs when the man has been drinking.

Q   Why do you think all men are refused entry to many Women's Refuges?

Voluntary support is growing for battered wives, with most areas in Britain now having Rape Crisis Centres and Women's Refuges. These are places of safety for women and their children, and men are forbidden entry to many of these centres, even if they are male doctors or social workers.

Psychological violence

DISCUSS

Would you agree with Leach's view of the modern family? What do you see as the main factors causing stress to individuals within a family? Why do you think 'granny bashing' or abuse of elderly people is increasing?

Although children are frequently victims of this kind of violence, the elderly and women also suffer. Children may suffer stress from the demands made on them by parents, and in extreme cases, may become mentally or physically ill as a result. The isolated nuclear family is frequently a place where individuals feel under strain and threatened by hostility, even if this does not develop into physical cruelty. The family has been described by *E Leach* as like:

'an overloaded electric circuit. The demands made on it are too great, and the fuses blow . . . the result is conflict.'

UNIT 4 FAMILY ROLES AND RELATIONSHIPS

The roles played by the different members of a family are the expected behaviour patterns that go with being an adult or a child. For example, family roles could be being a mother, wife, daughter or grandmother. The roles and the relationships between the family may depend on factors like the age of the married couple, whether they have children, their ethnic group, their social class, and whether they both work.

An important study of **conjugal roles**, i.e. the roles of husband and wife was done in 1957 by *Elizabeth Bott*. Her survey has been criticised because she only studied twenty couples, all of whom lived in London, so it is neither a large-scale study, nor necessarily representative of the whole of Britain. Despite this her work has been important to the understanding of conjugal roles.

Bott was interested to find out who did what in the home. Who was responsible for jobs, such as housework or decorating, and on what factors this depended. She found that couples had three different sorts of role. These were firstly **joint roles** where they worked together in the house, they might cook together or both do the gardening. Secondly, she found **complementary roles** where the couples helped one another, one might cook and the other wash up. Thirdly were the **segregated roles** where the husband and wife had separate jobs to do; the wife might be cleaning the house while the husband was cleaning the car.

Q Which sort of roles would these be; joint, complementary or segregated?
Couple A: She washes and he irons.
Couple B: She does the shopping while he mows the lawn.
Couple C: They both do the decorating together.
Couple D: She puts the children to bed while he cooks their supper. □

It was already known that social class affected roles. Working-class couples are more likely to live in close-knit extended families than the more socially and geographically mobile middle-class nuclear families. Bott found that although most working-class couples had segregated roles, some had joint roles, so class was not the only explanation of why couples had different roles.

Instead it was the **social relationships** that the couple brought with them to their marriage that was most important. If the couple came from a close-knit group of friends and relatives where they all met regularly, they were more like to have segregated roles. The new wife would spend time at her mum's, while the husband would go out with his friends. If their friendship group was loosely knit, without strong relationships, they were more likely to have joint roles. Couples with joint roles seemed more dependent on each other for emotional support and companionship.

These two theories were supported by the research of Peter Willmott and Michael Young in their study of family change *Family and Kinship in East London*, conducted in the 1950s. They found that when families were moved from the working-class area of Bethnal Green to a new housing estate some miles away their extended 'mum-centred' family with strongly segregated roles was replaced by a nuclear pattern where couples had joint roles.

For more details of this study by Willmott and Young see Module 14 on Urbanisation, page 261.

RESEARCH IDEA

Test out Bott's theory. Interview couples about their conjugal roles by asking them who does what job around the house. Then assess their social and kinship network by finding out how often they have been in touch with family and friends in the preceding week. Is there a correlation or a link between these as Bott suggests? □

MY WIFE DOESN'T WANT A JOB, SHE'S DEVOTED TO OUR CHILDREN.

In the early 1970s Willmott and Young conducted another survey which they called *The Symmetrical Family*. This term was used to describe a family where the conjugal bond, i.e. the bond between the husband and wife was strong, and both partners helped in the day-to-day running of the home. Male and female roles were balanced or **symmetrical**, although not always equal. Men and women were often working both inside and outside the home.

The symmetrical family was home-centred, the family spent much of their time at home, rather than visiting family or friends. Their leisure time was often spent at home perhaps decorating or playing with their children. Willmott and Young found this pattern was not typical of most of the working-class families in their survey. The old working-class communities had broken down. This was sometimes because of the movement of families to other areas in search of better jobs, and sometimes because of the other differences within the family with changing roles and relationships, the changing position of women and smaller family size.

Q How have conjugal roles changed in the last thirty years? What conjugal role would you prefer – segregated or joint? □

Social change takes place slowly. Although middle-class people adapt to social change more quickly than working-class, few couples today are really equal, there are only a few who both have careers. These 'Dual Career Families' were studied by ***Rapoport*** who found they usually depended on extra help in the home, which was given by women.

T A S K | | | | | | |

Read the following extracts, one by a male and one by a female. What do they indicate about the relationships and roles of the couples? □

> 'Tom's home so little that when he is home – even if it's for a fortnight – I feel I've got to cook something interesting, and the effort that goes into that every night is a bit much, really. If I were to provide him with just chops and vegetables he wouldn't think much of that. He's not a very critical person, but he's appreciative of good cooking – any man is.'

Source: A middle-class wife quoted in *Housewife* by Oakley, 1976

> 'I've got the right bird. I've been going with her for eighteen months now. Her's as good as gold. She's . . . done well, she's clean. She loves doing . . . housework. Trousers I bought yesterday. I took 'em up last night and her turned them up for me. She's as good as gold and I wanna get married as soon as I can.'

Source: 'Spike', a working-class lad in *Learning to Labour* by Paul Willis

DISCUSS

Is there women's work and men's work? Which sex should do the following jobs?
a Painting and decorating.
b Cleaning the toilet.
c Cooking.
d Shopping.
e Gardening.
f Changing a dirty nappy.

Can you suggest any activities that you could all agree are women's work or men's work? (See Module 12 on Gender, Unit 2 for a further discussion of gender roles.)

Reasons for the increasing divorce rate

The divorce rate increased between 1961 and 1971 and has continued to rise. In 1984 about 150 000 divorces were granted, most of them filed by women. The reasons for this rise include legal factors, the effects of the media, religious, class and family factors.

Family factors

There appears to be an increased likelihood of divorce if the couple marry young, particularly as teenagers, and even more so if a couple have a so-called 'shot gun wedding' to legitimise a pregnancy. Chances of divorce are also slightly increased if the couple's parents are divorced.

More important family factors that affect the divorce rate are thought to be:

1 The change in *family structure* from extended to nuclear. (See Unit 3.) Nuclear families are without the support of their wider kin, and divorce doesn't affect family relationships as much as it would with an extended family network.

2 Changes in the *functions of the family* may also affect the divorce rate, with single parents getting financial help from the State, and schools taking over part of the education, social control, and socialisation functions. (See Unit 2.)

3 Changes in *family size*, and the increasing independence of women, mean that women who are unhappy in their marriage are more likely to divorce. Today the wife is less dependent on her husband and has fewer children to support than would have been the case a hundred years ago.

4 The changing roles that go with the *symmetrical* family pattern may increase the stress felt by the married couple. *Joint* or *complementary* roles (see Unit 4) may mean that the husband resents doing housework, whilst a working wife may resent doing two jobs, one in the home and one outside.

DISCUSS

What advice would you give to a couple who are marrying because the girl is pregnant? What sort of things do they need to consider carefully?

What advice would you give to a young woman intending to leave work when she gets married? □

Social class and occupation

In Britain the lower middle class and lower working class have the highest divorce rates, perhaps because they are at the bottom of their respective class groups and may have money worries. Certain occupations also have higher rates, particularly those causing frequent absences from home, such as being a sales rep and long-distance lorry driving. If couples come from different class backgrounds they are also more likely to divorce.

TASK

Conduct a quick survey around your class. How many people expect to marry? How many of those expect to get divorced? If the present trends continue almost all of you will marry and one in every three will divorce. Were you realistic in your survey? If not why not? □

Religious factors

Couples from different religious backgrounds are also more likely to divorce, but most religions are now more tolerant towards divorce than they used to be, and divorcees can now remarry in church. This means that couples no longer feel that they have to stay married if they are religious. The changing attitude of the church means that there is less of a **stigma** attached to divorce, i.e. it is socially acceptable to be divorced. This is because society is becoming generally less religious and more secular. (See Module 9 on Religion.)

The effects of the media

The mass media which includes the television, radio, newspapers, and advertising constantly uses the image of the family. The family is presented in plays, serials and adverts, as a happy, usually nuclear, unit.

The media image of the family tends to be idealised with the emphasis on romantic love. This idea is thought by some sociologists to increase the chance of divorce because couples have unrealistic ideas about marriage and will not accept an imperfect relationship. Certainly studies done by *Sue Sharpe* and others, show that most girls intend to marry before they are twenty-one but they do talk of having 'a good time first' which suggests they are not unrealistic about the constraints of marriage. (See Module 12 on Gender, page 214 for more on Sue Sharpe's studies.)

T A S K

What does the following extract indicate about the media's attitude to love and marriage? Do you think that the happy-ever-after image affects the divorce rate? □

'Inside almost every girl there is a Cinderella dying to meet her Prince Charming: a handsome, caring, considerate man who will fall madly in love with her, marry her and cherish her forever and a day. In this modern day fairy tale, our heroine Sarah Ferguson . . .'

Source: *When Love Takes a Hand* by Katie Boyle, July 1986 *TV Times*

Legal factors

One of the most important factors affecting the divorce rate is the current divorce law, and whether it is easy or difficult to get a legal divorce. Not all couples opt for divorce. They may continue in an 'empty-shell' marriage, where they have a poor relationship but still live together, or they may **separate** and live apart without divorcing.

The laws on divorce have changed considerably in the last 150 years. Before 1857 a Private Act of Parliament was needed to get a divorce and this was very lengthy and costly, so divorce was rare. In 1857 the Matrimonial Causes Act enabled couples to divorce on the grounds of adultery (of the wife only) and since then successive acts have extended the grounds or legally acceptable reasons for divorce. The 1937 Matrimonial Causes Act widened the grounds to include cruelty, insanity and desertion.

The 1949 Legal Aid and Advice Act meant more couples could afford to divorce because they could get free legal advice; but it was the 1969 Divorce Act that made the biggest difference to the numbers of couples divorcing. This act made irretrievable breakdown of marriage the sole grounds for divorce between consenting couples. From 1969 any couple who both wanted a divorce could obtain one cheaply and easily by declaring their marriage had 'broken down' and there was no chance of their getting back together.

BRAINSTORM

Think of as many media images of the family as you can. How realistic are they, and how many include ideas of family breakdown, divorce, or one-parent families?

The impact of the 1969 Divorce Act can easily be seen in statistics on divorce. The divorce rate trebled between 1961 and 1971, from 2.1 to 6.0 per 1000. In 1984 the Matrimonial Proceedings Act reduced the time after marriage needed before divorce proceedings can begin, and this led to a further rise.

T A S K

Look at the table below. How much has divorce increased between 1961 and 1986? Suggest some reasons to explain why many more women than men petition for divorce. (Look at Module 12 on Gender for possible answers.) □

Most of the information about the amount of divorce in our society is in the form of statistical charts. Most of these are either in percentages or in thousands, so examine graphs and tables carefully to see which they are in before analysing them.

Divorce trends between 1961 and 1986

	1961	1971	1976	1981	1982	1983	1984	1985	1986
Petitions filed (thousands)									
England & Wales									
By husband	14	44	43	47	47	45	49	52	50
By wife	18	67	101	123	128	124	131	139	131
Total	32	111	145	170	174	169	180	191	180
Persons divorcing per thousand married people									
England & Wales	2.1	6.0	10.1	11.9	12.1	12.2	12.0	13.4	12.9

Source: *Social Trends* 18, 1988

The effects of divorce

When marriages break down there are emotional problems for the family members involved who frequently suffer stress as a result. Most children remain with their mother, and it is thought that boys in particular may suffer from not having a father while they are growing up. However, in most cases the individuals readjust with no long-term ill effects.

Many divorcees remarry. In 1984, 35 per cent of marriages were between couples who had been married before. A family may have to adjust to further changes, with perhaps additional children, such as step-sisters or step-brothers being introduced to the original siblings. A marriage pattern which consists of marriage, divorce and remarriage is called **serial monogamy**, and it is becoming increasingly common, not only for film stars like Elizabeth Taylor or Zsa Zsa Gabor.

Chester calls a family which includes step-brothers and/or step-sisters a 'Stepfamily'.

It was thought in the 1950s that the family might be breaking down as the main human group in society. Certainly, the family has changed a great deal as has been shown in this module. The rising divorce rate is one of many changes affecting the family as it adapts to meet broader changes that are going on in society. It is now thought that as the family exists in every known society, past and present, it will continue to alter in response to factors like changes in the economy, religion, the legal and political systems, housing and technology. The next unit examines some possible directions the family might take.

The charts opposite show some of the recent changes that have taken place. One-parent families are caused either by the death of one partner, by a birth to a single woman, or by divorce which is now the main cause.

DISCUSS

Some people argue that it is morally wrong to make divorce easy to obtain, because this may encourage people to get a divorce. What do you think about the advantages and disadvantages of separating, living an 'empty-shell marriage', or divorcing, for couples who feel their marriage is over? What is the law on divorce in Northern Ireland? Why is it not the same as in the UK? How does it differ? Ask your school or college librarian for help in finding this information.

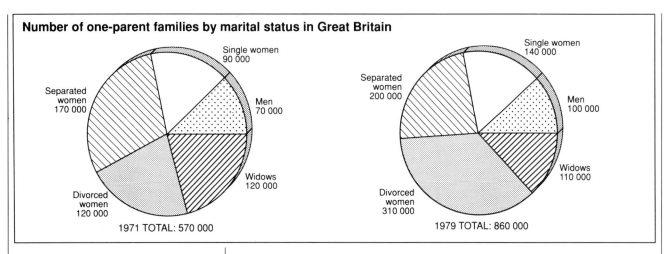

Number of one-parent families by marital status in Great Britain

Single women 90 000
Separated women 170 000
Men 70 000
Widows 120 000
Divorced women 120 000
1971 TOTAL: 570 000

Single women 140 000
Separated women 200 000
Men 100 000
Widows 110 000
Divorced women 310 000
1979 TOTAL: 860 000

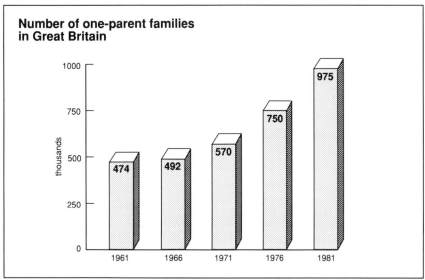

Number of one-parent families in Great Britain

thousands

474 — 1961
492 — 1966
570 — 1971
750 — 1976
975 — 1981

Source: National Council for One-parent Families Information Sheet

TASK

What does this data show about the numbers and types of one-parent families?

ROLE PLAYING THE FAMILY

Get into groups of four: mother, father, daughter aged fourteen, son aged sixteen. You are sitting watching the television discussing the following family problems.

1   Dad suddenly announces that he has been made redundant. It has come as a terrible shock to him. He feels very depressed and feels he is now 'on the scrap-heap'. He believes he has let the family down, especially as his wife doesn't work and he has always believed it was the man's job to bring in a wage.

2   Mum is worried that the people next door might be battering their baby. She has heard the parents screaming at the child in the middle of the night, and thinks she saw bruises and burn marks on its legs. She has recently read that child abuse has become increasingly common in the last ten years, and that often it is neighbours that notice something is wrong. She feels she ought to do something, but doesn't want to interfere in someone else's family life.

3   A letter has just arrived from the eldest daughter who is away at polytechnic. She has written to let them know that she is pregnant, and intending to live with, but not marry the father of the child. She says she hopes that they are not too upset, but that so many marriages end in divorce that she feels it is better just to live together.

4   The son has just decided to leave school. He was going to stay on and do
    A levels, but now feels it would be better to go on a YT scheme. This
    means that he will have to give up the idea of being a physiotherapist for
    a football team, which had been his ambition.

5   The daugher has started staying out late after going out with her friends
    on Saturday night. She thinks at fourteen she is old enough to stay out at
    least until midnight, but her parents are worried about what she may be
    doing. They want her to be in by ten o'clock at the latest.

6   The son has started bringing home things from school, such as library
    books, pens, chalk, and drawing equipment. He argues that it is not
    really wrong, after all his father occasionally brings similar things back
    from work.

7   Dad's mother has been ill and can no longer live alone. If she comes to
    live with them there may be problems. Mum does not like her very much
    and they don't have a spare bedroom.

DISCUSS

What sort of family did you create? Was it middle class or working class?
What were the roles and the relationships of the members of the family? Do
role plays like this contribute to a stereotyped picture of family life?   □

ALTERNATIVE TYPES OF FAMILY

Is it possible to have a society where people don't live in families? Many sociologists argue that it isn't and that the family is universal. Certainly there are many different family types, monogamous or polygamous, nuclear or extended. (Go back to Unit 1 for an explanation of these terms.) It has been suggested that the functions supplied by the family are neccessary to society, and therefore that it would be impossible to do without some form of family.

DISCUSS

Why do we live in families? Is it possible to do without them? How many alternatives to living in families can you suggest? □

There have been many attempts to live in alternative ways to the accepted family structures. This is either because individuals feel strongly about the way they should live; or because governments try to change family life for economic or political reasons. (See page 192 for details of an attempt to change the family in Russia.)

Two examples of possible alternatives to the family will be examined in this unit.
1   The current attempt by the Chinese government to alter family size.
2   A future type of family suggested as a possibility by some feminists.

There is information about an alternative type of family called the Oneida community in Module 9 on Religion, page 163.

The one-child family of China

The Chinese family of the 1990s is being deliberately changed by China's government in order to bring down the birth rate.

After the Communist government took control in 1949, the country remained relatively stable for the first time in many years. Most of the Chinese people settled down to a life of either factory work in the towns or working on agricultural collectives in the countryside. A **collective** is where a group of people work together on land that they jointly own.

However, by 1978 China had one major problem and that was the size of its population. This was estimated at about one billion people (1000 million), and if it continued to grow at the same rate the population might number four billion in a hundred years' time, the present total for the whole world! China already had to import 15 million tons of grain each year, and an increasing population would result in severe famine.

The government therefore decided in 1978 to try to solve this problem by introducing the one-child policy. This meant that each couple would be encouraged to have only one child, and if the government could get one third of all couples to agree then zero population growth would be achieved by the year 2000.

There are financial benefits for parents who take out a one-child policy, such as free child health care and free education. There are also strong social pressures to make sure most couples conform. There is less privacy in China than in the West, and workmates and neighbours are expected to remind each other to use contraception for the good of the whole country! Abortion is widely used if women do conceive a second time and children are taught in school to tell their parents that they don't want any brothers or sisters.

DISCUSS

Does a government have the right to tell its people how many children they can have? Is this a private matter or a public issue?

The birth rate is now dropping. It went down from 36 per 1000 in 1960 to 12 in 1979. The one child per family rule is only working really well in the urban areas, but already the birth rate has been significantly cut.

In some provinces however, many more males appear to be born than females, and it is suspected that first born girls are being killed. This practice is known as female infanticide. It is a custom found in some parts of the world where boys have a much higher status than girls, and where it is difficult to provide economically for both sexes. In China it means that parents can have a high-status male child, who will be able to help them on the land, look after them in their old age, and also bring them the state benefits from only having one child. Girls are less popular because they were traditionally considered inferior to boys, and on marriage wives go to live with their new husband's family. This can be very important in China today when the parents of an only girl may find themselves isolated when they are elderly.

DISCUSS

a If you were living in China would you agree to have only one child?
b If you were a poor peasant in China would you consider female infanticide if your first child was a girl? □

ROLE PLAY

Get into groups of four and act out a family discussion that might take place in modern China. The family consists of a wife and husband, and his parents. The wife is pregnant and only wants one child. The husband wants more than one child, particularly if the new baby is a girl. The husabnd's parents who live nearby are worried about who will support the elderly in society, if all couples comply with the government's wishes to have only one child.

You need to discuss the following:

a The reasons behind the one-child policy.
b The problem of the increasing numbers of old people in the society with fewer children to look after them. There are no state benefits, such as pensions in China.
c The possibility of killing the child if it is female. □

BRAINSTORM

Imagine Britain was facing a population crisis similar to that facing modern China. If you were a member of the Cabinet how would you advise the Prime Minister to solve the problem?

There are a number of alternatives including enforced sterilisation (this was actually done for a short time in India). A one-child policy similar to Chinas's could be introduced, or perhaps a lottery where some couples might win the chance to have one or two children! See how many ideas you can think of that would really be viable. □

For more about the population crisis, turn to Module 10 on Population, Unit 3 or Module 4 on Third World Studies, Unit 4.

The futuristic feminist family

Some feminists wish to abolish the family because they argue that it is the family that perpetuates the inferior status of females in society (see Module 12 on Gender, Unit 2). They argue that females are socialised into their domestic role by the family which expects them to do housework and look after the males. Females are then locked into these gender roles by the demands of pregnancy and child care.

Sociologists, such as **Shulasmith Firestone**, argue that if only women can be freed from their biological roles, by not having or rearing children, then they would become of equal status to men. This would create a new sort of society, perhaps without any sort of family at all. Adults could choose to live with each other if they wished, but children could be looked after by surrogate parents. Professional surrogate parents act out the roles of real parents by being pregnant, and caring for the children, but are not biologically related to them.

This sort of family frees women from their role as child bearers and child rearers, and it could therefore be called a 'futuristic feminist family'. It is not a fantasy as it is now theoretically possible. Medical advances in this country and in America have given us test-tube babies, whilst women are now paid to be surrogate mothers, i.e. they are pregnant with another couple's child.

In America 'sperm banks' are also in existence where women can choose and pay for sperm of a male who will be the biological, but not the social father of the child. Women can choose from a list of donors, and frozen sperm are delivered to her. This was a technique originally pioneered to help childless couples or couples where the husband was dying and the wife wanted his child after he died. An article about a woman who has has a child by choosing the 'father' from a sperm bank appears below.

QUESTIONS

Read the article and answer the following questions.
1 Who is Doron Blake's father?
2 How many babies are there from the 'Nobel spermbank'?
3 Why did Dr Blake decide to have a baby in this way?
4 Who originally founded the sperm bank and why?
5 Why do some feminists support the idea of women as surrogate mothers? ☐

DISCUSS

a Is the futuristic family a real possibility?
b Would you like to live in a society that reproduces like this? What would the advantages and disadvantages be?
c Do you think that gender roles really would change as a result, and women become equal to, or superior to men?

The woman who wanted a genius

If Doron Blake is a genius, his mother won't let it show. Doron, four on Sunday, is one of the first progeny of the famous and controversial "Nobel sperm-bank" in California. He is, beyond question, bright and precocious.

But his mother, Afton Blake, a clinical psychologist, has refused to have him tested again after he scored double the average for his age when he was two. Nor will she push him in the direction of any one of his interests: books, music and computers, to the exclusion of the others.

"I want Doran to grow up a normal little boy, not deprived of toys or friends or play time."

One thing Doran is deprived of is a Daddy. Then, as now, Dr Blake was single when she went to the sperm bank and chose "Number 28" to be the father of her child.

"Number 28" was not a Nobel prizewinner. He was too young for that recognition, being only in his thirties, but Dr Blake was told he had been honoured with other awards as a professor of computer science. She also learnt he was an extrovert who liked music, swimming, skiing and hiking. He has blond hair and green eyes, just like Doran. "Number 28's" identity, however, was concealed from her.

The "Nobel spermbank" wants to produce children of above-average intelligence by giving them the genetic endowment of sperm from donors who are highly accomplished. In six years there have been 28 healthy babies, with currently eight women pregnant. But the contributions of three venerable Nobel prize-winners for science were quietly dispensed with because mothers invariably requested younger donors.

Despite Dr Blake's feminist foray into this brave new world, she has not come close to resolving the "nurture-nature" conflict—are we more what we are from the nature of our genes or the nurturing of our upbringing? She said: "Some say it's 60-40 per cent one way, some say 40-60 the other, I don't know."

She believes Doron's structured education can wait until the age of six or seven, so he goes three days a week to an "alternative" school where the children each decide how they will pass the time. At home she leaves out paper, paint and other materials to stimulate his creativity but sees her role for now as helping rather than teaching.

At 44, Dr Blake is a forthright woman, a plump "earth mother" figure who wears flowing dresses and pulls her long fair hair back in a bun. She decided to have a baby by artificial insemination after three live-in relationships had failed, two of them over her wish to have children.

"I've never regretted my decision," she said, although she does not pretend that Doron is Supertot or she Supermum.

The intensity of her maternal dedication is reflected in the licence plate of her beat-up Honda—ME N DWB (for Doron William Blake).

Doron has asked about his absent father. Dr Blake said: "I've explained to him his Daddy doesn't live with us, that he is far away and there are just the two of us. There was one occasion when Doron got angry with me. He said he was going off to live with his dad. He meant it as a threat, but it was also kind of cute."

In time Doron will be told of his extraordinary conception: "I'll explain it to him when he starts to ask, in simple terms at first and the full story later on when he is old enough to understand."

Doron does have a half-sister, 18 months younger than he. She was born to another single mother who lives nearby and whose choice of donor at the sperm bank was also "Number 28." The two children play together frequently although the girl's mother shuns publicity.

In contrast, Dr Blake decided to be open about her patronage of the sperm banks as an encouragement and role-model to other women.

Source: *The Daily Telegraph*

RESEARCH IDEA

Find out more about scientific achievements in reproduction. Do an attitude survey on people's opinions of surrogate mothers and sperm banks. (For more about surveys turn to page 6 in Module 1 on research methods.

BRAINSTORM

What are the advantages and disadvantages of using sperm banks for reproduction? □

This module has examined the changes in the structure, roles and relationships of the family today. The family module has attempted to give an understanding of the functions of living in families, as well as some of the problems of family life. Alternatives to living outside a nuclear family structure have also been examined.

WHERE TO NOW?

You may now like to read some of the other modules that have been mentioned in these units. First turn to the next module on Gender, then either to Module 10 on Population, or Module 14 on Urbanisation.

MODULE · 12

GENGER

T W E L V E

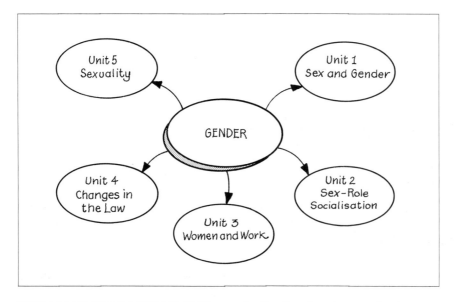

- Unit 5 Sexuality
- Unit 1 Sex and Gender
- GENDER
- Unit 4 Changes in the Law
- Unit 3 Women and Work
- Unit 2 Sex-Role Socialisation

WHAT THIS MODULE IS ABOUT

This module explores the controversial area of sex and gender. It looks at the causes and effects of the inequalities between males and females in Britain today, and asks why these inequalities still exist, despite changes in the law.

BY THE END OF THIS MODULE YOU SHOULD BE ABLE TO:

1   Demonstrate an understanding of the biological and cultural arguments regarding gender inequalities.
2   Discuss the effects of sex-role socialisation by the family, the school and the mass media.
3   Appreciate the reasons for the increase in the number of women going out to work since the Second World War and describe the inequalities suffered by women in work today.

4   Outline the changes that have taken place in the law in recent years and analyse the effects of these on the status of women in society and in producing equality between the sexes.
5   Consider the complex area of male and female sexuality and discuss the implications of sexual stereo-typing on a person's lifestyle.

Dustin Hoffman plays the role of a man playing the role of a woman.

UNIT 1 SEX AND GENDER

Q   Is it biology or culture that create the differences between males and females? ☐

Everyone has a **biological sex** when they are born, i.e. they are either *male* or *female*.

There are, of course genetic or biological differences between males and females; such as the differences in hormones and physical appearance. For example, males in general have greater physical strength than women and females are able to bear children whereas males cannot.

RESEARCH IDEA

What is strength? How many females do you know who are stronger than some of the men you know? How would you test this out? ☐

Some anthropologists argue that these biological or genetic differences between males and females are responsible for the differences in life-style between men and women in society. They suggest, for example, that since males are more aggressive and stronger by nature than females, that it is right and proper that males should undertake most of the work in society and also take the dominant positions of power. On the other hand, it is claimed that women are programmed to produce and care for children, are most suited to less strenuous tasks in society and to carrying out work in the home.

T A S K

List examples of heavy work and light work. Who tends to carry out this work – males or females? Why? ☐

Some sociologists suggest that since mothers bear and nurse children that they automatically have a closer and stronger relationship with them than anyone else. One of these writers *J. Bowlby*, argues that therefore 'a mother's place is in the home'; caring for her children especially during their early years. He argues that if a mother and child are separated in the early years, it can cause the child to be psychologically disturbed.

DISCUSS

Do you agree with *Bowlby*'s view that a mother's place is in the home? If you do, why? If you don't, why not? ☐

Another group of sociologists argue that there are major differences in brain structures between males and females. They suggest that males have a superior right-hand side of the brain giving them more highly developed spatial skills; whereas females have a stronger left-hand side of the brain which gives them superior skills in language.

DISCUSS

Do you agree with this theory? Does this explain why more females are involved in occupations using language and more males involved in areas such as technology? ☐

Many sociologists do not agree with the views expressed on this page. They do not believe that the only reason why women lead different lives from men is due to the sex they were born with; instead, these sociologists argue that it is the culture of society that is the most important factor. (When

Some women are stronger than men.

The **nature/nurture argument** is often referred to in sociology books. *Nature* refers to the characteristics you are born with and *nurture* refers to the characteristics or abilities you learn. You can read more about the nature/nurture argument in relation to intelligence and educational achievement in Module 7 on Education, Unit 4.

A pygmy man in child-caring role

Q Do you think the gender role differences in Britain are due more to biology or culture? Try to write a few paragraphs giving your own views on this question.

sociologists speak of the **culture** of society, they are referring to the way of life within that society, its values, attitudes, beliefs and traditions).

Children are born male or female, but they learn to become either *masculine* or *feminine*. These attitudes are known as **gender roles** and children learn them through the family, the education system and the mass media.

BRAINSTORM

What does the word masculine mean to you? What does the word feminine mean to you? You could divide into groups and then compare your ideas. □

The normal or expected gender role for a male is to be masculine and for a female to be feminine, any change in these roles, such as a male who acts in a feminine way or vice-versa, is regarded as deviant.

DISCUSS

Do you think it is *normal* for a male to be sensitive and to cry when unhappy or moved? □

Recently a group of 14 year-old students in Britain suggested that to be *feminine* is to be attractive, a good mother, good housewife, quiet, pretty, neat, a good cook, caring, loving, etc.

Q How do your groups brainstorms of the term feminine compare with this definition? □

The women of the Mundagumor tribe in New Guinea are almost exactly the opposite to this description. To be feminine in the Mundagumor is to be assertive, forceful and to detest child-bearing and child-rearing! Furthermore, it is the males in the Tchambuli tribe in New Guinea who decorate themselves, carve, paint and practise dancing, whilst their wives go fishing.

T A S K

Suggest ways in which girls in Britain learn to be caring, sensitive and quiet, as part of their feminine role, and how the Mundagumor women learn to be assertive and forceful. Which behaviour is really feminine? For more on this subject of women's gender role, look at the works of the social anthropologist, Margaret Mead. □

It can be seen from these brief examples that the way males and females behave in their gender roles, depends greatly on the culture or society to which they belong. Another example of a different culture with different, ways of behaving is that of the Mbuti pygmies, where there are very few distinctions or differences between the sexes. The Mbuti pygmy males often care for the children and both sexes go hunting and gathering food.

In Britain, on the other hand, where women do their hunting and gathering in the local supermarket, they usually take the children along too! In other words, child-caring and domestic work are traditionally part of the feminine gender role and are not usually shared equally by males in our society.

RESEARCH IDEA

Using the library as a resource, locate other examples of photographs, cartoons, articles, etc. depicting gender roles in British society and in other societies or cultures. Note whether there are any evident differences in the expected gender roles of males and females. □

DISCUSS

Using the examples given on this page and your own research or ideas, discuss which gender roles you prefer and why. □

SEX-ROLE SOCIALISATION

It is important to examine in detail *how* females and males learn their gender roles. This process of learning is called **socialisation** and it can be seen to take place in at least four areas or **subsytems** of society.

1 *The Family* This is where the first or **primary** socialisation takes place. Parents are of course very important to children, and children love to please their parents and copy them. Therefore, if they see their father going out to work and their mother taking responsibility for the house, then these will be the **role models** the children accept as normal for themselves. Many children's games reveal the way in which children identify with their parent's roles, playing 'mummy' and 'daddy' roles.

Furthermore, some parents tend to treat their children differently according to the particular sex of the child. For example, boys are perhaps expected to be tougher and more boisterous; they are given mechanical toys that are closely linked with the world of work, such as train sets, they are also encouraged to play strenuous games and are expected to get their clothes dirty.

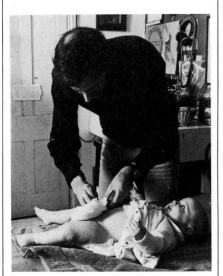

How many children experience this role-model?

| T | A | S | K |

Make a list of boys' toys and games. What do you think boys are learning through their play? □

As *Anna Coote* reveals, girls are often given dolls, dolls' houses, little housewife cleaning sets, toy kitchens containing utensils for the modern Miss to cook with, just like mother and they are encouraged to play cleaner games, such as skipping, which keeps their clothes neat and attractive.

| T | A | S | K |

Make a list of girls' toys and games. What do you think girls are learning about their role in society from these toys and games? □

Sociologists, such as *Ann Oakley*, argue that the toys and games children play with in the family and at school, teach them about their future adult roles in society. In this way, girls learn, or are socialised into the feminine role of child-rearing and domesticity, whilst boys learn about their future work roles. All of this primary socialisation takes place from a very early age and is the way in which boys and girls are taught to behave differently and to have different interests and attitudes which then affect the rest of their lives.

DISCUSS

Why do girls/females tend to wear dresses and boys/males to wear trousers? Why are there these differences in clothing? Which clothing is the more comfortable to wear? □

DISCUSS

Some young women decide not to change their names to that of their husband on marriage. They see this tradition as simply reinforcing male domination, or **patriarchy** as it is often called, and wish to retain their own identity.

Do you think this helps to bring more equality between males and females in society? □

RESEARCH IDEA

Construct a questionnaire asking people to suggest suitable toys to buy for a three-year-old boy and a three-year-old girl. Are there any differences?

| T | A | S | K |

Some writers suggest that boy and girl babies are even handled differently and spoken to in different tones and words right from birth. In pairs, conduct a simple role-play (in private if you prefer) of a parent speaking encouragingly to their young child so that they will eat the food prepared for them. Role play the parent speaking to a baby girl and then the parent speaking to a baby boy. Do you observe any difference in your tone of voice, behaviour, words used, etc? If so, why do you think this happens?

2 *The School* This is where the differences between males and females are reinforced. For example, in the choice of subjects taken by third year pupils in their options, there is a clear difference in terms of gender.

T A S K

Examine the bar chart given below and identify which subjects girls are most interested in, and which subjects are dominated by boys.

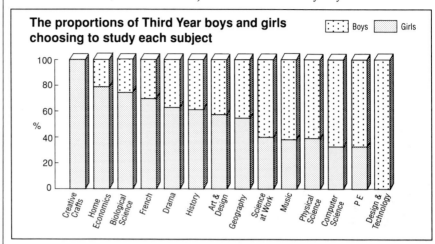

Source: *A study of option choices in a comprehensive school* by C Hales, 1981

You will notice that more girls take arts subjects, such as creative crafts, home economics, french, history, art and design. Whereas, subjects like science, computers and CDT are dominated by males. □

Now answer the following questions:

QUESTIONS

1 Are some subjects more feminine or more masculine than others? Give examples of each and explain why.
2 Which is the only science where there are more girls than boys opting for it? Suggest reasons why this happens.
3 Why are there no girls taking Design and Technology? What do you think will be the result of this in future years?
4 Although sociology does not appear in the options chart, more females tend to take sociology than males. Why do you think this happens? □

Source: MEG Sociology GCSE Specimen Questions, 1988

DISCUSS

Tessa Blackstone argues that since less girls take science, computing and CDT, that this explains why there are so few women scientists and engineers. Do you agree? Can you suggest ways to change this situation in schools? Will the National Curriculum help to redress the sex balance in these school subject areas? □

Other writers argue that teachers, like parents, also tend to have different expectations for their male and female pupils. They act differently towards girls as opposed to boys, and encourage or guide girls into following courses which lead to traditional feminine careers. Teachers, therefore, are often accused of **sex-stereotyping**, or, reinforcing what girls are/are not expected to do in society. For example, girls are not expected or encouraged to be mining engineers. Furthermore, teachers expect girls to be quieter in class (and therefore expect boys to be noisier) and research by *Dale Spender* has shown that teachers give the quieter, more conscientious girls less attention in class than the more extrovert, and noisier boys.

RESEARCH IDEA

Conduct your own research in school to see whether this study by *C Hales* in 1981 is still relevant today. How will you gain your information about the number of girls and boys in each subject?

RESEARCH IDEA

Do you agree with Dale Spender's research? Do teachers in your school or college give more attention to boys than girls? Conduct your own research to find out. Which would be the most appropriate method of research?

Would you use a *questionnaire* to ask teachers or pupils if teachers give more attention to boys or, would you *observe* teacher behaviour in class and decide for yourself? Which is the fairest method of finding out? For more details on these see Module 1 on research methods.

I'm sure Roger has the right answer...

Highest qualifications of school-leavers by sex 1980–1981

Highest qualifications	Percentages	
	Boys	Girls
2 or more GCE A-levels	14	13
1 GCE A-level	3	3
5 or more GCE O-levels	8	11
1 to 4 GCE O-levels	24	29
Other Grades	37	35
No Graded Qualifications	13	10

Source: DES statistical bulletin

Several sociologists suggest that the effects of the teacher paying less attention to the girls in class – and more attention to the lads – is to reinforce the belief that boys are more important and therefore deserve more attention; and, that girls are therefore less important requiring less attention by the teacher.

The evidence below would seem to indicate that girls are actually neglected by some teachers in class.

Interviewer:	Who does Mrs Symonds pay most attention to in this group?
Male Pupil:	She pays a lot of attention to Bob and me.
Interviewer:	Who gets paid the least attention, do you think, in this class?
Male Pupil:	Edith, I think. Then there's those other two girls, Judy and Eve. Those three, they are very quiet, they don't say very much. They are just bumbling along so they get left alone . . .
Interviewer:	Even though they don't understand?
Male Pupil:	Yeah, but you just completely don't notice Edith. You forget her existence. Whereas if me and Bob are away, Mrs Symonds notices that, because we usually make a lot of noise in the class.

Source: *Gender and Schooling* by M Stamworth, 1981

DISCUSS

Examine the suggestion that the single-sex schools, i.e. schools for girls or for boys only, are better than mixed-sex schools since girls would get more attention from teachers. □

Nevertheless, despite what goes on inside the classroom, girls at 16 years of age are generally more successful than boys in examinations. The table on the left reveals how more girls pass O-levels than boys – but it also reveals how fewer girls gain sufficient A-level passes, to enable them to get onto higher education courses, than boys.

DISCUSS

Suggest reasons why less girls take and obtain A-levels than boys? What happens to girls between GCSE/O-level at 16 years and A-level at 18 years? □

Research by *Sarah Bayliss* in 1982 revealed that girls were actually discouraged from entering higher education because teachers thought that most would get married at an early age! Similarly in *Just Like a Girl*, **Sue Sharpe** studied a group of secondary school girls in Ealing and found that they were primarily concerned about boy-friends and their future prospects of marriage. School and education in general, were seen as largely irrelevant in their eyes, as they would only be working for a few years at the most before settling down into marriage and child-bearing.

RESEARCH IDEA

Where do you think these girls in Ealing got their ideas from? Are girls different in your area? Is Sue Sharpe's research out-of-date now or do girls still see education as largely irrelevant and unimportant? Conduct your own research into:

a How long girls expect to work when they leave school
b Whether they would like to go on to higher education and
c What sorts of occupations girls want to go into.

Decide for yourself whether these occupations are typical women's work: teaching, nursing, office work, working as a shop assistant, etc. □

The Great 11+ Gender Robbery!

Did you know . . . that more girls passed the 11+ EXAM than boys? However, because boys had not reached the level of maturity of girls at 11 years it was felt to be unfair to boys. Therefore, the boys' scores were weighted, i.e. marks were added on to compensate for their lack of maturity, thus enabling more of them to pass the 11+ and since there were only a certain number of places available, some girls who actually passed the exam were failed in order to allow enough boys into the Grammar schools.

DISCUSS

Do you think this was fair?

Q With the National Curriculum do you think more 11 year-old girls will achieve higher levels of attainment?

The way in which some teachers differentiate between girls and boys in lessons is sometimes referred to as being part of the **hidden curriculum** (see Module 7 on Education, page 121). This is an important sociological concept to grasp and the following explanation should be considered carefully.

Teachers in school are, believe it or not, only human! They are part of society and therefore share the same values, attitudes and behaviour of most other people in society. This is referred to as sharing the **dominant culture** of society. If, in this dominant culture of British society, the traditional feminine role is to be primarily concerned with child-rearing and domesticity, and the traditional masculine role is to be mainly concerned with work, then it is perhaps not surprising that the teacher will also share these values and attitudes about gender roles and will therefore speak and behave differently towards girls as opposed to boys.

In sociology, this whole area of expectations, attitudes and relationships between teachers and pupils, and between pupils and pupils, is referred to as the *hidden curriculum* and it is far more powerful in reproducing the inequalities between males and females than is the **overt curriculum** i.e. the subjects on the timetable.

RESEARCH IDEA

The effects of the hidden curriculum can be seen on page 213 in the student's option choices. Investigate why girls in most schools do not tend to choose CDT. How is the hidden curriculum at work? □

Another example of the hidden curriculum can often be found in the form registers. Investigate whether girls and boys are differentiated according to sex in the registers in your school or college. If so, why are they? What message does this practice give to the pupils in school?

3 *The Mass Media* This term refers to the wealth of books, magazines, newspapers, films, radio and television programmes in society. In the mass media, it is possible to see how the traditional gender role differences are again continuously reinforced or strengthened.

T A S K

Take a look at some children's reading books. Do you remember the ones you had at your first school? Were they like these?

Note: The illustrations shown here are not from the Ladybird scheme

DISCUSS

Should both males and females be prepared or socialised into the caring roles in the family and society? How can children's books help to do this?

Sociologists argue that stories and pictures like these reinforce the ideas that girls should help Mummy to dust, sweep the floor and get the tea, just like Jane who is, of course, a 'good girl'.

a What sort of adult role are girls, like Jane, being prepared for by pictures and words like those in the early Ladybird books?
b What is Peter doing? Is he helping with the housework too? Why not?
c If girls are being prepared for their future 'caring roles' words like these, what sort of future roles are boys being prepared for in society? □

'Peter likes to play with toys. He plays with a toy station and a toy train. Jane says, 'Please can I play?' 'Yes,' says Peter, 'I have the train. You play with the station.'

Peter and Jane like to help Mummy. They go to the shops for Mummy. 'Come on,' says Peter, 'We have to go to the fish shop.' Peter and Jane like to help Daddy. They help Daddy with the car. Jane is in the car. Daddy and Peter have some water (to wash the car).

Jane and Peter want some flowers. 'Some flowers for you and some for me,' says Jane. 'Get some flowers, Peter. Get some for Mummy and Daddy.'

Q Do you feel that gender stereotypes are still being perpetuated in this reading book?

T A S K

Write a fairy story where the traditional gender roles are reversed and the female saves the male from disaster. Read it to friends, relatives and brothers and record their impressions or reactions to the story.

T A S K

Examine some of the these magazines critically to see whether the story content is nearly always about love and how to win your man.

Also examine boys' magazines. What is the content of these magazines? Are they concerned with love and advice on how to win a girl-friend?

T A S K

The text on the mini-pages on page 215 were taken from the early Ladybird reading scheme. The series was rewritten in 1972. Examine the extract on the left from the later stories and see if there are any differences in the way gender roles are portrayed here. □

RESEARCH IDEA

Collect as many examples of reading schemes from family, friends and local primary schools, as possible. Compare the gender roles portrayed in these reading books and report back to the group with your findings. □

Traditional gender roles or stereotypes are also reinforced by the nursery rhymes and fairy stories learnt, recited and acted out by children in their early years.

T A S K

Consider two of the most popular nursery rhymes learnt and recited by most children in Britain: *Little Miss Muffet* and *Little Bo Peep*. What sort of feminine image is portrayed by these rhymes? Describe the characters of Miss Muffet and Little Bo Peep. Decide whether they are portrayed as strong, active and clever, or weak, timid and in need of help. □

Now consider other nursery rhymes, such as *Tom, Tom the Piper's Son* and *Little Jack Horner*. What sort of masculine image is portrayed here? Investigate other nursery rhymes and interpret or decide for yourself what image or message these rhymes are giving to the young child who learns them by heart.

RESEARCH IDEA

Fairy stories are also very interesting to study. Investigate the plots or story lines in *Sleeping Beauty*, *Snow White*, *Rapunzel* and *Cinderella*. What does each have in common? Is there a damsel in distress in each of these stories? Who saves the damsel? What happens at the end of each story?

What sort of image of femininity do you think is being portrayed in each of these fairy stories – what is the princess like? Consider also the image of masculinity portrayed in Fairy Stories. What is the hero prince like? Considering that children grow up believing in these tales, what effect do you think this might have on children's ideas and expectations about what is normal behaviour for males and females in society? □

Teenagers do not read fairy stories and nursery rhymes of course, but the magazines they buy also reinforce gender stereotypes. Girls tend to buy magazines, such as *Jackie, 17, Oh Boy! PhotoLove* and *My Guy* which tend to concentrate on the theme of how to win a boy-friend. The stories usually portray the male as dominant and fully in charge of the relationship.

Advertisements also reinforce the idea that to be feminine means to be attractive and sexually desirable. Adverts suggests that females can achieve this femininity by buying perfume, deodorant, makeup, etc.

T A S K

Collect adverts from a range of magazines: teenage, women's, football, motorcycle, etc and newspapers. Examine them and decide on the particular image of femininity or masculinity that is being portrayed or used in the advert. Look at the examples below and also see Module 2 on Mass Media page 21. □

DISCUSS

Why will some women (and men) be offended by this advert? ☐

DISCUSS

Why do females pluck their eyebrows and shave under their arms? Why don't males? ☐

T A S K

Collect a range of women's magazines and examine the content to judge whether the traditional feminine role, i.e. of mother, housewife and cook is being reinforced through the romantic stories, recipes, knitting patterns and adverts. Are there some women's magazines that include articles and features on women's careers and other interests outside of the home? ☐

RESEARCH IDEA

Examine the Agony Aunt . . . Dear Cathy . . . letters in both teenage and women's magazines in order to discover the major problems for females identified in these. Discuss your findings.

Do boys' magazines have a 'problem' page?

It is common for boys to read girls' magazines when they are left lying around. If so why do they do this? ☐

DISCUSS

Page 3 girls, are they being exploited as sex objects by the media, or are they exploiting the media by using their femininity to their own personal advantage? ☐

RESEARCH IDEA

Examine advertisements on the **television** for washing-up liquid, soap powder, food, hand cream, etc. Do these advertisements portray females in their traditional domestic, child-caring roles? Are they guilty of sex-stereotyping? Are there any adverts using males to demonstrate washing-up liquid or soap powder, etc? Compare your findings and interpretations with the rest of the group. ☐

WOMEN AND WORK

One major change in British society since the Second World War has been the great increase in the number of married women going out to work. Now, approximately 50 per cent of all married women work and women make up 40 per cent of the total work-force of the country.

However despite the importance of women to the economy, women are paid less on average than men. For example, in 1983, the average weekly wage for men was £105.50p, but for women was £99.00 – women earned and still do earn only 70 per cent of the average male wage!

DISCUSS

Do you think this is fair? ☐

Sociologists have studied the persistence of this inequality of pay between men and women in society, and have looked at why it still occurs despite the fact that in 1970, the Equal Pay Act was passed which stated that males and females must be paid equally for equal work!

Ann Oakley argues that the reason why women earn only 70 per cent of men's wages is due to the way in which the labour force is largely segregated or divided into **women's jobs** and **men's jobs**. Two-thirds of all women workers are to be found in the ten 'worst' occupations, especially shop assistants, office workers and nurses. These jobs are not only low paid, but are often low status with often little opportunity or possibility of earning any overtime money.

QUESTIONS

Look at the tables below and opposite and answer the following:
1   Name two jobs in which 75 to 90 per cent of the workers are women.
2   Are these jobs well-paid?
3   Give examples of highly-paid, high-status jobs in society. Is there any reason why women cannot do these jobs? ☐

Source: MEG Sociology specimen paper GCSE, 1988

Range and type of women's jobs

Eight out of ten women who go out to work in Great Britain are employed in one of the four types of jobs.

Office and clerical work	30.3%
Catering and domestic services	20.4%
Unskilled and semi-skilled factory work	15.9%
Shop work	10.1%
Total	76.7%

This means that some jobs have come to be thought of as 'women's jobs', as shown below:

Jobs in which over 90% of the workers are women	Canteen assistant	Sewing machinist	Nurse	Maid	Typist
Jobs in which 75%–90% of the workers are women	Shop assistant	Telephone operator	Cleaner	Hairdresser	
Jobs in which 60%–75% of the workers are women	Cashier	Packer	Cook	Primary school teacher	

Who does what?

	Full-time women	Part-time women	All working women	Working men
	%	%	%	%
Management general	less than 1	less than 1	less than 1	1
Professionals supporting management	2	less than 1	1	6
Professionals in health, education and welfare	16	10	13	5
Literary, artistic and sports	1	1	1	1
Professionals in engineering and science	1	less than 1	1	5
Other managerial	5	1	4	12
Clerical	41	22	33	6
Selling	5	13	9	4
Security	0	less than 1	0	2
Catering, cleaning and hairdressing	10	41	23	3
Farming and fishing	1	2	1	2
Material processing (excluding metal	1	1	1	3
Making and repairing (excluding metal)	6	4	5	6
Metal processing, making, repairing	3	1	2	20
Painting, assembling, packing	8	3	5	5
Construction and mining	less than 1	less than 1	less than 1	6
Transport	1	1	1	11
Miscellaneous	less than 1	less than 1	less than 1	1
	100	100	100	100

DISCUSS

Why are women not allowed to work down the mines in Britain? They used to, as this article reveals; and there are women miners in America and Russia. □

Source: *The Evening Sentinel*, October 1986

Women who worked at the pit-heads

WOMEN have a long history in coal mines prior to industrialisation. The North Staffs Polytechnic have now put out an appeal for old photographs of Staffordshire women who worked at the pit-heads in the 18th and early 19th centuries.

They will tie in with a current exhibition in the Foyer Gallery at the Poly, "Our Lives — Our Struggle", which includes photographs of the women who worked at the "pit brow" of the Lancashire coalfields.

"The photographs tell us more of the gruelling work that was demanded of these women and suggest some achieved a dignity and independence in spite of it," says Zoe Munby, Department of History and Design.

'I KEEP IMAGINING THE CONGREGATION HAVING TO WAIT WHILE THE WOMAN PRIEST IN THE PULPIT RUMMAGES THROUGH HER HANDBAG FOR THE SERMON'

The reason that newspapers continue to print jokes like the one on the left is that very few of the **top jobs** in society are held by women, despite the fact that we have a female Prime Minister and a Queen.

Sociologists argue that the reason for this state of affairs is largely due to sex-role socialisation, as described in the previous unit. If girls are not encouraged or socialised into thinking of an important career, by their family, school or the mass media and instead are expected to take on the traditional mother and housewife role, then work outside the home will be regarded as of *secondary* or lesser importance for most females. It is because this happens, many writers argue, that women are then willing to accept low-paid, part-time work that fits in with their *primary* role in the family.

Many women are even willing to work as a **homeworker** – the lowest paid job in Britain, when women often earn less than *40* pence per hour!

DISCUSS

Why do you think some women will work as homeworkers when the pay is so poor? Why can't they go out to work? □

Despite the passing of the Sex Discrimination Act in 1975, there is little evidence that women are able to break down the barriers that guard the highly-paid professions. For example, only 10 per cent of all Bank Managers, less than 1 per cent of airline pilots and only 2 per cent of all doctors are female. Only 5 per cent of MPs are women and in 1989 there were no female Ministers in Mrs Thatcher's cabinet. Even in the female dominated industries, such as catering (see table on range and type of women's jobs on page 218) men are to be found occupying the top most positions, for example, Chef and Hotel Manager, whilst females occupy the lower-paid positions, such as catering assistant.

RESEARCH IDEA

Interview ten female workers to see whether the comment below is appropriate or not.
In a study of shiftworkers in 1979, *March* commented that 'women work with women, but are supervised more often than not by a man'. □

RESEARCH IDEA

Investigate how many female Heads of Department there are in your school, college or office. □

DISCUSS

Examine the reasons why few women teachers get to the top of the promotions ladder.

QUESTIONS

Look at this table and answer the following:

1 What percentage of male teachers are on Main Scale with no incentive allowance?
2 What percentage of female teachers are on this same scale?
3 What percentage of male teachers are on Main Scale incentive E allowance?
4 What percentage of female teachers are on this scale?

Note: incentive allowances are awarded for additional responsibilities, e.g. as Head of Department

Percentages of men and women secondary teachers on different pay scales, March 1988

	Men		Women	
	Full-time	Part-time	Full-time	Part-time
Head	4	1	1	–
Deputy head	7	–	4	–
Main scale with:				
incentive allowance:				
E	6	2	2	–
D	21	7	8	–
C	2	1	2	–
B	26	10	22	1
A	3	4	4	1
no incentive allowance	31	63	57	91
Other scales*	–	13	1	7
Total	100	100	100	100
All teachers (thousands)	103.0	3.6	88.4	26.0

Source: DES Survey of Secondary Staffing in England

© Times Newspapers Ltd, 1989

However, despite these inequalities of pay and status at work, an increasing number of women are going out to work, for the reasons given on page 222. They are taking on the **dual roles** of housewife/mother and of worker/paid employee. This **double identity**, as *Sue Sharpe* calls it, can cause great strains on the women and can produce changes in conjugal relationships. For example, the wife going out to work can either bring more democracy or equality into the relationship between husband and wife, with both sharing the housework and child-caring roles equally, or it can bring more stress and conflict.

DISCUSS

If both husband and wife go out to work, do you think the housework and child-caring roles should be equally shared? Does this actually happen in practice? Refer to your own research. □

QUESTIONS

1. In the list on the left, *Oakley* describes housework as alienating, i.e. as boring and lonely work. Do you agree?
2. Since housework is unpaid, is it real work? (See Module 8 on Work, page 130.)
3. Can you think of any ways to improve the life of a housewife?
4. Consider role-reversal. How many househusbands do you know of? What reasons lie behind a man's decision to swop roles do you think? □

DISCUSS

In groups, read this article, to see if you agree with the research. It might provoke a lively debate.

Source: *The Sunday Mirror*, (Mother's Day), March 1987.

PRICE OF A WIFE?

Here's something to think about on Mother's Day—the great British housewife is worth £370.25 a week.

That is how much she would earn if she were paid for her chores around the home.

It works out at £19,253 a year, more than twice the national average salary.

On those wages the typical housewife would be better off than a bishop, a fire chief, an Army major or a Second Division footballer.

A First World War munitions worker

Q What other jobs did women do during the First World War and the Second World War? □

Reasons for the increase in the number of married women working:

1 The work the women did in the two world wars, when they did men's jobs, together with the suffragettes and other female emancipation movements, who helped to fight for and bring about a rise in the status of women.

2 Birth control has enabled smaller families, and therefore a greater freedom for females who are no longer tied to the home for long periods of childbirth and rearing.

3 Technical developments have led to a growth in light industry, e.g. electronics and communications and have produced jobs that employers feel are suited to women. There has also been an increase in the service industries, e.g. shops and catering – both of which tend to be low paid and low status.

4 Better education for all, including females has meant that women are better qualified than ever before and therefore better able to compete with males in the labour market for work.

5 Women are attractive to employers because they are willing to work part time, which can legally be paid at a lower rate with no National Insurance contributions to pay. Women are therefore a cheap source of labour; and even full-time women workers still earn only 70 per cent of the wages of men.

QUESTIONS

1 Why are employers quite happy to employ part-time workers?
2 Why are 90 per cent of part-time workers women?
3 Why do women earn on average only 70 per cent of male earnings?
4 Why do you think women are absent from work more often than men? □

RESEARCH IDEA

Suffragettes used both peaceful protest and also more militant action. What did they do in order to gain the vote? □

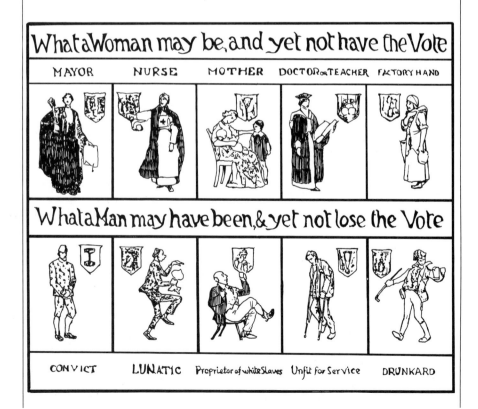

UNIT 4

CHANGES IN THE LAW

The **Equal Pay Act** of 1970 stated that women doing broadly similar work to men should get paid at the same rate.

The **Employment Protection Act** of 1975 gave women the right to paid maternity leave and the opportunity of returning to work afterwards.

The **Sex Discrimination Act** of 1975 stated that it was illegal to treat a person less favourably on the grounds of their sex in employment, training, education, housing, etc.

The **Equal Opportunities Commission** was set up in 1975, to promote equal opportunities for men and women and to deal with cases of discrimination.

The **Independent Taxation Legislation** came into effect in April 1990. A wife's income is no longer deemed to belong to her husband and she completes her own tax return.

Details of several recent changes in the law which *should* have helped women gain equality of pay and status at work are given in the margin.

RESEARCH IDEA

Take *one* of the following problems or hypotheses concerned with changes in the law and the equality of women in society. Conduct a fieldwork investigation to establish whether the problem still exists. □

1 Despite the Equal Pay Act, women earn only two-thirds the pay of men. One way in which employers have found a loop hole in the Act is by segregating women into areas of work where their job and pay could not then be compared to that of the men in the organisation.

Does this still happen in your area?

There has been a recent change in the law, which allows a woman to claim equal pay for a job of equal importance, e.g. a secretary or cook with an engineer or a miner. Has this recent change in the law brought about any real changes in pay in your area?

2 The problem with the Employment Protection Act is that a man cannot have the same right to paid maternity leave as a woman. He cannot claim paternity leave, and cannot therefore afford to stay at home and take over the child-caring role, whilst his wife goes out to work. This means that it will always be the female that stays at home to look after the children.
a How many weeks paid maternity leave is a woman entitled to?
b Has she any right to return to her employer? Is her job guaranteed? Would men really like the opportunity to take paid paternity leave?

3 In education it is unlawful to discriminate between boys and girls. Both must have the same educational opportunities. For example, girls must have the opportunity of doing CDT and boys of doing Home Economics if they wish. However, this provision of equality of opportunity is obviously not enough to actually encourage girls and boys to take these subjects, as the chart on page 213 shows. This is evidently a problem which the Sex Discrimination Act has not yet changed. What actually happens to influence girls against CDT and boys against Home Economics, before they reach 13 to 14 years of age and are ready to make their option choices?
a Do pupils have an equal experience in these subjects in their primary school and in the years 1 to 3 in their secondary school education?
b What are the pupils' views or perceptions of these subjects.

4 Employers who advertise for employees are not allowed to state which sex they prefer for the job. However, they often find ways of describing the job to indicate which sex they would prefer to apply.

Examine a sample of newspapers, especially local ones, to find examples of such advertisements.

It is still possible to find examples of adverts stating a particular sex of employee. This is, of course, illegal – unless sex is a genuine occupational qualification for the job. For example, 'actress required for the part of Lady Macbeth'. Can you think of or find any other examples like this?

5 As there are still great inequalities between men and women in society, can it be claimed that the Equal Opportunities Commission is really working?
a What powers has the EOC got to deal with practices of discrimination?
b How many complaints has it received and dealt with?
c How far has it helped to achieve equality between the sexes in your view?

UNIT 5 | SEXUALITY

This unit looks at the area of sexuality, which should be considered and discussed with great sensitivity and care.

One major role or image attributed to females in British society is that of the sexually-desirable/page 3/dolly-bird. This image is to be found in the daily newspapers, in advertisements and also in the many 'girlie' magazines sold above and below the counter of newsagents shops.

RESEARCH IDEA

It is interesting to consider why women are to be found half-naked in newspapers and advertisements and not half-naked men. Is the female body more attractive than the male body? Conduct a quick survey to gauge peoples' opinions on this issue. □

Many people believe that males have more sexual urges or needs than females. Whilst this is certainly not true, it could partly explain why there are huge businesses established which cater for the sexual needs of males. For example, there are strip-tease and sex-shops of Soho in London and in many other cities. There are also pornographic and sexually violent films and videos available, besides sexually-explicit magazines.

Many female writers point out the damaging effect pornography has on the image and status of women in society. They claimed that pornography is degrading to women and can encourage violent, sexual crimes against women, such as rape. (See also Unit 4 on Women and Crime, in Module 13 on Deviance)

In Britain, double standards exist with regards to sex. For example, many people believe that a casual sexual relationship is acceptable, even natural, for a male, but, for a female, it is something shameful and unfeminine.

A boy or man who has several girl-friends or sexual partners is often described as 'one of the lads' or as 'sowing his wild oats'; but, a girl or woman who does the same thing is referred to as easy, promiscuous or even worse.

Lads, then are expected to be promiscuous in society, but promiscuous girls are despised, as *P Willis* in *Learning To Labour*, 1977 describes:

'. . . the lads are after the easy lay at dances, though they think twice about being seen to go out with them. The girl-friend is a very different category from an easy lay.'

DISCUSS

What are your views about this? Why is it quite acceptable for a lad to have sex with a girl, but despicable for a girl to have sex with a boy? Is this a case of double standards? □

Has the spread of AIDS changed everyone's views about casual sex?

Although, in Britain it is the male that is expected to be more sexually assertive than the female, it is interesting to discover that other cultures do not share the same image or view of male and female sexuality. For example, among the Zuni Indians of North America, it is the women who are expected to be sexually aggressive, whilst the men are sexually timid and approach their wedding night with trepidation.

DISCUSS
Why are most prostitutes female?

The British image of male sexuality is of course very different. Males are taught to cultivate a macho image and to suppress their own emotions and feeling in public. *Andrew Tolson* has pointed out this male, macho stereotype can be just as limiting to men as the female sex-object stereotype is to women.

DISCUSS

The British may be famous for their 'stiff upper lip', meaning that it is a national characteristic for males to be reserved, and unemotional, especially in public. Discuss this and think of any societies or nationalities where it is the norm to show your feelings towards the opposite sex, even in public? How do these differences in behaviour, between societies come about? Is the younger British male more open in his emotional life than his father and grandfather before him? □

In further discussing the sensitive area of sexuality, it is important to remember that not all sexual relationships in Britain are **heterosexual**, i.e. between adult males and females. There are other forms of sexual relationship, such as that between adult male and male: this is called a **homosexual** relationship, and that between female and female, which is referred to as a **lesbian** relationship.

Whether people are born either heterosexual, homosexual or lesbian, or whether they learn through their environment to take on a particular sexual relationship, causes much debate. What is clear, however, is that in British society homosexuality and lesbianism are labelled as deviant. As *Ken Plummer* in *Sexual Stigma*, 1975 has pointed out, this labelling then causes considerable public shame, abuse and even physical attack against homosexuals and lesbians.

Q   People who prefer homosexual and lesbian relationships are often stereotyped by the media. How does the media depict gays through television characters, pictures, jokes, etc.? Are the images perpetuated by the media fair or accurate? □

Finally, then, it would appear that in the area of sexuality, there is a considerable degree of liberation to be achieved, not simply for females trapped in their sexual stereotype, but for both sexes and sexual relationships in our society. What do you think?

QUESTIONS

1   a   Look at cartoon A. What does the wife do which embarrasses her husband?
    b   A sociologist might call the husband's reaction an attempt to conform to social pressure. Briefly explain the meaning of the term 'social pressure'.
    c   What is meant by 'role conflict', give an example.
    d   Explain why the mothers of the female engineering candidates find it difficult to accept the career choice made by their daughters. See extract B.
    e   Examine table C. Which O-level subjects had a mainly male entry? Discuss the extent to which schools are responsible for continuing this entry pattern.

Q   Do you think it is a good thing for males to hide their feelings? Can you think of any problems in personal relationships that this can cause?

One in how many?

Homosexual disclosure

Judge 'victim of blackmail'

© Times Newspapers Ltd, 1988

Q   Is it shameful to be gay?

A

Things are different now that we're married Liz... people are talking!

Oh darling, Im sorry— I'll never fix the lawnmower for you again!

B

The candidate flushed. I had clearly embarrassed her but how? All I had asked was how she intended to spend the time between the end of her work with a well-known engineering company and starting university the following October. It's the sort of dull question that all interviewers ask when they cannot think up anything brighter.

She took a while to answer and this is what she said:
"Well, my mum thinks, after all this engineering, that I ought to do some normal things . . . you know, cooking and sewing . . ."

There was an awful silence. Both of us were embarrassed now. We had touched the delicate issue of the "female engineer", the collision of two opposing role models could be seen in my poor candidate's red face. Other female engineering candidates had told me similar stories, of mothers who allow bumbling dads to make messes of their toasters but won't allow daughters to change a plug.

C

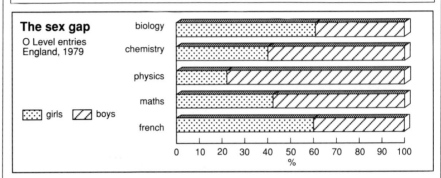

The sex gap
O Level entries
England, 1979

girls   boys

Source: *New Society*, March 1983

2   *Equal pay and sex discrimination*

In some ways legislation has helped women. It has helped to create a social climate in which women increasingly expect to be treated equally with men and it has prevented some of the more obvious forms of social and legal discrimination. But many people feel that the legislation does not go far enough. Loopholes have appeared which make it possible in practice for employers to find ways of avoiding paying women equal wages, and the Equal Opportunities Commission has turned out to be a rather moderate, secretive body, reluctant to campaign actively on behalf of women or to speak out strongly against continuing discrimination.

Source: *Examining Sociology* by Jane L Thompson, 1980

A woman's work

The Equal Pay Act, 1970, has lost its power to improve the lot of women. The main reason for the lack of progress is the entrenched segregation of 'men's jobs' and 'women's jobs', which in manual work is increasing. Some 47 per cent of female manual workers were hairdressers, cleaners, or in catering and services in 1975; by 1981 this total had risen to 57 per cent.

But outright prejudice still exists, too: men will still threaten to strike to prevent women taking 'men's' jobs.

There are slightly fewer women in the traditional clerical jobs that there were, but this could herald an invasion of offices by men eager to use the new technology.

Source: *New Society*, June 1982

a   i   According to the first passage, in what ways has equal pay legislation been a success?
   ii   What are the two reasons given in the second passage for the lack of any recent improvement in women's pay relative to men's pay?
b   Explain why women still tend to be concentrated in jobs like cleaning and catering.
c   The second passage suggests that more men are now working in clerical jobs. What are the reasons for this, and what may be the consequences?

3   Write a short essay on the following question.
   'Why do girls and women tend to get jobs which are low paid, low status and unskilled, usually caring for others and serving men?'   □

WHERE TO NOW . . .?
This module could lead you virtually anywhere. You might decide to read more about the powerful socialisation agencies of The Family, Education and the Mass Media . . . or you might turn to Module 13 on Deviance for more about women and crime. You could instead study another inequality in society. See Module 6 on Inequality and Module 5 on Social Stratification.

Source: UCLES Sociology GCSE, 1984

M O D U L E · 13

DEVIANCE

THIRTEEN

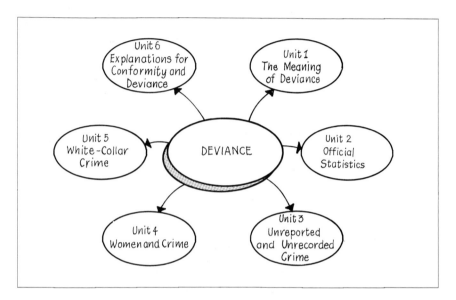

WHAT THIS MODULE IS ABOUT

This module aims to give the reader an understanding of deviance and to assess what official statistics really show about the amount of crime in society. There is also a focus on two areas of crime that are often neglected, those committed by women, and those committed by middle-class people. Finally, some of the sociological explanations for the increasing crime rate are assessed and contrasted with those offered by other disciplines, such as biology.

BY THE END OF THIS MODULE YOU SHOULD BE ABLE TO:

1 Explain what is meant by deviance and why deviance is called a relative concept.
2 Understand why official statistics of crime may not accurately reflect the actual amount of crime in society.
3 Show an understanding of white-collar crime.
4 Explain why statistics for female crime are increasing.
5 Illustrate the difference between informal and formal social controls.
6 Discuss different sociological theories of deviance.
7 Assess biological explanations of deviance and be aware of how they still influence the way people think about deviants.

THE MEANING OF DEVIANCE

Deviance means behaviour that goes against the accepted norms of society. Deviants are people who behave in an unacceptable way. This could include teachers coming to work in their underwear or a male pupil wearing a dress! Some deviant acts are also criminal. A **crime** is an act which breaks the law and it is usually considered deviant as well as criminal. A burglar for example is deviant because what he does is unacceptable, and criminal because it is also against the law.

DISCUSS

Which of the following acts are deviant? Which are criminal? Which are both deviant and criminal?
a   Writing graffitti on a wall with an aerosol can.
b   Exceeding the speed limit by five miles an hour.
c   Keeping pet snakes in the living-room.
d   Sunbathing in the nude.
e   Stealing from work.
f   Killing another person.
g   Taking drugs.
h   Dyeing your hair green. □

Behaviour that is considered by a society to be deviant at one time or one place may become perfectly acceptable in another and behaviour that was once acceptable may become deviant or even criminal if a new law is passed. This means that both crime and deviance are **relative** concepts, i.e. whether or not behaviour is deviant or criminal depends on the time, place, and society where they take place. Killing another person may be a criminal act in peace time, but in times of war it is acceptable behaviour. Medals are given to soldiers who are particularly good at killing the enemy as a sign of society's approval!

There have been many laws passed within the last twenty years that have changed previously acceptable behaviour into criminal behaviour, or criminal behaviour into deviant or normal behaviour. The Suicide Act of 1961 abolished the criminal offence of suicide, but included the offence of aiding and abetting, i.e. helping someone to commit suicide. This changed a criminal act into a deviant act. In 1983 an Act was passed making it illegal not to wear seat belts in the front seats of cars and this immediately created a lot of criminals!

There does not appear to be any behaviour that has always been considered universally deviant. Forms of behaviour that seem unacceptable to us, such as incest and murder, have all at one time been acceptable in some society. Even in our society attitudes to behaviour may change quickly between being seen as normal, deviant or criminal.

BRAINSTORM

Consider patterns of behaviour, such as nudity, murder, cigarette smoking, not wearing a crash helmet on a motorbike, homosexuality or suicide. Which of these have recently changed from acceptable to deviant behaviour or from criminal to deviant? □

Q   Which are more effective in controlling people's behaviour, formal controls, such as laws, or informal controls, such as behaviour being considered unacceptable? □

Q   Would you consider helping someone commit suicide, perhaps if it was an elderly person who was very ill?

If not, is it because you consider this to be morally wrong, i.e. deviant, or because it is against the law and therefore criminal?

There is further discussion of sexuality in Module 12 on Gender, Unit 5.
For more about designing questionnaires turn to page 8 in Module 1 on research methods.

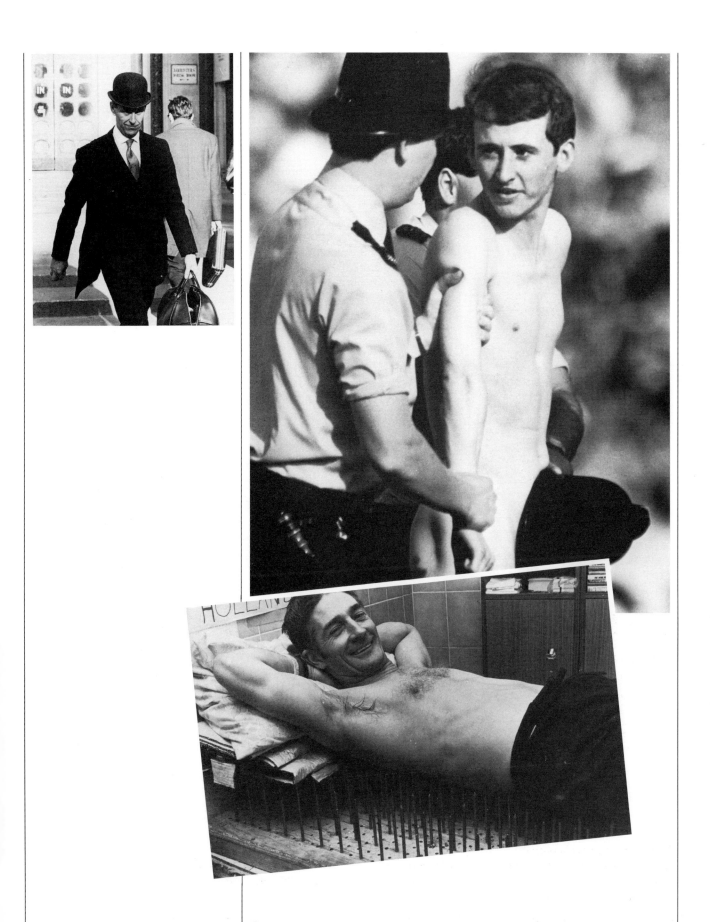

Q Deviance is a relative concept, depending on time, place and culture. Which of the people in the above images are deviant? □

U N I T 2

OFFICIAL STATISTICS

Official statistics of crime show how many people are found guilty in a court of law. The government publishes records each year of criminal statistics. In 1986 there were 3.8 million notifiable offences recorded in England and Wales, half of which were theft and handling stolen goods. **Notifiable** or **indictable offences** are the more serious crimes that could incur a prison sentence.

There has been a steady increase in the amount of crime in society in the last ten years, with the amount of recorded crime rising by 5 per cent a year between the mid 1970s and the mid 1980s. The amount of violent crime has increased even more, with nearly twice as many violent crimes in 1984 as in 1974 (85 599 in 1974 and 154 000 in 1984).

| **Q** | What is a notifiable offence? |

DISCUSS

Some people think that the death penalty should be reintroduced for some crimes, such as terrorism or multiple murder. The death penalty was dropped partly because it does not appear to deter criminals, and partly because many people felt it was wrong to kill anyone, even a criminal. Do you think there should be a death penalty for certain crimes?

T A S K

The table below shows the number of notifiable offences recorded in 1971 and 1984 and 1985.

Studying a table like this, it is useful to first read all the information surrounding the figures, such as the countries and years it deals with.

Next look carefully at the figures, are they in hundreds or thousands, or in percentages or averages? Then either read across the table or graph, here looking at each year in turn, or down the table looking at each offence for just one year.

Get into pairs and ask each other questions about the table, e.g. how much did robbery increase by between 1971 and 1986? □

Notifiable offences recorded by the police: type of offence, 1971, 1985 and 1986

(000)

	England & Wales			Scotland			Northern Ireland		
	1971	1985	1986	1971	1985	1986	1971	1985	1986
Notifiable offences recorded									
Violence against the person	47.0	121.7	125.5	5.0	10.7	11.6	1.4	3.5	4.2
Sexual offences	23.6	21.5	22.7	2.6	2.6	2.7	0.2	0.7	0.8
Burglary	451.5	866.7	931.6	59.2	100.7	96.9	10.6	20.2	20.0
Robbery	7.5	27.5	30.0	2.3	4.4	4.1	0.6	1.8	2.2
Drugs offences		8.0	7.3	0.9	5.1	5.3	—	—	0.3
Theft and handling stolen goods	1003.7	1884.1	2003.9	104.6	208.9	212.8	8.6	29.5	30.8
Fraud and forgery	99.8	134.8	133.4	9.4	30.6	30.6	1.5	3.7	4.2
Criminal damage	27.0	539.0	583.6	22.0	79.5	78.9	7.4	3.2	4.1
Other notifiable offences	5.6	8.7	9.4	5.0	19.5	21.0	0.5	2.0	1.7
Total notifiable offences	1665.7	3611.9	3847.4	211.0	462.0	463.8	30.8	64.6	68.3

Source: *Social Trends* 18, 1988.

DISCUSS

What do these official statistics show about the increase in crime in the last fifteen years? □

Less serious offences are dealt with by a Magistrates Court, where penalties, such as fines and probation orders can be given. Magistrates are ordinary members of the public who are elected to their post. The more serious indictable offences are more usually dealt with by a Crown Court. In a Crown Court specially trained judges deal with the cases, and decide on the sentence; but the jury is made up of ordinary people who decide whether the defendant is innocent or guilty. The death penalty was abolished in Great Britain in 1965, and the maximum sentence is now life imprisonment which is thirty years.

RESEARCH IDEA

Any member of the public can watch what happens inside a court so you could conduct an *observation study* inside a Magistrates Court or a Crown Court. What sort of cases are being heard, and what sentences do the courts give out? Also take notice of the sex, age and social class of the defendant, and the attitude of the court towards them and the offence they have committed. □

The official statistics of crime may not be an accurate assessment of the amount of crime in society. The tendency is to assume that official statistics give the actual amount of crime in society, and that criminals are somehow different from most people in society, but is this really so? Sociologists have discovered that most adults have committed acts that are criminal, although most of them have not been found out and so the offences do not appear on any official statistics of crime.

Answer the following questions to discover more about the criminal tendencies of so-called normal people. (See answers at foot of page.)

Formal dress or fancy dress?

Test yourself.
Are you a criminal?
Have you, or would you, do any of the following?

1 Have a ride on a train, bus, or tube intending not to pay?
2 Tip a garage man to ensure getting an MOT certificate?
3 Keep money when you have received too much change?
4 Smoke cigarettes under the age of sixteen?
5 Use the firm's telephone for personal calls?
6 Consume alcohol in a pub under the age of eighteen?
7 Exceed the speed limit?
8 Try to evade customs duty on a small item bought on holiday?
9 Take souvenirs (e.g. a glass or ashtray) from a pub or hotel?
10 Swear in public, such as at a football match?
11 Try a joint? (marijuana)
12 Keep money found in a street?
13 Drive a car knowing you are over the legal alcohol limit?
14 Write graffiti on a public wall?
15 Streak or debag in public?
16 Fiddle your expenses?
17 Buy a watch (or other goods) from someone, knowing it was stolen?
18 Take a newspaper from an unattended stand?
19 Use a television without a television licence?
20 Take anything, (e.g. stationery, books, pens), from work or school?

Many of these *are* offences although few would appear as official statistics of crime, because no one knows about them. Until the 1982 *British Crime Survey* there were no offical estimates of **unrecorded** crime, although it was known that certain crimes were not likely to be reported.

Answers 1 theft 2 corruption 3 theft 4 not an offence 5 theft 6 not an offence (selling it is) 7 speeding 8 intending to defraud the Crown of customs duty 9 theft 10 behaviour likely to occasion a breach of the peace 11 possession of cannabis 12 theft 13 driving a car with excess alcohol 14 criminal damage 15 indecent exposure 16 theft 17 handling stolen property 18 theft 19 using a tv set without a licence 20 theft.

U|N|I|T 3 UNREPORTED AND UNRECORDED CRIME

It is very difficult to estimate how much crime there is in society. Crime statistics are only the tip of the crime iceberg and much crime takes place that is never reported to the police. Some offences are not recorded because they have not been discovered. The amount of unrecorded and unreported crime is known as the **dark figure** of crime.

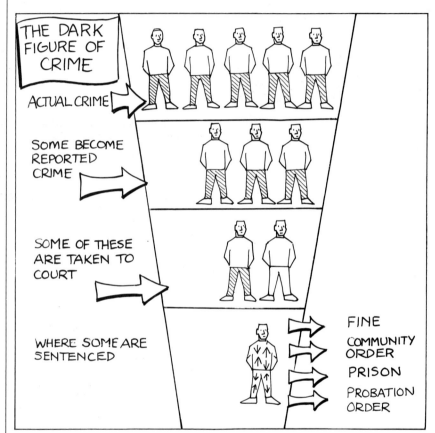

Q What is meant by the *dark figure* of crime?

Q Is this cartoon meant to be funny?

For more about rape see Unit 4 on Women and Crime in this module.

There are some crimes which rarely get reported. For example with rape, very few women will even report the attack because of embarrassment or shame, or from worries about the insensitive attitude of the police. A woman who has been raped also has to undergo a medical examination at the police station and face her attacker again at the trial. The attitude of the courts towards rape victims has also been criticised, many judges have in the past implied that raped women have 'asked for it', perhaps by accepting a lift from a stranger.

However in 1986 it was figures for rape that showed the largest increase, which many experts explained by the changing attitudes of the police, in encouraging more women to report the offence.

The crime rate is therefore the result of many factors. These include, the amount of crime in society, the seriousness of the crime (murder is usually reported), the attitude of the victim (as in rape), and police action. If the police are trying to catch people committing a particular offence, then the crime rate of that offence will go up because more police have been deployed in that area to trace and catch offenders.

A Christmas 'drink and drive' campaign for example, will result in an increase in the offical statistics for related crime. This does not necessarily mean that there are more drunk drivers, just that more of them are caught. When looking at official statistics for say, child abuse, football hooliganism, or drug abuse, one must bear this in mind.

BRAINSTORM

What sort of offences are unlikely to become official statistics, and why? Begin with offences, such as murder, incest, wife battering, car theft, fraud or granny bashing. □

TASK

The chart below shows the amount of recorded and unrecorded crime as estimated by the *British Crime Survey* in 1983. Which crimes are most likely to be reported and which are least likely? See if you can think of some explanations for the different rates of reporting. (Bicycle thefts for example, are thought to have increased because of the popularity of BMX bikes after 1981.) □

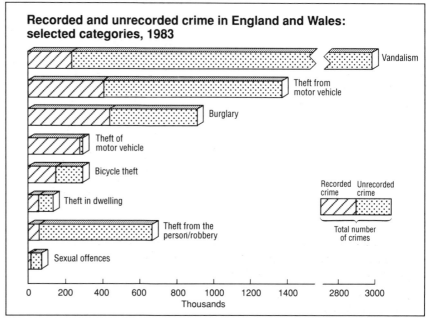

Recorded and unrecorded crime in England and Wales: selected categories, 1983

Source: *Social Trends* 16, 1986

'The first *British Crime Survey* (*BCS*) was conducted early in 1982 and related to crimes committed between the beginning of 1981 until the date of the interview (an average recall period of 14 months). It provides a new source of information not only about unrecorded crime, but also about victims and the risks and consequences of victimisation. However the survey is limited to those crimes which have clearly identified people as victims; it does not count crimes against organisations (such as company fraud, shop-lifting, or fare evasion) and 'victimless crimes' involving, for example, drug abuse.'

Source: *Social Trends* 16, 1986

Q   Is the *BCS* likely to provide completely accurate information about unrecorded crime? Give reasons for your answer. □

The official statistics on crime show that the highest number of criminals come in the category of 14 to 16 year-old working-class males. The second highest category is for 16 to 20 year-old working-class males.

However, this does not mean that other categories, such as women and middle-class people do not commit crimes, just because they do not appear in official statistics. The police and the courts may be more lenient towards girls than towards boys; and towards non-violent crimes. Crimes, such as company fraud, or fiddling tax are known as 'victimless crimes' because no one is directly hurt and no property is directly damaged by them. The courts often deal more leniently with these offenders than with those who steal directly from others. In the same way many people steal minor items from work, seeing this as the perks of the job, but would never steal from a friend.

DISCUSS

Which of the following events would you report to the police? If you would not report all of these, discuss the reasons for failing to notify the police. You discover:

a   a corpse.
b   that your house has been burgled.
c   that your bicycle has been stolen from outside a shop.
d   that your car has been dented while it was left outside a school.
e   that an old lady is hiding goods inside her coat, while you are shopping at the local supermarket.
f   that someone has taken money out of your pocket while you are having a drink at the pub.
g   that the person giving you a lift home from work has obviously had too much to drink.
h   that your best friend regularly steals small items from work, and has now also started stealing cash from his mother's handbag.
i   a purse containing £50 on the pavement.
j   that your neighbours children are stealing the flowers out of your garden to give to their mother. □

Q Many people fail to report minor crimes because they feel it is pointless, or because they feel the police would not be able to do anything anyway. What effect would different attitudes to crime, and different attitudes towards the police have on crime statistics? □

TASK

In the urban disturbances of 1984 and 1985 many black youths complained that they were being unfairly discriminated against, as they were being continually stopped by the police on 'sus', i.e. suspected of criminal intent. (See Module 14 on Urbanisation, pages 271–273 for more on urban riots.) The publicity about the 'sus' law led to a change in the law, but the police still have the power to stop and search suspects.

The attitude of the police towards certain groups, and their methods of policing can also affect the crime statistics. What sort of people are most likely to be stopped by the police and what sort of people are least likely to be stopped? What difference does age, sex or class make? □

RESEARCH IDEA

Conduct a survey on the attitudes of the public towards the police. You could discover whether many people have talked informally to a uniformed police officer, and whether they would report minor crimes. □

WOMEN AND CRIME

If an examination of official statistics of crime is made it appears that fewer females commit crimes than males; but that like males, female criminals are more likely to come from the lower socio-economic groups in society.

The unit on official statistics has shown that not all crime is reported or recorded. The following extracts highlight this with reference to crimes against women, or by women.

'In 1982 a seventeen-year-old girl hitched a lift back from a party, and was raped by the driver of the Jaguar car, a married man of 33 with three children. In passing sentence on Allen at Ipswich Crown Court on 5 Jan Judge Bertrand Richards stated that in taking a lift the woman was "guilty of a great deal of contributory negligence."

The Judge said the case was "a tragedy" for Allen, and fined him only £2000.'

Source: *Causes for Concern*, Eds Phil Scraten & Paul Gordon, 1984

DISCUSS

Here is an extract about a girl who has been the victim of two horrific crimes; rape and incest. Despite the seriousness of these crimes they are unlikely to be recorded, and the criminal will probably escape prosecution, why?

'I am just 16 and feel like committing suicide. The reason for this is that eight months ago I was raped by my father. I did not tell anyone but shut myself away from people as much as I could. I am at college but since it happened I have spent my days wandering in the park. I was a virgin when it happened. Now I am eight months pregnant. About three months ago I told my mother I was pregnant. But I could never tell her who the father is. She was very shocked and will not speak to me. She forbade me to have an abortion.' □

Source: *New Society*, January 1986.

DISCUSS

What do you think is an appropriate sentence for rape?

One of the rapists in this case was jailed for a total of ten years – five for rape and five for aggravated burglary. The rape victim is quoted as saying: 'I am however shocked at the way in which the judge in passing sentence seems to have treated rape and burglary as roughly comparable crimes.'

Clergyman's fury over 'inadequate' terms for rapists

PREBENDARY Michael Saward, beaten unconscious during a raid on his vicarage as he lay in a room within earshot of a young woman's rape, yesterday spoke of the physical and emotional trauma he and the other victims had suffered since their ordeal.

Mr Saward, 54, said the rape victim and her sister had needed psychiatric treatment. He himself had been seeing a neurologist, and David Kerr, a family friend, who was also bludgeoned by the gang during the raid, is receiving treatment for a hearing problem.

"One of the barristers and the judge seemed to assume that because we were all Christians everything was all right. But we are still suffering.

...I am frankly appalled at the lack of understanding evident in some of the statements made by the judge and some of the barristers."

Mr Saward added: "While I did not feel hatred, or any desire for personal revenge on my own behalf, I do feel strong anger. I feel angry at what those men did to a young woman and a young man and, not least, because she will always have to live with something of the emotional pain of that day.

"She has wonderfully overcome most of the horror, but there will always be something of it with her, and I feel angry that a trio of callous and brutal louts could do such a thing to her." Mr Saward praised the police and thanked all the medical staff who had "helped us in the process of recovery".

Victim speaks of shock at sentences

AS THE three men involved in the Ealing Vicarage rape began their jail terms yesterday, the young woman victim spoke of the distress caused by her rape ordeal and her "shock" at the sentences imposed on her attackers.

One of the rapists was jailed for a total of 10 years — five for the rape and five for aggravated burglary. The second was jailed for a total of eight years, three of them for the rape. Yesterday, a third man who organised the burglary, but took no part in the rape, was sentenced to a total of 14 years.

In a statement issued at the end of the trial, the rape victim said: "I am, as you would expect, glad that after such a long wait the trial is over and the sentences have been passed. I am, however, shocked at the way in which the judge in passing sentence seems to have treated rape and burglary as roughly comparable crimes."

Source: *The Independent*, February 1987

The graphs below show the difference in numbers of females and males recorded as having committed offences.

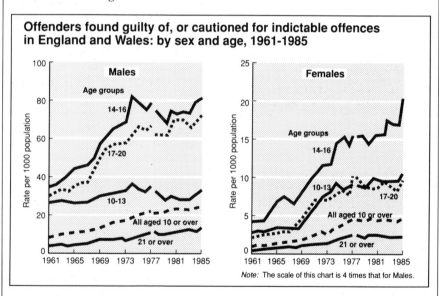

Offenders found guilty of, or cautioned for indictable offences in England and Wales: by sex and age, 1961-1985

Note: The scale of this chart is 4 times that for Males.

Source: *Social Trends* 17, 1987

A number of explanations have been offered for the different crime rates of males and females. These include the biological and social reason that females are less aggressive than males, and secondly that they form friendship groups of two or three individuals rather than the larger groups which may become delinquent gangs. It has also been suggested that the societal pressures on girls to be successful are not as great as the pressures on boys, who are more likely to turn to crime as a result.

Finally sociologists have also argued that females may receive preferential treatment from the police and the courts. Magistrates frequently perceive deviant girls as being in need of care and protection rather than as candidates for punishment. For all these reasons, crime statistics have indicated that few females in this society are deviant, so that those that are have always been seen as particularly mad or bad!

Q Do you think that boys are naughtier than girls? If so, why do you think this is?

DISCUSS

Do you think that males and females are treated differently by those in power? Are there differences in the way teachers treat and discipline boys and girls at school? For more on this read Module 12 on Gender, page 214, and Module 7 on Education, page 123.

More recent work on women criminals presents a slightly different picture, showing that women do *not* always get shorter sentences than men, or an easier time in prison. When a female ends up in court she is often assumed to have had lots of previous chances to leave crime and go straight.

The extract below is about a woman who ran a criminal company that was very successful for a time. After she had been prosecuted for fraud, she found both the top security Durham Prison and a freer open prison, Askham Grange, very difficult to cope with.

Going to Durham was a shocking experience. In 'H' Wing you are under maximum surveillance, twenty-four hours a day. My own crime and record didn't warrant maximum security but the Home Office sends women there who have been convicted of fairly minor crimes so that they can make up the numbers. So I was sent to Durham neither for my own good nor for the public good, but purely to suit the convenience of the Home Office.

At Durham a prisoner's every movement is monitored and controlled. You have to be very quiet and you can get told off for *laughing.* The regime is totally oppressive. Even when you're locked in your cell someone will look through the Judas-hole every hour, on the hour. There is an electronic lock on the door and once you're locked in you cannot get taken out of your room unless the Governor is called out of his bed. They can't even push a sanitary towel or a pill through to you if you get taken ill. You move about in very small spaces and only three women can talk together at one time — though never behind a closed door. You always have to leave the door open. Tension builds up. I met some interesting women in Durham and I took two Open University courses there but I changed physically, emotionally and mentally. My skin became grey and I looked harder. I began to walk differently — much more aggressively — and I learned to hate.

I remember learning to hate for the first time. One day I looked out through the barred window of my cell and saw male officers marching a man round and round a tiny exercise yard. Watching them were other officers with dogs and chains and batons. At that moment I felt absolute hatred.

I had been at Durham for twelve months when one day, completely out of the blue, I was told that I was to be sent to Askham Grange open prison. I was tipped straight out of a concrete tomb into an open prison in the middle of Yorkshire.

At first, Jenny hated Askham Grange. Being locked up in close confinement is totally debilitating and when Jenny first went to

Askham she could not even bring herself to plug in the kettle to make a cup of tea. For a year she had not engaged in routine domestic activities; for a year, her every move had been monitored; now that she was released into open conditions she could not cope with them! But although the Askham regime was more relaxed in some ways it was stricter in others. Spatially, the women were less confined but, because of the very high standards of behaviour required of them, they were even more closely regulated both physically and mentally. Hundreds of petty rules, violation of any of them possibly resulting in loss of pay and privileges, ensured that the women never forgot that they were in prison.

I hated the pettiness of it all, the kind of things you were put on report for. I'd managed to get that far without getting a report but at Askham I lost two weeks' pay just for picking a handful of blackberries. Someone else lost two days' remission for having a piece of bread in her room. You could be put on report for running up the stairs.

Source: *Criminal Women*, Ed Pat Carlen, 1985

DISCUSS

What impression of life in prison do you get from this extract? Why does Jenny find the open prison so difficult to adjust to after life inside Durham? □

Many girls who become criminal are dissatisfied with the traditional low-status, domestic role of females in this society, and turn to crime for status and success. As Jenny, the criminal in the previous extract says: 'I was out to prove something. I was determined to be respected and powerful as a woman in a man's world.' Some women like Jenny may become white-collar (i.e. middle-class) criminals, whilst many others may turn to crimes, such as shop-lifting.

The increasing crime rate for women may be the result of many factors. Certainly the changing positions of women in this society means that many females now want to be successful in areas outside the home, e.g. the changing roles for women often leads to disagreements within the family, where adolescent boys are still given greater freedom than adolescent girls. A boy who stays out all night is seen as a 'bit of a lad' wheras a girl may be seen as a 'slut' and morally bad.

Feminists argue that girls are expected to be docile and conformist in British society. Those that rebel are treated harshly because females have traditionally been seen both as belonging to men and as mother figures.

TASK

There are few alternatives to prison for a young female offender. Very few women are put on a community service order and there are few youth custody centres for females. Therefore many women, including those with babies and young children, find themselves in prison and separated from their families.

Find out what sentences a Magistrates Court can give a young offender; what is a youth custody centre? What is community service? □

Many female adolescents who are seen as being in moral danger end up in community homes, because they are not behaving in a way that is considered appropriate for a girl. Here is another extract from *Criminal Women* in which an offender called Diana describes how her Father's attitude towards her changed as she grew up.

Source: *Criminal Women*, Ed Pat Carlen, 1985

Q What does this extract show about the different treatment of adolescent boys and girls? On the basis of your own experience, would you agree that there are tighter controls on the behaviour of girls? □

Delinquent female gangs are now appearing for the first time, and the attitudes of the police towards female offenders now seem to be less lenient than a decade ago.

The greater number of female headed single-parent families may mean greater economic pressure is placed on these women, so that they may turn to crime to support their families. The growth of unemployment generally in the late 1970s and the 1980s may be seen as a contributory factor in the increasing crime rate for both men and women. Certainly the 1980s can be seen as a time when more crimes are being committed *against* women (or at

Q Do you think that people should be sent to prison for non-violent crimes? How do you think prisons should be run?

least appearing in the official statistics, e.g. rape and wife-battering) but also more crimes are being committed *by* women, e.g. shop-lifting, fraud, and soliciting as a prostitute. Many sociologists would argue that there have always been women criminals, but in the past society has preferred to ignore them.

RESEARCH IDEA

Find out about prisons in other societies. What proportion of offenders are sent to prison elsewhere in Europe? What sort of prisons are found in the United States and in Scandinavia?

You will need to use secondary data for this research. □

As part of a experimental project in a Swedish prison, this man served only four years of his sentence for murder before moving into this villa outside the prison compound after his marriage

Inmates in this US jail share a large common cell and enjoy some personal liberties, such as watching TV and the benefit of their own shower

For more about the differences in the way boys and girls are treated in British society, look again at Module 12 on Gender.

U N I T 5   **WHITE-COLLAR CRIME**

Q   White-collar crimes would include income tax evasion, fraud, and stealing from work. What other offences would be examples of white-collar crime?

Crimes committed by middle-class people are called **white-collar crimes** and they are underreported for two reasons. Firstly although the courts may take a serious view of theft, a company may prefer to dismiss the worker rather than risk damaging their reputation in a court case. Secondly, there is some evidence to suggest that middle-class people are treated more leniently by the police and the courts.

This means that not everyone receives the same punishment for the same offence. *Alan Cicourel*, an American sociologist, argues that 'what ends up being called justice is negotiable.' This idea of the **negotiation of justice** is one explanation for why more working-class people appear in the crime statistics. Middle-class people are more likely to be represented by a lawyer in court. Middle-class delinquents have parents who will *negotiate* on their behalf, apologise for a 'mistake', and thus appear as a respectable and caring family before the magistrate. The court may therefore decide to give the offender another chance.

Cicourel found in a study of two Californian cities, each of a similar size and with similar demographic (population) factors, that there was more crime in one city than in the other. Cicourel argues that this can only be explained by the different size, organisation, and methods of the policing in the two cities.

The sabotage of computer technology is one example of white-collar crime that demands the specialist knowledge of a skilled computer programmer.
These 'hackers' cause a lot of damage to the running of a business, as this extract shows, even if a virus was originally put into the system 'for fun'.

Q   What other white-collar crimes require a specialist skill?

T A S K

Make a list of new white-collar crimes that could not have existed fifty years ago.

Blind fall victim to 'Friday the 13th' computer plague

THE "Friday the 13th" computer plague affected the Royal National Institute for the Blind yesterday. The computers in the institute's employment unit failed to work and the department believes it may have been the victim of a computer virus – a self-replicating rogue programme introduced into the system by a hoaxer.

It had been widely feared that viruses, ready to be triggered by yesterday's date, were lurking in computer systems worldwide. There was a panic in the Netherlands about the "Datacrime" virus, which can obliterate data on a computer's hard storage disk.

Other "Friday the 13th" viruses perpetrated in the past still exist. These include the bouncing ball virus, which causes a ball to bounce across screens, and can damage the hard disk. Reports came in from Switzerland that

government computers had been hit by a virus, but that damage had been limited. In Australia, the government of Queensland said that a "Friday the 13th" virus had been discovered during a purge of some of its personal computers after warnings that viruses were poised to strike.

At the RNIB computer operators found that programmes which should translate ordinary print into large characters did not work. The employment unit, which produces programmes, equipment and advice for the blind and their employers, believes it has contained the virus, but acknowledged that it may have lost two years' information on its computer files. The RNIB sends software out to blind people on floppy disks, and there is concern that the virus may spread.

Source: *The Independent*. October 1989

Q   Why is it difficult to find out the amount of white-collar crime in society?

Q   What does this example indicate about attitudes towards white-collar crime?

T A S K

Turn to page 28 in Module 2 and read the section on media and deviance. Then explain what is meant by the following terms:

a   a moral panic,
b   a crime wave,
c   an amplification spiral.

Source: *The Independent*, April 1987

Fraudulent share applications, an example of white-collar crime in 1987

In 1986 the Conservative Government began selling off nationalised companies, so that it was possible for ordinary members of the public to buy shares in the new firms. Many people make large profits by buying shares and selling them when they are worth more than they paid for them; so share applications were limited to one application per person.

The first company to be sold off was British Telecom, and it was soon discovered that many fraudulent applications were being made. Some people who owned more than one house applied from both addresses, others used different combinations of their names to try and avoid detection.

The recent use of computer vetting of applications, by matching up names, addresses, and cheque numbers, revealed large numbers of white-collar criminals. One man who was found to have bought six times more than his allocation of shares was Keith Best, a Conservative MP, who stood down at the next election as a result.

At the beginning of 1987 more than 7000 suspected multiple applicants were reported to the Fraud Squad and the Director of Public Prosecutions over applications for British Gas shares and a similar figure was also suspected in the British Airways privatisation.

Best to quit Commons over Telecom shares row

KEITH BEST, the Conservative MP who broke a signed undertaking and bought six times more than his due allocation of British Telecom shares, last night bowed to Government whips' pressure and announced that he would not stand for his Anglesey seat of Ynes Mon at the next election.

But the immediate Labour and Alliance reaction was that the announcement would not defuse the controversy.

Even before Mr Best's announcement had been issued, Dale Campbell-Savours, the Labour MP who has been urging the Speaker to give priority to parliamentary contempt proceedings against Mr Best, said: "We won't be satisfied with offers to dump him for the election. We want a resignation." After the announcement, Mr Campbell-Savours said: "If he goes now, he won't get a penny. If he goes at the election, he gets a £9,250 pay-off."

Mr Best said in his statement, issued after another unseemly and embarrassing row over his share purchases in the Commons, that he had first offered his resignation as candidate for the next election last Wednesday.

He said his party executive had backed him at a meeting last Saturday. But that was before it became known that he had also made four irregular and successful applications for shares in the Jaguar privatisation.

Mr Best said last night: "I consider that my original decision was correct in order to uphold the high standards of those in public life."

Meanwhile, more than 7,000 suspected multiple applicants in the British Gas flotation will next week be reported to the Fraud Squad and the Director of Public Prosecutions by Touche Ross, the accountants policing the issue. The news yesterday coincided with the disclosure that thousands more suspected share cheats had been uncovered in the British Airways privatisation.

New evidence of major fraud in the recent spate of privatisations has been uncovered by computer vetting of all share applications matching up names, addresses and cheque numbers, Richard Lackburn, the Touche Ross partner in charge of the investigation, said.

No firm figure has been put on the number under scrutiny in the British Gas issue. But a spokesman said there were certainly more than the 6,600 suspect forms in the Telecom float.

U N I T 6 EXPLANATIONS FOR CONFORMITY AND DEVIANCE

The majority of people are not deviant, they conform to the norms of society. However, a minority within every society deliberately go against the accepted patterns of behaviour, although there are both formal and informal controls on behaviour.

Informal controls may include the disapproval of family or friends, or the fear of being gossiped about. For most people informal social controls are enough to ensure conformity, such as the threat 'I'll tell your Dad, if I see you doing that again.' Formal controls on behaviour are the police and the courts which are used by a society if the informal controls do not work.

Controls over behaviour do not prevent deviance, so experts from many different academic fields, including sociology and psychology, have attempted to explain why some people do not conform.

Sociological explanations

Some sociological explanations explain deviance as a response to the structure of society by people of a certain sex, age group, or class. Other explanations examine the relationships between groups in society in an attempt to understand why some people become deviant. Marxist sociologists are interested in why society appears to be more concerned about the petty thief than the white-collar criminal.

Robert Merton's theory of anomie

Merton's theory of anomie examines the links between the structure of society and the individual's response to it. Merton suggests that each society has certain goals that it's members aim to achieve, such as becoming rich, powerful, or important. Society also gives its members certain legitimate or acceptable ways of achieving these goals. In British society hard work and increasingly, educational qualifications provide the means for achieving these goals.

Many people realise that they will not be able to attain the goals society sets them, particularly if they are disadvantaged in some way. They may be from the bottom of the class system or from an ethnic minority group. This may lead people to feel frustrated, hopeless, or rejected; or in Merton's words, they suffer from a feeling of **anomie**.

People react to anomic feelings in different ways, as although people are all expected to 'play the game', many suffer negative feelings if they fail in a society that values success.

Q Do you agree with Merton that society sets us certain goals to achieve and certain legitimate ways of attaining them?

Q Can you explain in your own words what is meant by anomie?

Merton's theory of anomie may partly explain working-class deviance, because it is known that working-class people are less likely to succeed in education and are more likely to be unemployed (see Module 7 on Education). They are perhaps, therefore more likely to turn to crime to acquire the goals of society, such as money.

If Merton's theory offers explanation for some crime, it certainly does not explain 'motiveless crime', such as writing graffiti, joy-riding in cars, or vandalism. It also does not explain middle-class crime, such as the female shop-lifter who steals inexpensive items, or the middle-class computer expert who programs the firm's computer to give extra pay.

One particular criticism of Merton's theory comes from *Professor Laurie Taylor*, who says Merton is arguing that society operates like a slot machine which everyone can play. Some people play fair and hope that they will win, while others try inserting foreign coins or breaking into the machine. This is a good analogy for Merton's ideas, but Taylor takes it a step further and asks who benefits from the majority of people in society playing the game. In other words, who gets the profits from the slot machine of life?

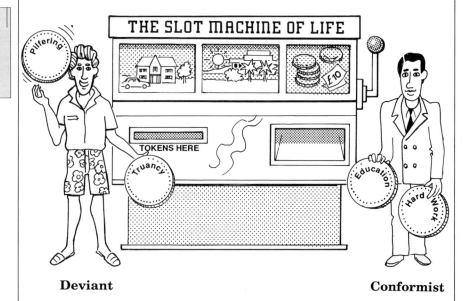

THE SLOT MACHINE OF LIFE

Deviant   Conformist

Whereas the theory of anomie sees the causes of deviance lying within the structures and systems of society, e.g. education, other sociologists have explained it as being the result of the interaction or inter-relationships of different groups within society.

Howard Becker's theory of labelling

Howard Becker argues that deviance is a result of the interaction between two groups in society, deviants and non-deviants. Becker suggests that any act can become defined as deviant if one group of people can successfully apply the label of deviant to another group. If this label sticks, they are separated from 'normal' people and seen as odd, or in Becker's words they are seen as **outsiders**. The two groups, the non-deviants who do the **labelling**, and the deviants who are **labelled**, therefore have a complementary relationship; one group cannot exist without the other.

Although there are many non-deviants in society, and only a few who are labelled as deviant, a small number of powerful people may be important in deciding what behaviour is seen as deviant.

There is more about labelling in Module 7 on Education, page 123.

There is more about labelling in Module 7 on Education, page 123.

The groups within society that are powerful enough to successfully label others include the mass media and the police, (see Module 2 on the Mass Media, Unit 4). The police may label potential suspects because of the way they have been trained to think about who is likely to commit crimes.

T A S K

The following extract is from a police training manual by David Powis, Deputy Assistant Commissioner to the Metropolitan Police. What does it show about the way police stereotype people as potential offenders and therefore label people as suspicious? ☐

> The following indices of suspiciousness emerge:
>   young people generally, but especially if in cars (and even more so if in groups in cars);
>   people in badly-maintained cars, especially if they have a tatty, dog-eared licence;
>   people of untidy, dirty appearance – especially with dirty shoes (even manual workers, if honest, he says, are clean and tidy);
>   people who are unduly nervous, confident or servile in police presence (unless they are doctors, who are 'naturally' confident);
>   people whose appearance is anomalous in some way – e.g. their clothes are not as smart as their car;
>   people in unusual family circumstances;
>   political radicals and intellectuals, especially if they 'spout extremist babble', and are in possession of a 'your rights' card (as supplied by the NCCL). These
>   people are also particularly likely to make unjust accusations against the police.
> Normal, unsuspicious people are those outside the above categories, especially if they are of smart conventional appearance (which commands natural authority and respect) and even more so if they smoke a pipe . . .
>
> These points add up to a fairly clear-cut picture; respectable, unsuspicious people conform to extremely conventional middle-aged, middle-class/respectable working-class modes of appearance, lifestyle, and political belief. Anything else is suspicious, and the further it deviates from that model, the more suspicious it becomes.

Source: *The Signs of Crime: A Field Manual for Police* by David Powis, 1977

T A S K

According to this extract how would the police stereotype
a You?
b Your friends?
c Your parents?

Would the labelling be justified, and could it affect the behaviour of those labelled?

The police would justify this stereotyping as being confirmed by crime statistics. After all, as can be seen in the graphs in the margin, most people who appear in court are male adolescents and most of these come from a working-class background. Sociologists would use the term *self-fulfilling prophecy* to explain this. The police are more likely to pick up these people, who then appear as part of the official statistics. The statistics confirm the correctness of the police behaviour, and fulfil the prophecy. For details of crime statistics turn to the graph on page 237.

Labelling theory gives an explanation for how and why some people are defined as deviant. Once someone has become labelled it may affect both their own behaviour and the behaviour of other people towards them. The label may become that person's **master status**, i.e. their most important characteristic. The master status of 'deviant' may be used to explain everything about that person's behaviour. This may make the person perceive themselves as deviant and perhaps make them more likely to commit further deviant acts as a result. Labelling of this kind may start a person on a deviant career in crime.

There have been many criticisms of labelling theory. In particular, many argue that it is one-sided in assuming that the deviant is the victim of people powerful enough to label them. Labelling theory does not explain why some people are labelled and others with similar characteristics are not. Neither does it explain why some people commit deviant acts and others do not. Many young people join groups or gangs, some of which commit motiveless crimes, such as joy-riding in cars or writing graffiti on walls. Theories of anomie or labelling do not successfully explain these patterns of behaviour which are not done for gain, nor appear to be the result of interaction with powerful non-deviants.

The following extracts are taken from a book written by **Stan Cohen** in the late 1960s which examines the Mods and Rockers groups of that time. Cohen argues that these groups represent modern-day devils, and symbolise all that is evil in society.

During the 1960s an initially trivial incident on a beach led to gang fights on the South Coast. Cohen suggests that the way these incidents were reported in the media led on increased police action and stiffer sentencing by the courts. (For more about media influence on crimes, see Module 2 on Mass Media pages 28–29.)

> 'A young journalist, who was trying to get into the Margate courtroom, was shown to the cells instead of the press bench because he had fairly long hair and was wearing jeans. "You look just like them," he was told.'
>
> 'Wearing a white shirt and tie with a conventional sportscoat, I was walking with a group of Mods down the promenade which had temporarily been made a 'one-way'. After we were moved along by the police, I turned round and together with a number of others started walking back the wrong way. Although I was pushed once, the police were not as abusive to me as to the others; the boys on either side of me were bodily turned around and pushed in the other direction.'

Source: *Folk Devils and Moral Panics* by Stan Cohen

Q In what way do these extracts illustrate labelling? Which groups of people are able to label others? Which groups are labelled in society today?

A clash between Mods and Rockers on the beach at Margate in 1964

Q Why might media coverage of the Mods and Rockers phenomenon make fights more likely to occur?

The Mods and Rockers have continued to exist up to the present day, and each Bank Holiday since the 1960s has seen rival groups appearing at coastal resorts in the South of England. The media continue to warn the public about potential trouble, and fights have regularly broken out.

Albert Cohen's theory of delinquent subcultures

This theory attempts to explain why working-class youths join gangs. *Albert Cohen* argues, as Merton does, that most people want to achieve the goals that society gives them; the goals of wealth, power or status.

Working-class males are less likely to achieve success through education than middle-class males, who are more likely to gain a well-paid job and to be able to afford to run a car and go on holiday. Cohen argues that the working-class adolescent will try to get status in other ways, perhaps by joining a gang whose goals can be achieved.

The gang may value a distinctive hair-style or way of dressing, or a certain form of behaviour, such as 'havin' a laff'. The gang may therefore be a **delinquent subculture**, because they are a group with different values and norms to that of the wider society.

The members of the gang can attain status by belonging to the gang and conforming to the goals and values of its subculture. Cohen suggests that working-class youths are suffering from **status frustration**, because they cannot achieve the legitimate goals of society. Group behaviour, such as stealing cars and driving them away, or vandalism, is both a way of getting status from the group and a way of rejecting middle-class values that they cannot achieve.

TASK

The following extracts are from two books about working-class lads at school and work. The first extract was written in the 1950s by P Willmott; the second was in the 1970s by P Willis. Both show working-class youths engaging in similar behaviour.

Can the behaviour of these boys be explained by Albert Cohen's theory of delinquent subcultures? □

A delinquent subculture?

In a more general sense, the 'laff' is part of an irreverent marauding misbehaviour. Like an army of occupation of the unseen, informal dimension 'the lads' pour over the countryside in a search for incidents to amuse, subvert and incite. Even strict and well-patrolled formal areas like assembly yield many possibilities in this other mode. During assembly Spanksy empties the side jacket pocket of someone sitting in front of him, and asks ostentatiously, 'Whose these belong to?', as Joey is clipping jackets to seats, and the others ruin the collective singing:

JOEY   The chief occupation when we'm all in the hall is playing with all the little clips what holds the chairs together. You take them off and you clip someone's coat to his chair and just wait until he gets up . . . and you never really listen . . . you have to be really discreet like, so as the Clark [the deputy head] won't see yer, call you out, the other teachers don't matter.

(. . .)

JOEY   Even on the hymn . . . when they mek you sing –

PW   But do they make you sing? I didn't notice many of you singing –

?   I was just standing there, moving my mouth.

?   We've only got one of them books between all our class. We've got one between twenty-five –

?   When we do sing we make a joke of it.

FUZZ   Sing the wrong verses . . . So if you're supposed to be singing verse one, you're singing verse three.
[Laughter]

Source: *Learning to Labour* by P Willis, 1978

Q If the theory of delinquent subcultures only explains male, adolescent, working-class crime, what sorts of deviance does it fail to explain?

Another boy, aged 17, described what happened one Sunday afternoon with three friends:

'We decided to go down to Southend in this little van – me and Charlie and Alan and Tom. Charlie was driving. We got down to Southend about 5.30, we jumped out and went in a telephone box to comb our hair in the mirror. We went to the Kursaal and started bilking the dodgem cars. You just jump over the fence, you see, and get in the queue; you say you've lost your ticket and get away with it. Then we went in the bar and had a few drinks. Then we went in the ghost train and Alan got off the train in the dark, I thought he would; we were all waiting for him to jump on us and somebody jumps on the top of us, it's Alan. Then we went on the scenic railway and they wouldn't strap us in [i.e. they were not allowed to ride]: they could see what we was like. Then we went on the beach and Charlie shouted out there was a lot of bottles down there. We filled them with water and started throwing them about; they smashed against the stones; I stood there and thought if someone's going to come down in the morning they'll cut their feet to pieces. Then Alan stood on the end of this pier and started swinging round a big tin can on a string, he was going to throw it out to sea, he misjudged it, instead of throwing it upwards he let go too late and it went straight over his shoulder, just missed this old lady. So we ran and jumped in the van and drove away.'

Source: *Adolescent Boys of East London* by P Willmott

Q What distinctive groups or gangs have emerged since the Mods and Rockers of the Sixties? What sort of identifying features do they have, in terms of dress or hair-style? (Reread Unit 5 on Youth Culture in Module 2 on Mass Media.) □

The three sociological theories explaining deviance that we have examined can be summarised as follows:

Anomie which explains deviance as being the result of certain groups within society not being able to achieve the goals by using the legitmate ways that society sets out.

Labelling which explains deviance as the result of the interaction between two groups in society, those with the power to label and those who are labelled as deviant.

Deliquent subcultures which sees deviance as the result of the lack of status of the male working-class adolescent.

T A S K

Which of the three sociological theories of deviance best explains the following type of deviant behaviour? If you think more than one theory is relevant then state why.

a	vandalism	f	fraud
b	drug abuse	g	football hooiganism
c	theft	h	shop-lifting
d	wife-battering	i	joy-riding (driving cars)
e	gang fights	j	streaking
		k	You give some examples!

You may well find that none of these theories adequately explain deviance. There are many other sociological theories on deviance but even so sociologists do not claim to have the answer to the crime problem! You might like to look at the following explanations for deviance given by biological theorists. □

Biological explanations of deviance

In the Nineteenth century *Lombroso*, an Italian criminologist, argued that deviant people could be detected by their abnormal physical characteristics, such as an extra finger, toe, or nipple, big ear lobes, large jaws or an insensitivity to pain. The picture below shows how *Havelock Ellis*, a Victorian writer with similar beliefs, thought that deviants could be identified by their build and facial features.

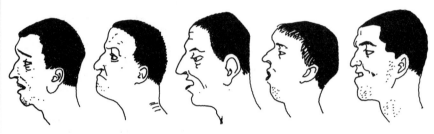

Source: *The Criminals* by Havelock Ellis

Biological theories, such as those of Ellis might appear ridiculous to people today, but it was accepted until recently that many criminals had a different genetic make-up to normal people. It was thought that the possession of an extra Y chromosome made people more likely to commit deviant acts.

As recently as 1964 *Sheldon and Eleanor Glueck* argued that there was a connection between someone's physical build and the likelihood of their becoming deviant. They argued that people with a short stocky build (mesomorphs), commit more deviant acts than people who are tall and slim (ectomorphs). It now appears that this relationship is caused by a third variable, that of social class. Working-class people are both more likely to be mesomorphs and to be deviant; it is not build that causes deviant behaviour.

Biological explanations of deviance are still accepted in some societies, and the deviant is therefore seen to be ill and in need of a cure, rather than suffering from group pressure or from anomie. This means that deviants in Russia, for example, may be sent to an asylum for a cure, rather than taken to court where they may be fined or imprisoned as in this society.

A biological cure for deviance that used to be widely practised is the **lobotomy**, and operation that involves slicing into part of the brain. The patient becomes less aggressive but also frequently suffers personality changes as well. The effects of a lobotomy mean that it is now rarely practised in the West, but other biological cures, such as **electro-convulsive therapy** (ECT) are widely used for aggression and depression.

Explanations for deviance therefore vary from sociological explanations, such as anomie, delinquent subcultures, and labelling, to biological explanations. You may well find that none of these theories adequately explain deviance. There are many other sociological theories on deviance, but sociologists do not claim to have found the solution to the crime problem. You might like to look at other subject areas, such as psychology to assess its explanations for deviance.

RESEARCH IDEA

Conduct a survey about stereotyping and deviance. You could present respondents with a series of photos and ask them to describe each person's character. You could combine with this opinion research about the causes of deviant behaviour in society today. You could ask respondents whether crime is caused by unemployment, lack of educational opportunity, group pressure. □

Q Although biological explanations new seem ludicrous, remnants of them still remain. People still say about someone 'he looks bad', as if physical appearance causes deviance. In films the villain is often made obvious with an evil face, moustache, or a scar!

Perhaps someone's facial features may lead to labelling taking place. What do you think?

Did you know that Ann Boleyn was thought to be a witch, because she had an extra little finger? She invented a new fashion for long sleeves in order to hide it!

T A S K

Take a particular example of deviant behaviour, such as football hooliganism, and assess how sociological, and biological explanations can help us to understand the causes of this type of deviance in society today. □

DISCUSS

a   Which theories offer the most convincing explanations for the six cases of deviance listed below?

b   What else might you need to know about the actual cases, in order to make sure you are not just stereotyping?

c   Which research methods would you want to use to gain additional information (e.g. experiments, documentary sources, such as case-histories, interviews, questionnaires, participant observation)? See Module 1 on research methods.

d   What sentence would you pass on these criminals, if you were a magistrate or jury member? (e.g. prison sentence, fine, community service, conditional discharge, probation order, etc.)

1   A famous football manager who illegally bets on matches for personal gain.

2   A seventeen-year-old girl caught shoplifting, whose parents say she was 'born bad', and has always been a trouble-maker.

3   A mother living in poverty in an inner-city area, who murders her three children, and then makes an unsuccessful suicide attempt.

4   A fourteen-year-old boy who plays truant from school to join a gang painting graffiti on walls and thieving minor items from shops.

5   A teacher who kills a pedestrian when driving with excess alcohol in her blood.

6   A working-class man caught stealing £500000 from a bank. □

WHERE TO NOW?

It is important that you now read the section linking deviance and the media in Module 2, page 28. You may then be interested in reading Module 12 on Gender and Module 14 on Urbanisation.

M O D U L E · 14

URBANISATION

FOURTEEN

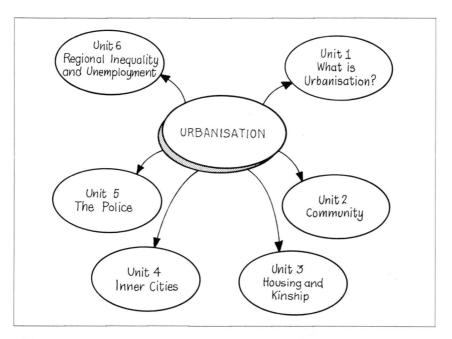

WHAT THIS MODULE IS ABOUT

Urbanisation is about the towns and cities we live in. It is also about the quality of life we expect from our environment and from one another. Urbanisation involves both the movement of people from rural to urban areas and the changes in values associated with this movement. This module also looks at the effects of urbanisation and migration on kinship, community, housing, employment and people's relationships. You could say that the study of towns and cities is the study of sociology itself, since the discipline analyses *where* people live, *how* they live and in what conditions they live.

BY THE END OF THIS MODULE YOU SHOULD BE ABLE TO:

1 Describe the main patterns of urban change over the past hundred years in Britain.

2 Explain the main differences and similarities between rural and urban communities.

3 Understand the links between migration, urbanisation and community change.

4 Discuss regional differences in employment, health, housing and employment.

5 Examine conflict in urban areas with reference to the police, community, housing and kinship.

6 Appreciate that there are different sociological interpretations of urban development.

UNIT 1 WHAT IS URBANISATION?

The term **urban** relates to the towns and cities that people live in while the term **rural** refers to country areas where people live in villages or in small towns. Part of the study of urbanisation involves comparing and contrasting urban and rural living – in particular the nature of community life in both.

Most of us live in or on the edge of large towns and cities. Very few people in Britain now live a *rural* way of life. This contrasts with the situation 200 years ago. Today less than 20 per cent of the population live in rural areas. Many inhabitants of villages in Britain are commuters or retired people leaving only a small proportion of the population dependent upon the land for their livelihood.

Q   What do you see as the main differences between young people growing up in urban and rural environments?

Large towns and cities in Britain are relatively new. Their development is linked with the rapid growth in industry and population from the 1750s onwards. By the mid 1850s, Britain's industrial strength was built on coal, iron ore, textiles, shipbuilding and other manufacturing industries. New inventions in agricultural machinery and production and land reforms through enclosure, altered the traditional feudal pattern of rural living and working. Fewer agricultural workers were required to work the land, resulting in the drift of the excess work-force to the towns and cities to find work in the new factories. Despite the change in life-style and living conditions, industrial cities at least offered employment and escape from rural poverty. Alongside such industrial and population changes, the new urban centres developed in an unplanned and largely haphazard fashion. In the mid 1850s, 50 per cent of the inhabitants of the new cities had been born in them; the majority being young migrants from rural areas seeking to escape unemployment in the villages. Although poverty and overcrowding were accepted by the new city dweller, factory conditions, tenement housing and the concentration of population in city areas posed new problems. But despite the hardships suffered by many people, the industrial city presented a new way of life and provided new types of organisations in response to urban problems, e.g. new town development, high density housing, public transport, public parks, museums, libraries, hospitals and schools.

BRAINSTORM

List some of the main advantages and drawbacks experienced by the new city migrants. On balance do you think they were better or worse off? Give reasons for your answers. □

DISCUSS

Look at the photograph above of Nineteenth century urban housing. What problems would people face living in these conditions?

Can you see any evidence of similar problems in the photograph of Twentieth century urban housing? Here are some issues to consider:

a   Noise pollution.
b   Air pollution.
c   Density of population.
d   Standard of housing.
e   Factory and office sites. □

Most people have a love-hate relationship with the city. Those who live in and around cities, and are both frustrated and excited by them. According to the sociologist, **C Wright-Mills**, cities are both beautiful and ugly places.

> 'Consider the horrible, beautiful, ugly magnificent sprawl of the great city. For many upper-class people, the personal solution to the 'problem of the city' is to have an apartment with a private garage under it in the heart of the city, and forty miles out, a house by Henry Hill, garden by Garrett Eckbo, on a hundred acres of private land. In these two controlled environments with a small staff at each end and a private helicopter connection – most people could solve many of the problems of personal milieux caused by the facts of the city. But all this, however splendid, does not solve the public issues that the city poses. What should be done with this wonderful monstrosity? Break it all up into scattered units, combining residence and work? Refurbish it as it stands? Or, after evacuation, dynamite it and build new cities according to new plans in new places? What should those plans be? And who is to decide and to accomplish whatever choice is made?'

Source: *The Sociological Imagination* by C Wright-Mills

Q What does Wright-Mills mean when he says that cities can be both beautiful and ugly places? □

A point to note about Britain's city areas is that they were largely unplanned and that they were established by the early 1900s, since which time their character has changed little. That legacy is perhaps best captured through the eyes of the modern traveller.

> 'Travelling by road or rail through one of Britain's great industrial cities gives the casual observer the feeling that they have always been there. Vast sprawling areas of mean housing, Victorian and modern, stretch to the horizon, relieved only by the outlines of factories and modern office developments. In the centres, tall slabs of concrete tower over the streets, dwarfing their inhabitants. But even here in the centre, the gloss of modernity is seldom complete. Old churches hide in the enormous shadows of the tower blocks; there is even the occasional old house. In Coventry, as an example of civic pride in the past, the few old houses that survived the bombing of the war and the designs of the planners, have been carefully dismantled and rebuilt along one street of oak beams and boutiques. Such gestures over-simplify the continuity of our urban history. Equally noticeable in the areas surrounding the historic cores of cities, are relics of the past that remain amidst the cheerless redevelopments of recent years. Among these relics the urban schools are often the most obvious, from the red brick 'three deckers' of the old school boards to the cottage-style primary schools of the progressive educationalists of the first half of this century.'

Source: *Urban Schooling* by L. Bash, D. Colby and C. Jones, 1988

The old and the new: the cathedral in Coventry

T A S K

Is the above too pessimistic a view? In your own words describe an urban scene near to you. If you have time, walk through parts of a local city area with friends and make notes on what you see. □

Urbanisation is not, of course, just about slabs of concrete, tower blocks and office buildings, it is also about *people*. Urban issues are present in our day-to-day lives, in school and at home, in the youth club, factory, office and elsewhere. When we talk about the neighbourhood in which we live, about recreational and leisure facilities, friends, the shops, crime, the police, etc., we are invariably talking about urban issues.

In terms of population size alone, larger concentrations of people in cities present problems of social organisation, where people are to live, work, play and so forth. The growth of cities requires, for example, an effective system of production, food distribution, law and order and government. It also requires that people are housed and healthy and that it is possible for them to come and go safely and in an orderly manner. As we shall see in this module, cities have developed forms of organisation to deal with such problems which differ markedly from those in rural societies. This has led to the argument that rural areas are essentially better places to live, since their social organisation and communities are more straightforward. Such arguments whether they are accurate or not indicate the kind of criticism urban planners are likely to face.

Q Is urban planning and organisation doomed to failure? How would you answer this? Bear in mind that there is a tendency for some people to romanticise traditional values and to pour scorn on all things modern. □

U N I T 2 | THE COMMUNITY

Views about rural and urban life vary enormously. What people mean by **community** is also open to wide interpretation. One issue currently under debate is whether or not traditional community values (whatever these may be) have been undermined by urbanisation.

One view suggests that the impersonal quality of city life has led to a breakdown in traditional norms and beliefs, notably those associated with religious and family life. This breakdown is connected with a loss of community spirit, resulting in rising crime rates and a growing disrespect for those in authority, e.g. teachers, social workers, police, the elderly, etc. Supporters of this view often point to the cohesion or well being found in traditional village and working-class communities which binds people together in a shared value system.

BRAINSTORM

Every picture tells a story. Describe and explain the three family types depicted in these illustrations. How do such families represent or reflect dominant values in the community?

Another group believe that city life offers people greater scope and freedom than close-knit communities allow. In cities people are less restricted by family and religious values and are better able to define their own way of life. From this viewpoint 'social problems' which arise in the city may not be *caused* by the breakdown of traditional community values, but by new found freedom or other factors associated with unemployment, poor housing or an inability to cope with difficult conditions. According to the Social Anthropologist **Ronald Frankenberg** in his famous study, *Communities in Britain*, there is no set definition of the term community. He maintains that what makes up a community is not simply a matter of size or scale, but rather a common set of interests shared by people.

Q Explain what Frankenberg means by 'All communities are societies, but not all societies are communities.'

All communities are societies, but not all societies are communities. Communities are peculiar in several ways . . . A group of two or three hundred people living together on an urban housing estate may or may not form a community . . . Size is not the only key.

Community implies having something in common. In the early use of the word it meant having goods in common. Those who live in a community have overriding economic interests which are the same or complementary. They work together and also play and pray together. Their common interest in things gives them a common interest in each other. They quarrel with each other but are never indifferent to each other. They form a group of people who meet frequently face-to-face, although this may mean they end up back-to-back.

Source: *Communities in Britain* by R Frankenberg, 1966

T·A·S·K

What do you understand by the term community? How would you define it in your own terms. Write down your answer and compare it with others in your group.

Miners from an urban community line up to get supplies from the company's store

As Frankenberg argues, confusion arises over what is meant by the term community. There is, for example, a tendency as we have seen to romanticise the past.

Popular understanding suggests that communities are small in size and are rurally based. Yet this perspective ignores the existence of urban communities found in areas associated with mining, shipbuilding, steel, fishing, textiles and so forth. In this case urban communities may not be exceptions, they may even be the norm. Perhaps a more promising method of distinguishing 'urban' from 'rural' communities is to focus on some of the similarities and differences between them.

The lack of care of the elderly is often cited as an example of the breakdown of traditional community values. The assumption is, of course, that in the past the elderly were looked after. In reality, there were far fewer elderly people in preindustrial society due to shorter life expectancy and different definitions of 'old age'. According to *Peter Laslett*, in his book *Family Life and Illicit Love in Earlier Generations*, he finds no evidence that past generations were more caring than today with regard to their elderly relatives. It was not the custom, for example, to move ailing parents into the homes of their children, nor did the elderly demand this. Why then is there a tendency to romanticise 'care' in the past with today's reality?

One answer is, of course, that society feels guilty about the elderly. The elderly are seen as a problem. Longevity, i.e. people living longer, and the increasing numbers of elderly people place a burden on the welfare state and on the young. In our society retirement is an ambiguous term. In theory it marks a time of recreation and leisure for the elderly, freed of the responsibilities of productive work. Yet, in practice, it represents for many a change in status and a decline in living standards.

Recent figures show that 23 per cent of around 8 million pensioners in Britain claimed supplementary benefit and that a further 750 000 pensioners were eligible but did not claim it.

RESEARCH IDEA

The loss of community fact or fiction?

Interview a sample of elderly people who have lived in your area for most of their lives. Ask them about the changes they have seen and how the changes have affected them.

Before you start, think about the kind of problems you envisage in carrying out this project. What methods will you use and how will you write it up as a report or present your results? □

UNIT 3 HOUSING AND KINSHIP

A homeless young person sleeps out under Waterloo Bridge in London

Q What are the main problems which young people face in looking for accommodation?

The deprivation described in the previous unit is not a new phenomenon. In the 1880s, *Frederick Engels* wrote scathingly about poverty and neglect in Manchester. *Charles Booth*'s famous survey of London slums at the turn of the century, *Life and Labour of the London Poor*, also pointed to the widespread incidence of poverty. Similar findings were made in *Rowntree*'s study of York. In various ways Engels, Booth and Rowntree pointed to the links between bad housing, unemployment, poverty and crime. Yet studies of poverty carried out in the affluent 1960s and 1970s by *Smith and Townsend* indicate that little has changed. More recent studies in the 1980s by *Charles Madge*, *Peter Willmott* and *Michael Young*, and by *Paul Harrison*, point to the despair felt by people living in modern high-rise slums. Harrison in his account of life in the East London Borough of Hackney writes:

'Many slums were cleared by the blitz or bulldozers, but the public housing that replaced them was in some respects worse. Local government was poor in resources, with a narrow and declining base on which to levy rates.

'Educational results were spectacularly poor, perpetuating the shortage of qualified labour. Redevelopment, emigration and immigration progressively ate away at the community, the extended family, even the nuclear family. Socialisation and social control of the young began to fail. Crime and vandalism blossomed. Good neighbourliness gave way to apathy'.

There can be little doubt that major rebuilding programmes from the late 1940s to the mid-1960s have had a major effect on family and kinship. These programmes included rehousing people from slum areas to new council estates on the edge of cities and building high-rise flats to accommodate inner-city dwellers. A number of new towns were built to provide housing for over three million people outside the largest cities. These include Milton Keynes, Stevenage, Harlow and Crawley in the South East, and Washington and Peterlee in the North East. While some of these new planned communities have proved successful, the building of high-rise flats has not.

Many high-rise estates have themselves turned into slums. The elderly and young mothers with children often find such estates remote and unfriendly. Residents complain that it is particularly difficult to build up community spirit, with no common ground or play areas and the architecture itself is frequently inhospitable, with walkways, staircases and broken lifts. The unpopularity of such estates has led to the further charge that they have become the 'dumping grounds' for problem families with nowhere else to go. If, in the early days, architects won awards for their design of such buildings it has proved harder in the years that followed for residents to live in them.

TASK

What are the main problems which mothers and young children face living in high-rise accommodation? □

The link between housing and kinship is an important factor in looking at community development. In their famous study *Family and Kinship in East London* of 1957, by *Michael Young* and *Peter Willmott*, looked at patterns of the extended family in Bethnal Green, in the East End of London, and 'Greenleigh', a suburban housing project where people from Bethnal Green had been rehoused. While official housing policy at the time was to encourage those who wanted a better home to leave Bethnal Green and move to the new town of Greenleigh, it accelerated the breakdown of community and kinship, i.e. the splitting up of sons, daughters, parents, grandparents, cousins, etc.

DISCUSS

Explain some of the main advantages and disadvantages of moving from one type of neighbourhood to another.

'Women feel the lack of friends, as of kin, more keenly than their menfolk. Those who do not follow their husbands into the society of the workplace – and loneliness is one of the common reasons for doing so - have to spend their day alone, "looking at ourselves all day", as they say. In one interview the husband was congratulating himself on having a house, a garden, a bathroom, and a TV – "the tellie is a bit of a friend down here" – when his wife broke in to say, "It's alright for you. What about the time I have to spend here on my own?". This difference in their life may cause sharp contention, especially in the early years. "When we first came," said Mrs Haddon, "I'd just had the baby and it was all a misery, not knowing anyone. I sat on the stairs and cried my eyes out. For the first two years we were swaying whether to go back. I wanted to and my husband didn't. We used to have terrible arguments about it. I used to say 'It's all right for you! I have to sit here all day. You do get a break."

'Not that all women resent it. A few, like Mrs Painswick, actually welcome seclusion. She had been more averse to the quarrels amongst the 'rowdy, shouty' Bethnal Greeners than appreciative of the mateyness to which quarrels are the counterpart, and finds the less intense life of Greenleigh a pleasant contrast. "In London people had more squabbles. We haven't seen neighbours out here having words." '

Source: *Family and Kinship in East London* by P Willmott and M Young, 1957

In a more recent edition of their book, published in 1986, Willmott and Young argue that recent urban disorders are directly connected to the failure of housing policies in the 1950s.

'When young families were rehoused away from Bethnal Green they were cut off from their relatives, and from the mutual aid this provided . . . government and municipal authorities were united in a gigantic act of folly . . . If the lessons had been learned in the 1950s London and the other big cities might not have suffered the 'anomie' and violence manifested in the urban riots of the 1980s.'

BRAINSTORM

What do Willmott and Young mean when they say '. . . if the lessons had been learned in the 1950s . . . cities might not have suffered . . . the violence manifested in the urban riots of the 1980s'? In your answer consider issues associated with urban planning, housing, migration and any other factors which you think are relevant. □

Urbanisation is also often associated with **conflict**. When a decision has to be made about opening or closing a factory, building an office block, closing a hospital, policing an area or rehousing families, people usually have different views about what ought to be done. Interest and pressure groups are likely to be involved (see Module 3 on Power and Politics, pages 51–53) and conflict arises when people feel that their views have not been heard. The question of whose view whould prevail arises.

The answer to this question is not straightforward. Much depends on the issues involved, what people value, and whether they are in a position to influence the change. Consider the following example about housing developments:

In their plans to redevelop part of a city area, the following figures have been presented by the developers to the Council for approval:

Present population of the area   14 500
Population after redevelopment   5 750

DISCUSS

What futher information would you need to know about the developer's plans and intentions?

Explain the discrepancy between the figures.

How should decisions about development and rehousing be made? □

The above example illustrates a common dilemma associated with urban planning and development: who makes the decisions and what happens to the people involved? A further question arises concerning the people involved. For example, when looking at housing there may be noticeable differences between the type, age and external conditions of the houses that ethnic minorities live in and those that Whites live in.

BRAINSTORM

Do you think it is preferable to own or rent accommodation? Give reasons for your answers.

Type and condition of dwellings for white and ethnic populations

	Ethnic minorities	Whites
Type of dwelling:	%	%
Detached	1	21
Semi-detached	15	36
Terraced	66	30
Flat/rooms/maisonette	15	12
Not stated	3	1
Age of dwelling:		
Built before 1914	46	24
Built before 1940†	86	48
External condition of dwelling:		
Very good	28	55
Very good or average†	58	89

†includes previous category.

Source: *Racial Disadvantage in Britain* by D J Smith

QUESTIONS

1 Compare the type, age and condition of the dwellings of minority groups and whites.
2 What reasons can you give for the differences in housing conditions which you have described.

What implications might such differences in housing conditions have
a for the minority communities themselves?
b for the way in which other groups react to these minorities? □

In 1980 there was rioting in St Pauls in Bristol. In 1981 there were riots in Brixton in London, Toxteth in Liverpool and Moss Side in Manchester. Autumn of 1985 saw a new spate of riots in Britain's deprived inner-city areas: Handsworth in Birmingham on 9 September, Brixton on 29 September, and Tottenham in London on 6 October. It is to these and related issues that we turn out attention in the next unit.

RESEARCH IDEA

The wealth of different types of community offers you a lot of scope for research projects on community issues. Some further ideas include:

a Looking at the way a local or national newspaper researches and reports various topical issues.
b Examining the contribution made to the local community by a small business, a shop or supermarket, a health or leisure centre, a citizen's advice bureau or local law centre, a charity or neighbourhood action group.
c Analysing local housing needs and local authority housing policy with reference to the homeless, the elderly, single-parent families, young homeless people, etc.

These are intended as starter ideas. Discuss among yourselves and with your teacher other ideas for projects. Remember your project will involve you in establishing contacts with local groups over time. You will need to plan your project carefully, paying attention to aims, methods and objectives. (See Module 1 on research methods.) □

UNIT 4 | INNER CITIES

There is a tendency to use expressions like 'inner-city', 'leafy suburb', 'stockbroker belt' and 'gentrification' to denote the status of particular residential districts. **Inner-city** is a convenient shorthand term to describe a particular type of area in the city. It is not, however, a geographically accurate description. While such areas a Toxteth in Liverpool, Moss Side in Manchester, and Brixton in London are near the centre of such cities, they are not central. Middle-class districts, such as Mayfair in London, Edgbaston in Birmingham and Hillhead in Glasgow are nearer to the centre of those cities than other localities designated as inner-city areas. Knowsley, St Helens, Huyton, Gateshead and Lambeth are not inner-city areas but have become defined as such because they conform to a certain pattern. According to *Michael Williams inner-city* describes a cluster of variables (or factors) which are manifested in particular districts. These include:

a   Architectural failures.
b   Long-term shifts in land use and values.
c   A loss of population and jobs.
d   Family breakdown.
e   Non-white immigration and racial discrimination.
f   Poverty of resources and income.
g   Poor environment.

BRAINSTORM

What do you understand by the term inner-city? Does the term necessarily signify those variables identified by Williams?

Q   How would you describe the main differences between the areas depicted in the photographs on the right?

The theory of zones

One way of looking at cities is in terms of *zones*. Most cities can be subdivided into recognisable areas of housing or residency. Neighbourhoods have their own distinct character, way of life and territorial demarcation. Very often zones are demarcated on race and class lines with the boundaries 'policed' by youth groups and gangs. *Burgess* in 1925 proposed the following model for looking at how cities evolve, adapt and survive over time.

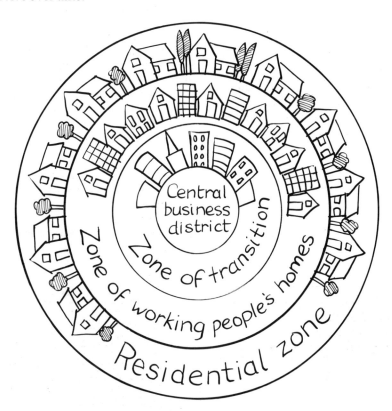

The model depicts the expansion of the urban population through a number of zones, shown as concentric circles. These suggest that individuals or groups move from one zone to the next. One theory is that as various immigrant or ethnic groups gain in status they move further and further away from the inner zones of transition. In residential terms this would seem to explain social and geographical mobility out of the inner-city ring into the outer suburban ring. Burgess saw such movement as a natural evolutionary process which explained stability and change.

Criticisms of the model:

a   It does not explain why certain groups remain in the centre.
b   It assumes that inner-city inhabitants wish to become suburban dwellers.
c   It ignores the issue of power, i.e. the power of businessmen, planners and politicans who have a major say in the running of cities, e.g. their development often means rehousing.
d   It ignores the 'yuppie' phenomenon of gentrification (moving into poor areas and doing up property).

A common feature associated with inner cities is **decline**. Essentially, inner cities have been neglected: as a result they have become **marginalised**, i.e. separated off, from the suburbs by poor housing, unemployment, migration out and inadequate investment and planning. The burden of

Q   What do you understand by the term 'gentrification'.

unemployment has not, for example, fallen evenly on the community. As the following figures indicate, by age, sex and race, ethnic minorities suffer the effects of unemployment far greater than others. Although poverty and unemployment exist elsewhere in society it has nevertheless been convenient for politicians and media to label inner cities as problem areas. Two possible explanations can be made for this:

a Ethnic minorities are concentrated in inner-city areas.

b Ethnic minorities have established identities and communities of their own.

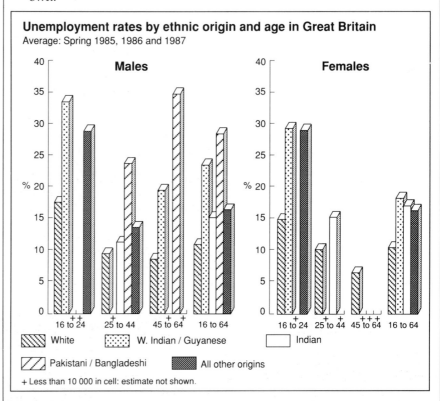

Unemployment rates by ethnic origin and age in Great Britain
Average: Spring 1985, 1986 and 1987

Males

Females

White   W. Indian / Guyanese   Indian

Pakistani / Bangladeshi   All other origins

+ Less than 10 000 in cell: estimate not shown.

Source: *Employment Gazette*, December 1988

QUESTIONS

1 With reference to the above charts, describe the link between unemployment, age, sex and race.

2 Is there a relationship between unemployment and inner-city decline? □

The dynamism of inner cities is that they are built on ethnic diversity and conflict. On the one hand, they have integrated successive generations of immigrants into wider society while, on the other, the people in them have had to fight against discrimination and for a better deal on housing, jobs, education and related services. It is perhaps this dynamic quality linked with increasing isolation from mainstream suburban society which has attracted suspicion about inner-city areas.

Sensational press coverage has, for example, reinforced the impression that certain sectors of our cities have become 'no go' areas, dominated by criminals and riotous youths. **Stuart Hall** and **Barry Troyna**, two sociologists, point to the ways in which Blacks and Asians have increasingly become featured in one dominant news context 'trouble', particularly crime. Hall charts the progress of a 'mugging moral panic' in which public fears about rising crime levels are fused through newspaper coverage with stereotyped images of face, to produce a new 'folk devil', the Black Mugger. Hall's research emphasises the absence of any statistical foundation for this image. Nevertheless, as the following headlines from *The Sun* newspaper indicate, this powerful symbol did register in the public mind. (For further discussion of this issue, see Module 2 on the Mass Media, page 28.)

Is this a stereotypical image?

Q What is the likely effect of such reporting on public attitudes among the White community and the Black community?

STREETS OF FEAR
Where packs of muggers prey on lonely women

CITY streets of fear, where elderly women live with the constant risk of being mugged by black youths, were highlighted by a judge yesterday.

Judge Gwyn Morris, QC, said hundreds of women had written to him about the gangs of muggers who bring terror to the streets of South London.

He added: 'It is pitiful to read their letters. One elderly woman wrote to say that she lived only two streets away from her married daughter, but was too afraid to go out at night and visit her. And equally the daughter was too frightened to visit her mother for fear of being attacked and robbed.'

Detective Constable Barry Donovan told the judge at the Old Bailey that 167 women were mugged in the streets of Clapham and Brixton in six weeks earlier this year.

And the judge said: 'It is an immense social problem.'

Source: *The Sun*, October 1976

Sensationalist headlines, such as those from *The Sun*, are designed to sell newspapers, not to accurately report the news. One effect, as we have seen, is that sensationalism creates an atmosphere of fear and terror by stereotyping all members of a particular community as deviant or violent. Consider, for example, the following headlines 'Hooded Animals out for Blood' from *The Sun* newspaper, reporting the death of PC Blakelock on the Broadwater Farm Estate in Tottenham.

HOODED ANIMALS OUT FOR BLOOD | # The killing of PC Blakelock

Source: *The Sun*, 1987

T A S K

Collect various sensational and non-sensational newspaper articles and examine the relationship between the headlines and the way the issues or incidents are reported. What are the similarities and differences between the different newspapers that you have examined? How would you explain these similarities and differences? □

Perhaps the major problem with reporting provided by such papers as *The Sun*, *The Daily Mail* and *The Daily Express*, in this area is that it fails to go beyond superficial descriptions of inner-city areas (see Module 2 on The Mass Media, pages 28–29). In the case of Broadwater Farm, for example, much 'news' was made of the physical structure of the buildings, such as its walkways and general design. Little was said about the people living there or the fact that the number of crimes on the Broadwater Farm had dropped over the year immediately preceeding the disturbances. Yet, beneath the claims and counter-claims about what actually happened at the Broadwater Farm Estate, it was not an isolated incident. The recent riots are part of a deeper underlying tension in society, part of which can be explained in terms of conflict between the community and the police. It is this aspect of the discussion that Unit 5 considers.

UNIT 5 | THE POLICE

The policeperson's role has dramatically changed in the past decade. The traditional image of *Dixon of Dock Green* has been replaced in the public's mind with a more sinister impression. The picture below of police in riot gear on the Broadwater Farm Estate in 1985 conveys an almost warlike image, more commonly associated with soldiers on the streets in Northern Ireland.

What accounts for this change in role? One answer is that rising crime figures and fear about crime has made law and order a political issue (see Module 13 on Deviance, page 235). At present, street crime, football hooliganism and inner-city riots appear to be the official confirmation of lawlessness in society. But despite the overall increase in white-collar crime, violence, rape, robbery and drug offences, increasing amounts of police time have been spent on maintaining **public order**, e.g. crowd control, strike picketing and riots. Perhaps not surprisingly, writes *Terrence Morris*, the traditional image of the 'caring copper' in the community has changed. Ambiguity now surrounds their role. At one moment the policeman is 'citizen' in uniform, the next he is 'soldier' in riot gear.

DISCUSS

Explain why increasing amounts of police time has been spent maintaining public order. How does this affect policing and detection in the areas of robbery, rape, drug offences and violent crime? ☐

The policeman must adopt a dual role. One day he is the kindly Mr Plod seeing children over the road, befriending old ladies and lost foreigners; the next he may be in flameproof overalls, bevisored and shielded, wielding his truncheon before a howling mob.

The riot control mode may be uncommon, but the carrying of guns has become routine. The growth in the number of armed police, and correspondingly of serious incidents of injury and death, have raised official anxieties to the point where there is now serious consideration of both reducing the number of permitted weapon carriers and at the same time an improvement in their training. That more criminals are carrying

1 Should the police carry guns? What are the main advantages and disadvantages of an armed police force?

2 What do you understand by the remark made in the extract that the policeman must adopt a 'dual role'.

3 Morris believes the police should be servants of the community and not the government in power. What do you think he means by this?

guns is an important, but by no means the only, factor in the situation.

The sympathy of conventional suburban Britain for the police in their far from enviable position may not be inexhaustible. People cannot go on being killed and injured, even by accident, and the more often public disorders are related to political dissent arising from the conduct of industrial relations, the policy for nuclear war or the condition of the poor in the inner city, the more chance the police have of being identified as the well-paid servants, not of the community, but of the government in power.

Yet much of the political debate about 'law and order' expenditure is quite misleading. In spite of massive investment in policing, notifiable criminal offences have risen from 2.3 million in 1979 to 3.4 million in 1985, while the proportion of cases cleared up has fallen steadily from 41 to 35 per cent in the same period.

Source: 'Police Force' by Terence Morris in *New Society*, March 1987

DISCUSS

With reference to these photographs and the information on Law and Order on page 270, explain the main changes which have occurred in the role of the police between 1979 and 86). □

LAW AND ORDER: 1979-1986

Police manpower: increased by 10,000 to 121,500.

Police expenditure: increased from £1.1 to £2.9 billion.

Increase in notifiable criminal offences: from 2.3 to 3.4 million.

Percentage of crimes cleared up: fallen from 42 to 35 per cent.

Prison population: increase from 42,000 to 50,000 (March 1987).

New restrictive legislation with implications for extended police powers with respect to: trade unions, police and criminal evidence, right of challenge in jury trials, public order (including political demonstrations of a non-violent nature).

Critical events involving the police:
- Inner city riots: Brixton and Toxteth 1981, Handsworth (Birmingham), St Pauls (Bristol), Broadwater Farm (London) 1985.
- Mineworkers' strike 1984: use of police in controlling pickets including events involving police horses at Orgreave and turning back of potential pickets at Dartford Tunnel.
- Printers dispute 1985-87: regular use of police at weekends to frustrate attempts to prevent movement of newspapers from News International plant at Wapping. Numerous allegations of violence and harassment of local inhabitants by police. Allegations of consequential depletion of police resources for crime control elsewhere.
- Hippie and peace convoys: broken up violently by police at Stonehenge (1985); dispersal of convoy at Stoney Cross (New Forest, 1986) without violence but with serious allegations concerning unlawful seizure of vehicles not on the highway and other instances of trespass to goods and personal possessions.
- Violence against students: riot-style dispersal of students and bystanders during visit to Manchester University by Leon Brittan (then home secretary; 1984). Allegations of violence and harassment towards complainants against police said to involve police "vigilantes" in plain clothes.
- Accidental shootings: including those of Stephen Waldorf (mistaken for dangerous suspect), John Shorthouse (sleeping child in home of suspected armed man wanted for questioning) and Cherry Groce (seriously wounded and permanently injured in tragic accident during house search). Death of Cynthia Jarret from natural causes during police search of domestic premises (riot on Broadwater Farm followed involving violent death of PC Blakelock).
- Police involvement in political contexts: alleged phonetapping of CND and trade union officials. (Alleged seizure and photocopying of documents found in panniers of journalist Duncan Campbell after being knocked off his bicycle. Later raids by Special Branch (1987) on home of Duncan Campbell and BBC Glasgow resulting in seizure of material relating to his *Secret Society* series believed to be deeply embarrassing to government).

Source: 'Police Force' by Terence Morris in *New Society*, March 1987

According to Morris, the police force face a dilemma in that their public order function, e.g. riot and picket control, is in conflict with their crime prevention, detection and community role. This is not, however, entirely accurate. As the 1983 Police Studies Institute Report, *The Police in Action* indicates, some policemen actually enjoy 'aggro' with the public, as this comment from a young police constable shows:

> 'I liked (the Grunwick dispute) best of all. It was such a fair, clean fight. The unions got all these blokes in from all over the country, they were a really tough lot, not rubbish mind you, but a really good class of demonstrator, they had a go at us and we had a go at them. If someone was hurt, both sides made a gangway so that the 'corpse' could be carried out to the ambulance . . . When it was all over I felt like shaking hands with the opposition and thanking them for such a good contest.'

Another officer recounted in similar manner how much he had enjoyed the Southall race riots in 1981.

> 'It was a great day out, fighting the Pakis. It ought to be an annual fixture. I thoroughly enjoyed myself.'

While much of the talk was probably exaggerated, many police officers do not appear to object to the occasional violent confrontation; and there is a distinct possibility that the police sometimes create the violence they are supposed to be controlling.

From the early 1980s various riots have occurred in major inner-city areas. Perhaps not surprisingly, most of these riots have involved conflict with the police, and criticism that the police contributed to the disturbances. As the following account indicates a common pattern of events is noticeable.

The Brixton Riot

The Brixton riot was sparked by the accidental shooting of a West Indian woman at her home when armed police raided the house in search of her 19–year-old son. Mrs Cherry Groce was paralysed. The raid was at 7 am, by the evening rioters had taken to the streets in protest. A press photographer later died from injuries. The incident occurred against a backdrop of severe social deprivation in Brixton aggravated by the withdrawal of special government aid, and against a new police strategy involving armed raids to pick up targeted suspects. In 1981 the riots in Brixton owed much to a different police strategy at the time – a mass stop and search exercise on the streets.

The Tottenham Riot

The Tottenham 1985 riot was sparked by the death of a black women, Mrs Cynthia Jarrett, during a police raid on her house. She died of a heart attack. In the riots that followed Police Constable Blakelock was stabbed to death, rioters used shotguns and petrol bombs, and 220 people were injured. Police were issued with CS gas and rubber bullets, but did not use them because of the problem imposed by the confined space of the blocks of flats at the centre of the rioting. Sir Kenneth Newman, London's Police Chief, emphasised in response to the Tottenham and Brixton riots that he would not shrink from using rubber bullets and 'tear gas' if he felt it was necessary for the protection of his officers and the mainten-ance of civil order.

BRAINSTORM

'It is sometimes easier to blame the events, situations and people involved in 'riots' rather than to explain them.' Discuss with reference to the photograph and the account of the Brixton and Tottenham Riots above. □

Lord Scarman's official enquiry into the Brixton riots in 1981 concluded that the riots resulted from a vicious circle of misunderstandings between young black people and the police.

> 'The riots were essentially an outburst of anger and resentment by young black people against the police . . .'
>
> 'They were neither premeditated nor planned, but the spontaneous reaction of angry young men, most of whom were black, against what they saw as a hostile police force. On the second day outsiders did participate and played a significant part in intensifying the riots by making and distributing petrol bombs. Some of them were clearly identified as whites.'
>
> 'Firstly they . . . (the police) . . . were partly to blame for the breakdown in community relations. Secondly, there were instances of harassment and racial prejudice among junior officers on the streets of Brixton which gave credibility and substance to the arguments of the police's critics. Thirdly, there was the failure to adjust policies and methods to meet the needs of policing a multi-racial society.'

Source: *The Scarman Report: The Brixton Disorder*, 1981

Four main recommendations arose from the Scarman Report:

1 The need to return to community policing by consent.
2 The need to establish improved community relations between the police and ethnic minority groups.
3 The need to improve police training in the field of race awareness.
4 The need to recruit ethnic minorities into the police force.

T A S K

To what extent do you think the four main recommendations from the Scarman Report have reduced conflict and tension between the community and the police force? □

Arguments about the causes of riots broadly fall into two camps:

> The **right-wing version** blames rioting on 'inadequate', 'evil', 'riff-raff' whose motives are criminal not political. Political agitators sometimes provoke and use these 'mindless' and 'violent' people, but the cause is essentially one of personal wickedness on the part of the rioters. The solution involves moral condemnation but, more pointedly, tougher policing and tougher sentencing by the courts to deter rioters. This vision of the problem and solution has much popular support amongst the police and Conservative politicians. It sees the rioters' acts as irrational and denies the significance of social factors like unemployment, poor housing, poverty and racism. (If you are not sure what the terms left wing and right wing mean see Module 3 on Power and Politics, page 41.)

Q How would you interpret the conclusions of Lord Scarman's report?

The **left-wing version** sees the cause rooted in social deprivation, aggravated by oppressive police tactics. The blame lies with the inadequacy of government policies to curb unemployment, poor housing, poor education, etc. in the inner-city 'ghettos', and with the police for tactless, racist handling of events, especially in connection with black youths. The left's solution, it follows, is to prevent the despair experienced in these areas by improving standards of living, job prospects and education, and by changing the style of policing to a more sensitive, democratically accountable form that meets the needs of the community better than repressive methods.

Source: *Sociology Up-date* by M Denscombe, 1986

The lessons of the riots

Unless you happened to live there nobody ever thought much about Toxteth or Brixton. But in the summer of 1981 and again in 1985, violent riots put them very much on the map.

The riots in Liverpool, London, Bristol and Birmingham have had ramifications at several levels. On the political right they reawakened old Tory fears of the mob: one response has been the atavistic cry for more "law and order". The left have taken the line that Mrs Thatcher's economic policies have been pushed too far and stirred up social discontent.

They were certainly a dramatic reminder that race and rebellion are two of the many elements in the inner city package. They were also a reminder that "benign neglect" of the cities as a policy leaves the door open, as happened in Brixton and Tottenham in 1985, to a chain reaction sparked by a single incident. It is significant that riots did not occur in, say, Glasgow or Gateshead, where deprivation is arguably as severe. The missing factor was race; more specifically, a local history of tense relations between inner city blacks and the front line agents of social control, the police.

Martin Kettle and Lucy Hodges, two journalists who studied the events of 1981 (*Uprising*, 1983), emphasise that the sparks that ignited the riots fell into the tinder box if inner city policing.

But behind the "failure" of policing lie objective facts about housing and job discrimination. A study of Hackney by the Commission for Racial Equality published in 1984 found that the Labour-controlled council was guilty of racial discrimination in allocating council houses. Black people were getting the worst houses on the "dump" estates. And Professor John Rex found in his studies of inner Birmingham that while blacks and Asians are not necessarily more likely to be unemployed, non-white groups often act as a "buffer" in the labour market – the first to go in recession and the last to be hired.

There have been efforts to repair relations between the black inner-city communities and the police, and enough progress has been made to disappoint those on the extreme left who welcomed the riots as the beginning of social revolution.

But in policing the inner city, there remains a gulf between the agents of law and order and blacks. A major study of the Metropolitan Police in 1984 by the Policy Studies Institute found substantial evidence of racism in the force. And as Paul Harrison notes in his study of Hackney: "It is an unfortunate fact of cultural diversity that many young Afro-Caribbeans, innocent or otherwise, behave in a way that makes hairs stand up on white policemen's necks."

Source: *Society Today* by M Williams, 1986

Q According to Williams' account, what are the main lessons of the riots?

T|A|S|K| | | | | | | | |

Neither vision of the problem and its solution holds all the truths. Explain the left- and right-wing versions of the riots.

What do you think remains unexplained by these accounts?

What factors other than race may explain recent riots?

How would you explain the involvement of White Youth in the riots? □

U N I T 6

REGIONAL INEQUALITY AND UNEMPLOYMENT

Following on from the previous unit, it is possible to see how wider regional factors reinforce some of the issues looked at so far. In particular, the pressing problem of unemployment is closely linked with urban and regional inequalities. In the Module 10 on Population, page 178 and Module 4 on Third World Studies, page 57 such inequalities have already been referred to as the *North–South Divide*.

Industrial recession has affected some sectors of the population more than others. As we have seen in other modules class, race and gender are important factors in looking at inequality, but there is also a growing awareness of regional inequalities within the UK, which reflect the uneven influence of the economic recession on different parts of the community. Consider, for example, these figures for unemployment in the regions in 1985.

Unemployment in the regions (October 1985)

South East	9.9%	Greater London*	10.7%
East Anglia	10.5%	South West	12.1%
West Midlands	15.6%	East Midlands	12.5%
Yorks and Humber	15.1%	North West	16.3%
North	18.9%	Wales	17.2%
Scotland	15.6%	Northern Ireland	21.0%
UK	13.5%		

*Greater London is also included in the South East.

Source: Incomes Data Services, Report 461, November 1985

Further information below regarding the regional breakdown of the 1.6 million employee jobs lost and gained between 1979 and 1986 provides additional evidence of regional variation.

Regional breakdown of the 1.6m employee jobs lost and gained between June 1979 and 1986

East Anglia	+ 23.000
South East	− 73,000
South West	− 39,000
West Midlands	−301,000
Noth West	−278,000
Yorkshire/Humberside	−266,000
The North	−215,000
East Midlands	−118,000
Scotland	−149,000
Wales	−130,000
Northern Ireland	− 64,000

Source: *New Statesman*, January 1987

DISCUSS

What main types of job have been lost during the recession and what main types of jobs have been gained? □

BRAINSTORM

Unemployment is not a new phenomenon. How would you compare the issues associated with unemployment in the 1930s with those of today?

Q   Describe some of the main differences in unemployment in the regions identified in these figures.

There are many explanations given for the changing distribution of jobs and population in the UK. Perhaps the most obvious has been the decline in manufacturing industry which has hit the North and Midlands particularly hard. The North has borne the brunt of this recession in traditional industries like steel, coal, shipbuilding and heavy engineering, while the West Midlands, with its heavy dependence on the car industry, has been affected by the decline in manufacturing. One consequence of this is that as regions become more depressed, industry becomes less likely to invest there. As employment and investment prospects decline so too does the quality of housing stock and with it the whole 'infrastructure', including shops, roads, public services, transport, schools and so forth. Migration of people and businesses from inner-city areas further accelerates this process, adding further to the frustrations of people living there. In regional terms, this is increasingly referred to as the 'North/South Divide'.

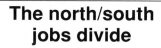

The north/south jobs divide

The current debate in Whitehall about regional policy will be given new urgency by the employment department's job census, which emerged this week. It shows that only some 6 per cent of the loss of jobs since 1979 has been in the south, while 94 per cent has been in the midlands, north, Wales, Scotland and Northern Ireland. The pressure on ministers to act to bridge the gap—in memoriam to Lord Stockton?—is growing.

In fact, the census figures paint an over-crude picture. They are for *net* job losses, the sum of old and new jobs together. In gross terms, many jobs have been lost in the south as well as the north. True, more new jobs have arisen to replace them—but they do not necessarily go to those who have been displaced. The lost opportunities were, in large measure, for full-time men; the new opportunities are, in large measure, for part-time women. If we look at *un*employment, it has risen by 144 per cent in the northern region since the government came to power—but by 215 per cent in the south east.

In the south east, 510,000 men are unemployed, 9.5 per cent of the male working population. Moreover, the south east is not homogeneous. Only 5.0 per cent of the population of Winchester is out of work, and 5.1 per cent in Crawley, but London suffers an overall unemployment rate of 10.4 per cent (much bigger in some boroughs) and Sittingbourne of 14.2 per cent.

Talk of the north/south divide is also misleading because it excludes by definition the region which had arguably been hit hardest of all by unemployment. In 1979, the West Midlands was still a haven of relative prosperity, with an unemployment rate (on today's definitions) of just 4.2 per cent. Since then, 302,000 manufacturing jobs have been lost in the region, the census shows, more than in Wales and Scotland put together. Unemployment in the West Midlands today stands at a massive 13.6 per cent. There are 234,000 men and 109,000 women in the region who have no jobs.

The overall north-south divide is still a fact, of course, and to any but the most blinkered, the inability of market forces to eliminate regional disparities is becoming apparent. The market mechanism—lower wages in the north attracting employers out of the south—has not worked, partly because of the extreme rigidities of the housing market.

But the debate about regional policy, important though it is, should not be allowed to obscure another, and more fundamental one, about our national policy for jobs. Misery shared is not misery spared.

Source: *New Society*, January 1987

Q What evidence is there that a North/South Divide exists? Do you think that the photographs complicate or simplify the arguments about this division? □

A major problem over the years has been that attempts to relocate business, industry and commerce from the South to the North have not worked. More recent attempts at setting up Development Corporations in the Regions, such as the Scottish Development Agency, have been more successful. These operate on the basis of attracting new industries and link them with employment programmes designed to build on existing local strengths. Yet, despite such initiatives, Regional aid to help regions worst affected by recession has been cut. While the government originally planned £700 million per year in regional aid, that figure was reduced to £400 million in the year 1987 to 1988.

Head of household by social class: percentage of population

	I	II	III		IV	V	Armed forces	Econom-ically inactive
			Non manual	Manual				
United Kingdom	4.5	18.8	9.1	26.1	12.2	4.1	2.5	22.7
N. Ireland	3.2	18.6	7.7	23.6	10.6	4.8	8.4	23.0
Wales	3.7	16.6	7.5	26.6	11.8	4.5	2.2	27.1
Scotland	4.2	16.4	8.4	27.3	13.2	5.0	2.4	23.2
England	4.6	19.2	9.3	26.1	12.1	3.9	2.4	22.4
North	3.5	14.6	7.6	29.8	13.0	5.3	1.6	24.7
North West	4.1	16.8	8.7	26.7	13.5	5.0	1.8	23.3
Yorks & Humberside	3.3	16.9	8.0	28.8	13.2	4.4	1.9	23.6
East Midlands	3.8	18.1	8.1	29.9	13.2	3.6	2.1	21.2
East Anglia	4.4	19.6	8.3	25.6	12.5	3.5	3.9	22.1
South East	5.8	22.2	11.1	23.0	10.5	3.5	2.5	21.3
South West	4.7	19.9	9.2	23.8	10.9	3.1	3.4	25.0
West Midlands	3.8	17.4	7.8	29.4	14.2	3.9	2.3	21.2

Source: *Regional Trends* 20, 1985

Certainly, following the publication of the Black Report on the state of the nation's health, major differences in the health of people in the North and the South of the country have been observed. Illnesses associated with smoking, drinking, eating stodgy and fatty foods have been found to be higher in the North than in the South. This, and more recent reports, have stimulated furious debate about whether the poor's disproportionate ill health is due to irresponsibility or poverty. It was Edwina Currie's view as Junior Health Minister that major health differences between North and South could be explained in terms of poor eating and drinking habits – not in terms of poverty or unemployment. (For further discussion of health issues see Module 6 on Inequality, Unit 3).

Currie chides the unhealthy North

Poor health among people in the North of England was caused by ignorance, Mrs Edwina Currie, the newly promoted junior health minister, said yesterday.

In a visit to Newcastle-upon-Tyne, she offered the South as an example of how people looked after themselves better.

Mrs Currie criticized a report published last week which linked poverty in the North with health problems. She rejected the suggestion that poor health was the Government's fault, or that it was directly linked to poverty and high unemployment.

"The problem very often for many people is, I think, just ignorance ... and failing to realize they do have some control over their lives," she said.

Source: *The Times*, September 1986
© Times Newspapers Ltd, 1986

BRAINSTORM

What do such figures tell us about the distribution of social classes in various regions? How might such figures be linked to unemployment, health and other social factors, including educational opportunities?

DISCUSS

What do you think of Mrs Curry's views? What evidence can you find to either support or refute her views?

It may be that Edwina Currie was right. The Black Report indicates that eating, drinking and smoking habits still vary between North and South. It also maybe, however, that the higher incidence of unemployment in the North affects dietary habits and is linked with *relative poverty*. Evidence indicates, for example, that the very poor tend to eat cheaper foods, which contain a higher fat and carbohydrate content.

BRAINSTORM

Discuss the relationship between social class, health, illness and mortality (see Module 10 on Population, page 175). □

The following illustration provides a convenient way of looking at North/South health differences. Depending upon where you live, it may reinforce various stereotypes or point to very real differences between the North and South.

Source: *New Society*, January 1987

|T|A|S|K| | | | | | | |

Discuss the various stereotyped images portrayed in the illustration.

Are the differences between North and South displayed in the illustration based on fact?

What evidence is there that such a thing as North/South divide exists? Discuss your answer with reference to health, social class and employment. □

WHERE TO NOW?

Reading this Module may make you interested in reading more on Work in Module 8. You may also like to learn more about Inequalities and Poverty. You could continue, therefore, by reading Module 6 on Inequality, and Module 5 on Social Stratification next.

Index

Acknowledgements

The Publishers would like to thank all those who gave permission to reprint copyright material in this book.

Illustrations by:

Mark Hackett
Peter Joyce
Maggie Ling
Chris Price
Val Saunders/Oxford Illustrators
Shaun Williams/Cartoon Communication

Additional artwork by permission of the following:

The Centre for World Development Education, p.56
The Daily Mirror, p.14

Photographs by permission of the following:

Bryan & Cherry Alexander p 110;
Andes Press Agency pp 59, 62, 74, 154;
Barnabys Picture Library p 106, Barnabys Picture Library/T Simpson p 141, Barnabys Picture Library/Max Hunn p 95, Barnabys Picture Library p 256, Barnabys Picture Library/H Kanus p 65; Camera Press pp 31, Camera Press/C J Edwards 31, 36, 38, 79, 80, 166, Camera Press/Interpress 167, Camera Press/L Smillie 189, 201, 222, 229, Camera Press/J Drysdale 229, 241, 247;
J Allan Cash p 141;
Courtesy of Prestel/Jenny Baily Associates p 137;
Crown Copyright p 7;
Format/Brenda Prince pp 11, 30, 36, 71, Format/Pam Isherwood 74, Format/Maggie Murray 74, 79, Format/M Murray p 264, Format/B Friend p 275;
Sally & Richard Greenhill pp 36, 106, 127, 176, 212, 229, 248;
Greenpeace p 51;
Robert Harding Picture Library pp 154, 211, 255;
Hulton Picture Company p 259;
Hutchison Library p 59;
Courtesy of IBM p 275
I M Keill p 157;
Kobal Collection p 106;
Magnum Photos Ltd/Peress p 168;
Master & Fellows of Trinity College, Cambridge p 219;
Network/G Franklin p 100, Network/J Sturrock pp 268, 269;
Photo Co-op/Crispin Hughes pp 6 Photo Co-op/Sarah Saunders 74;
Photo Co-op/Vicky White 81, Photo Co-op/D Stewart 145, Photo Co-op/Janis Dustin 173, Photo Co-op 254, Photo Co-op/V White 257;
Photo Co-op/C Hughes 266;
Popperfoto p 31;
Press Association pp 231, 271;
Syndication International p 145;
The Independent/Jeremy Nicholl p 52;
Topham Picture Source pp 99, 146, 192, 241, 255, 260;
USSR Photo Library p 83;
Wiedel Janine p 111, 120, 122, 124, 235, 254, 269.

Examination questions by permission of the following:

The Associated Examining Board; University of Cambridge Local Examinations Syndicate; Midland Examining Group; and Southern Examining Group.

Advertisements by permission of the following:

The British Broadcasting Corporation (Logo, p.20); British Gas (p.143); Christian Aid (p.167); Elida Gibbs Ltd. (p.21); The Independent Broadcasting Authority (Logo, p.20);
Volvo Concessionaires Ltd. (p.217); Josiah Wedgwood & Sons Ltd. (p.21); and J.D. Williams Group Ltd. (Swan, p.21).

Charts, graphs and tables by permission of the following:

The Association for the Teaching of the Social Sciences, for W.A. BRADFORD: from *Development*, (ATSS Monograph Services); Broadcasters' Audience Research Board Ltd.; Economic and Social Research Council; European Schoolbooks Ltd., for J.B. HARRISON: from *Britain Observed*; The Fabian Society for H. Glennersten & R. Pryke: from *The Public Schools* (1964) Gower Publishing Group, for R. JOWELL & C. AIREY (Eds.): from *British Social Attitudes, The 1984 Report*; The Controller of Her Majesty's Stationery Office, for material from *Social Trends*, *Regional Trends*, and *Annual Abstract of Statistics*, (CSO), and *Employment Gazette*, and *National Food Survey*, (HMSO); The Home Office; National Society for the Prevention of Cruelty to Children, from *Trends in Child Abuse*; New Statesman & Society; Office of Population Censuses and Surveys; Penguin Books Ltd., for DAVID J. SMITH: from

Racial Disadvantage in Britain: The PEP Report, copyright © PEP, 1977; Routledge & Kegan Paul, for M. YOUNG & P. WILLMOTT: from *The Symmetrical Family*; South Publications Ltd.; and Times Newspapers Ltd., from *T.E.S.*, © Times Newspapers Ltd., 1989.

Text extracts by permission of the following:

Academic Press Inc. (London) Ltd., for THOMAS J. COTTLE: from 'The Cost of Hope', in *British Journal of Social Work*, Vol. 7 No. 2; The Association for the Teaching of the Social Sciences, for CHRIS FARLEY: from *World Population and Poverty*, (ATSS Resource Unit); Basil Blackwell, for PAT CARLEN (Ed.): from *Criminal Women*, (Polity Press, 1985), ANNE OAKLEY: from *Sociology Of Housework*, (1984), and SYLVA & LUNT: from *Child Development*; Jonathan Cape Ltd., for DESMOND MORRIS: from *The Human Zoo*, (1969); Centre for World Development Education, from CWDE Cartoonsheet 3, 'Drinking Water and Sanitation Decade', and Cartoonsheet 4, 'Food and Agriculture'; Century Hutchinson Ltd., for JANE L. THOMPSON: from *Examining Sociology*, (1980); Chatto & Windus/The Hogarth Press, for RICHARD NORTH: from *The Real Cost*, (1986); Colorific Photo Library Ltd., for MARY ELLEN MARK: front cover *The Sunday Times Magazine*, (28 Nov. 1982); Confederation of British Industry, for CBI leaflets; Curtis Brown Ltd., for HUGH BEYNON: from *Working for Ford*, (Penguin, 1973); Martyn Denscombe, from *Sociology Update*; Express Newspapers plc, for BRIAN APPLEBY: 'The Gambols' in *The Daily Express*; Professor Ronald Frankenberg, for R. FRANKENBERG: from *Communities in Britain*, (Penguin, 1966); Gower Publishing Co. Ltd., for P. WILLIS: from *Learning to Labour: How Working-Class Kids Get Working-Class Jobs*, (Saxon House, 1978); *The Guardian*, from articles by Dennis Barker, Maev Kennedy, and David McKie; A.M. Heath & Co. Ltd., on behalf of the estate of the late Sonia Brownell Orwell, for GEORGE ORWELL: from *The Road to Wigan Pier*, (Secker & Warburg); The Controller of Her Majesty's Stationery Office, for Lord SCARMAN: from *The Scarman Report: The Brixton Disorders*, (1981), and for Crown copyright leaflets; Holt, Rinehart & Winston, for L. BASH, D. COULBY & C. JONES: from *Urban Schooling*, (1985); Independent Television Publications Ltd., from *TV Times*; Ladybird Books Ltd., from Ladybird Key Words Reading Scheme; *The Leek Post & Times*; McGraw Hill Book Company (UK) Ltd., for D. POWIS: from *Signs of Crime: A Field Manual for Police*, (1977); MacMillan Publishers Ltd., for M. WILLIAMS: from *Society Today*, (1986); Ewan MacNaughton Associates, from articles by Ian Brodie and Harvey Lee in *The Daily Telegraph*; National Society for the Prevention of Cruelty to Children, for NSPCC leaflets; New Statesman & Society, for articles by M. McFadyean, Terence Morris, Jonathan Steinberg, and others in *New Society*; News (UK) Ltd., from *Today*; News Group Newspapers Ltd., from *The Sun*; Newspaper Publishing plc, from articles by Anthony Bevins & Patrick Donovan, Mary Fagan, Oliver Gillie, and Heather Mills in *The Independent*; The Observer, for front cover *The Observer Magazine*, (2 Dec. 1984); Open Books Publishing Ltd., for M. RUTTER: from *Fifteen Thousand Hours*, (1979); Oxford University Press, Inc., for C. WRIGHT MILLS: from *Sociological Imagination*, copyright © 1959 by Oxford University Press, Inc., renewed 1987 by Yaraslava Mills; Penguin Books Ltd., for PAUL HARRISON: from *Inside the Inner City: Life Under the Cutting Edge*, (1983), copyright © Paul Harrison, 1983, and SHEILA JEFFREYS & JILL RADFORD: from 'Contributory Negligence or Being a Woman? The Car Rapist Case', in Phil Scraton and Paul Gordon (Eds.): *Causes for Concern: Questions of Law and Justice*, (1984), copyright © Phil Scraton and Paul Gordon, 1984; The Press Association, from article in *The Shropshire Star*; Routledge & Kegan Paul, for G. DRIVER: from 'West Indian Families: An Anthropoligal Perspective' in R.N. Rapoport (Ed.): *Families in Britain*, (1982), G. HURD (Ed.): from *Human Societies*, (1973), MARY WILLES: from *Children Into Pupils: Study of Language in Early Schools*, (1983), PETER WILLMOTT: from *Adolescent Boys of East London*, (1966), and P. WILLMOTT & M. YOUNG: from *Families and Kinship in East London*, (1957); Staffordshire Sentinel Newspapers Ltd., from *Evening Sentinel*; Syndication International (1986) Ltd., from articles by Victor Knight, and Keith Richmond in *The Sunday Mirror*, and John Kelly in *The Daily Mirror*; Stanley Thornes (Publishers) Ltd., for PATRICK MCNEIL & CHARLES TOWNLEY: from *Fundamentals of Sociology*, (1981); Times Newspapers Limited, from articles in *The Times*, and by Philip Norman in *The Sunday Times Magazine*; University of Chicago Press, for W. FOOTE WHYTE: from *Street Corner Society*, (1943), © 1943, 1955, 1981 by The University of Chicago, All Rights Reserved; Unwin Hyman Ltd., for A. PILKINGTON: from *Race Relations in Britain*, (1984), and MICHELLE STANWORTH: from *Gender and Schooling: Study of Sexual Divisions in the Classroom*, (1983), © Michelle Stanworth, 1983; and Virago Press, for M. SPRING-RICE: from *Working Class Wives*, (1981).

Although every effort has been made to contact copyright holders, this has not always been possible. If notified, the publishers will be pleased to rectify any errors or omissions at the earliest opportunity.